LAND OF LISP

LAND OF LISP

Learn to Program in Lisp, One Game at a Time!

by Conrad Barski, M.D.

no starch
press

San Francisco

LAND OF LISP. Copyright © 2011 by Conrad Barski, M.D.

Printed in Canada

14 13 12 11 10   1 2 3 4 5 6 7 8 9

ISBN-10: 1-59327-281-2
ISBN-13: 978-1-59327-281-4

Publisher: William Pollock
Production Editors: Ansel Staton and Serena Yang
Developmental Editor: Keith Fancher
Technical Reviewers: Philip Fominykh and Heow Eide-Goodman
Copyeditor: Marilyn Smith
Compositor: Susan Glinert Stevens
Proofreader: Linda Seifert
Indexer: Nancy Guenther

For information on book distributors or translations, please contact No Starch Press, Inc. directly:

No Starch Press, Inc.
38 Ringold Street, San Francisco, CA 94103
phone: 415.863.9900; fax: 415.863.9950; info@nostarch.com; www.nostarch.com

Library of Congress Cataloging-in-Publication Data

```
Barski, Conrad.
 Land of Lisp : learn to program in Lisp, one game at a time! / by Conrad Barski.
     p. cm.
 Includes index.
 ISBN-13: 978-1-59327-281-4
 ISBN-10: 1-59327-281-2
 1.  Computer games--Programming 2.  COMMON LISP (Computer program language) 3.  LISP (Computer program language)
I. Title.
 QA76.76.C672B3693 2010
 794.8'1526--dc22
                                          2010026755
```

For Lauren

BRIEF CONTENTS

Acknowledgments xvii

Introduction 1

SECTION I: LISP IS POWER

Chapter 1: Getting Started with Lisp 15

Chapter 2: Creating Your First Lisp Program 21

Chapter 3: Exploring the Syntax of Lisp Code 31

SECTION II: LISP IS SYMMETRY

Chapter 4: Making Decisions with Conditions 49

Chapter 5: Building a Text Game Engine 67

Chapter 6: Interacting with the World: Reading and Printing in Lisp 85

Chapter 6.5: lambda: A Function So Important It Deserves Its Own Chapter.......103

Chapter 7: Going Beyond Basic Lists..107

Chapter 8: This Ain't Your Daddy's Wumpus...129

Chapter 9: Advanced Datatypes and Generic Programming 153

SECTION III: LISP IS HACKING 191

Chapter 10: Looping with the loop Command 195

Chapter 11: Printing Text with the format Function...221

Chapter 12: Working with Streams 237

Chapter 13: Let's Create a Web Server! 253

Functional Programming Is Beautiful 269

SECTION IV: LISP IS SCIENCE

Chapter 14: Ramping Lisp Up a Notch with Functional Programming 291

Chapter 15: Dice of Doom, a Game Written in the Functional Style 303

Chapter 16: The Magic of Lisp Macros 339

Chapter 17: Domain-Specific Languages...355

Chapter 18: Lazy Programming 375

Chapter 19: Creating a Graphical, Web-Based Version of Dice of Doom 401

Chapter 20: Making Dice of Doom More Fun..417

Epilogue 429

Index...465

CONTENTS IN DETAIL

ACKNOWLEDGMENTS   xvii

INTRODUCTION   1
What Makes Lisp So Cool and Unusual? 2
If Lisp Is So Great, Why Don't More People Use It? 3
Where Did Lisp Come From? 4
Where Does Lisp Get Its Power? 10

SECTION I: LISP IS POWER

1
GETTING STARTED WITH LISP   15
Lisp Dialects 15
    A Tale of Two Lisps 16
    Up-and-Coming Lisps 17
    Lisp Dialects Used for Scripting 17
    ANSI Common Lisp 17
Getting Started with CLISP 18
    Installing CLISP 18
    Starting Up CLISP 19
What You've Learned 19

2
CREATING YOUR FIRST LISP PROGRAM   21
The Guess-My-Number Game 21
Defining Global Variables in Lisp 23
    Defining the small and big Variables 23
    An Alternative Global Variable Definition Function 23
Basic Lisp Etiquette 24
Defining Global Functions in Lisp 25
    Defining the guess-my-number Function 25
    Defining the smaller and bigger Functions 27
    Defining the start-over Function 28
Defining Local Variables in Lisp 28
Defining Local Functions in Lisp 29
What You've Learned 30

3
EXPLORING THE SYNTAX OF LISP CODE   31

Syntax and Semantics 31
The Building Blocks of Lisp Syntax 32
    Symbols 33
    Numbers 34
    Strings 35
How Lisp Distinguishes Between Code and Data 35
    Code Mode 36
    Data Mode 37
Lists in Lisp 37
    Cons Cells 38
    List Functions 38
    Nested Lists 41
What You've Learned 45

SECTION II: LISP IS SYMMETRY

4
MAKING DECISIONS WITH CONDITIONS   49

The Symmetry of nil and () 49
    Empty Equals False 50
    The Four Disguises of () 51
The Conditionals: if and Beyond 52
    One Thing at a Time with if 52
    Going Beyond if: The when and unless Alternatives 55
    The Command That Does It All: cond 56
    Branching with case 57
Cool Tricks with Conditions 58
    Using the Stealth Conditionals and and or 58
    Using Functions That Return More than Just the Truth 60
Comparing Stuff: eq, equal, and More 62
What You've Learned 65

5
BUILDING A TEXT GAME ENGINE   67

The Wizard's Adventure Game 68
    Our Game World 68
    Basic Requirements 69
Describing the Scenery with an Association List 70
Describing the Location 71
Describing the Paths 72
    How Quasiquoting Works 73
    Describing Multiple Paths at Once 73
Describing Objects at a Specific Location 77
    Listing Visible Objects 77
    Describing Visible Objects 78

Describing It All 79
Walking Around in Our World 81
Picking Up Objects 82
Checking Our Inventory 83
What You've Learned 84

6
INTERACTING WITH THE WORLD: READING AND PRINTING IN LISP
85

Printing and Reading Text 86
    Printing to the Screen 86
    Saying Hello to the User 87
    Starting with print and read 88
    Reading and Printing Stuff the Way Humans Like It 90
The Symmetry Between Code and Data in Lisp 91
Adding a Custom Interface to Our Game Engine 92
    Setting Up a Custom REPL 93
    Writing a Custom read Function 94
    Writing a game-eval Function 96
    Writing a game-print Function 96
Trying Out Our Fancy New Game Interface 99
The Dangers of read and eval 101
What You've Learned 101

6.5
LAMBDA: A FUNCTION SO IMPORTANT IT DESERVES ITS OWN CHAPTER
103

What lambda Does 103
Why lambda Is So Important 105
What You've Learned 106

7
GOING BEYOND BASIC LISTS
107

Exotic Lists 107
    Dotted Lists 108
    Pairs 109
    Circular Lists 110
    Association Lists 111
Coping with Complicated Data 113
    Visualizing Tree-like Data 113
    Visualizing Graphs 114
Creating a Graph 114
    Generating the DOT Information 115
    Turning the DOT File into a Picture 120
    Creating a Picture of Our Graph 123
Creating Undirected Graphs 124
What You've Learned 127

8
THIS AIN'T YOUR DADDY'S WUMPUS   129

The Grand Theft Wumpus Game 131
Defining the Edges of Congestion City 135
    Generating Random Edges 135
    Looping with the loop Command 136
    Preventing Islands 137
    Building the Final Edges for Congestion City 139
Building the Nodes for Congestion City 142
Initializing a New Game of Grand Theft Wumpus 144
Drawing a Map of Our City 145
    Drawing a City from Partial Knowledge 146
    Walking Around Town 148
Let's Hunt Some Wumpus! 149
What You've Learned 152

9
ADVANCED DATATYPES AND GENERIC PROGRAMMING 153

Arrays 153
    Working with Arrays 154
    Using a Generic Setter 154
    Arrays vs. Lists 156
Hash Tables 157
    Working with Hash Tables 157
    Returning Multiple Values 159
    Hash Table Performance 160
    A Faster Grand Theft Wumpus Using Hash Tables 161
Common Lisp Structures 163
    Working with Structures 163
    When to Use Structures 165
Handling Data in a Generic Way 166
    Working with Sequences 166
    Creating Your Own Generic Functions with Type Predicates 170
The Orc Battle Game 172
    Global Variables for the Player and Monsters 173
    Main Game Functions 174
    Player Management Functions 175
    Helper Functions for Player Attacks 177
    Monster Management Functions 178
    The Monsters 179
    To Battle! 187
What You've Learned 189

SECTION III: LISP IS HACKING

loop and format: The Seedy Underbelly of Lisp 193

10
LOOPING WITH THE LOOP COMMAND   195

The loop Macro 195
    Some loop Tricks 196
    Everything You Ever Wanted to Know About loop 202
Using loop to Evolve! 202
    Growing Plants in Our World 204
    Creating Animals 205
    Simulating a Day in Our World 212
    Drawing Our World 212
    Creating a User Interface 213
    Let's Watch Some Evolution! 214
    Explaining the Evolution 218
What You've Learned 219

11
PRINTING TEXT WITH THE FORMAT FUNCTION   221

Anatomy of the format Function 221
    The Destination Parameter 222
    The Control String Parameter 222
    Value Parameters 223
Control Sequences for Printing Lisp Values 223
Control Sequences for Formatting Numbers 225
    Control Sequences for Formatting Integers 225
    Control Sequences for Formatting Floating-Point Numbers 226
Printing Multiple Lines of Output 226
Justifying Output 228
Iterating Through Lists Using Control Sequences 231
A Crazy Formatting Trick for Creating Pretty Tables of Data 232
Attack of the Robots! 233
What You've Learned 235

12
WORKING WITH STREAMS   237

Types of Streams 238
    Streams by Type of Resource 238
    Streams by Direction 238
Working with Files 242
Working with Sockets 244
    Socket Addresses 245
    Socket Connections 246
    Sending a Message over a Socket 246
    Tidying Up After Ourselves 248
String Streams: The Oddball Type 249
    Sending Streams to Functions 249
    Working with Long Strings 250
    Reading and Debugging 250
What You've Learned 251

13
LET'S CREATE A WEB SERVER! 253

Error Handling in Common Lisp 253
    Signaling a Condition 254
    Creating Custom Conditions 254
    Intercepting Conditions 255
    Protecting Resources Against Unexpected Conditions 255
Writing a Web Server from Scratch 256
    How a Web Server Works 256
    Request Parameters 258
    Parsing the Request Header 261
    Testing get-header with a String Stream 262
    Parsing the Request Body 263
    Our Grand Finale: The serve Function! 263
Building a Dynamic Website 265
    Testing the Request Handler 265
    Launching the Website 266
What You've Learned 267

FUNCTIONAL PROGRAMMING IS BEAUTIFUL 269

SECTION IV: LISP IS SCIENCE

14
RAMPING LISP UP A NOTCH WITH
FUNCTIONAL PROGRAMMING 291

What Is Functional Programming? 292
Anatomy of a Program Written in the Functional Style 295
Higher-Order Programming 298
    Code Composition with Imperative Code 298
    Using the Functional Style 299
    Higher-Order Programming to the Rescue 300
Why Functional Programming Is Crazy 300
Why Functional Programming Is Fantastic 301
    Functional Programming Reduces Bugs 301
    Functional Programs Are More Compact 301
    Functional Code Is More Elegant 302
What You've Learned 302

15
DICE OF DOOM, A GAME WRITTEN IN
THE FUNCTIONAL STYLE 303

The Rules of Dice of Doom 304
A Sample Game of Dice of Doom 304

Implementing Dice of Doom, Version 1 306
    Defining Some Global Variables 306
    Representing the Game Board 307
    Decoupling Dice of Doom's Rules from the Rest of the Game 309
    Generating a Game Tree 311
    Calculating Passing Moves 312
    Calculating Attacking Moves 313
    Finding the Neighbors 314
    Attacking 315
    Reinforcements 316
    Trying Out Our New game-tree Function 317
    Playing Dice of Doom Against Another Human 318
Creating an Intelligent Computer Opponent 321
    The Minimax Algorithm 323
    Turning Minimax into Actual Code 323
    Creating a Game Loop with an AI Player 324
    Playing Our First Human vs. Computer Game 325
Making Dice of Doom Faster 326
    Closures 326
    Memoization 328
    Tail Call Optimization 331
    A Sample Game on the 3-by-3 Board 334
What You've Learned 336

16
THE MAGIC OF LISP MACROS   339

A Simple Lisp Macro 340
    Macro Expansion 341
    How Macros Are Transformed 342
    Using the Simple Macro 345
More Complex Macros 345
    A Macro for Splitting Lists 346
    Avoiding Repeated Execution in Macros 347
    Avoiding Variable Capture 348
    A Recursion Macro 350
Macros: Dangers and Alternatives 352
What You've Learned 353

17
DOMAIN-SPECIFIC LANGUAGES   355

What Is a Domain? 355
Writing SVG Files 356
    Creating XML and HTML with the tag Macro 357
    Creating SVG-Specific Macros and Functions 361
    Building a More Complicated SVG Example 362
Creating Custom Game Commands for Wizard's Adventure Game 365
    Creating New Game Commands by Hand 366
    Let's Try the Completed Wizard's Adventure Game! 371
What You've Learned 373

18
LAZY PROGRAMMING   375

Adding Lazy Evaluation to Lisp 376
 Creating the lazy and force Commands 378
 Creating a Lazy Lists Library 380
 Converting Between Regular Lists and Lazy Lists 381
 Mapping and Searching Across Lazy Lists 383
Dice of Doom, Version 2 384
Making Our AI Work on Larger Game Boards 387
 Trimming the Game Tree 387
 Applying Heuristics 389
 Winning by a Lot vs. Winning by a Little 389
 Alpha Beta Pruning 393
What You've Learned 400

19
CREATING A GRAPHICAL, WEB-BASED VERSION OF
DICE OF DOOM   401

Drawing the Game Board Using the SVG Format 402
 Drawing a Die 403
 Drawing a Tile 405
 Drawing the Board 406
Building the Web Server Interface 408
 Writing Our Web Request Handler 408
 Limitations of Our Game Web Server 409
 Initializing a New Game 410
 Announcing a Winner 410
 Handling the Human Player 410
 Handling the Computer Player 412
 Drawing the SVG Game Board from Within the HTML 412
Playing Version 3 of Dice of Doom 413
What You've Learned 415

20
MAKING DICE OF DOOM MORE FUN   417

Increasing the Number of Players 417
Rolling the Dice 418
 Building Chance Nodes 419
 Doing the Actual Dice Rolling 420
 Calling the Dice Rolling Code from Our Game Engine 420
 Updating the AI 422
Improving the Dice of Doom Reinforcement Rules 423
Conclusion 425

EPILOGUE   429

INDEX   465

ACKNOWLEDGMENTS

First of all, I'd like to thank my wife Lauren for letting me spend so many weekends on this book project. I am also particularly grateful to Philip Fominykh, the main technical reviewer for this book, whose extensive experience with proper Common Lisp form and style helped to reign in many (but not too many) quirks in the source code and in the discussions of Lisp philosophy. I also owe a great deal to Heow Eide-Goodman, who reviewed the final chapters and helped complete this project.

Many folks at No Starch Press had to wrestle with the idiosyncratic prose and structure of this book to bring it into publishable form. First and foremost, I want to thank Keith Fancher, my primary editor for most of this project. Great effort was also put in by Bill Pollock, Serena Yang, Ansel Staton, Riley Hoffman, Alison Petersen, Magnolia Molcan, Kathleen Mish, Don Marti, Tyler Ortman, and Adam Wright. I'd also like to thank Aaron Feng for early feedback on the style of the book.

This book project originally began as an expansion of my "Casting SPELs in Lisp" web tutorial. I want to thank everyone who emailed or talked with me about this tutorial and helped me expand my understanding of Lisp along the way. rms (Richard Stallman), in particular, gave me a lot of feedback on Lisp style and helped me put together the Emacs Lisp version of the tutorial. Please consider donating to the Free Software Foundation (*http://www.fsf.org/*), a nonprofit organization he founded to support the development of open source and free software, which includes many great Lisp tools. James Webb also helped greatly with the Emacs Lisp version. And among the countless folks who gave feedback and/or corrections on "Casting SPELs in Lisp," I'd especially like to thank Kenny Tilton, Marshall Quander, Wei-Ju Wu, Christopher Brown, Stephen Gravrock, Paul Schulz, Andy Cowell, and Johan Bockgård.

INTRODUCTION

So, you've decided to pick up a book on Lisp and read
the introduction. Perhaps you were surprised to see
something that looks like a comic book mixed in with
the other computer programming books on the shelf.
Who would bother writing a comic book about a weird
academic programming language like Lisp? Or maybe
you've heard other people raving about the Lisp language and thought, "Boy, Lisp sure sounds different
from other languages people talk about. Maybe I should
pick up a Lisp book sometime." Either way, you're now
holding a book about a programming language that is
very cool but also very unusual.

What Makes Lisp So Cool and Unusual?

Lisp is a very *expressive* language. Lisp is designed to let you take the most complicated programming ideas and express them in a clear and appropriate way. Lispers have the freedom to write a program in exactly the way that is most helpful for solving any problem at hand.

The power at your fingertips when writing Lisp code is what makes it so different. Once you "get" Lisp, you'll be forever changed as a programmer. Even if you end up never writing Lisp code again for the rest of your life, learning Lisp will fundamentally change you as a coder.

In a way, learning a typical programming language is similar to learning a foreign language as an adult. Suppose you go out tomorrow and decide you're going to learn French. You may take every course on French that you can find, read materials that are only in French, and even move to France. But no matter what you do, your understanding of French will always remain a little imperfect. And no matter how good of a French speaker you eventually become, in your dreams you probably will still be speaking in your native language.

Lisp is different. It's not just like learning any foreign language. Once you've learned Lisp, you'll even dream in Lisp. Lisp is such a powerful idea that it will crowd out your previous programming experience and become your new mother tongue! Whenever you encounter a new programming idea in any language, you'll always say to yourself, "That's kind of how I'd do it in Lisp, except . . . ." That's the kind of power only Lisp will give you.

At this point, all you may know about Lisp is that at least one person (me) is extremely excited about it. But your time is valuable, and learning something new is bound to require some effort.

The good news is Lisp isn't really as difficult as it may seem at first glance. For instance, the following is a valid Lisp expression:

```
(+ 3 (* 2 4))
```

Can you guess what the value of this expression is? If you answered 11, then you've already figured out how to read basic Lisp code. It is written just like math, except that the functions—in this case, addition and multiplication—come before the numbers, and everything is in parentheses.

If Lisp Is So Great, Why Don't More People Use It?

Actually, a fair number of large companies *do* use Lisp for some serious work (you'll find a long list of industrial Lisp projects at *http://snipurl.com/e3lv9/*). Other programming languages are constantly "borrowing" features of Lisp and presenting them as the latest and greatest ideas. Also, the Semantic Web, which many believe will play a big role in the future of the Web, uses many tools written in Lisp.

NOTE   *The idea behind the Semantic Web is to create a set of protocols for websites to follow so that a computer can determine the "meaning" of information on a web page. This is done by annotating web pages with special metadata (usually in a format called Resource Description Framework, or RDF) that links to common vocabularies, which different websites may share. Many of the tools used for working with description logics and RDF data are written in Lisp (for example, RacerPro and AllegroGraph).*

So, Lisp certainly has a promising future. But some may think that learning Lisp is not worth the effort.

How did Lisp get this undeserved reputation?

I think that people use a rule of thumb when deciding what things in life are worth learning. Most people seek knowledge in one of the following three categories:

- What many other people learn (calculus, C++, and so on)
- What is easy to learn (hula-hooping, Ruby, and so on)
- What has value that is easy to appreciate (thermonuclear physics, for example, or that ridiculously loud whistle where you stick your fingers in your mouth)

Lisp doesn't fall into any of these categories. It's not as popular as calculus, particularly easy to learn, or as obviously valuable as that loud whistle. If we were to follow these (usually very sensible) rules of thumb, we would conclude that a reasonable person should stay away from Lisp. However, in the case of Lisp, we're going to throw out these rules. As you'll see from reading this book, Lisp gives you insights into computer programming that are so profound that every serious programmer should have some experience with this unusual language, even if it requires a little effort.

If you're still not convinced, you might want to take a peek at the comic book epilogue way at the end of the book. You might not be able to understand everything in there right now, but it will give you a feel for the advanced features available within Lisp and what makes Lisp programming different from other types of programming.

Where Did Lisp Come From?

The Lisp family of languages is truly ancient, with a history that differs from other languages. We'll need to travel far back in time to get to the beginning of it all.

A long time ago (way back in the 1940s), the Earth was covered by a giant ocean called the Panthalassic Ocean, along with a single barren land mass named Pangaea. In this unforgiving environment, the first computer programs evolved, written in pure machine language (or "ones and zeros," as they say).

These protolanguages were tightly bound to specific computer systems, such as the ENIAC, the Zuse Z3, and other early vacuum-tube contraptions. Often, these early computers were so primitive that "programming" them involved simply flipping switches or patching cables to physically encode each operation.

The dark days of these protolanguages saw a lot of experimentation with different computer architectures and an explosion of different computer instruction sets. Competition was fierce. While most of these primitive language experiments ultimately disappeared—victims of ancient battles for survival—others thrived.

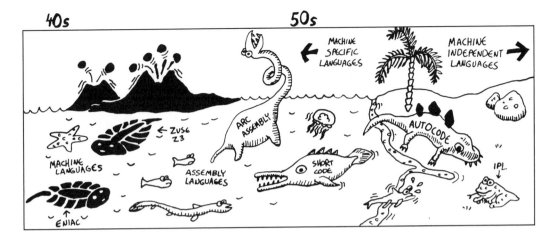

At a certain point, computers acquired their own in memory to store programs, along with primitive *assemblers* that allowed programs to be written in text, instead of with just pure numbers. These *assembly* languages included Short Code, ARC assembly, and EDSAC Initial Orders.

Assembly languages made software development much more efficient, enabling ancient assemblers to evade the many predators in this primordial ocean. But assembly languages still had significant limitations. They were always designed around the instruction set of a specific processor and so they were not portable across different machine architectures. Programming languages needed to evolve to survive beyond the confines of a specific machine instruction set.

The 1950s saw the arrival of the first machine-independent programming languages. Languages like Autocode and Information Processing Language accomplished this independence not only through lungs and legs, but also through new types of software, such as compilers and interpreters.

With compilers and interpreters, computer programs could now be written in a human-friendly syntax. A *compiler* can take a human-written computer program and convert it automatically into a machine-friendly binary format that the computer can execute. An *interpreter*, on the other hand, performs the actions described in a human-written program directly, without converting them all the way down to a machine-friendly binary format.

For the first time, programmers could use languages that were designed to make computer programming a pleasant activity, without needing to operate at the primitive level of the computer hardware. These interpreted and compiled programming languages are what we now think of as the first "true" programming languages. One of the most imposing of these early languages, FORTRAN (developed in 1957), was widely supported on different architectures and is still used heavily to this day.

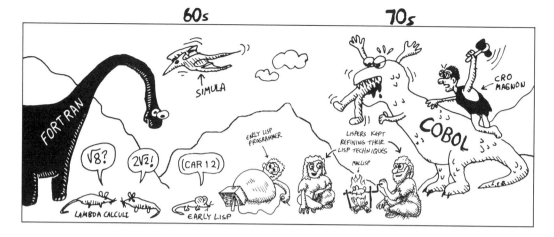

Up until this point, the most successful languages had been designed around one central idea: to offer a general design and syntax that would make programming as easy as possible for novices. However, designing a good programming language turns out to be very difficult. Hence, most of these languages, like FORTRAN, BASIC, and C, were really just a mishmash of older ideas, copied from one another and thrown together in a way that lacked any real beauty. They were usually easy to use in only superficial ways. Nonetheless, these fierce languages roamed the jungles for decades in search of easy prey.

In the shadows of these fearsome beasts lurked a small, humble, and entirely different sort of creature—mostly hidden from view, but present almost since the very first machine-independent languages crawled onto land. These were languages that used mathematical syntax, such as the lambda calculus, developed by mathematicians in the 1930s.

Not the least bit concerned with being pragmatic or easy for novices to learn, these languages were highly intelligent and wanted to push the limits of language design. They posed questions about program notation, language semantics, and the simplest possible language syntax.

From these highly intelligent mathematical syntaxes evolved one most notable creature: the original Lisp programming language. Unlike most other programming languages, it did not evolve from FORTRAN or other languages that were concerned with pragmatism or ease of use. Its lineage is a completely separate one, drawn straight from mathematics. But where did Lisp come from?

Some people claim that the story behind Lisp's origins has been forever lost in the fog of time. Others (who are probably more correct) say Lisp's creation was the work of John McCarthy in 1959. One day, it is said, he gathered together his tribe at MIT and presented an ingenious idea. McCarthy envisioned a completely theoretical programming language, which would have minimal syntax and semantics but, at the same time, create incredibly elegant programs. These programs were so elegant that even writing an interpreter for Lisp in Lisp itself would take only around 50 lines of computer code!

NOTE *John McCarthy published the paper "Recursive Functions of Symbolic Expressions and Their Computation by Machine, Part I," Communications of the ACM (April 1960): 184–195. You can read it at* http://www-formal.stanford.edu/jmc/recursive.pdf.

When McCarthy first published his idea, it was intended only as an intellectual exploration of mathematical syntax. But soon, the Lisp language evolved and could work with compilers and interpreters. It now ran on real computers, just like FORTRAN and the other programming languages! But unlike these other languages, Lisp retained a beauty derived from its mathematical ancestry.

Soon after the first Lisps appeared, the first Lisp programmers appeared, capturing these docile creatures and transforming them into ever-more-refined programming languages. Over time, these programmers turned the primal Lisps into dialects such as MACLISP and Interlisp.

2000

Although the hunting of early Lisps was a successful avocation for early Lisp programmers, it soon became clear that these hunters had a competitor: Cro-Magnon man. The Cro-Magnons were more aggressive than the peaceful Lisp programmers, attacking ever-bigger software development projects using fearsome languages such as COBOL. Developed for business applications, COBOL was an ugly and vile behemoth that nonetheless made lucrative prey for the Cro-Magnons. Lisp programmers, on the other hand, were more content contemplating elegant programming and hunting the occasional Lisp.

Now, while Lisp was an incredibly powerful idea, other programming languages already had a head start in mind share and more mature development tools. This made it a challenge for Lisps, and the Lisp programmers dependent on them, to get the traction they needed for mainstream success. However, the gentle Lispers were not concerned with such petty things. Despite their differing dispositions, the Lispers and the Cro-Magnons lived side by side in relative harmony.

In their own way, the Lispers were thriving. At that time, they benefited heavily from highly academic research in areas such as image recognition, computerized data classification, and other problems that fall under the general umbrella of *artificial intelligence (AI)*. The highly mathematical nature of these problems lent their investigation to a Lispy approach, and Lisp programmers built new dialects of Lisp into ever-more-advanced computer systems to attack them. Many consider this the Golden Age of Lisp.

Unfortunately, after this brief golden period, the winds unexpectedly turned on the poor Lispers. In the mid-1980s, a sudden tilt in the axis of the Earth altered the climate, causing shortages in the food sources that the Lisp languages needed to survive. Disappointments in the progress of AI research caused many grants for academic research to dry up, and much of the hardware favored by the Lisps (such as Lisp machines from Symbolics, Lisp Machine, Inc., and Texas Instruments) fell behind the capabilities of more traditional complex instruction set computer (CISC) and reduced instruction set computer (RISC) hardware architectures. The world had become an unwelcoming place for Lisps and the Lisp programmers that depended on them for survival. The "AI winter" had arrived, and Lisp was doomed.

This finally gave the Cro-Magnons the definite advantage in the language race. The new craze of megalithic, FORTRAN-derived, object-oriented languages—such as C++, developed in 1983—had slowly conquered commercial software development. This gave the Cro-Magnons complete immunity from the AI winter, which was afflicting the Lispers. Furthermore, the wily Cro-Magnons borrowed some of the ideas pioneered by the Lispers to patch up the problems of mainstream languages. Thus, garbage collection and parametric polymorphism, originally found in the Lisps, became common in the languages used by mainstream programmers.

Eventually, through immense effort, the language behemoths of olden days had been tamed by the Cro-Magnons into C#, Java, and similar languages. The belief arose that these languages were more pleasant to use as tools than anything available in the past, with the Golden Age of Lisp long forgotten. More recently, languages such as Python and Ruby have further refined these Cro-Magnon languages into more modern directions.

But what has happened to the Lisp programmers during all this time? Have they completely succumbed to the AI winter? Are they once again lurking in the shadows, waiting for another day in the sun? No one knows for sure. But if you look hard enough, maybe in the highest mountains, in the deepest jungles, or on the lowest basement levels of MIT, you may catch a glimpse of an odd sort of creature. Some call it the Windigo; others refer to it as a yeti, Sasquatch, or rms. But those who really know think it just might be—that it could only be—a Lisp programmer.

Where Does Lisp Get Its Power?

I've said that Lisp is a particularly powerful language. So what were the key insights that John McCarthy (and the other, later innovators of Lisp) had that made this power possible?

To make a programming language powerful, you need to make it expressive. Having an expressive language means that you can do a lot of stuff with very little actual code. But what traits does a language need to make this possible? I think there are two that are most important.

One trait is a lot of features built into the language. That way, for most things you need to get done, someone has already performed some of the work for you, and you can leverage that work to make your own code look pithy. Many modern languages have this trait. The Java language, for instance, is renowned for powerful libraries that, for example, let you acquire data from another PC over a socket with ease.

The second trait that gives a language power is letting you muck around inside it as deeply as possible to make it do your bidding. That way, even if the designers of the language never conceived of what you're trying to do, you can make your own changes to the language until it does exactly what you need to solve your problems elegantly. This trait is much more difficult to provide in a language. Suppose you wanted to add something like nested function definition support to Java. If you know Java well, thinking about how to add such support is in the realm of nightmares.

The reason most languages aren't good at supporting both of these traits simultaneously is that they conflict with each other. The richer a language is at the start, the more complicated it is. And the more complicated the language, the more painful it is to muck with that language. That's why making your own changes to the most mature programming languages is close to impossible.

Of course, if you try hard enough, you can always make fundamental changes to any language. For instance, when C++ was developed, it originally took the form of a C preprocessor. A special C program was written that could take code written in the new C++ dialect and convert it into plain-old C, which you could then just run through a standard C compiler. This is how Bjarne Stroustrup, the inventor of C++, was able to tweak the C language and add features to turn it into his own. However, writing a translator such as this is an extremely difficult and tedious process that you would consider only as a last resort.

In contrast, Lisp languages make it extremely easy for an experienced Lisper to alter the compiler/interpreter that runs a program, while still supporting rich language features with extensive libraries. In fact, messing around with the language within Lisp is easier than in any other language ever created!

For example, writing a function in Lisp to calculate the distance between two points would be simple, as in most other languages. But an experienced Lisper would find it equally easy to invent a new way to nest function definitions or devise a funky if-then command. Even writing your own object-oriented programming support inside Lisp is not complicated (and most Lispers have probably done so at some point). In Lisp, everyone gets to be a mini-Stroustrup!

How does Lisp make this neat feat possible? One of Lisp's core characteristics is that writing a Lisp directly in Lisp is, itself, unbelievably simple. It turns out that *this is the key property* that allows Lisp to break the paradox of the two traits. By starting out as a language that could perform a cool mathematical trick of elegantly writing itself, it ended up possessing the very property needed to be both feature-rich *and* tweakable. That, in turn, makes it the perfect tool for actually writing just about any kind of program at all!

Think of it this way: Give a programmer a fish command in his programming language, and he will eat Chinese takeout and drink Jolt for a day. Give a programmer a programming language that allows him to write his own fish command, and he'll eat Chinese takeout and drink Jolt for a lifetime (which, admittedly, would probably be cut short by nutritional deficiencies, and let's not even discuss the probable heart arrhythmias).

So, now you have an idea of why Lisp is a very cool and very unusual programming language. It has a long and atypical history compared with most programming languages. Most languages came from the world of engineering, whereas Lisp originated from a more mathematical background. It has a lot to offer to those willing to spend a little time learning something new.

SECTION **I**:
LISP IS POWER

1

GETTING STARTED WITH LISP

This chapter begins with an introduction to the various dialects of Lisp. Then we'll talk a bit about ANSI Common Lisp, the dialect that we'll be using in this book. Finally, you'll get started by installing and testing CLISP, the implementation of ANSI Common Lisp that will let you run all the Lisp games you're going to be creating!

Lisp Dialects

Any language that obeys the central principles of Lisp is considered a Lisp dialect. Since these principles are so simple, it's not surprising that literally hundreds of dialects of Lisp have been created. In fact, since so many budding Lispers create their own Lisp dialect as an exercise, there may be *thousands* of partially completed Lisps slumbering in long-abandoned directories on hard drives across the planet. However, the vast majority of the Lisp community uses two Lisps: ANSI Common Lisp (often abbreviated CL) and Scheme.

In this book, we'll be talking exclusively about the ANSI Common Lisp dialect, the slightly more popular of the two. Nevertheless, most of the knowledge you'll gain from reading this book will also be relevant to Scheme (although the names of functions tend to differ somewhat between the dialects).

A Tale of Two Lisps

Some deep philosophical differences exist between ANSI Common Lisp and Scheme, and they appeal to different programmer personalities. Once you learn more about Lisp languages, you can decide which dialect you prefer. There is no right or wrong choice.

To aid you in your decision, I have created the following personality test for you:

If you chose A, you like raw power in your language. You don't mind if your language is a bit ugly, due to a lot of pragmatic compromises, as long as you can still write tight code. ANSI Common Lisp is the best language for you! ANSI Common Lisp traces its ancestry most directly from the ancient Lisp dialects, built on top of millions of programmer hours, giving it incredibly rich functionality. Sure, it has some baroque function names due to countless historical accidents, but this Lisp can really fly in the right hacker's hands.

If you chose B, you like languages that are clean and elegant. You are more interested in fundamental programming problems and are happy to while away on a beautiful meadow, contemplating the beauty of your code, occasionally writing a research paper on theoretical computing problems. Scheme is the language for you! It was created in the mid-1970s by Guy L. Steele and Gerald Jay Sussman and involved some soul-searching about the ideal Lisp. Code in Scheme tends to be slightly more verbose, since Schemers care more about mathematical purity in their code than creating the shortest programs possible.

If you chose C, you're someone who wants it all: the power of ANSI CL and the mathematical beauty of Scheme. At this time, no Lisp dialect completely fits the bill, but that could change in the future. One language that might work for you (although it is sacrilege to make this claim in a Lisp book) is Haskell. It is not considered a Lisp dialect, but its followers obey paradigms popular among Lispers, such as keeping the syntax uniform, supporting native lists, and relying heavily on higher-order functions. More important, it has an extreme mathematical rigor (even more so than Scheme) that allows it to hide very powerful functionality under a squeaky clean surface. It's essentially a wolf in sheep's clothing. Like Lisp, Haskell is a language that any programmer would benefit from investigating further.

Up-and-Coming Lisps

As just mentioned, there really isn't a true Lisp dialect available yet that possesses both the power and flexibility of ANSI Common Lisp and the elegance of Scheme. However, some new contenders on the horizon may attain the best-of-both-worlds crown in the near future.

One new Lisp that is showing promise is Clojure, a dialect developed by Rich Hickey. Clojure is built on the Java platform, allowing it to leverage a lot of mature Java libraries right out of the box. Also, Clojure contains some clever and well-thought-out features to ease multithreaded programming, which makes it a useful tool for programming seemingly ubiquitous multicore CPUs.

Another interesting challenger is Arc. It is a true Lisp language being principally developed by Paul Graham, a well-known Lisper. Arc is still in an early stage of development, and opinion varies widely on how much of an improvement it is over other Lisps. Also, its development has been progressing at a glacially slow pace. It will be a while before anyone can say if Arc might be a meaningful contender.

We'll be dipping our toes in some Arc and Clojure in the epilogue.

Lisp Dialects Used for Scripting

Some Lisp dialects are used for scripting, including these:

- Emacs Lisp is used for scripting inside the popular (and overall awesome) Emacs text editor.
- Guile Scheme is used as a scripting language in several open source applications.
- Script-Fu Scheme is used with the GIMP image editor.

These dialects are forks from older versions of the main Lisp branches and are not typically used for creating stand-alone applications. However, they are still perfectly respectable dialects of Lisp.

ANSI Common Lisp

In 1981, in order to cope with the dizzying number of dialects of the language, members of the varying Lisp communities drafted a specification for a new dialect named Common Lisp. In 1986, this language, after further adjustments, was turned into the ANSI Common Lisp standard. Many of the developers of older versions of Lisp modified their interpreters and compilers to conform to this new standard, which became the most popular version of Lisp and remains so to this day.

NOTE *Throughout this book, the term* Common Lisp *refers to the version of Common Lisp defined by the ANSI standard.*

A key design goal with Common Lisp was to create a *multiparadigm language*, meaning it includes support for many different styles of programming. You've probably heard of *object-oriented programming*, which can be done quite nicely in Common Lisp. Other programming styles you may not have heard of before include *functional programming*, *generic programming*, and *domain-specific language programming*. These are all well supported within Common Lisp. You'll be learning about each of these styles, along with others, as we progress through this book.

Getting Started with CLISP

Many great Lisp compilers are available, but one in particular is easiest to get started with: CLISP, an open source Common Lisp. CLISP is simple to install and runs on any operating system.

Other popular Lisps include Steel Bank Common Lisp (SBCL), a fast Common Lisp that's considered a bit more heavy-duty than CLISP and also open source; Allegro Common Lisp, a powerful commercial Lisp by Franz, Inc; LispWorks; Clozure CL; and CMUCL. Mac users may want to consider LispWorks or Clozure CL, which will be easier to get running on their machines. However, for our purposes, CLISP is the best choice.

NOTE *Starting with Chapter 12, we'll be using some CLISP-specific commands that are considered nonstandard. However, up until that point, any implementation of Common Lisp will work for running the examples in this book.*

Installing CLISP

You can download a CLISP installer from *http://clisp.cons.org/*. It will run on Windows PCs, Macs, and Linux variants. On a Windows PC, you simply run an install program. On a Mac, there are some additional steps, which are detailed on the website.

On a Debian-based Linux machine, you should find that CLISP already exists in your standard sources. Just type `apt-get install clisp` at the command line, and you'll have CLISP installed automatically.

For other Linux distributions (Fedora, SUSE, and so on), you can use standard packages listed under "Linux packages" on the CLISP website. And experienced Linux users can compile CLISP from source.

Starting Up CLISP

To run CLISP, type `clisp` from your command line. If all goes according to plan, you'll see the following prompt:

```
$ clisp
  i i i i i i i      ooooo   o      ooooooo   ooooo   ooooo
  I I I I I I I     8     8 8          8    8   o 8   8
  I \ `+' / I       8       8          8    8       8   8
   \ `-+-' /        8       8          8    ooooo   8oooo
    `-__|__-'       8       8          8         8 8
        |           8     o 8          8    o    8 8
  ------+------      ooooo   8oooooo ooo8ooo  ooooo  8
```

Copyright (c) Bruno Haible, Michael Stoll 1992, 1993
Copyright (c) Bruno Haible, Marcus Daniels 1994-1997
Copyright (c) Bruno Haible, Pierpaolo Bernardi, Sam Steingold 1998
Copyright (c) Bruno Haible, Sam Steingold 1999-2000
Copyright (c) Sam Steingold, Bruno Haible 2001-2006

```
[1]>
```

Like all Common Lisp environments, CLISP will automatically place you into a *read-eval-print loop* (*REPL*) after you start it up. This means you can immediately start typing in Lisp code.

Try it out by typing **(+ 3 (* 2 4))**. You'll see the result printed below the expression:

```
[1]> (+ 3 (* 2 4))
11
```

This shows how the REPL works. You type in an expression, and then the Lisp will immediately evaluate it and return the resulting value. When you want to shut down CLISP, just type **(quit)**.

Now that you have CLISP working on your computer, you're ready to write a Lisp game!

What You've Learned

In this chapter, we discussed the different dialects of Lisp and installing CLISP. You learned the following along the way:

- There are two main dialects of Lisp: Common Lisp and Scheme. Both have a lot to offer, but we'll focus on Common Lisp in this book.

- Common Lisp is a multiparadigm language, meaning that it supports many different programming styles.

- CLISP is a Common Lisp implementation that is easy to set up, making it a great choice for a Lisp novice.
- You can type in Lisp commands directly from the CLISP *REPL*.

2

CREATING YOUR FIRST LISP PROGRAM

Now that we've discussed some of the philosophy of Lisp and have a running CLISP environment, we're ready to write some actual Lisp code in the form of a simple game.

The Guess-My-Number Game

This first game we'll write is pretty much the simplest game imaginable. It's the classic guess-my-number game.

In this game, you pick a number from 1 to 100, and the computer has to guess it.

The following shows what game play might look like if you pick the number 23. The computer starts by guessing 50, and with each successive guess, you enter (smaller) or (bigger) until the computer guesses your number.

```
> (guess-my-number)
```

```
> (smaller)
25
> (smaller)
12
> (bigger)
18
> (bigger)
21
> (bigger)
23
```

To create this game, we need to write three functions: guess-my-number, smaller, and bigger. The player simply calls these functions from the REPL. As you saw in the previous chapter, when you start CLISP (or any other Lisp), you are presented with the REPL, from which the commands you type will be *read*, then *evaluated*, and finally *printed*. In this case, we're running the commands guess-my-number, smaller, and bigger.

To call a function in Lisp, you put parentheses around it, along with any parameters you wish to give the function. Since these particular functions don't require any parameters, we simply surround their names in parentheses when we enter them.

Let's think about the strategy behind this simple game. After a little thought, we come up with the following steps:

1. Determine the upper and lower (big and small) limit of the player's number. Since the range is between 1 and 100, the smallest possible number would be 1 and the biggest would be 100.

2. Guess a number in between these two numbers.

3. If the player says the number is smaller, lower the big limit.

4. If the player says the number is bigger, raise the small limit.

By following these simple steps, cutting the range of possible numbers in half with every guess, the computer can quickly hone in on the player's number.

This type of search is called a *binary search*. As you may know, binary searches like this are used all the time in computer programming. You could follow these same steps, for instance, to efficiently find a specific number given a sorted table of values. In that case, you would simply track the smallest and largest row in that table, and then quickly hone in on the correct row in an analogous manner.

Defining Global Variables in Lisp

As the player calls the functions that make up our game, the program will need to track the small and big limits. In order to do this, we'll need to create two global variables called *small* and *big*.

Defining the small and big Variables

A variable that is defined globally in Lisp is called a *top-level definition*. We can create new top-level definitions with the defparameter function:

```
> (defparameter *small* 1)
*SMALL*
> (defparameter *big* 100)
*BIG*
```

The function name defparameter is a bit confusing, since it doesn't really have anything to do with parameters. What it does is let you define a *global variable*.

The first argument we send to defparameter is the name of the new variable. The asterisks surrounding the names *big* and *small*—affectionately called *earmuffs*—are completely arbitrary and optional. Lisp sees the asterisks as part of the variable names and ignores them. Lispers like to mark all their global variables in this way as a convention, to make them easy to distinguish from local variables, which are discussed later in this chapter.

NOTE *Although earmuffs may be "optional" in a strictly technical sense, I suggest that you use them. I cannot vouch for your safety if you ever post any code to a Common Lisp newsgroup and your global variables are missing their earmuffs.*

An Alternative Global Variable Definition Function

When you set the value of a global variable using defparameter, any value previously stored in the variable will be overwritten:

```
> (defparameter *foo* 5)
FOO
> *foo*
5
```

```
> (defparameter *foo* 6)
FOO
> *foo*
6
```

As you can see, when we redefine the variable *foo*, its value changes.

Another command that you can use for declaring global variables, called defvar, won't overwrite previous values of a global variable:

```
> (defvar *foo* 5)
FOO
> *foo*
5
> (defvar *foo* 6)
FOO
> *foo*
5
```

Some Lispers prefer to use defvar instead of defparameter when defining global variables. In this book, however, we'll be using defparameter exclusively.

NOTE   *When you read about Lisp in other places, you may also see programmers using the term* dynamic variable *or* special variable *when referring to a global variable in Common Lisp. This is because global variables in Common Lisp have some special abilities, which we'll be discussing in future chapters.*

Basic Lisp Etiquette

The way commands are called and the way code is formatted in Lisp is somewhat strange compared with other languages. First of all, you need to surround the command (and its arguments) with parentheses, as with the defparameter function:

```
> (defparameter *small* 1)
*SMALL*
```

Without the parentheses, a command will not be called.

Also, spaces and line breaks are completely ignored when Lisp reads in your code. That means you could call this command in any crazy way, with the same result:

```
> (              defparameter
        *small* 1)
*SMALL*
```

Because Lisp code can be formatted in such flexible ways, Lispers have a lot of conventions for formatting commands, including when to use multiple lines and indentation. We'll loosely follow some of the common indentation conventions in the code examples in this book. However, we're more interested in writing games than in discussing source code indentation rules, so we're not going to be spending too much time on code layout rules in this book.

Defining Global Functions in Lisp

Our guess-my-number game has the computer respond to the player's request to start the game, and then to requests for either smaller or bigger guesses. For these, we need to define three global functions: guess-my-number, smaller, and bigger. We'll also define a function to start over with a different number, called start-over. In Common Lisp, functions are defined with defun, like this:

```
(defun function_name (arguments)
  ...)
```

First, we specify the name and arguments for the function. Then we follow it up with the code that composes the function's logic.

Defining the guess-my-number Function

The first function we'll define is guess-my-number. This function uses the values of the *big* and *small* variables to generate a guess of the player's number. The definition looks like this:

```
> (defun guess-my-number ()
❶    (ash (+ *small* *big*) -1))
❷ GUESS-MY-NUMBER
```

The empty parentheses, (), after the function name guess-my-number indicate that this function doesn't require any parameters.

Although you don't need to worry about indentation or line breaks when entering code snippets at the REPL, you must be sure to place parentheses correctly. If you forget a parenthesis or put one in the wrong place, you'll most likely get an error.

Whenever we run a piece of code like this in the REPL, the resulting value of the entered expression will be printed. Every command in Common Lisp generates a return value. The defun command, for instance, simply returns the name of the newly created function. This is why we see the name of the function parroted back to us in the REPL after we call defun ❷.

What does this function do? As discussed earlier, the computer's best guess in this game will be a number in between the two limits. To accomplish this, we choose the average of the two limits. However, if the average number ends up being a fraction, we'll want to use a near-average number, since we're guessing only whole numbers.

We implement this in the guess-my-number function by first adding the numbers that represent the high and low limits, then using the arithmetic shift function, ash, to halve the sum of the limits and shorten the result. The code (+ *small* *big*) adds together those two variables. Because the addition happens within another function call, ❶, the resulting sum is then passed to the ash function.

The parentheses surrounding the ash function and the addition (+) function are mandatory in Lisp. These parentheses are what tell Lisp, "I want you to call this function."

The built-in Lisp function ash looks at a number in binary form, and then shifts its binary bits to the left or right, dropping any bits lost in the process. For example, the number 11 written in binary is 1011. We can move the bits in this number to the left with ash by using 1 as the second argument:

```
> (ash 11 1)
22
```

This produces 22, which is 10110 in binary. We can move the bits to the right (and lop off the bit on the end) by passing in -1 as the second argument:

```
> (ash 11 -1)
5
```

This produces 5, which is 101 in binary.

By using the ash function in guess-my-number, we are continually halving our search space of possible numbers to quickly narrow down to the final correct number. As already mentioned, this halving process is called a *binary search*, a useful technique in computer programming. The ash function is commonly used for such binary searches in Lisp.

Let's see what happens when we call our new function:

```
> (guess-my-number)
50
```

Since this is our first guess, the output we see when calling this function tells us that everything is working as planned: The program picked the number 50, right in between 1 and 100.

When programming in Lisp, you'll write many functions that won't explicitly print values on the screen. Instead, they'll simply return the value calculated in the body of the function. For instance, let's say we wanted a function that just returns the number 5. Here's how we could write this:

```
> (defun return-five ()
❶    (+ 2 3))
```

Because the value calculated in the body of the function ❶ evaluates to 5, calling (return-five) will just return 5.

This is how guess-my-number is designed. We see this calculated result on the screen (the number 50) not because the function causes the number to display, but because this is a feature of the REPL.

NOTE *If you've used other programming languages before, you may remember having to write something like* return... *to cause a value to be returned. In Lisp, this is not necessary. The final value calculated in the body of the function is returned automatically.*

Defining the smaller and bigger Functions

Now we'll write our smaller and bigger functions. Like guess-my-number, these are global functions defined with defun:

```
❶ > (defun smaller ()
❷     (setf *big* (1- (guess-my-number)))
❸     (guess-my-number))
   SMALLER
   > (defun bigger ()
❹     (setf *small* (1+ (guess-my-number)))
       (guess-my-number))
   BIGGER
```

First, we use defun to start the definition of a new global function smaller. Because this function takes no parameters, the parentheses are empty ❶.

Next, we use the setf function to change the value of our global variable *big* ❷. Since we know the number must be smaller than the last guess, the biggest it can now be is one less than that guess. The code (1- (guess-my-number)) calculates this: It first calls our guess-my-number function to get the most recent guess, and then it uses the function 1-, which subtracts 1 from the result.

Finally, we want our smaller function to show us a new guess. We do this by putting a call to guess-my-number as the final line in the function body ❸. This time, guess-my-number will use the updated value of *big*, causing it to calculate the next guess. The final value of our function will be returned automatically, causing our new guess (generated by guess-my-number) to be returned by the smaller function.

The bigger function works in exactly the same manner, except that it raises the *small* value instead. After all, if you call the bigger function, you are saying your number is bigger than the previous guess, so the smallest it can now be (which is what the *small* variable represents) is *one more* than the previous guess. The function 1+ simply adds 1 to the value returned by guess-my-number ❹.

Here we see our functions in action, with the number 56 as our guess:

```
> (bigger)
75
> (smaller)
62
> (smaller)
56
```

Defining the start-over Function

To complete our game, we'll add the function start-over to reset our global variables:

```
(defun start-over ()
   (defparameter *small* 1)
   (defparameter *big* 100)
   (guess-my-number))
```

As you can see, the start-over function resets the values of *small* and *big* and then calls guess-my-number again to return a new starting guess. Whenever you want to start a brand-new game with a different number, you can call this function to reset the game.

Defining Local Variables in Lisp

For our simple game, we've defined global variables and functions. However, in most cases you'll want to limit your definitions to a single function or a block of code. These are called *local* variables and functions.

To define a local variable, use the command let. A let command has the following structure:

```
❶ (let (variable declarations)
❷    ...body...)
```

The first thing inside the let command is a list of variable declarations ❶. This is where we can declare one or more local variables. Then, in the body of the command (and only within this body), we can use these variables ❷. Here is an example of the let command:

```
❶ > (let ((a 5)
❷         (b 6))
❸    (+ a b))
  11
```

In this example, we've declared the values 5 and 6 for the variables a ❶ and b ❷, respectively. These are our variable declarations. Then, in the body of the let command, we added them together ❸, resulting in the displayed value of 11.

When using a let expression, you must surround the entire list of declared variables with parentheses. Also, you must surround each pair of variable names and initial variables with another set of parentheses.

NOTE *Although the indentation and line breaks are completely arbitrary, because the names of the variables and their values in a* let *expression form a kind of simple table, common practice is to align the declared variables vertically. This is why the b is placed directly underneath the a in the preceding example.*

Defining Local Functions in Lisp

We define local functions using the `flet` command. The `flet` command has the following structure:

```
❶ (flet ((function_name (arguments)
❷          ...function body...))
❸   ...body...)
```

At the top of the `flet`, we declare a function (in the first two lines). This function will then be available to us in the body ❸. A function declaration consists of a function name, the arguments to that function ❶, and the function body ❷, where we put the function's code.

Here is an example:

```
❶ > (flet ((f (n)
❷            (+ n 10)))
❸     (f 5))
  15
```

In this example, we define a single function, f, which takes a single argument, n ❶. The function f then adds 10 to this variable n ❷, which has been passed in it. Then we call this function with the number 5 as the argument, causing the value 15 to be returned ❸.

As with `let`, you can define one or more functions within the scope of the `flet`.

A single `flet` command can be used to declare multiple local functions at once. Simply add multiple function declarations in the first part of the command:

```
❶ > (flet ((f (n)
             (+ n 10))
❷          (g (n)
             (- n 3)))
     (g (f 5)))
  12
```

Here, we have declared two functions: one named f ❶ and one named g ❷. In the body of the `flet`, we can then refer to both functions. In this example, the body first calls f with 5 to yield 15, then calls g to subtract 3, leading to 12 as a final result.

To make function names available in defined functions, we can use the `labels` command. It's identical in its basic structure to the `flet` command. Here's an example:

```
❶ > (labels ((a (n)
               (+ n 5))
❷            (b (n)
```

```
❸              (+ (a n) 6)))
❹     (b 10))
      21
```

In this example, the local function a adds 5 to a number ❶. Next, the function b is declared ❷. It calls the function a, and then adds 6 to the result ❸. Finally, the function b is called with the value 10 ❹. Since 10 plus 6 plus 5 equals 21, the number 21 becomes the final value of the entire expression. The special step that requires us to use labels instead of flet is where the function b calls the function a ❸. If we had used flet, the function b would not have "known" about the function a.

The labels command lets you call one local function from another, and it allows you to have a function call itself. This is commonly done in Lisp code and is called *recursion*. (You will see many examples of recursion in future chapters.)

What You've Learned

In this chapter, we discussed the basic Common Lisp commands for defining variables and functions. Along the way, you learned the following:

- To define a global variable, use the defparameter command.
- To define a global function, use the defun command.
- Use the let and flet commands to define local variables and functions, respectively.
- The function labels is like flet, but it lets functions call themselves. Functions that call themselves are called *recursive* functions.

3

EXPLORING THE SYNTAX
OF LISP CODE

As you've learned so far, Lisp commands must be entered in a rather unorthodox way, with parentheses surrounding each command. In this chapter, we'll explore why Lisp works this way.

To understand why any language—whether it's a programming language or a human language—looks a certain way, we need to begin with two concepts from the field of linguistics: syntax and semantics.

Syntax and Semantics

Here is a typical sentence in the English language:

My dog ate my homework.

This sentence has the correct syntax for a sentence in English. The *syntax* of a piece of text represents the basic rules that it needs to follow to be a valid sentence. Here are some of the rules of sentences in the English language that this text obeys:

- The sentence ends in a punctuation mark.
- The sentence contains a subject and a verb.
- The sentence is made up of letters in the English alphabet (as opposed to Egyptian hieroglyphics or Sumerian cuneiform).

However, there is more to a sentence than just its syntax. We also care about what the sentence actually means. When we talk about the *semantics* of a sentence, we're referring to its meaning.

For instance, here are some sentences that all roughly have identical semantics:

My dog ate my homework.

The canine, which I possess, has consumed my school assignment.

Der Hund hat meine Hausarbeit gefressen.

The first two are just different ways of saying the same thing in English. The third sentence is in German, but it still has the same meaning and, hence, semantics as the first two.

The same distinction between these two ideas exists in programming languages. For instance, here is a valid line of code written in C++:

```
((foo<bar>)*(g++)).baz(!&qux::zip->ding());
```

This line of code obeys the rules of C++ syntax. To make my point, I put in a lot of weird syntax that is unique to C++, which differentiates it from other languages. If you were to place this line of code in a program of another programming language with a different syntax, it would probably be invalid and cause an error.

Of course, this C++ programming code also means something. If we were to put this line of code in a C++ program (in the proper context), it would cause your computer to *do* something. The actions that a program performs are the *semantics* of the program. It is usually possible to write a program that has the same semantics in different programming languages; that is, the program will do the same thing in both languages.

What all this boils down to is that most programming languages have similar semantic powers. However, basic Lisp code is different from code in any other major programming language in that it has a far simpler syntax. *Having a simple syntax is a defining feature of the Lisp language.*

The Building Blocks of Lisp Syntax

From the crazy line of C++ code in the previous section, you can get the idea that C++ has a lot of weird syntax—for indicating namespaces, dereferencing pointers, performing casts, referencing member functions, performing Boolean operations, and so on.

If you were to write a C++ compiler, you would need to do a lot of hard work so that the compiler could read this code and obey the many C++ syntax rules, before you could make any sense of the code.

Writing a Lisp compiler or interpreter is much easier. The part of a Lisp compiler or interpreter that reads in the code (which Lispers actually call the *reader*) is simpler than in C++ or any other major programming language. Take a random piece of Lisp code:

```
(defun square (n)
    (* n n))
```

This function declaration, which creates a function that simply squares a number, consists of nothing more than parentheses and symbols. In fact, you can view it as just a bunch of nested lists, delimited by parentheses.

Lisp only has one way of organizing bits of code: It uses parentheses to organize the code into *lists*.

All basic Lisp code uses this simple list-like syntax:

But what sorts of things can we put into these lists? Well, besides other lists, we can also put symbols, numbers, and strings into our code. Here, we'll look at these basic building blocks, or datatypes, you'll use in Lisp. (We'll discuss many other Common Lisp datatypes in later chapters.)

Symbols

Symbols are a fundamental type of data in Lisp and are used extensively. A symbol in Lisp is a stand-alone word. Common Lisp symbols are typically made up of letters, numbers, and characters like + - / * = < > ? ! _. Some examples of valid Lisp symbols are foo, ice9, my-killer-app27, and even --<<==>>--.

Symbols in Common Lisp are *case-insensitive* (although most Lispers avoid using uppercase). To illustrate this, we'll use a function called eq, which lets us see if two symbols are identical:

```
> (eq 'fooo 'FoOo)
T
```

As you can see, this function returned T, which tells us that Lisp considers these two symbols to be identical. (For now, ignore the quotation mark in front of the symbols. This will be explained shortly, when we discuss *data mode*.)

Numbers

Lisp supports both floating-point numbers and integers. When you write a number, the presence of a decimal point determines whether your number is seen as a floating-point number or an integer. The numbers 1 and 1.0 are two different entities in Common Lisp.

For instance, if you use most math functions with both an integer and a floating-point number, the integer will become "poisoned," and a floating-point number will be returned. Here's a case in point:

```
> (+ 1 1.0)
2.0
```

Note that the decimal point in the returned number, 2.0, indicates that it is a floating-point number.

Lisp can perform some amazing feats with numbers, especially when compared with most other languages. For instance, here we're using the function expt to calculate the fifty-third power of 53:

```
> (expt 53 53)
24356848165022712132477606520104725518533453128685640844505130879576720609150223301256150373
```

Isn't that cool? Most languages would choke on a calculation involving such a large number.

Finally, you should know that something weird could happen if you divide two integers:

```
> (/ 4 6)
2/3
```

The division function is dividing the 4 by 6. But instead of returning a fraction (0.66666...) as you might expect, it returns a *rational number*, represented as two integers with a division symbol between them. So the 2/3 result represents a single rational number, which is the mathematically ideal way to encode a fraction such as this.

Note that we get a different answer if there is a floating-point number in our calculation:

```
> (/ 4.0 6)
0.6666667
```

As in the previous example, the number with the decimal point (4.0) has poisoned our numbers to give us a fraction as a result.

If you're not a math geek, this might not be of much use to you, but at least you now know what's happening if you see this sort of thing while you're coding. You can also rest assured that Lisp will do the right thing with this number when you use it later on in another calculation. Lisp is smart.

Strings

The last basic building block in Lisp is the *string*. Although strings aren't really that fundamental to Lisp from a theoretical standpoint, any program that communicates with a human will usually need strings, because humans like to communicate with text.

To indicate a string in Lisp, surround characters with double quotes. For example, "Tutti Frutti" is a valid string.

We can display a string using a function called princ:

```
> (princ "Tutti Frutti")
❶ Tutti Frutti
❷ "Tutti Frutti"
```

Notice that printing our text at the REPL[1] will cause the text to appear twice. First, we see the actual printing caused by the princ command ❶. However, since the REPL will always show the result of evaluating the entered expression, we see our string parroted back to us ❷. This is because the princ function also returns a value, which happens to be the source string.

A string can also contain so-called *escaped characters*. If you want a string to include double quotes or a backslash, you'll need to prefix these characters with a backslash. For example, this string has two escaped quotes:

```
> (princ "He yelled \"Stop that thief!\" from the busy street.")
He yelled "Stop that thief!" from the busy street.
```

As you can see, the backslashes in front of the two quotes tell Lisp that these are literal quotation marks in the string, shown in the displayed string just like any other character.

How Lisp Distinguishes Between Code and Data

When we write our Lisp program, how does Lisp decide which parts of our program consist of code (stuff to be executed) and which parts are just data? The syntax of Lisp has a special way of distinguishing between the two.

Common Lisp uses two modes when it reads your code: a *code mode* and a *data mode*. You can switch between these two modes when writing Lisp code.

---

1. As discussed in Chapter 2, in a read-eval-print loop (or REPL), the functions we enter will be read, then evaluated, and finally printed.

Code Mode

Whenever you type something into the Lisp REPL, the compiler assumes that you're entering a command you want to execute. In other words, Lisp always assumes that you're writing code and defaults to code mode.

As we've already discussed, Lisp will expect Lisp code to be entered as a list. However, the code should be in a special type of list: a *form*. So when you're in code mode, as you are when you start typing into the REPL, the commands you enter need to be structured as forms:

A form is simply a list with a special command at the beginning—typically the name of a function.

When reading a form, Lisp sends all other items in the list to the function as parameters. For example, enter the following into your REPL:

```
> (expt 2 3)
8
```

This calculates 2^3 = 8. It does this by calling expt, which computes an exponent. This command was entered in the standard way for Lisp: as a form with the function name at the beginning.

When Lisp reads the text for the parameters of such a command, it usually assumes that these parameters are *also* in code mode. Here's an example:

```
> (expt 2 (+ 3 4))
128
```

This example has two nested forms. Lisp first looks at the entire expression in code mode. It determines that we've entered a form for the expt command. Then Lisp looks at the arguments to this command, also in code mode. One of these arguments (+ 3 4) is a form in its own right. This form is then executed, yielding 7. Afterward, this result is passed to the outer expt form, which is then executed.

Data Mode

As you might imagine, any stuff written in data mode is treated as data. This means the computer will not try to "execute" it, which allows us to have information in our code that's just plain old data.

Let's take a look at data mode in action. We'll enter the same form that we entered in code mode in the previous example, with one difference:

```
> '(expt 2 3)
(expt 2 3)
```

This time, we put a single quote in front of the list. Instead of responding with the sum of the numbers 1 and 2, Lisp simply parrots our expression to us. The single quote tells Lisp to treat the subsequent form as a chunk of data—simply a list of items. Lisp then prints the result of evaluating what we entered, which is the list itself. It ignores any functions or variables in our list, treating everything as data.

Placing a quote in front of lists so that they won't be evaluated as a command is called *quoting*. By using quoting, you can tell Lisp, "This next part isn't a command. It's just a chunk of data for my program."

Lists in Lisp

Lists are a crucial feature in Lisp. They are what hold all your Lisp code (as well as data) together. Take any basic piece of Lisp code, such as the following:

```
(expt 2 3)
```

This piece of code contains a symbol (expt) and two numbers, all tied together as a list, indicated by the parentheses.

You can think of a Lisp program as a house. If you were to build a house in Lisp, your walls would be made out of lists. The bricks would be made out of symbols, numbers, and strings. However, a wall needs mortar to hold it together. In the same way, lists in Lisp are held together by structures called *cons cells*.

Cons Cells

Lists in Lisp are held together with cons cells. Understanding the relationship between cons cells and lists will give you a better idea of how Lisp works.

A cons cell looks like this:

It's made of two little connected boxes, both of which can point at other things. A cons cell can point to another cons cell or another type of Lisp data. By being able to point to two different things, it's possible to link cons cells together into lists. In fact, lists in Lisp are just an abstract illusion—all of them are actually composed of cons cells.

For instance, suppose we create the list '(1 2 3). Here's how this list is represented in computer memory:

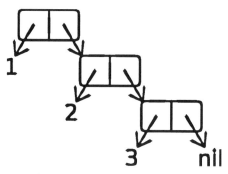

It's created using three cons cells. Each cell points to a number, as well as the next cons cell for the list. The final cons cell then points at nil, to terminate the list. (If you've ever used a linked list in another programming language, this is the same basic idea.) You can think of this arrangement like a calling chain for your friends: "When I know about a party this weekend, I'll call Bob, and then Bob will call Lisa, who will call . . ." Each person in a calling chain is responsible for only one phone call, which activates the next call in the list.

List Functions

Manipulating lists is extremely important in Lisp programming. There are three basic functions for manipulating cons cells (and hence lists) in Lisp: cons, car, and cdr.

The cons Function

If you want to link any two pieces of data in your Lisp program (regardless of type), the usual way to do that is with the cons function. When you call cons, the Lisp compiler typically allocates a small chunk of memory, the cons cell, that can hold two references to the objects being linked. (Usually, the second of the two items being linked will be a list.) For example, let's link the symbol chicken to the symbol cat:

```
> (cons 'chicken 'cat)
(CHICKEN . CAT)
```

As you can see, cons returns a single object, the cons cell, represented by parentheses and a dot between the two connected items. Don't confuse this with a regular list. The dot in the middle makes this a cons cell, just linking those two items together.

Notice how we prefix our two pieces of data with a single quote to make sure that Lisp sees them as just data and doesn't try to evaluate them as code.

If instead of another piece of data, we attach the symbol nil on the right side of the list, something special happens:

```
> (cons 'chicken 'nil)
(CHICKEN)
```

Unlike with our cat, the nil does not show in the output this time. There's a simple reason for this: nil is a special symbol that is used to terminate a list in Lisp. That said, the Lisp REPL is taking a shortcut and just saying that we created a list with one item, our chicken. It could have displayed the result by explicitly showing our cons cell and printing (CHICKEN . NIL). However, because this result is coincidentally also a list, it instead will show the list notation.

The lesson here is that Lisp will always go out of its way to "hide" the cons cells from you. When it can, it will show your results using lists. It will show a cons cell (with the dot between the objects) only if there isn't a way to show your result using lists.

The previous example can also be written like this:

```
> (cons 'chicken ())
(CHICKEN)
```

The *empty list*, (), can be used interchangeably with the nil symbol in Common Lisp. Thinking of the terminator of a list as an empty list makes sense. What do you get when you add a chicken to an empty list? Just a list with a chicken in it. The cons function also can add a new item to the front of the list. For example, to add pork to the front of a list containing (beef chicken), use cons like so:

```
> (cons 'pork '(beef chicken))
(PORK BEEF CHICKEN)
```

When Lispers talk about using cons, they say they are *consing* something. In this example, we consed pork to a list containing beef and chicken.

Since all lists are made of cons cells, our (beef chicken) list must have been created from its own two cons cells, perhaps like this:

```
> (cons 'beef (cons 'chicken ()))
(BEEF CHICKEN)
```

Combining the previous two examples, we can see what all the lists look like when viewed as conses. This is what is *really* happening:

```
> (cons 'pork (cons 'beef (cons 'chicken ())))
(PORK BEEF CHICKEN)
```

Basically, this is telling us that when we cons together a list of three items, we get a list of three items. No wholesale copying or deleting of data ever needs to take place.

The REPL echoed back to us our entered items as a list, (pork beef chicken), but it could just as easily (though a little less conveniently) have reported back the items exactly as we entered them: (cons 'pork (cons 'beef (cons 'chicken ()))). Either response would have been perfectly correct. *In Lisp, a chain of cons cells and a list are exactly the same thing.*

The car and cdr Functions

Lists are just long chains of two-item cells.

The car function is used for getting the thing out of the *first* slot of a cell:

```
> (car '(pork beef chicken))
PORK
```

The cdr function is used to grab the value out of the *second* slot, or the remainder of a list:

```
> (cdr '(pork beef chicken))
(BEEF CHICKEN)
```

You can string together car and cdr into new functions like cadr, cdar, or cadadr. This lets you succinctly extract specific pieces of data out of complex lists. Entering cadr is the same as using car and cdr together—it returns the second item from a list. (The first slot of the second cons cell would contain that item.) Take a look at this example:

```
❶ > (cdr '(pork beef chicken))
  (BEEF CHICKEN)
❷ > (car '(beef chicken))
  BEEF
```

❸ > (car (cdr '(pork beef chicken)))
BEEF
❹ > (cadr '(pork beef chicken))
BEEF

We know that cdr will take away the first item in a list ❶. If we then take that shortened list and use car, we'll get the first item in the new list ❷. Then, if we use these two commands together, we'll get the second item in the original list ❸. Finally, if we use the cadr command, it gives us the same result as using car and cdr together ❹. Essentially, using the cadr command is the same as saying that you want the second item in the list.

The list Function

For convenience, Common Lisp has many functions built on top of the basic three—cons, car, and cdr. A useful one is the list function, which does the dirty work of creating all the cons cells and builds our list all at once:

```
> (list 'pork 'beef 'chicken)
(PORK BEEF CHICKEN)
```

Remember that there is no difference between a list created with the list function, one created by specifying individual cons cells, or one created in data mode using the single quote. They're all the same animal.

(CONS 'PORK (CONS 'BEEF (CONS 'CHICKEN ())))

(LIST 'PORK 'BEEF 'CHICKEN)

'(PORK BEEF CHICKEN)

ALL THE SAME

Nested Lists

Lists can contain other lists. Here's an example:

```
'(cat (duck bat) ant)
```

This is a list containing three items. The second item of this list is (duck bat), which is a list itself. This is an example of a *nested list*.

However, under the hood, these nested lists are still just made out of cons cells. Let's look at an example where we pull items out of nested lists. Here, the first item is (peas carrots tomatoes) and the second item is (pork beef chicken):

❶ > (car '((peas carrots tomatoes) (pork beef chicken)))
  (PEAS CARROTS TOMATOES)
❷ > (cdr '(peas carrots tomatoes))
  (CARROTS TOMATOES)
❸ > (cdr (car '((peas carrots tomatoes) (pork beef chicken))))
  (CARROTS TOMATOES)
❹ > (cdar '((peas carrots tomatoes) (pork beef chicken)))
  (CARROTS TOMATOES)

The car function gives us the first item in the list, which is a list in this case ❶. Next, we use the cdr command to chop off the first item from this inner list, leaving us with (CARROTS TOMATOES) ❷. Using these commands together gives this same result ❸. Finally, using cdar gives the same result as using cdr and car separately ❹.

As demonstrated in this example, cons cells allow us to create complex structures, and we use them here to build a nested list. To prove that our nested list consists solely of cons cells, here is how we could create this nested list using only the cons command:

```
> (cons (cons 'peas (cons 'carrots (cons 'tomatoes ())))
        (cons (cons 'pork (cons 'beef (cons 'chicken ()))) ()))
((PEAS CARROTS TOMATOES) (PORK BEEF CHICKEN))
```

Here are some more examples of functions based on car and cdr that we could use on our data structure:

```
> (cddr '((peas carrots tomatoes) (pork beef chicken) duck))
(DUCK)
> (caddr '((peas carrots tomatoes) (pork beef chicken) duck))
DUCK
> (cddar '((peas carrots tomatoes) (pork beef chicken) duck))
(TOMATOES)
> (cadadr '((peas carrots tomatoes) (pork beef chicken) duck))
BEEF
```

Common Lisp already defines all these functions for you. You can use any function with the name c*r right out of the box, up to four levels deep. In other words, cadadr will already exist for you to use, whereas cadadar (which is five levels deep) does not (you would need to write that function yourself). These functions make it easy to manipulate cons cells-based structures in Lisp, no matter how complicated they might be.

What You've Learned

In this chapter, we discussed the basic Lisp syntax. Along the way, you learned the following:

- Parentheses in Lisp are there to keep the amount of syntax to a minimum.
- Lists are created from cons cells.
- You can create lists by making cons cells with the cons command.
- You can inspect the pieces of a list with car and cdr.

SECTION II:

LISP IS SYMMETRY

4

MAKING DECISIONS
WITH CONDITIONS

In the previous chapters, you learned some basic Lisp commands, as well as some of the philosophy behind Lisp. In this chapter, we'll be looking in detail at commands for handling conditions. The elegance of these commands shows that the unusual philosophy and design of Lisp has real practical benefits.

The Symmetry of nil and ()

One thing is particularly striking when we look at how Lisp commands and data structures work: They are imbued with symmetry in every conceivable way. This symmetry can give your Lisp code a certain elegance that other languages cannot have, and Lisp's simple syntax is an important factor in making this symmetry possible.

Empty Equals False

Since the Lisp philosophy strongly emphasizes the use of lists to store and manipulate information, it will come as no surprise that the design of Common Lisp favors behaviors that make it easy to slice and dice such lists. The most profound design decision made in Common Lisp, with regard to lists, is that it automatically treats an empty list as a false value when evaluating a condition:

```
> (if '()
      'i-am-true
      'i-am-false)

I-AM-FALSE

> (if '(1)
      'i-am-true
      'i-am-false)

I-AM-TRUE
```

This example shows that when we pass the empty list () into an `if` form, it evaluates as a false value, whereas a list that contains an item evaluates as true.

Because we can easily detect an empty list, we can process lists using *recursion*. With this technique, we can take items from the front of a list and send the rest of the list back to the same function until the list is empty. (It's a good thing that detecting empty lists is so easy, because so many functions in Lisp end up being list-eaters.)

Let's look at a common list-eating function, which calculates the length of a list.

```
> (defun my-length (list)
    (if list
        (1+ (my-length (cdr list)))
        0))

> (my-length '(list with four symbols))

4
```

This function is written in classic Lisp style. It calls itself recursively as it chomps items off the front of the list. Calling yourself in this way is not only allowed in Lisp, but is often strongly encouraged. Lists in Lisp are recursive (conses of conses of conses . . .), so the act of consuming a list maps naturally onto functions that are recursive.

NOTE   *Calling yourself recursively can sometimes make for slow code. In Chapter 14, we'll rewrite the my-length function using a special, potentially faster, type of recursion.*

The Four Disguises of ()

Not only does the empty list evaluate to false, but it is the *only* false value in Common Lisp. *Any value not equivalent to an empty list will be considered a true value.* This explains why the expression '(1) in the earlier example was treated as true. However, there are some other expressions in Lisp that are disguises for the one and only empty list:

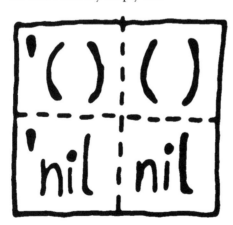

We can see that the expressions in this table are equivalent by comparing them with one another:

```
❶ (eq '() nil)  ==> T
❷ (eq '() ())   ==> T
❸ (eq '() 'nil) ==> T
```

Notice that the only value in the table that seems normal is the quoted list on the left side of the comparisons. The other three all seem to break the rules of Lisp forms that we talked about in the previous chapter.

The first two examples are particularly puzzling. They are missing the quotation mark that tells the Lisp environment, "Hey, this item is a piece of data, not code!" In the case of nil, you would expect that this would actually be the name of a variable that could have some kind of arbitrary value. In the case of the unquoted (), there's no way you could tell what would happen. The parentheses look like a form of code that needs to be evaluated, but a Lisp form always has a symbol at the beginning, telling it what to do. What do we do when there's nothing inside the form at all?

The bottom line is that Common Lisp is architected behind the scenes to make sure all four of these values look like an empty list when you use them in your program, allowing most Lisp conditionals to be written with an elegant brevity. For instance, there is a constant named nil that evaluates to itself and allows you to omit the quotation mark in the first case ❶. The second case ❷ is a natural by-product of how Common Lisp parses an empty form. The third case ❸ is due to a requirement in the Common Lisp spec that says that () and nil should be treated the same.

Although there's a certain beauty to having all of these values be the same, not every Lisper agrees with this sentiment. After all, are false and empty list really the same kind of thing? The creators of the other popular dialect of Lisp, Scheme, felt differently about this issue, and preferred to keep the concepts of falsity and empty list completely separate, at a slight cost to code brevity.

The Conditionals: if and Beyond

Now that you understand how Lisp handles true and false, let's look at if and some of the other conditional commands.

One Thing at a Time with if

The if command can be used to make different things happen when things are true (such as when $1 + 2 = 3$) or false (such as when $1 + 2 = 4$).

```
> (if (= (+ 1 2) 3)
      'yup
      'nope)

YUP

> (if (= (+ 1 2) 4)
      'yup
      'nope)

NOPE
```

The `if` command can also be used to check whether a list is empty:

```
> (if '(1)
      'the-list-has-stuff-in-it
      'the-list-is-empty)

THE-LIST-HAS-STUFF-IN-IT

> (if '()
      'the-list-has-stuff-in-it
      'the-list-is-empty)

THE-LIST-IS-EMPTY
```

So far, the only way to branch on a condition that we've looked at has been the `if` command:

```
> (if (oddp 5)
      'odd-number
      'even-number)

ODD-NUMBER
```

All we're doing here is checking whether the number 5 is odd, then, depending on the result, evaluating one of the two following expressions in the `if` form. Since 5 is odd, it evaluates the first such expression, and the form as a whole returns `odd-number`.

There's a lot happening in this harmless-looking little command—stuff that's important to understanding Lisp. Here are two important observations:

- Only one of the expressions after the `if` is actually evaluated.
- We can only do one thing in an `if` statement.

Usually, when a function is executed in Lisp, all the expressions after the function name are evaluated, before the function itself is evaluated. However, `if` does not follow these rules. To see this, consider the following example:

```
> (if (oddp 5)
      'odd-number
      (/ 1 0))

ODD-NUMBER
```

Any self-respecting, law-abiding Lisp function would kick your butt to the curb if you tried to run this code, because you're dividing by zero.

But `if` is not just a function. It's a *special form*, which gives it special privileges, such as the right to not evaluate all its parameters in the normal way. This makes sense, since the whole point of a condition is to run some stuff but not other stuff. In this case, it just merrily ignores the division by zero, since it's in the part of the branch that applies only to even numbers. Conditional commands in Lisp are typically special forms.

NOTE *Some of the conditional commands may be macros, which are something like user-created special forms. Being a special form usually implies that a command is directly "baked in" to the language. In Chapter 16, you'll learn how to write such macros yourself.*

Since only one expression inside an if is ever evaluated, it's impossible to do two or more separate things inside your branch.

There is actually a clever style of programming (called *functional programming*, as we'll discuss in Chapter 14), which considers this a Good Thing. However, for cases when you really want to do more than one thing, you can use a special command, progn, to wedge in extra commands in a single expression. With progn, only the last evaluation is returned as the value of the full expression. In this next example, for instance, we use the command to set a special global variable directly inside our conditional branch.

```
> (defvar *number-was-odd* nil)

> (if (oddp 5)
      (progn (setf *number-was-odd* t)
             'odd-number)
      'even-number)
```

ODD-NUMBER

```
> *number-was-odd*
```

T

Going Beyond if: The when and unless Alternatives

Since it's kind of a pain to use progn every time you want to do multiple things inside an if, Lisp has several other commands that include an *implicit* progn. The most basic of these are when and unless:

```
> (defvar *number-is-odd* nil)
> (when (oddp 5)
        (setf *number-is-odd* t)
        'odd-number)
```

ODD-NUMBER

```
> *number-is-odd*
```

T

```
> (unless (oddp 4)
        (setf *number-is-odd* nil)
        'even-number)
```

EVEN-NUMBER

```
> *number-is-odd*
```

NIL

With when, all the enclosed expressions are evaluated when the condition is true. With unless, all the enclosed expressions are evaluated when the condition is false. The trade-off is that these commands can't do anything when the condition evaluates in the opposite way; they just return nil and do nothing.

The Command That Does It All: cond

But what do you do if you're the kind of coder who wants it all? Maybe you just ain't in a compromisin' mood and want a function that will do everything! Well, Lisp has you covered.

The cond form is the classic way to do branching in Lisp. Through the liberal use of parentheses, it allows for an implicit progn, can handle more than one branch, and can even evaluate several conditions in succession. Since cond has been around since the Lisp Stone Age, and it's comprehensive in its abilities, many Lisp programmers consider it to be the one true Lisp conditional.

Here's an example:

```
> (defvar *arch-enemy* nil)
> (defun pudding-eater (person)
      (cond ((eq person 'henry) (setf *arch-enemy* 'stupid-lisp-alien)
                                '(curse you lisp alien - you ate my pudding))
            ((eq person 'johnny) (setf *arch-enemy* 'useless-old-johnny)
                                '(i hope you choked on my pudding johnny))
            (t                  '(why you eat my pudding stranger ?))))

> (pudding-eater 'johnny)
(I HOPE YOU CHOKED ON MY PUDDING JOHNNY)
> *arch-enemy*
JOHNNY
```

```
> (pudding-eater 'george-clooney)
(WHY YOU EAT MY PUDDING STRANGER ?)
```

As you can see, the body of a cond uses a layer of parentheses to separate the different branches of the condition. Then the first expression of each parenthesized part contains the condition for making that branch active. In our example, we have different branches for each type of pudding thief: one for Henry ❶, one for Johnny ❷, and one for everyone else ❸. We use eq to compare the supplied person's name with each potential perpetrator.

The conditions in a cond form are always checked from the top down, so the first successful match drives the behavior. In this example, the last branch ❸ has a condition of t (for true), guaranteeing that at least the last branch will always be evaluated. This is a common cond idiom.

As with when and unless, the triggered branch may contain more than one command, since there is an implicit progn. In this case, the first two branches ❶❷ set an extra *arch-enemy* variable, besides supplying a return variable.

Branching with case

Let's look at one final Lisp command: the case form. It is common to use the eq function for conditionals, and case lets you supply a value to compare against. Using case, we can rewrite the previous example as follows:

```
> (defun pudding-eater (person)
    (case person
       ((henry)    (setf *arch-enemy* 'stupid-lisp-alien)
                   '(curse you lisp alien - you ate my pudding))
       ((johnny)   (setf *arch-enemy* 'useless-old-johnny)
                   '(i hope you choked on my pudding johnny))
       (otherwise '(why you eat my pudding stranger ?)))))
```

This version of the code is a lot easier on the eyes. The name of the person handled by each part of the case statement is clearly visible—it's not hidden inside an equality check. Depending on which version of Lisp you use, a case statement like this may also be more efficient, especially with longer statements, where larger numbers of cases are handled.

WARNING *Because the case command uses eq for comparisons, it is usually used only for branching on symbol values. It cannot be used to branch on string values, among other things. See "Comparing Stuff: eq, equal, and More" on page 62 for details.*

Cool Tricks with Conditions

The fundamental design of Lisp lets you get a lot of mileage out of a few simple commands. Specifically, a couple of counterintuitive tricks involving conditions in Lisp can help you write cleaner code. The first involves two new conditional commands. The second takes advantage of Lisp's simple conception of true and false.

Using the Stealth Conditionals and and or

The conditionals and and or are simple mathematical operators, which allow you to manipulate Boolean values in the same way you might manipulate numbers using addition and subtraction.

For example, here's how we could use and to see if three numbers are odd:

```
> (and (oddp 5) (oddp 7) (oddp 9))

T
```

Because 5, 7, and 9 are odd, the entire expression evaluates as true.

Similarly, we can use or to see whether at least one of a set of numbers is odd:

```
> (or (oddp 4) (oddp 7) (oddp 8))

T
```

Because 7 is odd, the or command still evaluates as true, despite the fact that 4 and 8 are even.

But there's something a bit more interesting about and and or that you might not notice just by looking at these first two examples. So far, these two commands look like completely ordinary mathematical operators; they do not look like conditional commands, such as if or cond. However, they can be used for conditional behavior.

For instance, here's how we could use these conditionals to set a global variable to true only when a number is even:

```
> (defparameter *is-it-even* nil)

*IS-IT-EVEN*
```

```
> (or (oddp 4) (setf *is-it-even* t))

T

> *is-it-even*

T
```

If we do the same thing using an odd number, the variable remains unchanged:

```
> (defparameter *is-it-even* nil)

*IS-IT-EVEN

> (or (oddp 5) (setf *is-it-even* t))

T

> *is-it-even*

NIL
```

This example illustrates that Lisp uses *shortcut Boolean evaluation*. This means that once Lisp determines that an earlier statement in a list of or values is true, it simply returns true and doesn't bother evaluating the remaining statements. Similarly, once it determines that an earlier statement in a list of and values is false, it stops without bothering to evaluate the rest of the statements.

While this may seem like a minor esoteric observation, it can actually be very useful in many situations. For instance, imagine if you want to save a file to disk, but only if the file was modified, and only when the user wants it to be saved. The basic structure could be written as follows:

```
(if *file-modified*
    (if (ask-user-about-saving)
        (save-file)))
```

Here, the function ask-user-about-saving would ask the user about the file, and then return true or false based on the user's wishes. However, since short-cut Boolean evaluation is guaranteed to be used for Boolean operations under Common Lisp and most other Lisp dialects, we could write this instead:

```
(and *file-modified* (ask-user-about-saving) (save-file))
```

Using this cleaner style for evaluating conditional code is possible only if you think beyond the typical use of the Boolean operators as simply mathematical operators. This form has an elegant symmetry between the three expressions, which some Lispers may like. However, others would argue that a reader of your code may easily miss the fact that (save-file) does something beyond returning a Boolean value. A bit of time is required to wrap your head around this more-general conception of what and and or actually mean.

A third way to write this code, which is a compromise between the previous approaches, is as follows:

```
(if (and *file-modified*
         (ask-user-about-saving))
    (save-file)))
```

Many experienced Lispers will consider this version a bit clearer than the previous two versions, because only expressions that are expressly designed to return a Boolean value are treated as part of the condition.

Using Functions That Return More than Just the Truth

Now let's look at another benefit of Lisp's simple way of thinking about true and false. As we've already discussed, any value in Common Lisp (except for the different variations on nil) is true. This means that functions that are commonly used in conditions have the option of returning *more than just the truth.*

For instance, the Lisp command member can be used to check for list membership for an item:

```
> (if (member 1 '(3 4 1 5))
      'one-is-in-the-list
      'one-is-not-in-the-list)

'ONE-IS-IN-THE-LIST
```

This seems pretty straightforward. However, once again, there is something happening behind the scenes that you may not expect. Let's run the member command in isolation:

```
> (member 1 '(3 4 1 5))

(1 5)
```

What the heck happened here? Why is it returning (1 5)?

Actually, there's a perfectly rational explanation for this. Whenever a Lisper writes a function that returns true and false, she will think to herself, "Is there anything else I could return other than just t?" Since all non-nil values in Common Lisp evaluate to true, returning some other value is essentially a freebie. The implementers of the member function decided that some crazy Lisper somewhere may see the value in having the tail of the list for some calculation that uses this function.

NOTE   *Remember from Chapter 3 that the list '(3 4 1 5) is the same as the nested contraption (cons 3 (cons 4 (cons 1 (cons 5 nil)))). This should make it clear why the value (cons 1 (cons 5 nil)) is an easy thing for the member function to return.*

But why doesn't it just return the value it found, instead of the tail? In fact, this would have been a useful way to define the member function, because it would allow passing the original value to some other function in such a manner. Unfortunately, one edge case in particular would ruin this plan:

```
> (if (member nil '(3 4 nil 5))
      'nil-is-in-the-list
      'nil-is-not-in-the-list)

'nil-is-in-the-list
```

As you can see in this example, the member function still gives the correct answer, even when we search for nil as the member! If the member function had actually returned nil (in other words, the original value we were searching for), it would have evaluated as false, and the example would have incorrectly stated that nil isn't in the list. However, since the member function returns the tail of the list at the point of the found item, it can be guaranteed to always be a true value. A successful discovery of the desired value will always return a list with at least one value, which we know always evaluates as true.

One function that really benefits from rich return values is find-if, as follows:

```
> (find-if #'oddp '(2 4 5 6))

5

> (if (find-if #'oddp '(2 4 5 6))
      'there-is-an-odd-number
      'there-is-no-odd-number)

'there-is-an-odd-number
```

The find-if function actually takes another function, in this case oddp, as a parameter. find-if will find the first value in the list for which oddp returns true. In this case, it will find the first number (if any) that is an odd number.

You can see clearly how find-if can fill dual roles: either as a retriever of values matching some constraint or as a true/false value inside a condition.

NOTE *Don't worry yet about the weird hash mark (#) in front of oddp in the example. We'll discuss the find-if function, and other so-called higher-order functions, in greater detail in Chapters 7 and 14.*

Alas, the elegant symmetry of the find-if function has a single, small, ugly wart. If we try our edge case again, searching for a nil value, we get a rather disappointing result:

```
> (find-if #'null '(2 4 nil 6))

NIL
```

The null function, which returns true for any of the nil values, correctly finds the nil. Unfortunately, in this one annoying case, we would not want to use find-if inside a conditional statement, because a correctly found value still returns a result that evaluates as false. The symmetry has been broken.

These are the kinds of small things that make even grown Lispers shed a tear.

Comparing Stuff: eq, equal, and More

There's a lot of beautiful symmetry in Lisp. One part of Lisp that isn't so beautiful, though, involves the commands for comparing things.

If you want to compare two values in Lisp to find out if they are "the same," you will find a bewildering assortment of different functions that purport to accomplish this. Of these, equal, eql, eq, =, string-equal, and equalp are the most commonly used. A Lisper must understand the subtleties of these functions intimately in order to know how to compare values correctly.

Before we start dissecting this madness, let me give you Conrad's Rule of Thumb for Comparing Stuff. Follow this rule, and though you may not be writing the world's cleanest Lisp code, you will probably be able to post some samples to a newsgroup without more seasoned Lispers running you out of town with torches and pitchforks.

CONRAD'S RULE OF THUMB FOR COMPARING STUFF:

1. USE **EQ** TO COMPARE SYMBOLS
2. USE **EQUAL** FOR EVERYTHING ELSE

Symbols should always be compared to other symbols with eq:

```
> (defparameter *fruit* 'apple)

*FRUIT*

> (cond ((eq *fruit* 'apple) 'its-an-apple)
        ((eq *fruit* 'orange) 'its-an-orange))

ITS-AN-APPLE
```

The eq function is the simplest of all the Lisp comparison functions, and it's also very fast. It doesn't really work for comparing items besides symbols, but if you consider the central role symbols play in Lisp, you'll realize how useful this function can be. Experienced Lispers might look down on code if it compares two things, known to be symbols, with something other than eq.

NOTE   *eq can also be used to compare conses (the links created by the cons command). However, it returns true values only when a cons is compared directly to itself, created by the same cons call. This means, two unrelated conses that "look" exactly the same can fail an eq test. Since eq can check a cons cell only against itself, using eq with conses isn't really that useful for a beginner. However, an advanced Lisper may want to compare conses with eq under certain circumstances.*

If you're not dealing with two symbols, just use equal. This command will tell you when two things are *isomorphic*, meaning they "look the same." It works for the whole suite of basic Lisp datatypes, as shown here:

```
;;comparing symbols
> (equal 'apple 'apple)

T
```

```
;;comparing lists
> (equal (list 1 2 3) (list 1 2 3))

T

;;Identical lists created in different ways still compare as the same
> (equal '(1 2 3) (cons 1 (cons 2 (cons 3))))

T

;;comparing integers
> (equal 5 5)

T

;;comparing floating point numbers
> (equal 2.5 2.5)

T

;;comparing strings
> (equal "foo" "foo")

T

;;comparing characters
> (equal #\a #\a)

T
```

As you can see, most items in Lisp can be effectively compared with equal, including strings and characters (which are discussed in the next chapter).

Now that you know the bare minimum about Lisp comparisons to fake your way through your next cocktail party, let's look at all the other comparison commands.

The eql command is similar to the eq command, but unlike eq, it also handles comparisons of numbers and characters:

```
;;comparing symbols
> (eql 'foo 'foo)

T

;;comparing numbers
> (eql 3.4 3.4)

T

;;comparing characters
> (eql #\a #\a)

T
```

The equalp command is essentially the same as the equal command, except that it can handle some difficult comparison cases with a bit of extra sophistication. For instance, it can compare strings with different capitalizations and can compare integers against floating-point numbers:

```
;;comparing strings with different CAPS
> (equalp "Bob Smith" "bob smith")
T
;;comparing integers against floating point numbers
> (equalp 0 0.0)
T
```

The remaining comparison commands are just specializations for specific datatypes. Otherwise, they are similar to equal. For instance, the = (equal sign) function handles numbers, string-equal handles strings, and char-equal handles characters.

I hope that you can now appreciate just how seriously Lispers take comparisons.

What You've Learned

In this chapter, we discussed how conditions work in Lisp. Along the way, you learned the following:

- The values nil, 'nil, (), and '() are all basically the same thing in Common Lisp.

- Lisp makes it easy to check for empty lists. This makes it simple to write list-eaters.

- Lisp conditionals, such as the if command, cause Lisp code to be evaluated only under the right conditions.

- If you need a conditional command that does everything, then you want to use cond.

- Comparing stuff in Lisp is complicated, but you can get by if you just use eq for comparing symbols and equal for comparing everything else.

5

BUILDING A TEXT GAME ENGINE

When you write a program, no matter which programming language you're using or what your program does, it will probably need to work with text. Sure, one day we may all have Ethernet ports at the base of our skulls (100Mbps Ethernet will have been fully adopted by then, of course). But until the day arrives when you can just exchange thoughts with your MacBook using a direct hookup, you'll be stuck using alphabetic text for input and output in your software.

Computers have always had a bit of a tenuous relationship with text. Although we tend to think of text processing as a central task for computer hardware and software (indeed, the 8-bit byte is the standard design element in modern computers, in large part, due to how well suited it is for encoding Western character sets), the truth of the matter is that the human concept of *text* is really alien to a computer.

In this chapter, you'll learn how to use Lisp to manipulate text. You'll see, once again, that the Lispy approach to solving problems allows you to create code that is full of elegance and symmetry. To demonstrate this approach, we will do something that would seem to make thinking with text unavoidable: build the engine for a simple text adventure game. However, we'll do this in a way that avoids constraining our code by artificially forcing the human notion of text into its design. This will allow us to write code that focuses on the strengths of a computer.

As you read this chapter, remember that handling text is not a computer's strength. It is a necessary evil best kept to a minimum.

The Wizard's Adventure Game

In this game, you are a wizard's apprentice. You'll explore the wizard's house. When we complete the game (in Chapter 17), you'll be able to solve puzzles and win a magical donut.

Our Game World

Here is a picture of our game world:

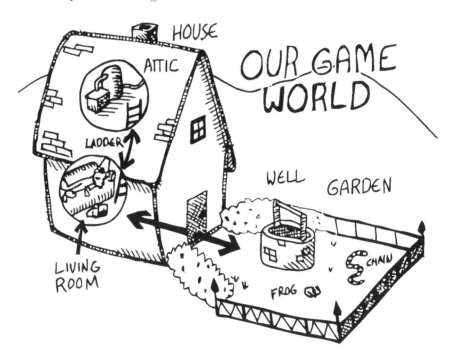

As you can see, we can visit three different locations: a living room, an attic, and a garden. Players can move between places using the door and the ladder to the attic.

Think of this game world as a simple directed graph with three nodes (represented as ellipses) and four edges (represented as arrows):

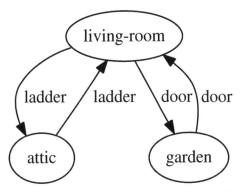

Players move between nodes by traveling along the edges in either direction. Wherever the players are, they can interact with various objects around them.

Basic Requirements

Our game code will need to handle a few basic things:

- Looking around
- Walking to different locations
- Picking up objects
- Performing actions on the objects picked up

In this chapter, we'll address the first three of these requirements. To perform more complex actions on objects, we'll use the more advanced Lisp techniques covered in later chapters. Because of this, our game engine will be somewhat limited in its abilities until we finish it in Chapter 17.

When looking around in our game world, you will be able to "see" three kinds of things from any location:

- Basic scenery
- One or more paths to other locations
- Objects that you can pick up and manipulate

Let's add features for these one at a time.

Describing the Scenery with an Association List

The world inside our adventure game is very simple, containing only three locations. Let's first create a top-level variable, *nodes*, to contain descriptions of the locations that exist in our game:

```
(defparameter *nodes* '((living-room (you are in the living-room.
                             a wizard is snoring loudly on the couch.))
                        (garden (you are in a beautiful garden.
                            there is a well in front of you.))
                        (attic (you are in the attic.
                            there is a giant welding torch in the corner.))))
```

This variable contains a list and description of our three locations. In essence, the *nodes* variable basically gives us a way to find a piece of data associated with a lookup key. In this case, the key is the name of the place (living-room, garden, or attic), and the data is a text description of the scenery at that place. This type of structure is called an *association list*, or *alist* for short (alists are covered in greater detail in Chapter 7).

One thing is rather unusual about the definition of this *nodes* variable: Even though it contains descriptions of the various locations in our game world, it does not actually contain any text strings. Since Common Lisp has a string datatype, we could have written descriptions using quotes. For instance, we could have written "You are in a beautiful garden. There is a well in front of you." Instead, we use more fundamental datatypes—symbols and lists—to encode this information.

Why wouldn't we just use strings? As I mentioned at the beginning of this chapter, the manipulation of text is not really a fundamental computing concept. In this game, we'll manipulate the messages displayed to players based on their interaction with the game world in complicated ways. For most real-world programs, the information you'll generate as output (such as HTML, PDFs, or even richer graphical formats) will probably be far more complicated than just simple text.

By keeping your source data structures free from assumptions regarding the output format from the start, your coding can take full advantage of your programming language. Since the easiest things to manipulate in Lisp are symbols and lists, most experienced Lispers will try to focus on these datatypes in the design of their software whenever possible. So, we will stay away from strings in our design. (In the next chapter, we will translate these lists and symbols into properly formatted text.)

NOTE *Common Lisp doesn't force you to represent strings with lists and symbols in this way. If it's more convenient, you can work with strings directly. (You'll see examples of working with strings later in the book, especially in Chapter 11.) Using lists and symbols as an intermediary for manipulating text is definitely an old-school Lisp technique. However, it can often lead to very elegant code, since list operations are so fundamental to Lisp.*

Describing the Location

Now that we've created an alist of our game world, we need to create a command to describe a location. To accomplish this, we'll use the assoc function to find the correct item in the list using a key:

```
> (assoc 'garden *nodes*)
(GARDEN (YOU ARE IN A BEAUTIFUL GARDEN. THERE IS A WELL IN FRONT OF YOU.))
```

Using assoc, we can easily create the describe-location function:

```
(defun describe-location (location nodes)
  (cadr (assoc location nodes)))
```

To use this function, we pass in a location and the *nodes* list:

```
> (describe-location 'living-room *nodes*)
(YOU ARE IN THE LIVING-ROOM. A WIZARD IS SNORING LOUDLY ON THE COUCH.)
```

Why don't we just reference the *nodes* variable directly from the describe-location function? Because this function is written in the *functional programming* style. In this style, a function will reference only parameters or variables declared in the function itself, and it will do nothing besides return a value, which is the description of the location in this case.

By writing functions that don't reference variables in the "outside world" directly and that don't perform any actions other than returning a value, you can write code that can easily be tested in isolation. You should try to write your Lisp functions in this style whenever possible. (We will discuss the functional programming style in greater detail in Chapter 14.)

Describing the Paths

Now that we have basic descriptions of each location, we need descriptions of paths to other locations as well. We'll create a second variable, *edges*, that contains the paths that players can take to move between places on our map. (We use the term *edges* because that's the proper math term for the lines connecting nodes in a graph.)

```
(defparameter *edges* '((living-room (garden west door)
                                     (attic upstairs ladder))
                        (garden (living-room east door))
                        (attic (living-room downstairs ladder))))
```

Using this structure, we create the describe-path function, which builds a textual description of a given edge using our symbols system.

```
(defun describe-path (edge)
  `(there is a ,(caddr edge) going ,(cadr edge) from here.))
```

This describe-path function looks pretty strange—almost like a piece of data more than a function. Let's try it, and then figure out how it works.

```
> (describe-path '(garden west door))
(THERE IS A DOOR GOING WEST FROM HERE.)
```

This function basically returns a piece of data with small bits of calculated information inserted into it. This feature of Lisp, called *quasiquoting*, allows us to create chunks of data that have small pieces of Lisp code embedded in them.

How Quasiquoting Works

To enable quasiquoting, you must use a backquote [`] not a single quote [']
when switching from code to data mode. The describe-path function has just
such a backquote in it.

Both the single quote and backquote in Lisp "flip" a piece of code into
data mode, but only a backquote can also be *unquoted* using the comma character, to flip back into code mode.

With a little imagination, this should make sense to you. After all, a comma
does look just like an upside-down backquote, doesn't it? Here's how the flip-
flop in the describe-path function works (the parts in code mode are shaded):

Lisp attempts to make list manipulation as easy as possible. Here, you
can see how our program, which uses lists of symbols to store our text, can
now leverage the quasiquoting feature to construct sentences in a very concise and clear way.

Describing Multiple Paths at Once

Now let's use our describe-path function to create a more advanced function.
Since a location may have any number of paths exiting from it, we need a
function that can generate descriptions for all edges from a given location by
looking up the location from our data structure of edges:

```
(defun describe-paths (location edges)
  (apply #'append (mapcar #'describe-path (cdr (assoc location edges)))))
```

This function uses a bunch of commands that may seem very exotic to a person not accustomed to the world of Lisp. Many programming languages would use some kind of for-next loop to run through the edges, and then cram the descriptions of each path together using a temporary variable. Lisp uses a much more elegant approach. Let's see it in action:

```
> (describe-paths 'living-room *edges*)
(THERE IS A DOOR GOING WEST FROM HERE. THERE IS A LADDER GOING UPSTAIRS FROM
HERE.)
```

The describe-paths function takes the following steps:

1. Find the relevant edges.
2. Convert the edges to descriptions.
3. Join the descriptions.

Let's see how it performs each of these steps.

Finding the Relevant Edges

The first, inner part of the describe-paths function is pretty straightforward. To find the relevant paths and edges leading from the living room, we use assoc again to look up the location in our list of edges:

```
> (cdr (assoc 'living-room *edges*))
((GARDEN WEST DOOR) (ATTIC UPSTAIRS LADDER))
```

Converting the Edges to Descriptions

Next, the edges are converted to descriptions. Here is just the code to accomplish this, shown in isolation:

```
> (mapcar #'describe-path '((GARDEN WEST DOOR) (ATTIC UPSTAIRS LADDER)))
((THERE IS A DOOR GOING WEST FROM HERE.)
 (THERE IS A LADDER GOING UPSTAIRS FROM HERE.))
```

The mapcar function is used frequently by Lispers. This function takes another function and a list, and then applies this function to every member of a list. Here's an example:

```
> (mapcar #'sqrt '(1 2 3 4 5))
(1 1.4142135 1.7320508 2 2.236068)
```

This example passes the sqrt (square root) function, along with the (1 2 3 4 5) list, into mapcar. As a result, the function generates a list of the square roots of the original numbers by applying sqrt to every member of the list and creating a new list.

Functions that take other functions as parameters, such as `mapcar`, are very useful and a distinguishing feature of Lisp. Such functions are called *higher-order functions*.

Here is another example:

```
> (mapcar #'car '((foo bar) (baz qux)))
(foo baz)
```

This time, our source list contains two smaller lists. The `car` function, which grabs the first item in a list, causes `mapcar` to return the first items from each smaller list, `foo` and `baz`.

You may be wondering why the function names we pass into `mapcar` have the #' symbols in front of them. This symbol sequence is a shorthand for the function operator. The Lisp reader (the part of your Lisp environment that reads the code you type) will convert the previous example into the following longer version:

```
> (mapcar (function car) '((foo bar) (baz qux)))
(foo baz)
```

Common Lisp requires you to use the `function` operator when referring to a function as a value directly like this, because the name of a function may conflict with other named items in a program, causing unpredictable errors. For instance, imagine if we added more stuff to the previous example, like this:

```
❶ > (let ((car "Honda Civic"))
❷    (mapcar #'car '((foo bar) (baz qux))))
(foo baz)
```

In this version, the `car` symbol could have two different meanings. The first meaning of `car` is that it is a standard function built into Lisp (introduced in Chapter 3). However, we're also creating a local variable named `car` ❶. Because we prepended the word `car` with #' in our call to `mapcar` ❷, there is no confusion about which `car` we are talking about.

Now let's look at the `describe-paths` function again:

```
(defun describe-paths (location edges)
  (apply #'append (mapcar #'describe-path (cdr (assoc location edges)))))
```

Notice how the `append` and `describe-path` functions are passed in as values to the `apply` and `mapcar` functions, which are designed to receive and use the functions.

Common Lisp tracks function names differently from variable names. It has multiple *namespaces*, including one for variables and one for functions. (We'll learn more about namespaces later, especially in Chapter 16.) Scheme, the other popular Lisp dialect, doesn't force you to mark functions with a function operator when using them as values.

In other words, Scheme has only one namespace for both functions and variables. For instance, in Scheme, you can just write `(map sqrt '(1 2 3 4 5))` to generate the square roots of the numbers 1 through 5 without generating an error (`map` is the Scheme version of `mapcar`). As a result of this design, in Scheme, a variable and a separate function can't be available in the same block of code. That design decision is one of the great benefits (or curses) of Scheme, depending on your point of view. Because of this difference in the number of namespaces, Scheme is sometimes called a *Lisp-1*, whereas Common Lisp is sometimes referred to as a *Lisp-2*.

Joining the Descriptions

Once we've used `mapcar` to generate a list of descriptions for all the paths and edges, we need to combine them into a single description. We accomplish this with the `append` function, which joins several lists into one big list:

```
> (append '(mary had) '(a) '(little lamb))
(MARY HAD A LITTLE LAMB)
```

We use the `append` function to cram the list of path descriptions into one list that describes the whole enchilada, in one swoop. The problem is that `append` needs all of the lists handed to it as separate parameters. In `describe-paths`, we have our lists in one big list, not as separate objects we can pass as parameters. Heck, we don't even know how many paths there may be from any given spot.

The `apply` function solves this problem. You pass it a function and a list of objects, and it pretends that the items in the list are separate objects and passes them to the given function as such. For example, if we have the nested list `'((mary had) (a) (little lamb))`, the `apply` function will add in that little bit of duct tape needed to make the `append` function work with a single big list:

```
> (apply #'append '((mary had) (a) (little lamb)))
(MARY HAD A LITTLE LAMB)
```

WARNING   *Since the `apply` function passes each item in a list as an argument to the `target` function, you can run into problems when calling it on very large lists that have thousands of items or more. You can check the value of the `call-arguments-limit` variable in the REPL to see the maximum number of allowed arguments to a function. (More recent dialects of Lisp are typically designed to allow argument lists of any size, without an artificial limit.)*

You can see how `apply` enables the `describe-paths` function to build one long list describing all paths leading from a single location. Let's use this same approach on the path description lists we constructed:

```
> (apply #'append '((THERE IS A DOOR GOING WEST FROM HERE.)
                    (THERE IS A LADDER GOING UPSTAIRS FROM HERE.)))
(THERE IS A DOOR GOING WEST FROM HERE. THERE IS A LADDER GOING UPSTAIRS FROM
HERE.)
```

Now that we've looked at each part of the describe-paths function, let's review how it works:

```
(defun describe-paths (location edges)
  (apply #'append (mapcar #'describe-path (cdr (assoc location edges)))))
```

The function takes two parameters: the current player's location, as well as an alist of edges/paths for the game map. First, it uses assoc to look up the correct location from the edge alist. Since assoc returns both the key and the value from the alist, we call cdr to retrieve only the value. Next, we use mapcar to map the describe-path function against each edge that we found. Finally, we concatenate the lists for describing all the paths into one long list by applying append against the list.

The programming style used by describe-path is very typical for Lisp code. It involves passing along a complicated chunk of data and manipulating it in several steps, often using higher-order functions. To become a proficient Lisp programmer, you should try to get comfortable reading code written in this way.

Describing Objects at a Specific Location

To create the final piece of code to help us visualize our game world, we need to describe the objects on the floor at a given location, which a player can pick up and use.

Listing Visible Objects

To do so, we first create a list of the objects:

```
> (defparameter *objects* '(whiskey bucket frog chain))
*OBJECTS*
```

We can also create a second variable, *object-locations*, to track the location of each object in the form of an alist:

```
(defparameter *object-locations* '((whiskey living-room)
                                   (bucket living-room)
                                   (chain garden)
                                   (frog garden)))
```

Next, we write a function that lists the objects visible from a given location:

```
(defun objects-at (loc objs obj-locs)
❶  (labels ((at-loc-p (obj)
❷             (eq (cadr (assoc obj obj-locs)) loc)))
❸    (remove-if-not #'at-loc-p objs)))
```

This objects-at function declares a new function named at-loc-p using the labels command ❶. (Remember that the labels function allows you to define functions locally.) Since the at-loc-p function won't be used elsewhere, we can just declare it directly within objects-at, hiding it from the rest of the code in our program.

The at-loc-p function takes the symbol for an object and returns t or nil, depending on whether that object exists at the location loc. It does this by looking up the object in the obj-locs alist. Then, it uses eq to see whether the location it finds matches the location in question ❷.

Why did we name this function at-loc-p? When a function returns nil or a truth value, it's a Common Lisp convention to append a p to the end of that function's name. For instance, you can check that the number 5 is odd by calling (oddp 5). Such true/false functions are called *predicates*, which is why we use the letter p.

The remove-if-not function in the last line of the listing ❸, as you might expect, removes all things from a list for which a passed-in function (in this case, at-loc-p) doesn't return true. Essentially, it returns a filtered list of objects consisting of those items for which at-loc-p is true.

Here's what object-at looks like in action:

```
> (objects-at 'living-room *objects* *object-locations*)
(WHISKEY BUCKET)
```

Describing Visible Objects

Now we can write a function to describe the objects visible at a given location:

```
(defun describe-objects (loc objs obj-loc)
❶  (labels ((describe-obj (obj)
❷             `(you see a ,obj on the floor.)))
❸    (apply #'append (mapcar #'describe-obj (objects-at loc objs obj-loc)))))
```

In this listing, describe-objects first creates the describe-obj function ❶. This function generates a pretty sentence stating that a given object is on the floor, using quasiquoting ❷. The main part of the function consists of calling objects-at to find the objects at the current location, mapping describe-obj across this list of objects, and finally appending the descriptions into a single list ❸.

Let's try running describe-objects:

```
> (describe-objects 'living-room *objects* *object-locations*)
(YOU SEE A WHISKEY ON THE FLOOR. YOU SEE A BUCKET ON THE FLOOR)
```

Perfect!

Describing It All

Now we'll tie all of these description functions into one easy command called look. Because this will be the actual command players can enter to look around them in the game, look will need to know a player's current location. So, we need a variable to track the player's current position. Let's call it *location*:

```
(defparameter *location* 'living-room)
```

Because the *location* value is initialized to the living-room symbol, which occurs at the very start of the game, players will find themselves in the living room of the wizard's house. At this point, we can write a look function to describe everything we need by having it call all of our descriptor functions:

```
(defun look ()
  (append (describe-location *location* *nodes*)
          (describe-paths *location* *edges*)
          (describe-objects *location* *objects* *object-locations*)))
```

Since the look function uses global variable names (such as *location*, *nodes*, and so on), the player won't need to pass in any funky values in order to look out at the world. However, this also means that the look function is not in the functional programming style, because functions in the functional programming style reference only parameters or variables declared in the function itself. *location* and its ilk are global variables, so the look function doesn't hold up muster.

Since the player's location changes as the game progresses, look will do *different things at different times* in the game. In other words, the things you see when looking around will change depending on your location. In contrast, a function in the functional programming style always returns the same result, as long as the same values are given as parameters. The earlier functions we created, such as describe-location, describe-paths, and describe-objects, always return the same thing, no matter when they are called, *as long as their parameters are kept the same.*

Now here's what we see when we use look:

```
> (look)
(YOU ARE IN THE LIVING-ROOM OF A WIZARD'S HOUSE.
THERE IS A WIZARD SNORING LOUDLY ON THE COUCH.
THERE IS A DOOR GOING WEST FROM HERE.
THERE IS A LADDER GOING UPSTAIRS FROM HERE.
YOU SEE A WHISKEY ON THE FLOOR.
YOU SEE A BUCKET ON THE FLOOR)
```

THE LOOK FUNCTION READS GLOBAL VARIABLES. IT IS NOT FUNCTIONAL!

Walking Around in Our World

Now that we can see things in our world, let's write some code so that we can walk around. The walk function (not in the functional style) takes a direction and lets us walk there:

```
(defun walk (direction)
❶   (let ((next (find direction
❷                     (cdr (assoc *location* *edges*))
❸                     :key #'cadr)))
❹   (if next
❺       (progn (setf *location* (car next))
❻              (look))
❼       '(you cannot go that way.)))))
```

First, this function looks up the available walking paths in the *edges* table, using the current location ❷. This is used by the find function to locate the path marked with the appropriate direction ❶. (find searches a list for an item, then returns that found item.) The direction (such as west, upstairs, and so on) will be in the cadr of each path, so we need to tell find to match the direction against the cadr of all the paths in the list.

We can do this by passing find a *keyword parameter* ❸. In Common Lisp, many functions (such as find) have built-in features that can be accessed by passing in special parameters at the end of the function call. For instance, the following code finds the first item in a list that has the symbol y in the cadr location:

```
> (find 'y '((5 x) (3 y) (7 z)) :key #'cadr)
(3 Y)
```

A keyword parameter has two parts:

- The first is the name (in this case :key), which begins with a colon. (We'll discuss the meaning of this colon in more detail in Chapter 7.)
- The second is the value, which in this case is #'cadr.

We use keyword parameters the same way in our walk function to find the proper path based on the given direction.

Once we have the correct path, we store the result in the variable next ❶. The if expression then checks whether next has a value ❹ (the next variable isn't nil). If next has a value, if adjusts the player's position because this is a valid direction ❺. The call to look ❻ retrieves the description for the new location and returns it as a value. If the player chooses an invalid direction, look will generate an admonishment instead of a new description ❼.

Here's what our walk function looks like now:

```
> (walk 'west)
(YOU ARE IN A BEAUTIFUL GARDEN.
THERE IS A WELL IN FRONT OF YOU.
THERE IS A DOOR GOING EAST FROM HERE.
YOU SEE A CHAIN ON THE FLOOR.
YOU SEE A FROG ON THE FLOOR.)
```

There's a quote in front of the direction, since the direction name needs to be written in data mode. It's kind of awkward to force a player to put a quote in a game command, but the interface we are creating now is intended for easy debugging and development. Heck, it's almost not even worth calling an "interface," since we just enter the game commands directly into the REPL. In the next chapter, we'll create a much nicer interface using a custom REPL designed for playing text games that will take care of this wart.

NOTE   *You could use Lisp macros to create a command in a vanilla Lisp REPL that doesn't require the quote in front of the direction, so that you could just write (walk west), for instance. You'll learn more about macros in Chapter 16.*

Picking Up Objects

Next, let's create a command to pick up objects in our world. To do so, we modify the variable *object-locations* that we're using to track the location of objects:

```
(defun pickup (object)
❶  (cond ((member object
❷            (objects-at *location* *objects* *object-locations*))
❸       (push (list object 'body) *object-locations*)
           `(you are now carrying the ,object))
          (t '(you cannot get that.)))))
```

The pickup function uses the member ❶ function to see if the object is indeed on the floor of the current location. (The member function checks to see if a particular item is found in a list of items.) We use the objects-at command ❷ to generate the lists of objects at the current location.

If the object is at the current location, we use the push command ❸ to push a new item onto the *object-locations* list, consisting of the item and its new location. The new location will just be body, for the player's body.

The push command ❸ simply adds a new item to the front of a list variable's list. For example, the following example adds the number 7 to the list 1 2 3:

```
> (defparameter *foo* '(1 2 3))
*FOO*
> (push 7 *foo*)
(7 1 2 3)
> *foo*
(7 1 2 3)
```

This push command is basically a convenience function built on top of setf. For example, we could have replaced the preceding push command with (setf *foo* (cons 7 *foo*)) and obtained the same result. It's just easier to use push.

Pushing a new location for an object onto our *object-locations* alist does seem a bit odd. Since we're never removing old locations for objects, just pushing new ones, it means that *object-locations* may contain multiple entries for a single object, and that this list now has two stored locations for the object in question. Fortunately, the assoc command, which we use to find objects in a given location (within the objects-at command), always returns the first item it finds in a list. Therefore, using the push command makes the assoc command behave as if the value in the list for a given key has been replaced altogether.

Using the push and assoc commands together in this way allows us to pretend that values in an alist are changing, while still preserving old values. Old values are simply suppressed by newer values, thus preserving a history of all old values. The push/assoc idiom is a common technique used by Lispers.

Now let's walk back to the living room and try to pick up an object:

```
> (walk 'east)
(YOU ARE IN THE LIVING-ROOM OF A WIZARDS HOUSE. THERE IS A WIZARD SNORING
 LOUDLY ON THE COUCH. THERE IS A DOOR GOING WEST FROM HERE. THERE IS A LADDER
 GOING UPSTAIRS FROM HERE. YOU SEE A WHISKEY ON THE FLOOR. YOU SEE A BUCKET ON
 THE FLOOR.)
> (pickup 'whiskey)
(YOU ARE NOW CARRYING THE WHISKEY)
```

It worked. We're carrying the whiskey, which means that we can now pick up things in our world!

Checking Our Inventory

Finally, let's create a function that lets players see an inventory of objects they are carrying:

```
(defun inventory ()
  (cons 'items- (objects-at 'body *objects* *object-locations*)))
```

This inventory function uses the objects-at function to retrieve a list of objects at a requested location. What location does it search for? If you remember, when an object was picked up by the player, we changed its location to 'body: This is the location we now use to query.

Let's try out this inventory function:

```
> (inventory)
(ITEMS- WHISKEY)
```

As you can see, we are carrying only one item right now: the whiskey bottle we just picked up.

There you have it! We now have a basic engine for a text adventure game. We can look around the world with look; walk between places with walk; pick up objects with pickup; and check our inventory with inventory.

Of course, we don't really have much of a game, since we can't *do* anything with the objects we find. We'll add a mechanism for actually manipulating objects in Chapter 17. In the next chapter, we'll focus on improving our game's user interface. Even though the REPL is perfect for prototyping our game, adding a custom text game interface will make the game play more seamless for the player.

What You've Learned

In this chapter, we put together a simple engine for a text adventure game. Along the way, you learned the following:

- A game world can be represented by a mathematical graph, consisting of *nodes* for the places the player can visit and *edges* for the paths between these places.

- You can store these nodes in an *association list (alist)* called *nodes*. This *alist* allows you to look up properties of a node/place by using its name. In the case of our game, the property we're storing is a description of each node/place.

- You use the assoc function to look up a key (location name in our example) in an alist.

- *Quasiquoting* is a technique that allows you to insert small bits of computer code into larger pieces of data.

- Some Lisp functions accept other functions as arguments. These are called *higher-order functions*. The mapcar function is the most popular higher-order function in Common Lisp.

- To replace a value from an alist, you push new items onto the list. Only the most recent value will be reported by the assoc function.

6

INTERACTING WITH THE WORLD: READING AND PRINTING IN LISP

So far, we haven't written any code that directly interacts with the outside world. Instead, all the results generated by commands are just returned as values, which we can see by calling functions from our Lisp REPL.

However, code can't just spend its whole life sitting in a black box. At some point, it's going to need to interact with the world, so it will need a user interface. Luckily, Lisp has much to offer to help you create user interfaces. There are many graphical user interface libraries for different flavors of Common Lisp, as well as libraries for building web interfaces. In fact, we'll be building our own toy web interface in Chapter 13.

In this chapter, we'll focus on the most basic of all user interfaces, the *command-line interface*.

Printing and Reading Text

For a command-line interface, we need commands that can directly print text from the screen and read in text entered by the user. The two commands that do this are, appropriately enough, print and read. As you might expect by now, there is a lot of symmetry between these two commands.

Printing to the Screen

The print function simply lets you print stuff to the console:

```
> (print "foo")
```

❶ "foo"
❷ "foo"

Don't get confused by the fact that calling the print function caused "foo" to be printed twice. The first "foo" ❶ is what the print function *actually printed*. The second "foo" ❷ is there because, as you know, the REPL always prints the value of any expression that is entered. It so happens that the value of (print "foo") is "foo", causing the word to be shown twice. In the examples that follow in this chapter, I'll typically omit this extra final value printed by the REPL, just to avoid confusion.

The print function is an easy way to print a Lisp value to the screen. However, advanced Lispers often favor a related function called prin1. To understand the difference, let's try both of these functions out in the REPL:

```
> (progn (print "this")
         (print "is")
         (print "a")
         (print "test"))

"this"
"is"
"a"
"test"
```

The print function causes each item to be printed on a separate line. Now, let's try prin1:

```
> (progn (prin1 "this")
         (prin1 "is")
         (prin1 "a")
         (prin1 "test"))
"this""is""a""test"
```

As you can see, prin1 does not put the printed items on separate lines. To be precise, the print and prin1 commands are the same in every way, except that print will start a new line before printing a value. Additionally, print places a space character at the end of the printed value.

Because prin1 does less, it is really a simpler, more fundamental function. It is more flexible and, therefore, is commonly used in more serious Lisp code. We'll use the print function more frequently in this book, but you should be aware of the prin1 command, as well.

Saying Hello to the User

The following example is a simple function, say-hello, that you can call from your Lisp prompt. It asks users for their name and responds with a greeting. *When you run the program, be sure to type quotes around your name, even if this may seem odd.*

```
> (defun say-hello ()
❶     (print "Please type your name:")
❷     (let ((name (read)))
❸         (print "Nice to meet you, ")
❹         (print name)))
SAY-HELLO.
> (say-hello)
"Please type your name:" "bob"
"Nice to meet you,"
"bob"
```

In the first line of the say-hello function, we print a message asking users for their name ❶. Next, we define a local variable called name, which is set to the value returned by the read function ❷. The read function will cause Lisp to wait for the user to type in something at the REPL. Only after the user has typed something in at the prompt and pressed ENTER will the variable name be set to the result. Once we know the user's name, a personalized message is printed, greeting the user ❸❹.

As you can see from this simple function, the print and read functions do (almost) exactly what you would expect. The print function prints something on the screen. The read function lets the user enter something into the program. However, there is one glaring idiosyncrasy in these functions: Every value displayed and entered is surrounded by quotation marks.

Starting with print and read

When you need to print something on the screen, you should first think of the print command. If you need to read something in, you should first think of the read command. Other printing commands let you create the previous example without having superfluous quotes, but whenever you have an input or output task in Lisp, you should ask yourself, "Can print or read do the job?" You will save yourself a lot of trouble if you always use these two functions as your starting point.

WARNING   *The read command can be dangerous if used in the wrong way. See "The Dangers of read and eval" on page 101 for details.*

The print and read functions think about values with the mind of a computer, not the mind of a human. A computer loves having strings of text surrounded by quotes. It doesn't have a human brain, and consequently, it can't understand what we mean when we feed it raw textual information. However, if a text fragment is surrounded by quotes, even a dumb old computer can figure out that the value we're handing it is probably a string of text.

The print and read commands actually take this philosophy to the extreme. Almost any conceivable type of data in Lisp (with the exception of actual functions and some advanced data structures) can be printed and read using these commands, without the slightest bit of loss along the way. You can probably already imagine some scenarios where this feature would be immensely valuable, such as writing some hairy and huge piece of data to a file, and loading it in again at a later date.

As a simple example, the following code has *exactly* the same design as the previous function, but amazingly, it can read and print a number instead of a string. Notice how the program prints and reads numbers without the use of quotes, since Lisp knows when something is a number just by seeing the number in its raw form.

```
> (defun add-five ()
      (print "please enter a number:")
      (let ((num (read)))
          (print "When I add five I get")
          (print (+ num 5))))
ADD-FIVE
> (add-five)
"please enter a number:" 4
"When I add five I get"
9
```

Let's look at some more examples of what happens when we use print to write out values.

(print '3)	=> 3	*An integer*
(print '3.4)	=> 3.4	*A float*
(print 'foo)	=> FOO	*A symbol. It may be printed in all caps, since Common Lisp symbols are blind to letter case.*
(print '"foo")	=> "foo"	*A string*
(print '#\a)	=> #\a	*A character*

These examples are all really boring, since print pretty much just prints out exactly what we put in. Note that we put an explicit quote on the front of each value. It could be omitted and would be implicit in all cases but the symbol name, since a symbol can also refer to functions.

The last example shows how literal characters are entered in Lisp. To create a Lisp character, just place the #\ symbols in front of the actual character. Lisp also has special literals defined for nonvisible characters. The most important for everyday use are #\newline, #\tab, and #\space.

A table of output from the read function would look just as boring as this table for print, in the same symmetrical way.

NOTE   *In the examples above I stated that Common Lisp symbols are blind to letter case. While this is true for most strings, it is in fact possible to create case-sensitive symbols by surrounding the symbol with the vertical pipe |. So the symbol |CaseSensitiveSymbol| will retain its case. Symbols surrounded by vertical pipes can even contain punctuation. Hence |even this is a legal Lisp symbol!|*

Reading and Printing Stuff the Way Humans Like It

Of course, our initial little say-hello function does a pretty awful job of greeting people, even if it has some interesting properties. It would be much better if we had more functions that could make it friendlier for humans. Actually, we can create a (very symmetrical) little table that summarizes what we would like:

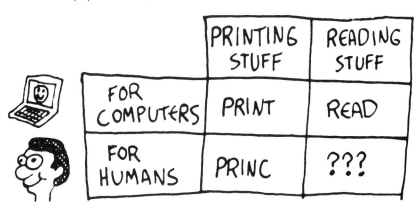

As you can see, Lisp has a command that can print pieces of data in a way that is appealing to humans. The princ function can take any piece of Lisp data, and it tries to print that data in a way humans would prefer. It will do the basic things you might expect: leave off the quotes on a string, print characters in their raw form, and so on. Here are some examples:

```
(princ '3)      => 3
(princ '3.4)    => 3.4
(princ 'foo)    => FOO
(princ '"foo")  => foo
(princ '#\a)    => a
```

Here's an example of princing a character that has a special meaning:

```
> (progn (princ "This sentence will be interrupted")
         (princ #\newline)
         (princ "by an annoying newline character."))
This sentence will be interrupted
by an annoying newline character.
```

By its nature, princ could be used to print any arbitrary output of characters you want. This is fundamentally different from print. As we've discussed, the cool thing about the print command is that it prints objects in such a way that they can always be "read" back into their internal representation. However, this means print can't be used to generate any arbitrary bit of text. On the other hand, princ can be used to print anything you want.

Therefore, although princ can print stuff in a way that humans prefer, it's a one-way street. Once we've printed things with princ, only a humanlike intelligence could decipher how to change things back into a meaningful, appropriate Lisp data structure. Since computers are too stupid to do this right now, it means our beloved symmetry has been broken.

Of course, we could always cheat and come up with some arbitrary rules for how the computer should interpret what the human enters. An obvious way to do this would be to say to the computer, "Just let the users type in whatever they want until they hit the ENTER key, then treat the whole thing as a string." The function that does this in Common Lisp is called read-line. However, it has none of the sophistication of the read, print, and princ functions, since it knows about nothing beyond characters and strings.

With this new knowledge, we can finally go full circle and create a proper function for greeting someone, without ugly quotes or other oddities:

```
> (defun say-hello ()
❶    (princ "Please type your name:")
❷    (let ((name (read-line)))
❸      (princ "Nice to meet you, ")
❹      (princ name)))
SAY-HELLO
> (say-hello)
Please type your name: Bob O'Malley
Nice to meet you, Bob O'Malley
```

This version of the say-hello function is similar to our first version. However, when the computer asks users for their name ❶, it now does so without printing quotes around the text string. The same holds true to when we print the greeting ❸❹. Also, users can now enter in *any* name (including a name with spaces and quotes), since the read-line command ❷ captures and returns all the text entered until the ENTER key is pressed, without any fuss.

The Symmetry Between Code and Data in Lisp

You have seen that Lisp has very elegant and symmetrical facilities for translating raw string data from the outside world and converting it to and from Lisp syntax expressions. But Lisp has an even deeper symmetry. It can treat program code and data interchangeably. A programming language that uses the same data structures to store data and program code is called *homoiconic*.

You saw an example of homoiconicity in Chapter 3, when we discussed code mode and data mode. In that example, we used the quote to change between the two modes:

```
> '(+ 1 2) ;data mode
(+ 1 2)
> (+ 1 2) ;code mode
3
```

In the previous chapter, we took this concept one step further by using a quasiquote when defining the describe-path function.

But the quoting and quasiquoting facilities in Lisp are somewhat limited in their abilities. What if we generate a piece of Lisp code from scratch somehow and wish to execute it as if it were a piece of code? For example, let's store a raw chunk of code inside a variable:

```
> (defparameter *foo* '(+ 1 2))
*FOO*
```

How could we execute the code that's in the *foo* variable? We need an even more powerful command to make this possible. This is the eval command:

```
> (eval *foo*)
3
```

Because the eval command is so powerful and yet so simple, it is extremely enticing to beginning Lispers. You want to write a program with self-modifying code? Then eval will be your best friend. In fact, this is probably the main reason why the artificial intelligence (AI) freaks back in the day loved Lisp so much. Go ahead and try writing some programs that use the eval command. You'll find that it's a lot of fun.

However, an experienced Lisper will only rarely use eval. Until you have a few thousand lines of Lisp code under your belt, you really won't know when it is appropriate to use this extremely powerful command. Often, a beginning Lisper will use the eval command instead of defining a Lisp macro. We will discuss macros in Chapter 16.

The bottom line is that the symmetry of data and code in Lisp pretty much makes Lisp the poster child of homoiconicity. Quoting, quasiquoting, the eval command, and macros allow you to take advantage of this property in your code.

WARNING   *Inexperienced use of eval can pose a security risk. See "The Dangers of read and eval" on page 101 for more information.*

Adding a Custom Interface to Our Game Engine

So far, we've been using the Lisp REPL to enter our game commands. It's amazing how well this works for prototyping our game. But now that you've gained an understanding of the basic Common Lisp input and output commands, we can begin to put in place our own custom text game interface, which will be better suited for interacting with the player.

Setting Up a Custom REPL

Creating your own REPL in Lisp is almost laughably easy. Here's a simple custom REPL for our game, which lets us call the look command in exactly the same way as the standard REPL did:

```
> (defun game-repl ()
    (loop (print (eval (read)))))
GAME-REPL
> (game-repl)
(look)

(YOU ARE IN THE LIVING-ROOM. A WIZARD IS SNORING LOUDLY ON THE COUCH. THERE IS
 A DOOR GOING WEST FROM HERE. THERE IS A LADDER GOING UPSTAIRS FROM HERE. YOU
 SEE A WHISKEY ON THE FLOOR.)
```

Stop me if this explanation of game-repl is confusing: First it reads a command, then evals it, and finally prints it. The only command you haven't seen before is loop (covered in detail in Chapter 10), which as you might expect, simply loops forever. (In CLISP, you'll need to hit CTRL-C and type :a to get out of the infinite loop.) As you can see, it's easy to build your own REPL by simply calling read, eval, print, and loop.

Of course, to customize the behavior of our REPL, we'll want to call our own versions of these functions. Also, we'll want a way to exit from our game in a more graceful manner. So, let's redefine game-repl as follows:

```
(defun game-repl ()
❶   (let ((cmd (game-read)))
❷     (unless (eq (car cmd) 'quit)
❸        (game-print (game-eval cmd))
❹        (game-repl)))))
```

In this version, we first capture the command the player types using a local variable, cmd ❶. This way, we can intercept any attempt to call quit and use it to exit our game-repl. In other words, we want to continue running our REPL unless the user typed quit ❷. Otherwise, the function evals and prints ❸, but using our custom versions of these functions, which we'll write shortly. Finally, the game-repl function calls itself recursively ❹, causing it to loop back, as long as we had not decided to quit earlier.

Writing a Custom read Function

The purpose of our game-read function is to fix the two annoyances that make the standard Lisp read function wrong for playing our game:

- The standard Lisp read forces us to put parentheses around our commands. As any old-school text adventure player knows, we should be able to just type look without any parentheses. To accomplish this, we can just call read-line and stick in our own parentheses.

- With read, we must put a quote in front of any function commands. We should be able to type walk east without a quote in front of east. To do this, we'll stick a quote in front of the parameters after the fact.

DURING THE DAY, LISA WORKS AT THE CITY LIBRARY HELPING PEOPLE LEARN THE DEWEY-DECIMAL SYSTEM...

BUT AT NIGHT, SHE BECOMES GAME-READ, UNDERSTANDING ANY WRITTEN TEXT!

GAME READ

JANE AUSTEN IS MY BFF!

Here's a definition of game-read that does both of these things:

```
(defun game-read ()
❶   (let ((cmd (read-from-string
❷                (concatenate 'string "(" (read-line) ")"))))
```

```
❸        (flet ((quote-it (x)
                 (list 'quote x)))
❹          (cons (car cmd) (mapcar #'quote-it (cdr cmd)))))))
```

The `read-from-string` command ❶ works just like the `read` command, but lets us read a syntax expression (or any other basic Lisp datatype) from a string instead of directly from the console.

The string we use for this is a tweaked version of a string we get from `read-line` ❷. We tweak it by adding quotes around it using the `concatenate` command, which can be used for concatenating strings together, as well as some parentheses. The result is that the `cmd` variable will be set to the player's requested command and converted into a Lisp syntax expression. For example, if the player types in `walk east`, the `cmd` variable will be set to the expression `(walk east)`, which is a list containing two symbols.

Next, we define a local function called `quote-it` ❸, which we can use to quote any arguments the player has in a command. How exactly does it manage to quote a parameter? Well, it turns out that the single quote is just shorthand for a Lisp command called `quote`. This means that `'foo` and `(quote foo)` are the same. We can quote a raw parameter by simply putting the parameter in a list with the `quote` command in front.

Remember that local functions can be defined with `labels` or `flet`. Since we are not using any recursion in the `quote-it` function ❸, we can use the simpler `flet` command. The final line in the `game-read` function applies `quote-it` to every argument in the player's command. It does this by mapping `quote-it` across the `cdr` of the `cmd` variable ❹ (and then attaching the first word in the command back on front with `car`).

Let's try our new function:

```
> (game-read)
walk east
(WALK 'EAST)
```

As you can see, the `game-read` function is able to add parentheses and quotes—just what our game needs!

NOTE   *Our custom reader has some limitations that a sufficiently boneheaded game player could conceivably bring to the surface. The player could enter a weird string like* `"(look"`, *with mismatched parentheses, and it would cause a Lisp exception in the* `game-read` *command. There's nothing wrong with this, per se, since the standard* `read` *command will also act strangely when given garbled input. (In this case, it will let you enter another line of input in the hopes that you will eventually supply it with the missing parenthesis.) However, our* `game-repl` *doesn't handle this situation properly, causing the actual* `game-repl` *to crash. This would be as if you were playing Zork and typed in a command so vile that it took down the Zork game itself. This rare situation could be addressed by having additional exception handling, as discussed in Chapter 13.*

Writing a game-eval Function

Now that we've created a nigh-perfect Lisp reader, let's think about how we could improve the eval command. The main problem with using eval in a game is it allows you to call any Lisp command, even if that command has nothing to do with playing the game. To help protect our program from hackers, we'll create a game-eval function that allows only certain commands to be called, as follows:

```
(defparameter *allowed-commands* '(look walk pickup inventory))

(defun game-eval (sexp)
❶   (if (member (car sexp) *allowed-commands*)
❷       (eval sexp)
        '(i do not know that command.)))
```

The game-eval function checks if the first word in the entered command is in the list of allowed commands, using the member function ❶. If it is, we then use the standard eval to execute the player's command ❷. By checking that the command called by the player is in the official list, we protect ourselves against any attempts to call malicious commands.

WARNING *Our game-eval function does not offer 100 percent protection against hacking. See "The Dangers of read and eval" on page 101 for details.*

Writing a game-print Function

The final missing piece in our game-repl system is the game-print function. Of all the limitations in the Lisp REPL version of our game, one was the most obvious: All the text descriptions printed in the game were in uppercase.

Last I checked, throughout the current millennium, computers have been able to display both uppercase *and* lowercase characters. By writing our own game-print function, we can solve this problem.

Before we step through the game-print function's code, let's look at an example of its output:

```
> (game-print '(THIS IS A SENTENCE. WHAT ABOUT THIS? PROBABLY.))
This is a sentence. What about this? Probably.
```

As you can see, the game-print function converts our symbol-based writing into properly capitalized text. By having this function available, we can store the text in our game engine in the most comfortable format possible: lists of symbols. This format makes it easier to manipulate the text. Then, at the point of presentation, we can decorate these symbol lists with presentation details.

Of course, in this example, the decorations are very simple. All we do is adjust the case. But you can already see some small benefits of separating the presentation details from the data model. For instance, suppose we changed the describe-path function to write sentences like "Left of here lies a door." No further changes would be needed; the program would automatically know to capitalize the *Left* at the beginning of the sentence.

However, the real benefits come into play when you want to use more sophisticated methods of presentation, such as generating HTML code. You might want to incorporate custom semantics for your text game to enhance the appearance of the text, such as changing colors, fonts, and so on. For instance, you could allow your game descriptions to contain phrases such as "You are being attacked by a (red evil demon)." Then you could just catch the keyword red in the game-print function to write the enclosed text in red. We will be creating an HTML presentation system similar to this in Chapter 17.

Now we're ready to look at the game-print function's code:

```
(defun tweak-text (lst caps lit)
  (when lst
❶   (let ((item (car lst))
          (rest (cdr lst)))
```

```
❷    (cond ((eq item #\space) (cons item (tweak-text rest caps lit)))
❸          ((member item '(#\! #\? #\.)) (cons item (tweak-text rest t lit)))
❹          ((eq item #\") (tweak-text rest caps (not lit)))
           (lit (cons item (tweak-text rest nil lit)))
❺          ((or caps lit) (cons (char-upcase item) (tweak-text rest nil lit)))
❻          (t (cons (char-downcase item) (tweak-text rest nil nil)))))))))

    (defun game-print (lst)
❼      (princ (coerce (tweak-text (coerce (string-trim "() "
❽                                                      (prin1-to-string lst))
                                         'list)
                                 t
❾                               nil)
                    'string))
      (fresh-line))
```

The game-print function and its helper function are a bit more complicated
than the other functions we've looked at so far. The first important part of
the code that is executed is in game-print, where it converts the symbol list
(containing the text whose layout we want to fix) into a string with prin1-to-
string ❽, one of Lisp's many print variants. The to-string part means this
function doesn't dump the result to the screen, but just returns it as a string.
The 1 means it will stay on a single line. The standard print command precedes
its output with a newline character and also follows it with a space. The functions prin1 and prin1-to-string variants don't add these extra characters.

Next, game-print converts the string to a list of characters with the coerce
function ❼. By coercing our string into a list, we can reduce the bigger goal
of the function into a list-processing problem. This is smack-dab in the Lisp
comfort zone. In this case, we're creating a list of the characters making up
the text we want to fix.

We can now send the data to the list-eater function tweak-text ❼. Notice
that some of the arguments used in the code of the game-print function are
printed on their own line for clarity. You can easily see which arguments are
meant for which commands by looking at the indentation. For instance, the t
and nil arguments ❾ belong to tweak-text.

The tweak-text function looks at each character in the list and modifies it
as needed. At the top of this function, we define two local variables, item and
rest, which we get by chewing off an item from the front of the sentence we're
tweaking ❶. Then, the tweak-text function uses a cond to check the character
at the top of the list for different conditions ❷.

The first condition it checks for is whether the character is a space
character ❷. If so, it just leaves the space unchanged and processes the next
character in the list. If the character is a period, question mark, or exclamation point ❸, we turn on the cap parameter for the rest of the string (by using
the value t as an argument in the recursive call) to indicate that the next symbol is at the beginning of a sentence and needs a capital letter.

We also track whether we've encountered a quotation mark ❹. We do
this because, infrequently, a symbol list is not adequate for encoding English
text. Examples include having a comma (commas are not allowed in standard

Common Lisp symbols) or product names with nonstandard capitalization. In these cases, we can just fall back on using text strings. Here's an example:

```
> (game-print '(not only does this sentence have a "comma," it also mentions
the "iPad."))
Not only does this sentence have a comma, it also mentions the iPad.
```

Our sample game doesn't actually need the fallback facility. Nonetheless, this feature allows the game-print function to handle many basic exceptional text situations that you may encounter if you try to expand the game on your own. We tell the function to treat the capitalization as shown literally by turning on the lit variable in the recursive call. As long as this value is set, the tweak-text function prevents the capitalization rules (which start at ❺) from being reached.

The next thing the tweak-text function checks is whether the next character is supposed to be capitalized. If it is, we use the char-upcase function to change the current character to uppercase (if it isn't already) before processing the next item in the list ❺.

If none of the other conditions were met, we know that the current character should be lowercase ❻, and we can convert it using the char-downcase function.

After tweak-text is finished correcting the text in the character list, the game-print function coerces it back into a proper string and princs it ❼. The fresh-line function at the end of game-print makes sure that the next item appearing on the screen will start on a fresh line.

We have now completed the task of printing the original list of symbols to the screen, using a set of decorations appropriate for the needs of an adventure game engine.

Trying Out Our Fancy New Game Interface

We have now completed all the pieces needed for a custom REPL for our game engine. Simply call the game-repl function and explore our new game world. Remember that we will be expanding this engine into a full game, with additional commands, in Chapter 17.

```
> (game-repl)
look
You are in the living-room. A wizard is snoring loudly on the couch. There is
a door going west from here. There is a ladder going upstairs from here. You
see a whiskey on the floor. You see a bucket on the floor.
walk west
You are in a beautiful garden. There is a well in front of you. There is a
door going east from here. You see a frog on the floor. You see a chain on
the floor.
pickup chain
You are now carrying the chain
scratch head
I do not know that command.
```

```
pickup chicken
You cannot get that.
walk east
You are in the living-room. A wizard is snoring loudly on the couch. There is
  a door going west from here. There is a ladder going upstairs from here. You
  see a whiskey on the floor. You see a bucket on the floor.
walk upstairs
You are in the attic. There is a giant welding torch in the corner. There is a
  ladder going downstairs from here.
inventory
Items- chain
walk china
You cannot go that way.
walk downstairs
You are in the living-room. A wizard is snoring loudly on the couch. There is
  a door going west from here. There is a ladder going upstairs from here. You
  see a whiskey on the floor. You see a bucket on the floor.
pickup bucket
You are now carrying the bucket
look
You are in the living-room. A wizard is snoring loudly on the couch. There is
  a door going west from here. There is a ladder going upstairs from here. You
  see a whiskey on the floor.
quit
```

Success! We now have an extremely flexible text game engine. It can be expanded and debugged within the Lisp REPL. It also has a fully customizable interface to offer the player a seamless text adventure experience. As we put it together, you saw some mind-bending Lisp techniques that let us construct this engine with a minimum of filler code or other overhead.

The Dangers of read and eval

We've used both the eval and the read commands in creating a custom Lisp REPL. These commands are very powerful, but also very dangerous. Using them without taking the proper precautions might allow a hacker to attack your software by running malicious commands.

For example, suppose our program needed a function called format-harddrive. This is *not* a function we would want just any person to have access to, and it could be very dangerous if a hacker somehow tricked our game REPL into calling it.

The game-eval function we created earlier in this chapter has some crude safeguards to prevent a player from entering format-harddrive as a game command. Here's what happens if we try to run this command in our new game REPL:

```
> (game-repl)
format-harddrive
I do not know that command.
```

Our game-eval function will run only commands that are in an approved list. This gives our game a sort of firewall, which lets us access the powers of Lisp to evaluate commands while still preventing the player from hacking the game.

However, there are also more sophisticated exploits players could try. For instance, they could enter walk (format-harddrive). Fortunately, our game-read function forces all function parameters into data mode by using quote-it. By using quote-it in game-read, the actual code that is executed is (walk '(format-harddrive)). The quote in front of (format-hardrive) puts the malicious command into data mode, so nothing bad can happen.

One attack method that *will* break our program is to use *reader macros*. These are an advanced set of features, built into the Common Lisp read command, that open another avenue for executing malicious computer code. (Remember that before we use eval on game commands, they first pass through read.) An example of a game command that will successfully execute evil code is walk #.{format-harddrive}.

The bottom line is that you can never be sure that a Lisp program using eval or read is completely safe from a hacker. When writing production Lisp code, you should try to avoid these two commands when possible.

What You've Learned

In this chapter, we created a custom REPL to supercharge our text adventure game. Along the way, you learned the following:

- The print and read functions let you directly communicate with the user through the console. These two functions work in a computer-friendly way.
- Other input/output functions are not as elegant as read and print, but are friendlier for interacting with humans. Examples include princ and read-line.

- A *homoiconic* programming language stores its program code and program data in a similar format. Lisp's quoting, quasiquoting, eval, and macro features make it extremely homoiconic.

- It's easy to write your own custom REPL.

- It's simple to transform your internal Lisp data into the format most suitable for your program's interface. This makes it easy to separate presentation details from your program's internal data structures.

6.5

LAMBDA: A FUNCTION SO IMPORTANT IT DESERVES ITS OWN CHAPTER

It's impossible to overstate the importance of the `lambda` command in Lisp. In fact, this command is pretty much the entire reason that Lisp exists in the first place.

What lambda Does

In short, `lambda` lets you create a function without giving it a name. For example, let's say we create a `half` function that takes a number and divides it in half. Until now, we've written such a function this way:

```
(defun half (n)
   (/ n 2))
```

It turns out that, in Lisp, functions are actually values that we can view and pass around just as if they were numbers or lists. An experienced Lisp programmer would say that functions are *first-class values* in Lisp. As you saw in Chapter 5, you can actually get at the function represented by the word half by using the function operator:

```
> #'half
#<FUNCTION HALF ...>
```

The lambda command just lets you do these same two things in a single step. You can define a function and then get it, without giving your function a name:

```
> (lambda (n) (/ n 2))
#<FUNCTION :LAMBDA ...>
```

The first parameter to the lambda command is a parameter list, no different from the parameter list used in defun. The rest of the parameters are just the commands for the body of the unnamed function.

Once you have a value representing your unnamed halving function, you can pass it directly to other Common Lisp commands, such as the mapcar or apply commands. For instance, we could do the following to elegantly halve all the values in a list:

```
> (mapcar (lambda (n) (/ n 2)) '(2 4 6))
(1 2 3)
```

Because not all parameters of the lambda command are evaluated, lambda itself is not actually a true function. It is something called a *macro*. Remember from Chapter 2 that all parameters to a Lisp function are evaluated before the function itself is evaluated. Macros, on the other hand, have special powers and are allowed to break those rules. You'll learn more about macros in Chapter 16.

Also, to confuse matters a bit, the actual value that lambda returns is a regular Lisp function—in this case, a function that cuts a number in half. When Lispers talk about lambda functions—which they pretty much do for breakfast, lunch, and dinner—they're talking about functions created using lambda. They're not talking about the lambda macro itself, which is not a function. Got that?

lambda lets your programs do very complicated things.

The lambda form allows your programming code to take a conceptual leap.

While most programming languages try to keep the worlds of functions and values separate, Lisp lets you bridge these worlds as desired. For instance, if you want to package up a little ad hoc function and pass it off to another part of your program, lambda does exactly what you need.

You will see that most Lisp programs use this command very heavily. The same holds true for the remaining examples in this book.

Why lambda Is So Important

The ability to pass around functions as if they were just plain old pieces of data is incredibly valuable. Once you get used to doing this, you open up all kinds of conceptual possibilities in the design of your programs. Eventually, your programs will start looking very different from programs in more (dare I say) pedestrian languages, such as Java or C. The name for the style of programming that relies heavily on passing functions as values is called *higher-order functional programming*. We will look at this style in more detail in Chapter 14.

An even more important reason why Lispers go gaga over lambda is that, as it turns out, in a purely mathematical sense, lambda is actually the only Lisp command there is!

Recall that Lisp is unusual among programming languages in that it was derived directly from a mathematical concept called the *lambda calculus*. In short, the lambda calculus is a theoretical programming language that contains only one command: the lambda command. By having only this single command and using special code transformations, it's possible to create a fully functioning (though perhaps not practical) programming language.

The take-home point is that the lambda special form is the most fundamental command in a Lisp system, and the central concept from which other functions in Lisp derive. In fact, it is the central concept from which the very idea of Lisp itself originated.

Now that you have a basic understanding of lambda, you're ready to tackle some more complicated programming examples that would be hard to write without the anonymous functions this command permits.

What You've Learned

This short chapter discussed how to create anonymous functions. Here are the main points:

- By using lambda, you can create a function without needing to give it a name.
- Many functions in Lisp accept functions as parameters. If you use these functions, you are using a technique called *higher-order functional programming*.

7

GOING BEYOND BASIC LISTS

In this chapter, we'll go beyond basic list concepts. We'll talk about special kinds of lists, and we'll write a game that will take list manipulation to a new level.

Exotic Lists

As you learned in Chapter 3, lists in Lisp are built out of cons cells—small data structures that allow you to link together two pieces of data. The right slot in the last cons cell in a list should contain a nil.

By stringing together several cons cells, you can create a list of any length. For instance, this is how we would use cons cells to create a list of the numbers 1, 2, and 3:

```
(cons 1 (cons 2 (cons 3 nil)))
```

Since it's so cumbersome for humans to think of a chain of cons cells as a list, Lisp has a special, simplified syntax for printing out such lists. You can see this for yourself by evaluating a chain of cons cells in the REPL:

```
> (cons 1 (cons 2 (cons 3 nil)))
(1 2 3)
```

Lisp uses the simpler list syntax when it parrots our chain back to us in the REPL. It shows our string of cons cells as a list of three items. The important point to remember is that *this difference in appearance is entirely superficial.* No matter how a Lisp list is displayed, fundamentally, it always remains a chain of cons cells.

Dotted Lists

So, what happens if we deviate from the classic "string of conses" formula? How will a Lisp environment deal with this when printing lists?

Suppose we try to create a list of the numbers 1, 2, and 3, like this:

```
(cons 1 (cons 2 3))
```

Here, instead of creating a third cons cell for the third number of our list, we stuff it into the right slot of the previous cell. What would the printed response look like if we were to enter this structure into a Lisp REPL? Let's try it out:

```
> (cons 1 (cons 2 3))
(1 2 . 3)
```

To indicate that the final item in the list wasn't found in the proper location for a nil-terminated list, Lisp places a dot in front of this final item. This dot is basically Lisp's way of saying, "I tried to print this structure you entered using list notation, but the last item in the list didn't contain the usual nil I expected; instead, it contained 3."

A list in Lisp that ends in something other than a nil is referred to as a *dotted list*. Dotted lists are kind of an oddity in the Land of Lisp. In and of themselves, they are not that useful a tool for Lisp programming. It would be quite unusual for a Lisp programmer to store data in dotted lists as a regular practice. However, given the pervasiveness of cons cells in Lisp, you will frequently encounter a non-nil value at the end of a chain of cons cells. That's why you should become familiar with dotted lists, even if you may never use them directly.

Another way of thinking about this dot notation is to consider it as simply an alternate syntax for the cons command, used in data mode. In fact, if we wanted to make life hard for ourselves, we could even create regular, proper lists using the dot notation, like this:

```
> '(1 . (2 . (3 . nil)))
(1 2 3)
```

Using this line of thinking, the dot appears in a dotted list simply because Lisp is forced to show the final cons cell in order to maintain the consistency of its list-printing mechanism.

Pairs

One common and practical use for dotted lists in Lisp programs is to elegantly represent pairs. For instance, suppose we wanted to represent a pair of the numbers 2 and 3. One way to do this would be to cons together these two numbers:

```
> (cons 2 3)
(2 . 3)
```

Essentially, all we're doing here is creating a dotted list of length two. As expected, Lisp uses dot notation to display this pair.

Creating pairs in this manner in Lisp is very convenient and efficient. It's convenient because we can extract members from the pair using the standard car and cdr commands. It's relatively efficient because the Lisp environment needs to allocate only a single cons cell to connect the two items.

These types of pairs are commonly used in Lisp programs. For instance, you could use them to store the x- and y-coordinates of a point or a key/value pair in a complex data structure. You will see this latter use for pairs when we discuss association lists.

Circular Lists

Here is the picture we used in Chapter 3 to illustrate the cons cells that make up the list '(1 2 3):

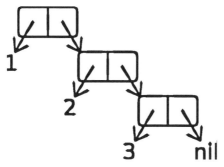

Now suppose that we created a weird mutant of this list. Let's have the cdr of the third cons cell point back to the first cons cell, rather than to nil:

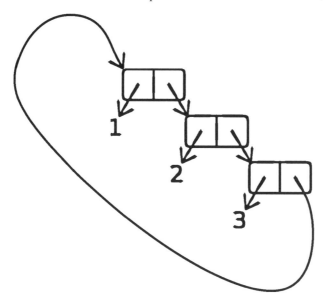

Every cons cell in a list theoretically exists as a separate object in memory. Since the car and cdr slots in a cell can point to any other object in memory, a cons cell can point to an upstream cons cell of a list. We call this a *circular list.*

But before you experiment with circular lists in any Common Lisp environment, you should run this command:

```
(setf *print-circle* t)
```

Setting *print-circle* to true warns Lisp that you plan on playing shenanigans with self-referential data structures, and that it needs to be extra careful when printing on the screen any of the monstrosities you may create. If you were to print a circular list without this variable set, there's no telling what would happen, but whatever the outcome, it wouldn't be pretty (unless you find some beauty in stack overflows and infinite loop printing).

When you have *print-circle* set to true, Common Lisp will use more complex printing routines for printing data structures. These routines (which are disabled by default to improve performance) will check to see if you've run into a previously seen cons cell, so that printing doesn't end up putting you into an infinite loop.

So how would you go about creating a circular list? The most straightforward way is to use the setf command to put extra stuff in the first parameter, like so:

```
> (defparameter foo '(1 2 3))
FOO
> (setf (cdddr foo) foo)
#1=(1 2 3 . #1#)
```

In this example, we've created an infinite list of '(1 2 3 1 2 3 1 2 3 ...) by replacing the nil at the end of a simple list with a reference to the list itself.

The ability to place complex expressions in the first parameter of a setf command, as in this example, is very cool, and we'll explore it in greater detail in Chapter 9.

NOTE   *CLISP (and other Common Lisps) can deal with the printing of circular lists very sensibly. Somehow, it must address the fact that one part of the list refers to another part. As you can see, it uses an esoteric, but quite clever, notation to link the self-referential parts of the expression. However, I'm sure you can also appreciate that, as the complexity of any self-referential data increases, the printed results offered by a Lisp printer for this type of data can become hard for a programmer to grok.*

Association Lists

One particularly useful data structure that can be created out of cons cells is an *association list*, or *alist* for short. An alist consists of key/value pairs stored in a list.

By convention, if a key appears multiple times in the list, it is assumed that the first appearance of the key contains the desired value. For instance, here is an alist representing an order for coffee drinks placed by Bill, Lisa, and John:

```
(defparameter *drink-order* '((bill . double-espresso)
                              (lisa . small-drip-coffee)
                              (john . medium-latte)))
```

To look up the order for a given person, use the function assoc:

```
> (assoc 'lisa *drink-order*)
(LISA . SMALL-DRIP-COFFEE)
```

This function searches the list from the beginning for the desired key, and then returns the key/value pair. Now suppose that, before picking up the drink order, Lisa flags you down and opts to change her order to something slightly more decadent. You can change her order using the push function:

```
> (push '(lisa . large-mocha-with-whipped-cream) *drink-order*)
((LISA . LARGE-MOCHA-WITH-WHIPPED-CREAM)
 (BILL . DOUBLE-ESPRESSO)
 (LISA . SMALL-DRIP-COFFEE)
 (JOHN . MEDIUM-LATTE))
```

This function simply adds a new item to the front of an existing list.

Because, by default, the first reference to a key in an association list takes precedence over later references to the same key, the order Lisa placed for a small drip coffee is superseded by her more recent order:

```
> (assoc 'lisa *drink-order*)
(LISA . LARGE-MOCHA-WITH-WHIPPED-CREAM)
```

As you can see, alists are a great way to keep track of any changeable collection of key/value pairs. Alists are easy to understand, to manipulate with Lisp functions, and to comprehend when printed out (they're just lists of pairs, after all).

Furthermore, once a value is stored in an alist, it remains there forever, making it easy to audit the history of any data. For instance, in our coffee example, the order Lisa placed for her drip coffee is still available even after it has been replaced.

However, alists do have one serious limitation: They are not a very efficient way to store and retrieve data, unless you're dealing with very short lists (under a dozen items). Because of this inefficiency, although alists are often one of the first tools in the Lisp programmer's toolbox, they may be replaced by other types of data structures as a program matures. (In Chapter 9, we'll discuss the performance limitations of list-based data structures, such as alists, in greater detail.)

Coping with Complicated Data

Cons cells are a great tool for representing a wide variety of list-like structures. In fact, most Lisp programmers, when faced with a programming task that is not bound by performance constraints, will rely on them almost exclusively. Because the manipulation and visualization of structures made of cons cells are central to the design of Lisp, these structures are extremely convenient to use and debug.

In fact, even if you do have performance constraints, structures made of cons cells can often be a great choice. A Lisp compiler can often reduce a change to a cons cell down to a single assembly instruction!

Visualizing Tree-like Data

As discussed in Chapter 3, the data (and code) in a Lisp program is represented with syntax expressions. In this format, data is represented using nested lists, often with Lisp symbols at the front of each list explaining the structure of the data.

For example, suppose we wanted to represent the component parts of a house in Lisp:

```
(defparameter *house* '((walls (mortar (cement)
                                       (water)
                                       (sand))
                               (bricks))
❶               (windows (glass)
                         (frame)
❷                        (curtains))
                (roof (shingles)
                      (chimney))))
```

This data structure very elegantly captures the hierarchical nature of the parts that make up a house. Since it is structured as a Lisp syntax expression, we can see the lists that make up the levels of the hierarchy. Also, it follows the convention of a syntax expression by putting a symbol at the front of each list. For instance, we can see how the list describing the windows first contains the Lisp symbol windows ❶, which is then followed by three items, representing the glass, frame, and finally the curtains ❷.

As you can see, data that is hierarchical and tree-like in nature can be very naturally expressed in this way. In fact, many Lispers consider XML (a popular format for representing hierarchical data) somewhat of a reinvention of the syntax expression format that Lisp pioneered.

If, however, we move beyond tree-like structures, data stored in a syntax expression can start becoming hard to visualize, even if it's relatively easy to store the data in cons cells. For instance, suppose we have a mathematical graph stored in a syntax expression. These types of graphs, where any arbitrary node of the graph may be connected to another by an edge, are notoriously hard to visualize in a computer program. Even Lisp's elegant system for representing cons cells can't help much for such data. Next, we'll look at our options for visualizing such graphs.

Visualizing Graphs

In mathematics, a *graph* consists of a bunch of nodes connected by edges. These nodes or edges might have additional data associated with them.

Such graphs can be stored in cons cells, but they are difficult to visualize. We saw this in Chapter 5, when we stored the map of the wizard's house (which consisted of a directed graph) in two alists: one containing the node information and one containing the edge information. I've renamed them *wizard-nodes* and *wizard-edges* for this chapter, as shown here:

```
(defparameter *wizard-nodes* '((living-room (you are in the living-room.
                                a wizard is snoring loudly on the couch.))
                               (garden (you are in a beautiful garden.
                                there is a well in front of you.))
                               (attic (you are in the attic. there
                                is a giant welding torch in the corner.))))
(defparameter *wizard-edges* '((living-room (garden west door)
                                            (attic upstairs ladder))
                               (garden (living-room east door))
                               (attic (living-room downstairs ladder))))
```

As you can see, it is hard to get a decent understanding of the structure of this game world from these raw data tables. Unfortunately, data that has the shape of a graph or contains other properties that go beyond simple tree structures are very common. Wouldn't it be great if we had a tool that could optimally arrange this data to create a pretty drawing of a graph? Luckily, there is a fantastic open source tool that performs exactly this task, which you'll try out next.

Creating a Graph

Graphviz generates graphs from your data. Indeed, you saw a simple Graphviz representation of the wizard's house in Chapter 5:

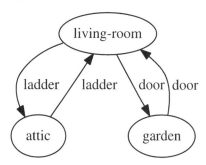

Graphviz is open source and available from the Graphviz website (*http://www.graphviz.org/*). After you've downloaded and installed it, creating a graph is easy. First, you'll create a DOT file that describes the shape of your graph. For example, in Graphviz, create a file named *test.dot* on your computer and enter the following information:

```
digraph {
    a->b;
}
```

This defines a directed graph with nodes A and B connected by an arrow. (There are numerous syntax options available in the DOT file format, as documented at the Graphviz website.)

Now, to generate a graphical bitmap from the DOT file, run neato (one of the Graphviz utilities) from the command line, as follows:

```
neato -Tpng -O test.dot
```

This should create a picture in the file *test.dot.png* that looks like this:

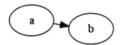

As you can see, Graphviz is simple to use. It can even generate large, complicated graphs quickly, with only minor graphical glitches. (Since perfect graph layouts are still an unsolved problem in computer science, Graphviz layouts aren't perfect. They are, however, closer to perfect than you might expect.)

Now that you have Graphviz up and running, let's create a library of commands that will let us conveniently draw graphs with Lisp. We can use this to draw some graphs of our adventure game world.

NOTE *The graph utilities used in the examples in this chapter perform certain system calls in a way that is not part of the Common Lisp standard. They are available only in the CLISP environment. The code would require some modifications to run within other Lisp systems.*

Generating the DOT Information

In order to create a graph drawing library, we want to generate a Graphviz DOT file that captures all the details of a graph. To do this, we will need to convert the identifiers of the nodes the player can visit, convert the edges connecting these nodes, and generate labels for every node and edge. We will test our library using the nodes representing the map of the wizard's world.

Converting Node Identifiers

When converting nodes into DOT format, the first thing we need to do is to convert the node identifiers into valid DOT identifiers. We do this by writing a dot-name function:

```
(defun dot-name (exp)
  (substitute-if #\_ (complement #'alphanumericp) (prin1-to-string exp)))
```

A node in DOT format can contain only letters, digits, and the underscore character. To make sure the node identifier we're using is legal, we'll change any forbidden characters to underscores. Here are examples of the dot-name function in use:

```
> (dot-name 'living-room)
"LIVING_ROOM"
> (dot-name 'foo!)
"FOO_"
> (dot-name '24)
"24"
```

This function accepts any basic Lisp type, which we can then convert to a string using the prin1-to-string function. We can process the resulting string and substitute underscores as needed.

NOTE   *For the sake of simplicity, our* dot-name *function assumes that no node identifiers differ only in their nonalphanumeric components. For instance, if we had one node called* foo? *and another node called* foo*, *the* dot-name *function would convert them both to* foo, *causing the names to clash.*

The substitute-if function substitutes values based on the result of a test function:

```
> (substitute-if #\e #'digit-char-p "I'm a l33t hack3r!")
"I'm a leet hacker!"
```

The test function in this example, digit-char-p, tells us if a character in a string is a numerical digit. Test functions like this, which accept a value and determine truth based on that value, are often referred to as *predicates*.

Another interesting property of the substitute-if function is that we can use it on lists as well:

```
> (substitute-if 0 #'oddp '(1 2 3 4 5 6 7 8))
'(0 2 0 4 0 6 0 8)
```

Here, all odd numbers in a list have been replaced by the number 0. The substitute-if function is one example of a *generic function*—a function that can accept multiple datatypes as parameters and handle them appropriately. (Generic programming is discussed in Chapter 9.)

When we use `substitute-if` in our `dot-name` function, we substitute only those characters that aren't alphanumeric. While no predicate that tests for exactly this is available for us in Common Lisp, it is easy to create this predicate on the fly. The following fragment in the `dot-name` function creates a predicate function for us with exactly the right behavior:

```
(complement #'alphanumericp)
```

Lisp already has a predicate function that tells us if a character is alphanumeric, called `alphanumericp`. However, we want to substitute only characters that are *not* alphanumeric. We can create this opposite (or *complement*) function to `alphanumericp` by passing it to a higher-order function named `complement`.

By passing this function into `substitute-if`, we get the behavior we want, without needing to use `defun` to pollute the top level with a new function just to feed to `substitute-if`.

NOTE *Common Lisp has a function called `substitute-if-not` that could have been used in the `dot-name` function in lieu of `substitute-if` to allow us to leave the `not` out of the lambda function. However, Lisp functions that end in `not` are better avoided. They may be removed from future versions in the ANSI Common Lisp standard, which means they are considered deprecated.*

Adding Labels to Graph Nodes

Now that we can tweak our node identifiers to make them appropriate for DOT, let's write another function that will generate the label that should appear in the node when it is drawn. The label will consist of the node name and the data linked to the node in the node alist. But we also need to make sure that we are not trying to put too much text in the label. Here is the code that generates the label:

```
❶ (defparameter *max-label-length* 30)

(defun dot-label (exp)
  (if exp
❷    (let ((s (write-to-string exp :pretty nil)))
❸      (if (> (length s) *max-label-length*)
❹          (concatenate 'string (subseq s 0 (- *max-label-length* 3)) "...")
          s))
    ""))
```

`*max-label-length*` ❶ is a global variable that determines the maximum number of characters for the label. If a node label is larger than the limit ❸, it gets cropped, and an ellipsis is added to indicate that fact ❹. The `write-to-string` function ❷ is similar to the `prin1-to-string` function we used earlier—it writes an expression to a string.

The `:pretty` parameter is an example of a *keyword parameter*, which is used by certain Lisp functions to let you choose which parameters you want to pass in. In the case of `write-to-string`, it tells Lisp not to alter the string to make it pretty. Without this, Lisp would place new lines or tabs into our converted string to make it look more pleasing to the eye. By setting the :pretty keyword parameter to `nil`, we are telling Lisp to output the expression without any decorations. (Having new lines in a label can confuse Graphviz, so we don't want to give Lisp any ideas.)

Generating the DOT Information for the Nodes

Now that we can generate both a name and label for each node, we can write a function that takes an alist of nodes and generates the DOT information that encodes them, like so:

```
(defun nodes->dot (nodes)
❶  (mapc (lambda (node)
           (fresh-line)
❷          (princ (dot-name (car node)))
           (princ "[label=\"")
❸          (princ (dot-label node))
           (princ "\"];"))
         nodes))
```

This function uses `mapc` to go through every node in the list of nodes ❶, and `princ` prints each node in the DOT format directly to the screen. `mapc` is a slightly more efficient variant of `mapcar`; the difference is that it does not return the transformed list. The `nodes->dot` function uses the `dot-name` ❷ and `dot-label` ❸ functions we created to convert the data.

Later, when we want to generate a file that contains this information, we'll write a function that takes this data from the console.

It may seem a bit odd to use the console as an intermediary for generating a file, instead of just writing directly into a file, but this is actually a common paradigm in Lisp. One immediate benefit of this approach is that we can easily debug the code in the REPL, where the printed lines are easy to see.

Now let's try using the `nodes->dot` function to generate the DOT information for the nodes in the wizard's house:

```
> (nodes->dot *wizard-nodes*)
LIVING_ROOM[label="(LIVING-ROOM (YOU ARE IN TH...)"];
GARDEN[label="(GARDEN (YOU ARE IN A BEAUT...)"];
ATTIC[label="(ATTIC (YOU ARE IN THE ATTI...)"];
```

Here, you can see the nodes of the wizard's house and an abbreviated version of the information attached to each node, shown in DOT format. Notice that we are not interested in the value returned from the `nodes->dot` function—only in the information it prints in the REPL. Lispers would say that we are only interested in the *side effects* of this function. Although `mapc` does not return the list, it still causes the code to iterate through the list and generate the same printed output that using `mapcar` would have, so it generates the same side effects as `mapcar`, a bit more quickly.

Converting Edges into DOT Format

The next step is to generate the DOT information for the edges that link our nodes. These will become the arrows in our visual graph. The function edges->dot generates the necessary data, again by printing it directly to the console.

```
(defun edges->dot (edges)
  (mapc (lambda (node)
          (mapc (lambda (edge)
                  (fresh-line)
                  (princ (dot-name (car node)))
                  (princ "->")
                  (princ (dot-name (car edge)))
                  (princ "[label=\"")
                  (princ (dot-label (cdr edge)))
                  (princ "\"];"))
                (cdr node)))
        edges))
```

Let's use this function to generate the DOT information for the edges of the wizard's house:

```
> (edges->dot *wizard-edges*)
❶ LIVING_ROOM->GARDEN[label="(WEST DOOR)"];
LIVING_ROOM->ATTIC[label="(UPSTAIRS LADDER)"];
GARDEN->LIVING_ROOM[label="(EAST DOOR)"];
ATTIC->LIVING_ROOM[label="(DOWNSTAIRS LADDER)"];
```

Here, we can clearly see the relationships between the nodes in the wizard's house, in the DOT format. For instance, the first line ❶ indicates that the player can walk from the LIVING_ROOM node to the GARDEN node by using an edge labeled (WEST DOOR).

Generating All the DOT Data

To complete our generation of the DOT data, we call both nodes->dot and edges->dot, and wrap it up with some extra decoration, as follows:

```
(defun graph->dot (nodes edges)
❶  (princ "digraph{")
❷  (nodes->dot nodes)
❸  (edges->dot edges)
   (princ "}"))
```

This function ties everything together by defining our graph as a directional graph ❶, and then calling our nodes->dot ❷ and edges->dot ❸ functions.

Here's what the final DOT information for our wizard game looks like, as created by our new library:

```
> (graph->dot *wizard-nodes* *wizard-edges*)
digraph{
```

```
LIVING_ROOM[label="(LIVING-ROOM (YOU ARE IN TH..."];
GARDEN[label="(GARDEN (YOU ARE IN A BEAUT..."];
ATTIC[label="(ATTIC (YOU ARE IN THE ATTI..."];
LIVING_ROOM->GARDEN[label="(WEST DOOR)"];
LIVING_ROOM->ATTIC[label="(UPSTAIRS LADDER)"];
GARDEN->LIVING_ROOM[label="(EAST DOOR)"];
ATTIC->LIVING_ROOM[label="(DOWNSTAIRS LADDER)"];}
```

We can now generate a proper Graphviz DOT file that captures all the details of our wizard map that we need to generate a pretty picture. These include the nodes the player can visit, the edges connecting these nodes, and labels for every node and edge.

Turning the DOT File into a Picture

To turn the DOT file into an actual bitmap, we capture the DOT file data, put it into a file, and then execute the dot command directly from the system command line, like this:

```
❶ (defun dot->png (fname thunk)
❷   (with-open-file (*standard-output*
                     fname
                     :direction :output
                     :if-exists :supersede)
    (funcall thunk))
  (ext:shell (concatenate 'string "dot -Tpng -O " fname)))
```

This function performs the most critical actions in our graph drawing library, using some advanced Lisp techniques.

First, to keep this dot->png function as reusable as possible, the graph->dot function isn't called directly. Instead, we write dot->png to accept a thunk ❶.

Using Thunks

It is common in Lisp to create small functions that have zero arguments. These functions are officially called *nullary functions*. However, Lispers will often create such functions in order to describe a computation that they don't want to run until later. In this scenario, a function without arguments is commonly called a *thunk* or a *suspension*. In this case, the thunk our dot->png function needs would be a function that, when called, prints a DOT file to the console.

Why is a thunk useful in our dot->png function? Remember that the easiest way for us to write and debug graph->dot and other DOT file functions is to have them print their results directly to the console. When we call graph->dot, it doesn't return its results as a value, but, instead, prints them at the console as a side effect. Therefore, we can't just pass the value of graph->dot to dot->png. Instead, we pass in graph->dot as a thunk. Then dot->png is responsible for calling graph->dot, capturing the results, and sending them to a file.

Since it is so common to generate textual data with a computer program, this particular technique is used a lot in Lisp code: First, we print stuff right to the console; next, we wrap it in a thunk; finally, we redirect the results to some other location.

As you'll see in Chapter 14, Lispers who follow the functional programming style eschew this technique, because side effects are required when printing to the console.

Writing to a File

The function with-open-file enables dot->png to write information to a file ❷. To give you a feel for how this function works, here's an example that creates a new file named *testfile.txt* and writes the text "Hello File!" to it:

```
❶ (with-open-file (my-stream
                   "testfile.txt"
                   :direction :output
                   :if-exists :supersede)
     (princ "Hello File!" my-stream))
```

In this example, you can see that the first item ❶ passed into with-open-file becomes the name of a special Common Lisp datatype called a *stream*, which is created for us by with-open-file.

Creating a Stream

Printing functions, such as princ, can accept a stream as an optional parameter. In this case, these printing functions won't print anything to the console, but instead will print to the stream object.

It is important to understand that with-open-file creates a stream variable from a stream variable name, in the same way that let creates a variable from a variable name:

```
❶ (with-open-file (my-stream ...)
❷    ...body has my-stream defined...)

❸ (let ((my-variable ...))
❹    ...body has my-variable defined...)
```

So if we pass the name my-stream in at the front of the first list to with-open-file ❶, this is analogous to defining my-variable at the start of a let ❸. A variable named my-stream will be available to us in the body of with-open-file ❷, in the same way that my-variable will be available to us in the body of the let ❹.

But don't worry too much about exactly what a stream is just yet. We'll be looking at them more closely in Chapter 12. For now, you just need to know that a stream is an object that can be connected to a file, and we can pass it to functions (such as princ) to write stuff to the connected file.

Understanding Keyword Parameters

The `with-open-file` command also makes heavy use of keyword parameters. Let's look at our previous example of this command again:

```
(with-open-file (my-stream
                 "testfile.txt"
❶               :direction :output
❷               :if-exists :supersede)
  (princ "Hello File!" my-stream))
```

A keyword parameter has two parts: the name of the parameter and the value of the parameter. The name of the parameter is always a symbol beginning with a colon. This example has two keyword parameters: `:direction` ❶, which is set to `:output` (we're only writing to the file and not reading it), and `:if-exists` ❷, which is set to `:superseded` (if a file by that name already exists, just toss out the old version).

`with-open-file` has keyword parameters because opening a file is a complex operation, and many esoteric options are available. If `with-open-file` just gave you regular parameters to set all this, every call to `with-open-file` would be long and cumbersome due to all the parameters. Also, humans have a hard time looking at a long list of parameters and remembering which one does what.

As you've probably noticed, symbols in Common Lisp sometimes begin with a colon. This includes keyword parameters, which always start with a colon. This is because a regular symbol in Lisp can refer to something else. For instance, we could set a variable `cigar` equal to 5 and then return it:

```
> (let ((cigar 5))
    cigar)
5
```

However, sometimes we don't want a symbol to refer to something else. We want to use the symbol outright, and we want it to have its own meaning. A colon-prepended symbol in Common Lisp (not surprisingly, called a *keyword symbol*) always means itself:

```
❶ > :cigar
  :CIGAR
❷ > (let ((:cigar 5))
      :cigar)
  *** - LET: :CIGAR is a constant, may not be used as a variable
```

As you can see, the keyword symbol `:cigar` can be evaluated right at the REPL and already has a value ❶. Its value is, conveniently, `:cigar`. If we try to redefine `:cigar` to something else, Common Lisp won't let us ❷. The fact that it is constant is useful, because a Lisp compiler can potentially optimize this simple type of symbol more than it can optimize other types. Also, we can reduce errors in our code by using keyword symbols in places where we know a symbol just has a meaning in its own right. Sometimes a cigar is just a cigar.

Capturing the Console Output

Our dot->png sends our data to the file in a slightly different way than is shown in this example: by declaring the name of the stream to be *standard-output* (a special global variable in Common Lisp that controls the default location to which printing functions send their output). As a result, any printing done inside the thunk will be redirected to our DOT file.

Let's look at our dot->png function again to see this:

```
(defun dot->png (fname thunk)
❶  (with-open-file (*standard-output*
                    fname
                    :direction :output
                    :if-exists :supersede)
❷    (funcall thunk))
    (ext:shell (concatenate 'string "dot -Tpng -O " fname)))
```

So how exactly does the dot->png function cause our DOT data to get saved to a file instead of just going to the console? To answer this, you'll need to exercise your brain a bit. Also, you'll need to recall our discussion of local and dynamic variables in Chapter 2.

Remember that the let command usually creates a *lexical*, or local, variable. As we've discussed, the stream variable created by with-open-file is analogous to using let to create a variable. Hence, it usually leads to the creation of a lexical stream variable for us.

However, if a dynamic variable already exists with the same name, let will instead, temporarily, override the value of the dynamic variable to the new value. *standard-output* is such a dynamic variable. This means that we can temporarily override the value of *standard-output* to a new value by passing it into our with-open-file command ❶.

In the body of the with-open-file, where we call our thunk ❷, any values printed to the console will now be automagically routed to our file, instead. The surprising thing (enabled by the design of lexical and dynamic variables in Common Lisp) is that this is also true for the princ statements in our graph->dot function, even though they are called indirectly from dot->png.

Creating a Picture of Our Graph

Lastly, we need a function that ties together all the pieces to let us easily create a graph from some nodes and edges:

```
❶ (defun graph->png (fname nodes edges)
❷   (dot->png fname
❸            (lambda ()
❹              (graph->dot nodes edges))))
```

This function takes the name of a DOT file (as the variable fname), as well as the graph's nodes and edges ❶, and uses them to generate the graph. To do this, it calls dot->png ❷ and creates the appropriate thunk—a lambda function ❸. As is usual for a thunk, it takes no parameters.

The graph->dot function is called inside the thunk ❹ as a *delayed computation.* Specifically, if we had called graph->dot directly, its output would just show up in the console. However, when inside the thunk, it will be called at the leisure of the dot->png function, and the output will be used to generate the DOT file with the filename passed in as the first parameter to graph->png.

Let's try out our new function to draw a graph of the wizard's house!

```
(graph->png "wizard.dot" *wizard-nodes* *wizard-edges*)
```

After calling this function, you should now see a file named *wizard.dot.png,* a picture of the map of the wizard's house:

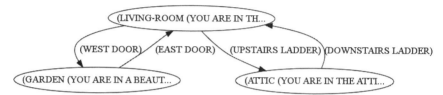

This may not be the prettiest graph on the planet, but it's packed with information and is very easy to understand. Also, the code is extremely flexible, and places few dependencies on our node and edge data.

With these utilities in our arsenal, we can now easily create graphs from any interconnected data in our Lisp programs. You'll find this technique to be a valuable debugging tool when you need to deal with complicated data.

Creating Undirected Graphs

A graph that has arrows on its edges is called a *directed graph*:

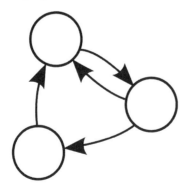

But sometimes we have data that is undirected, allowing us to travel in both directions along an edge. Such a graph is less busy than a directed graph, and can be easier to understand:

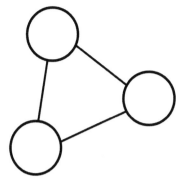

The following code expands our graph utilities with new functions that let us draw undirected graphs:

```
    (defun uedges->dot (edges)
❶    (maplist (lambda (lst)
                 (mapc (lambda (edge)
❷                        (unless (assoc (car edge) (cdr lst))
                            (fresh-line)
                            (princ (dot-name (caar lst)))
                            (princ "--")
                            (princ (dot-name (car edge)))
                            (princ "[label=\"")
                            (princ (dot-label (cdr edge)))
                            (princ "\"];")))
                       (cdar lst)))
              edges))

❸ (defun ugraph->dot (nodes edges)
❹   (princ "graph{")
     (nodes->dot nodes)
     (uedges->dot edges)
     (princ "}"))

❺ (defun ugraph->png (fname nodes edges)
     (dot->png fname
               (lambda ()
                 (ugraph->dot nodes edges)))))
```

This code is very similar to the code for creating our directed graphs. Let's look at some of the differences.

The uedges->dot function is very similar to the edges->dot function ❶. However, the graph we're drawing may have multiple directed edges between the same nodes that we want to replace with a single, undirected edge. For instance, on our wizard map, we can walk from the garden to the living room by going *east* through the door. Of course, we can also walk from the living room to the garden by going *west* through the exact same door. In our undirected graph, we'll want to collapse this; in essence, we just want to say, "There's a door between the garden and living room."

The uedges->dot function erases such duplicate edges by running through the list of edges using the maplist function. This is like the mapcar function, except that the function inside it receives the entire remainder of the list, not just the current item in the list:

```
> (mapcar #'print '(a b c))
A
B
C
...
> (maplist #'print '(a b c))
(A B C)
(B C)
(C)
...
```

The maplist function sends the print function everything in the list from the current item until the end. uedges->dot ❶ then uses the information about future nodes it gets from maplist to check whether the destination of the node appears later in the edge list. The actual checking is done with the assoc function, looking for the current edge in the list of remaining edges, calculated as (cdr lst) ❷. In this case, it skips the edge so that only one of any pair of edges will be printed.

The ugraph->dot ❸ function is similar to the graph->dot function, except that it describes the graph as just a graph ❹ when generating the DOT data, instead of a digraph. The ugraph->png function ❺ is essentially identical to the graph->png function, except that it calls ugraph->dot instead of graph->dot.

We designed the dot->png function to accept different thunks so it could work with different DOT data generators. Now we've used this flexibility to generate these functions that output pictures for undirected graphs. For example, let's try generating an undirected graph for the wizard's house:

```
(ugraph->png "uwizard.dot" *wizard-nodes* *wizard-edges*)
```

Here, `"uwizard.dot"` is the name of the DOT file we want to create. The
`*wizard-nodes*` and `*wizard-edges*` variables contain the data describing the
nodes and edges of the map of the wizard's world. This code generates the
uwizard.dot.png file, which looks like this:

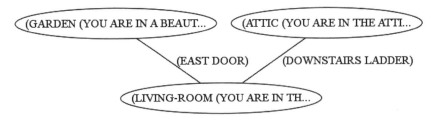

Now that you have a full suite of utilities for both directed and undirected
graphs, write these functions to a file named *graph-util.lisp*, so you can access
them from other programs.

What You've Learned

In this chapter, we discussed exotic types of lists and created a drawing
library for mathematical graphs. Along the way, you learned the following:

- You can create lists in Lisp that end in a value other than nil. Such lists are
  displayed with an extra dot before the last item and are called *dotted lists*.
- *Pairs* are what you get when you cons together two items that are not lists
  themselves. They can also be thought of as dotted lists that contain only
  two items.
- *Circular lists* are lists where the last cons cell points to an earlier cons cell
  in the same list.
- *Association lists* (*alists*) are lists of pairs. They can be used to store data that
  is in the form of keys associated with values.
- Lisp syntax expressions are great for storing and visualizing list-like and
  hierarchical data. Extra tools may be helpful for visualizing more complex data.
- If your data is in the form of a mathematical graph, it's helpful to be able
  to generate pictures of your data using Graphviz.
- A common technique for generating textual data in a Lisp program is to
  write functions that print the text to the console for easy debugging and
  wrap these functions in thunks. Then you can send these thunks to other
  functions, which capture the console output and route the text to the
  appropriate destination, such as writing it to a file.

8

THIS AIN'T YOUR DADDY'S WUMPUS

In the previous chapter, we worked with mathematical graphs in a simple game. However, as an old-school geek, the first thing I think of when I see these graphs is the old game Hunt the Wumpus. When I was nine, I could think of nothing more fun than sitting in front of my TI-99/4A and playing this excellent game.

Here is the original title screen:

In Hunt the Wumpus, you are a hunter searching through a network of caves to find a mysterious monster—the fabled Wumpus. Along the way, you also deal with bats and tar pits. Ah, those were the days!

But, unfortunately, those days are long gone. We're in a new millennium now, and no one would be impressed by these crude graphics anymore. And the story line, well, let's just say it sounds a bit corny by modern standards. I think we can all agree that Hunt the Wumpus is in serious need of a makeover. That's quite a challenge, but one I think we can handle.

Therefore, I present to you . . .

GRAND THEFT WUMPUS

VROOM!

THE MOST VIOLENT PROGRAMMING EXAMPLE EVER PUT INTO A TEXTBOOK

The Grand Theft Wumpus Game

In this new version of Hunt the Wumpus, you are the Lisp alien. You and the Wumpus have just robbed a liquor store and made off with the loot. However, during the escape, the Wumpus decides to double-cross you and run off with the money and your car. But before he drives off, you manage to cap him a couple of times in the kidney.

Now you're in a pretty tough situation. You don't have a car or any money, and no way to track down your former partner in crime. But you also have no choice. You have your principles, so you're going to *hunt the Wumpus*. You know he won't be able to get very far with his injuries. He will most likely need to lie low for a few days to recover, which means he will still be somewhere in Congestion City. The problem is that the roads in this town are impossibly convoluted, and no one can find their way around, especially an out-of-towner like yourself. How are you ever going to find the Wumpus in this impossible maze?

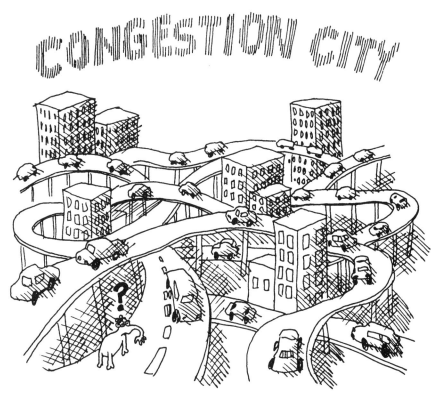

CONGESTION CITY

Luckily, being the Lisp alien, you always carry your trusty pocket computer. Using Lisp and your graph utilities, you're fully equipped to analyze complicated data such as the Congestion City roadways and intersections. Surely, you have the tools to conquer this impenetrable road system.

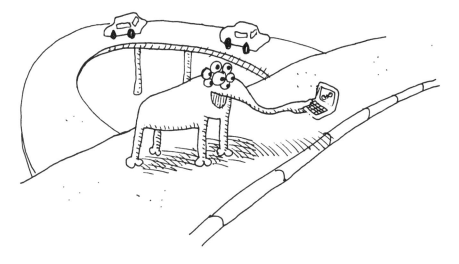

The Wumpus has been your partner in crime for a while now, so you know his MO quite well. He will always carefully scout out any new hiding place before he uses it. And since he is injured, any location one or two blocks away (that is, one or two graph edges away) from his hiding place should be marked with some telltale signs: his blood stains.

A problem is that he still has his trusty AK-47, while you have only a handgun with a single bullet. If you're going to take him out, you'll need to be absolutely sure you've tracked him down. You'll need to charge into his hideout and shoot him down immediately, and you'll have only one chance to pull this off.

Unfortunately, you and the Wumpus aren't the only criminals in this town. The most feared outlaw group in Congestion City is the Gruesome Glowworm Gang. These guys are a band of ruthless kidnappers. If you run into them, they will kidnap you, beat you up, rob you, blindfold you, and then kick you out of their car and leave you in some random part of town.

Luckily, they can be avoided if you know to keep an eye out for their glowing thoraxes (hence their name). If you see some blinking lights, you know that these guys are one street away from your current location. Also, you know the gang has exactly three separate teams that work the city from three separate locations.

THE GRUESOME GLOWWORM GANG

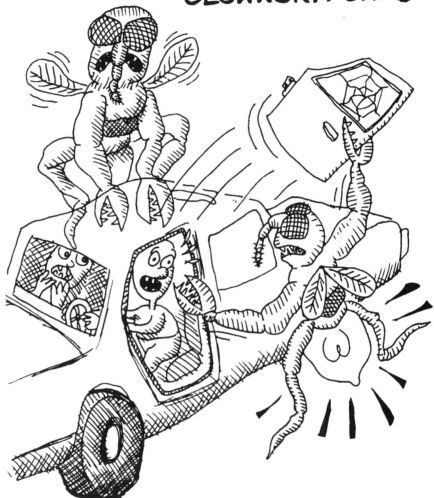

Finally, you still need to contend with the cops. You know they've probably set up some roadblocks in town to try to catch you and the Wumpus. You should still be able to visit any location in Congestion City, but you need to be careful which streets you travel. (In other words, the cops will catch you if you travel along the wrong edge.) Unfortunately, you don't know how many of these roadblocks there may be.

As you can see, finding the Wumpus and getting back your money and car will be tough. If you think you're Lisp alien enough to take on the Wumpus, then let's write this game and hunt him down!

Defining the Edges of Congestion City

The map of Congestion City will be an undirected graph with data associated with each node stored in the variable *congestion-city-nodes*. The possible data at each node will include the presence of the Wumpus, a Glowworm team, and various danger signs.

A set of edges stored in *congestion-city-edges* will connect the nodes, and data linked to these edges will alert us to the presence of any police roadblocks. We declare these and other global variables at the top of our program using defparameter:

```
❶ (load "graph-util")

  (defparameter *congestion-city-nodes* nil)
  (defparameter *congestion-city-edges* nil)
  (defparameter *visited-nodes* nil)
❷ (defparameter *node-num* 30)
❸ (defparameter *edge-num* 45)
❹ (defparameter *worm-num* 3)
❺ (defparameter *cop-odds* 15)
```

We first load our graph utilities with the load command ❶, which evaluates all the code in *graph-util.lisp* (which we created in the previous chapter) so the graph utility functions will be available. Notice that Congestion City will have 30 locations ❷ (nodes, defined with *node-num*), 45 edges ❸ (roads, defined with *edge-num*), and 3 worm teams ❹ (defined with *worm-num*). Each street will have a 1-in-15 chance ❺ of containing a roadblock (defined with *cop-odds*).

Generating Random Edges

Next, we create a random list of edges to connect all the nodes:

```
❶ (defun random-node ()
    (1+ (random *node-num*)))

❷ (defun edge-pair (a b)
    (unless (eql a b)
      (list (cons a b) (cons b a))))

❸ (defun make-edge-list ()
❹   (apply #'append (loop repeat *edge-num*
❺                         collect (edge-pair (random-node) (random-node)))))
```

First, we declare the random-node function ❶, which returns a random node identifier. It uses the random function, which returns a random natural number less than the integer you pass to it. Since we're going to be showing the node identifiers in our user interface, we use the 1+ function to number our nodes 1 through 30 (the upper limit because the *node-num* variable is set to 30), instead of 0 through 29.

The make-edge-list function ❸ generates the actual list of random edges. It uses the loop command to loop *edge-num* times ❹, and then collects the requisite number of edges ❺. We'll take a closer look at the loop command in the next section. The graph of the city is undirected, so this function uses a helper function, edge-pair ❷, to create *two* directed edges between the randomly selected nodes. This extra step makes sense once you remember that an undirected graph is the same as a directed graph, with two opposing directed edges mirroring each undirected edge. (When we build our edges into an alist later in this chapter, this step will ensure that the list is properly formed.)

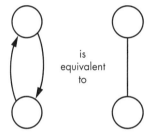

Let's try the make-edge-list function in the CLISP REPL:

```
> (make-edge-list)
((16 . 20) (20 . 16) (9 . 3) (3 . 9) (25 . 18) (18 . 25) (30 . 29) (29 . 30)
(26 . 13) (13 . 26) (12 . 25) (25 . 12) (26 . 22) (22 . 26) (30 . 29) (29 .
30) (3 . 14) (14 . 3) (28 . 6) (6 . 28) (4 . 8) (8 . 4) (27 . 8) (8 . 27) (3 .
30) (30 . 3) (25 . 16) (16 . 25) (5 . 21) (21 . 5) (11 . 24) (24 . 11) (14 .
1) (1 . 14) (25 . 11) (11 . 25) (21 . 9) (9 . 21) (12 . 22) (22 . 12) (21 .
11) (11 . 21) (11 . 17) (17 . 11) (30 . 21) (21 . 30) (3 . 11) (11 . 3) (24 .
23) (23 . 24) (1 . 24) (24 . 1) (21 . 19) (19 . 21) (25 . 29) (29 . 25) (1 .
26) (26 . 1) (28 . 24) (24 . 28) (20 . 15) (15 . 20) (28 . 25) (25 . 28) (2 .
11) (11 . 2) (11 . 24) (24 . 11) (29 . 24) (24 . 29) (18 . 28) (28 . 18) (14 .
15) (15 . 14) (16 . 10) (10 . 16) (3 . 26) (26 . 3) (18 . 9) (9 . 18) (5 . 12)
(12 . 5) (11 . 18) (18 . 11) (20 . 17) (17 . 20) (25 . 3) (3 . 25))
```

You see the pairs of node numbers that make up the edges. This list of edge pairs will form the skeleton of the Congestion City road system.

Looping with the loop Command

Our make-edge-list function employs the powerful loop command, which can be used to loop over various types of data. We'll be looking at loop in detail in Chapter 10. However, our game uses loop a few times, so let's consider some simple examples to clarify how it works.

One handy thing you can do with loop is create a list of numbers. For instance, the following command will create a list of 10 ones:

```
> (loop repeat 10
     collect 1)
(1 1 1 1 1 1 1 1 1 1)
```

Within the loop command, we specify how many times to repeat, and then specify an object to collect with every loop (in this case, the number 1).

Sometimes, we want to keep a running count as we're looping. We can do this with the following syntax:

```
> (loop for n from 1 to 10
     collect n)
(1 2 3 4 5 6 7 8 9 10)
```

In this example, we are saying that n should loop from 1 to 10. Then we collect each n and return it as a list.

Actually, we can put any Lisp code in the collect part of the loop. In the following example, we add 100 as we do our collecting:

```
> (loop for n from 1 to 10
     collect (+ 100 n))
(101 102 103 104 105 106 107 108 109 110)
```

Preventing Islands

We now can generate random edges. Of course, if we just connect random nodes with random edges, there's no guarantee that all of Congestion City will be connected because of all that randomness. For example, some parts of the city might form an island, with no connections to the main road system.

To prevent this, we'll take our list of edges, find unconnected nodes, and connect these islands to the rest of the city network using this code:

```
❶ (defun direct-edges (node edge-list)
❷   (remove-if-not (lambda (x)
                    (eql (car x) node))
                  edge-list))

❸ (defun get-connected (node edge-list)
❹   (let ((visited nil))
      (labels ((traverse (node)
                 (unless (member node visited)
❺                   (push node visited)
❻                   (mapc (lambda (edge)
                           (traverse (cdr edge)))
                         (direct-edges node edge-list)))))
        (traverse node))
      visited))

  (defun find-islands (nodes edge-list)
    (let ((islands nil))
❼     (labels ((find-island (nodes)
                 (let* ((connected (get-connected (car nodes) edge-list))
                        (unconnected (set-difference nodes connected)))
                   (push connected islands)
❽                   (when unconnected
                     (find-island unconnected)))))
        (find-island nodes))
      islands))

  (defun connect-with-bridges (islands)
❾   (when (cdr islands)
      (append (edge-pair (caar islands) (caadr islands))
              (connect-with-bridges (cdr islands)))))

❿ (defun connect-all-islands (nodes edge-list)
    (append (connect-with-bridges (find-islands nodes edge-list)) edge-list))
```

First, we declare a utility function called direct-edges ❶, which finds all the edges in an edge list that start from a given node. It does this by creating a new list with all edges removed (using remove-if-not ❷) that don't have the current node in the car position.

To find islands, we write the get-connected function ❸. This function takes an edge list and a source node and builds a list of all nodes connected to that node, even if it requires walking across multiple edges.

The usual way to find connected nodes is to start a visited list ❹, and then perform a search along connected nodes, starting with the source node. Newly found nodes are added to the visited list with the push command ❺. We also traverse all the children of this found node, using mapc ❻.

If, on the other hand, we encounter a node that has already been visited, we know we can ignore it. Once the search is complete, the visited list will consist of all connected nodes.

Now that we have a function for finding nodes that are connected, we can use it to create a function that will find all the islands in our graph. The find-islands function first defines a local function, called find-island ❼. This function checks which nodes are connected to the first node in our list of nodes using the connected function. It then subtracts these nodes from the full list of nodes using the set-difference function. (set-difference takes two lists, and returns all items that are in the first list but not the second.)

Any remaining nodes are deemed unconnected. If any unconnected node exists ❽, we call the find-islands function again recursively to find additional islands.

Once we've found all the islands, we need a way of bridging them together. This is the job of the connect-with-bridges function. It returns a list of additional edges that join all the islands together. To do this, it takes the list of islands and checks if there is a cdr in this list ❾. If there is, it means there are at least two land masses, which can be connected with a bridge. It uses the edge-pair function to create this bridge, and then calls itself recursively on the tail of the island list, in case additional bridges are needed.

Finally, we tie all of our island prevention functions together using the function connect-all-islands ❿. It uses find-islands to find all the land masses, and then calls connect-with-bridges to build appropriate bridges. It then appends these bridges to the initial list of edges to produce a final, fully connected land mass.

Building the Final Edges for Congestion City

To complete our edges for Congestion City, we need to convert the edges from an edge list into an alist. We also will add the police roadblocks, which will appear randomly on some of the edges. For these tasks, we will create the make-city-edges, edges-to-alist, and add-cops functions:

```
    (defun make-city-edges ()
❶    (let* ((nodes (loop for i from 1 to *node-num*
                         collect i))
❷           (edge-list (connect-all-islands nodes (make-edge-list)))
❸           (cops (remove-if-not (lambda (x)
                                     (zerop (random *cop-odds*)))
                                 edge-list)))
❹      (add-cops (edges-to-alist edge-list) cops)))

    (defun edges-to-alist (edge-list)
❺    (mapcar (lambda (node1)
                (cons node1
❻                     (mapcar (lambda (edge)
                                 (list (cdr edge)))
                             (remove-duplicates (direct-edges node1 edge-list)
❼                                              :test #'equal))))
            (remove-duplicates (mapcar #'car edge-list))))
```

```
   (defun add-cops (edge-alist edges-with-cops)
❽   (mapcar (lambda (x)
             (let ((node1 (car x))
                   (node1-edges (cdr x)))
               (cons node1
❾                  (mapcar (lambda (edge)
                             (let ((node2 (car edge)))
❿                              (if (intersection (edge-pair node1 node2)
                                                 edges-with-cops
                                                 :test #'equal)
                                   (list node2 'cops)
                                   edge)))
                            node1-edges))))
           edge-alist))
```

These are the most cumbersome functions in Grand Theft Wumpus. Let's take a closer look at them.

The make-city-edges Function

First, the make-city-edges function creates a list of nodes, using a loop ❶. (This is simply a list of numbers from 1 to *node-num*.) Next, it creates a random (but fully connected) edge list by calling the make-edge-list and connect-edge-list functions ❷. This result is stored in the edge-list variable. It then creates a random list of edges that contains cops ❸. We define these variables with the let* command, which allows us to reference previously defined variables.

The following example shows the difference between defining variables with let and let*:

```
> (let ((a 5)
        (b (+ a 2)))
    b)
*** - EVAL: variable A has no value
> (let* ((a 5)
         (b (+ a 2)))
    b)
7
```

As you can see, let won't allow you to refer to other defined variables (the variable b can't reference the value of a). When defining variables with let*, on the other hand, this kind of reference is allowed. For our purposes, using let* allows our definition of cops ❸ to contain a reference to edge-list.

Once we've created the edge list and determined where the cops are, we need to convert our edge list into an alist and add the cops to it ❹. The edges are converted to an alist with the edges-to-alist function, and the cops are added with the add-cops function.

The edges-to-alist Function

The edges-to-alist function converts a list of edges into an alist of edges. For example, assume we have the following city, with only three locations and two edges connecting those locations:

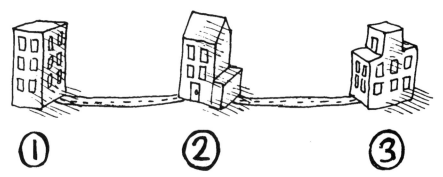

We would describe this using an edge list as '((1 . 2) (2 . 1) (2 . 3) (3 . 2)). Remember that each of the edges is repeated, since the edges are undirected and can be used in both directions. If we described this same city as an alist, what would that look like?

Remember that an alist is a list that lets us look up a key (in this example, one of the three nodes in our city) and find the information associated with that key (in this case, a list of the roads connected to it). For this small city, the alist would be '((1 (2)) (2 (1) (3)) (3 (2))).

To build this alist, the edges-to-list function first mapcars ❺ over the nodes found in the edge list. To build the list of nodes, we use the remove-duplicates function, which removes duplicate items from a list. By default, remove-duplicates uses the eql function to check for equality, though it also allows you to choose a different test function using the :test keyword parameter. Since we're checking for equality of cons pairs in our make-city-edges function, we set :test to #'equal ❼.

Within this outer mapcar ❺, we use another mapcar ❻ to map across all the direct-edges to this node. Together, these nested mapcar functions allow edges-to-alist to convert the edges of a city into an alist.

The add-cops Function

When we wrote the make-city-edges function, we randomly marked some of the edges to show that they have cops on them ❹. We are now going to use this list of cop edges to mark the edges in our alist that contain cops. This is the job of the add-cops function.

To do this, we use nested mapcar commands to map across the edges within each node ❽❾. We then check whether there are any cops on a given edge, using the intersection function ❿. (The intersection function tells us which items are shared between two lists.)

To understand exactly what the add-cops function is doing, it will help to once again imagine our city with only three locations and two streets. In this example, one of the streets has cops on it:

The generated alist for this city, created by add-cops, would look like this:

```
((1 (2)) (2 (1) (3 COPS)) (3 (2 COPS)))
```

This is actually a *nested* alist. The outer alist is organized based on the first node, and the inner alists are organized based on the second node.

With the edges in this format, we can easily find all edges connected to a given node by calling (cdr (assoc node1 edges)). To see if a given edge contains cops, we can call (cdr (assoc node2 (cdr (assoc node1 edges)))), which goes down two levels to grab the actual data linked to a specific edge between two nodes. (One additional benefit of using this nested alist format is that it is fully compatible with our graph libraries—a feature that we'll take advantage of shortly.)

Building the Nodes for Congestion City

Now we'll build an alist for the nodes in our city. These nodes may contain the Wumpus or the Glowworms, or they might contain various clues, such as blood, lights, or sirens.

Most of the clues in our game are based on proximity to another node, so we need to write some functions that tell us if two nodes are one node apart in the city graph. The neighbors function looks up the node's neighbors using the alist of edges. If the second node is in that list, we know we're one away.

```
(defun neighbors (node edge-alist)
  (mapcar #'car (cdr (assoc node edge-alist))))

(defun within-one (a b edge-alist)
  (member b (neighbors a edge-alist)))
```

First, this function looks up the first node (a) in the alist of edges with neighbors. Then it uses member to see if the other node (b) is among these nodes.

The blood stain clues for the Wumpus can also be seen from two nodes away. We can write a second function for checking two nodes like this:

```
(defun within-two (a b edge-alist)
❶  (or (within-one a b edge-alist)
       (some (lambda (x)
❷              (within-one x b edge-alist))
❸            (neighbors a edge-alist))))
```

First, we check if we are within one node of our goal ❶, since if we're within one, we're also within two. Next, we extract all the nodes that are one away ❸ (similar to what we did in the within-one function). Finally, we check if any of *these* new nodes are within one ❷, which would make them within two of the original node.

Now that we have those utility functions, let's write the function that builds the final node alist (basically, the final map of our city.) Here's the listing:

```
(defun make-city-nodes (edge-alist)
❶  (let ((wumpus (random-node))
❷        (glow-worms (loop for i below *worm-num*
                           collect (random-node))))
❸    (loop for n from 1 to *node-num*
❹       collect (append (list n)
❺                       (cond ((eql n wumpus) '(wumpus))
❻                             ((within-two n wumpus edge-alist) '(blood!)))
❼                       (cond ((member n glow-worms)
                               '(glow-worm))
❽                             ((some (lambda (worm)
                                       (within-one n worm edge-alist))
                                     glow-worms)
                               '(lights!)))
❾                       (when (some #'cdr (cdr (assoc n edge-alist)))
                          '(sirens!)))))))
```

The make-city-nodes function first picks random nodes for the Wumpus ❶ and the Glowworms ❷, and then it uses loop ❸ to run through the node numbers. As it runs through the nodes, it builds a list describing each node in the city, appended together from various sources ❹. By using append, each part of the code that describes these nodes (and is within the body of the append) can choose to add zero, one, or multiple items to the description, creating its own child lists with zero, one, or multiple items.

At the front of the list, we put the node name, n ❹. If the Wumpus is at the current node, we add the word *Wumpus* ❺ (but wrapped in a list, as we just described). If we're within two nodes of the Wumpus, we show its blood ❻. If the node has a Glowworm gang, we show it next ❼, and if the Glowworm gang is one node away, we show its lights ❽. Finally, if an edge from the node contains cops, we indicate that sirens can be heard ❾.

To check for the sirens clue, we simply grab the edges with (cdr (assoc n edges)) and see if some of these nodes have a value in the cdr. The 'cops symbol would be attached to the edges at the cdr. Since we have only one data point for edges in this game, looking for the presence of a cdr is an adequate check for the presence of cops. For example, if we use our earlier example of an alist with cops on it:

```
((1 (2)) (2 (1)❶ (3 COPS)❷) (3 (2 COPS)))
```

You can see that if an edge in the list has cops, such as here ❷, the cdr will lead to a non-nil value. An edge without cops ❶ will have a cdr that is nil.

Initializing a New Game of Grand Theft Wumpus

With our graph construction stuff out of the way, we can write a simple function that initializes a brand-new game of Grand Theft Wumpus:

```
(defun new-game ()
  (setf *congestion-city-edges* (make-city-edges))
  (setf *congestion-city-nodes* (make-city-nodes *congestion-city-edges*))
❶ (setf *player-pos* (find-empty-node))
  (setf *visited-nodes* (list *player-pos*))
  (draw-city))
```

There are two new functions here. One, the find-empty-node function ❶, ensures that the player doesn't end up on top of a bad guy right at the beginning of the game. Here's the code for that function:

```
   (defun find-empty-node ()
❶   (let ((x (random-node)))
❷     (if (cdr (assoc x *congestion-city-nodes*))
❸         (find-empty-node)
           x)))
```

The `find-empty-node` function is pretty simple. First, it picks a random node ❶ to consider as the player's starting position. Then it checks whether it is a completely empty node ❷. If there's stuff in that node, it simply calls itself again, trying another random spot ❸.

WARNING   *If you ever decide to modify the game and make it more crowded with bad guys, you could end up in a situation where no empty nodes exist. In that case, this function will search forever and lock up your Lisp REPL, since we didn't put in any checks to detect this situation.*

The other new function in our `new-game` command is `draw-city`, which we'll write next.

Drawing a Map of Our City

We're finally ready to draw a map of our new city. We're using a standard format for our graph data, so writing this function is a breeze:

```
(defun draw-city ()
  (ugraph->png "city" *congestion-city-nodes* *congestion-city-edges*))
```

We created the `ugraph->png` function in the previous chapter, as part of our graph library.

Now call (new-game) from the REPL, and open the *city.dot.png* picture in your web browser:

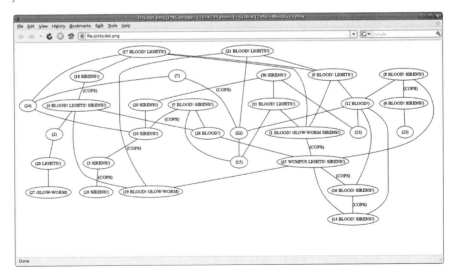

NOTE   *Since every city map created by our code is unique, your map will look completely different from the one in this picture.*

Finally, we can marvel at the results of our urban planning!

Drawing a City from Partial Knowledge

Of course, it's awfully boring to hunt something if you already know where it is before the hunt starts. To solve this problem, we want a map of the city that shows only the nodes that we've visited so far. To that end, we use a global list called *visited-nodes* that is initially set to the player's position only, but which we'll update as we walk around the city visiting other nodes. Using this *visited-nodes* variable, we can calculate a smaller graph that includes only those parts of the city that are known to us.

Known Nodes

First, we can build an alist of just the known nodes:

```
(defun known-city-nodes ()
❶   (mapcar (lambda (node)
❷             (if (member node *visited-nodes*)
                  (let ((n (assoc node *congestion-city-nodes*)))
❸                   (if (eql node *player-pos*)
                        (append n '(*))
                        n))
❹                 (list node '?)))
          (remove-duplicates
❺           (append *visited-nodes*
❻                   (mapcan (lambda (node)
                              (mapcar #'car
                                      (cdr (assoc node
                                                  *congestion-city-edges*))))
                            *visited-nodes*)))))
```

At the bottom of known-city-nodes, we need to figure out which nodes we can "see" based on where we've been. We'll be able to see all visited nodes ❺, but we also want to track all nodes within one node of a visited node ❻. (We will discuss the mapcan function shortly.) We calculate who is "within one" using code similar to the previously discussed within-one function.

Next, we mapcar over this list of relevant nodes, processing each ❶. If the current node is occupied by the player, we mark it with an asterisk ❸. If the node hasn't been visited yet ❷, we mark it with a question mark ❹.

Known Edges

Now, we need to create an alist stripped of any cop sirens that we haven't reached yet:

```
(defun known-city-edges ()
  (mapcar (lambda (node)
            (cons node (mapcar (lambda (x)
                                 (if (member (car x) *visited-nodes*)
                                     x
❶                                    (list (car x))))
                               (cdr (assoc node *congestion-city-edges*)))))
          *visited-nodes*))
```

This function is similar to the known-city-nodes function. The noteworthy line of code is here ❶ where we strip the cdr from the edge list for edges so that cops are indicated on the map only if we've visited the nodes on both ends of an edge containing cops.

The mapcan Function

The mapcan function we used in known-city-nodes is a variant of mapcar. However, unlike mapcar, mapcan assumes that the values generated by the mapping function are all lists that should be appended together. This is useful when there isn't a one-to-one relationship between the items in a list and the result you want to generate.

For example, suppose we run a burger shop and sell three types of burgers: the single, the double, and the double cheese. To convert a list of burgers into a list of patties and cheese slices, we could write the following function:

```
> (defun ingredients (order)
    (mapcan (lambda (burger)
              (case burger
                (single '(patty))
                (double '(patty patty))
                (double-cheese '(patty patty cheese))))
            order))
INGREDIENTS
> (ingredients '(single double-cheese double))
'(PATTY PATTY PATTY CHEESE PATTY PATTY)
```

Drawing Only the Known Parts of the City

Because we now have functions that can generate the known information about nodes and edges, we can write a function that turns this information into a picture, as follows:

```
(defun draw-known-city ()
  (ugraph->png "known-city" (known-city-nodes) (known-city-edges)))
```

Now let's redefine our new-game function to draw the known city when the game starts:

```
(defun new-game ()
  (setf *congestion-city-edges* (make-city-edges))
  (setf *congestion-city-nodes* (make-city-nodes *congestion-city-edges*))
  (setf *player-pos* (find-empty-node))
  (setf *visited-nodes* (list *player-pos*))
  (draw-city)
❶ (draw-known-city))
```

This function is almost exactly the same as the previous version of new-game, except that we also create a drawing composed only of the known parts of the city ❶.

Now, if we call the new-game function from the REPL, we'll get a new picture named *known-city.dot.png* that we can view in our browser. It will look something like this:

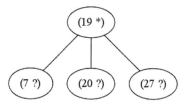

Now we're ready to walk around our map of Congestion City!

Walking Around Town

We'll need two functions for traveling between the nodes in our city: a regular walk function and one for when we think we've found the Wumpus, and we want to charge that location with our final bullet. Since these two functions are very similar, we'll have both of them delegate the bulk of the work to a common handle-direction function:

```
(defun walk (pos)
  (handle-direction pos nil))

(defun charge (pos)
  (handle-direction pos t))
```

The only difference between these two functions is the flag they pass to handle-direction, which is set to either nil or t, depending on the kind of traveling.

The handle-direction function's main job is to make sure that a move is legal, which it does by checking the edges of the city:

```
(defun handle-direction (pos charging)
  (let ((edge (assoc pos
❶               (cdr (assoc *player-pos* *congestion-city-edges*)))))
    (if edge
❷       (handle-new-place edge pos charging)
❸       (princ "That location does not exist!"))))
```

First, this function looks up the legal directions players can move to from their current location ❶. It then uses the pos the player wants to move to and looks it up in that list of possible directions. Once we've determined that a direction is legal (that is, a node with that number shares an edge with the player's current position), we need to find out what surprises are waiting as the player travels to this new place, using the `handle-new-place` function, which we'll create next ❷. Otherwise, we display a helpful error message ❸.

Now let's create the `handle-new-place` function, which gets called when the player has traveled to a new place:

```
     (defun handle-new-place (edge pos charging)
❶     (let* ((node (assoc pos *congestion-city-nodes*))
❷            (has-worm (and (member 'glow-worm node)
                            (not (member pos *visited-nodes*)))))
❸       (pushnew pos *visited-nodes*)
❹       (setf *player-pos* pos)
❺       (draw-known-city)
❻       (cond ((member 'cops edge) (princ "You ran into the cops. Game Over."))
❼             ((member 'wumpus node) (if charging
                                         (princ "You found the Wumpus!")
                                         (princ "You ran into the Wumpus")))
❽             (charging (princ "You wasted your last bullet. Game Over."))
❾             (has-worm (let ((new-pos (random-node)))
                          (princ "You ran into a Glow Worm Gang! You're now at ")
                          (princ new-pos)
                          (handle-new-place nil new-pos nil))))))
```

First, we retrieve the node the player is traveling to from the alist of nodes ❶. Next, we figure out if the node contains a Glowworm gang ❷. We ignore the gang if they're in a node already visited, because they'll only attack once.

Next, the `handle-new-place` function updates *visited-nodes* ❸ (adding the new position to the list) and *player-pos* ❹. Then it calls `draw-known-city` ❺ again, since we now have a new place we know about.

Next, it checks to see if there are any cops on the edge ❻, and then whether the Wumpus is at that location ❼. If the player encounters the Wumpus, our `handle-new-place` function needs to know whether we were charging the location. If we are charging at the Wumpus, we win the game. Otherwise, the Wumpus kills us and the game is over.

If, on the other hand, we charge at a location that does not contain the Wumpus, we waste our single bullet and we lose the game as well ❽. Finally, if the location has a previously unencountered Glowworm gang, jump to a random new location, calling `handle-new-place` recursively ❾.

Our game is now complete!

Let's Hunt Some Wumpus!

To play our game, simply enter the traveling commands we created (`walk` and `charge`) at the REPL, then switch to your browser and refresh *known-city.dot.png* to plan your next move.

For example, here's where we left off in our sample game:

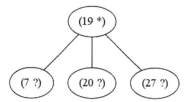

Since we have no clues, we know that any of these nodes will be safe to visit. Let's try (walk 20):

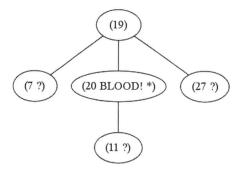

Uh oh! There's blood here. That means the Wumpus must be two nodes away! It should still be safe to (walk 11) though, because that's only one node away:

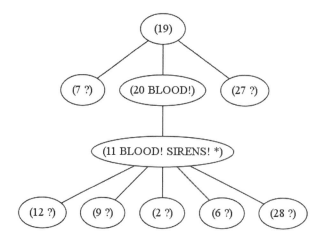

Oh no! One of these streets has a police roadblock. Let's backtrack with (walk 20) (walk 19), and then we can try (walk 7):

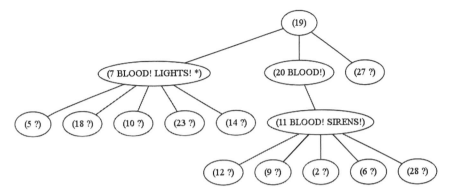

Darn! Now we have the Wumpus and some Glowworms nearby. Let's take a shot in the dark and try (walk 10):

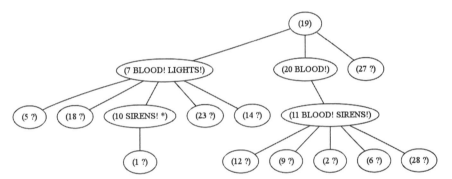

Well, that didn't help, since there are cops down this path. However, because node 10 has only one other unexplored street, we can say with certainty that the street between 1 and 10 has cops on it.

You can see that it takes some serious thinking to become a master in Grand Theft Wumpus! Remember, you can always start a new game, with a new map, by using the new-game function. Once you've tracked down the Wumpus, use the charge function to attack him.

If you master the basic version of this game, try increasing the number of nodes, edges, cops, and Glowworms for an even greater challenge!

What You've Learned

In this chapter, we've used graph utilities with Lisp to make a more sophisticated game. Along the way, you learned the following:

- The `loop` function allows us to loop across various types of data. It will be discussed in more detail in Chapter 10.
- The `set-difference` function tells you which items are in one list but not in another list.
- The `intersection` function tells you which items are shared by lists.
- The `remove-duplicates` function removes duplicate items from a list.

9

ADVANCED DATATYPES AND GENERIC PROGRAMMING

As you've seen so far, a lot can be accomplished in Lisp by using cons cells, symbols, strings, and numeric datatypes. As a very mature language, Common Lisp contains many more datatypes that move well beyond these basics. In this chapter, we will discuss the most useful of these advanced datatypes, including arrays, hash tables, and structures.

Arrays

The *Common Lisp array* is very similar to a list. The main advantage of using arrays is that they require only a constant amount of time to access a value at any specific location. We'll be discussing what this means shortly.

Working with Arrays

To create a new array, use the `make-array` command, specifying the array's size:

```
> (make-array 3)
#(NIL NIL NIL)
```

This creates an array of length 3. In order to indicate that the value created is not just a list, Common Lisp prepends a hash mark (#) in front of the array.

To get and set items in an array, use the `aref` function. For example, here's how we get the item at index 1:

```
> (defparameter x (make-array 3))
#(NIL NIL NIL)
> (aref x 1)
NIL
```

Of course, our array is just filled with `nils` right now, so there's not much worth getting. To set items in the array to more interesting values, use `aref` in conjunction with the `setf` command:

```
> (defparameter x (make-array 3))
#(NIL NIL NIL)
> (setf (aref x 1) 'foo)
FOO
> x
#(NIL FOO NIL)
> (aref x 1)
FOO
```

Although `aref` is usually a command used to *get* a value out of an array, when used in this special way indicated in the example, it lets us *set* a value in an array, instead. This ability to use the `setf` and `aref` commands together shows off a feature in Common Lisp: its support for generic programming. Let's take a closer look at the `setf` command to learn more about how this feature works.

Using a Generic Setter

The Common Lisp language is said to support *generic setters*. This means that in most cases, the code for *pulling a value out of* a data structure (whether an array, list, string, or something else) is identical to the code for *putting data into* that same data structure. The `setf` command can be used in conjunction with functions that perform getting operations and can use the same functions to perform setting operations, instead.

We've already seen that `aref` can be used to get values out of an array, and when used with `setf`, it can be used for setting values in the same array. The `setf` command can perform this trick in a general way across most of the commands in Common Lisp that get items from a data structure. Take, for instance, the following example involving a list:

```
> (setf foo '(a b c))
(A B C)
> (second foo)
B
❶ > (setf (second foo) 'z)
Z
> foo
(A Z C)
```

As you would expect, the expression (second foo) returns B. But, when we pass (second foo) to the setf command ❶, it somehow knows where the B came from, and it is able to treat the expression (second foo) as if it were a regular variable. Basically, the setf command asks itself the question, "Where did the item in my first argument originally come from?" In this case, the value came from the second item in the list named foo. Therefore, if we try to setf this location, the source variable, foo, is modified in response.

In fact, the first argument in setf is a special sublanguage of Common Lisp, called a *generalized reference*. Not every Lisp command is allowed in a generalized reference, but you can still put in some pretty complicated stuff:

```
> (setf foo (make-array 4))
#(NIL NIL NIL NIL)
❶ > (setf (aref foo 2) '(x y z))
(X Y Z)
> foo
❷ #(NIL NIL (X Y Z) NIL)
❸ > (setf (car (aref foo 2)) (make-hash-table))
#S(HASH-TABLE)
❹ > (setf (gethash 'zoink (car (aref foo 2))) 5)
5
> foo
#(NIL NIL (#S(HASH-TABLE (ZOINK . 5)) Y Z) NIL)
```

This example demonstrates the true power of setf in Common Lisp. In the first use, we put the list (x y z) into an array as the third item ❶. If we now print foo, we can see that it worked ❷. In the second use, we replace the first item in this list inside the foo array with a hash table ❸. Hash tables are another advanced data type we'll be learning about shortly, on page 157. It is surprisingly easy to do this with setf, because the generalized reference in the first argument to setf can be arbitrarily complicated.

Finally, we go all out and insert the value 5 into this hash table with the key of zoink ❹. The gethash function lets you get a value out of a hash table, as we'll see shortly. Here, with the help of setf, we are putting the number 5 into the hash table instead.

I hope you can appreciate from this example how useful setf can be when modifying complicated data structures in a program.

Another cool feature of setf is that you can expand the generalized reference syntax to support new ways of accessing values. setf is a truly generic way of modifying values, regardless of the level of nesting or the datatypes being used.

Arrays vs. Lists

You've now seen some basic examples of working with arrays in Lisp. However, to fully understand the benefits of arrays, we need to compare them with lists.

Almost anything that can be done with a list can also be done with an array. However, arrays are usually much faster than lists when accessing specific elements, so the difference is in performance.

For example, the array-handling function aref is very similar to a list-handling function called nth, which allows you access to an item at a specific location in a regular list without using an array. Here is an example using nth on a list:

```
> (nth 1 '(foo bar baz))
BAR
```

However, it makes sense to use the nth function only with very small lists. If, for example, list X had thousands of items in it, running the command (nth 1000 x) would be excruciatingly slow, because Lisp lists are made out of chains of cons cells. Hence, the only way Lisp can find the thousandth item in a list is to churn through the 999 preceding objects first.

In contrast, running the command (aref x 1000) on a large array accesses the thousandth item directly, without counting through the previous 999 items. This means aref will execute much more quickly on a large array than the nth command would on a large list. In fact, an aref call will happen very quickly no matter how large the array. Even if you had an array with a billion items, retrieving the last item would still happen very quickly. The only real limiting factor is your system: the amount of RAM your computer has and how capable your Lisp environment is of taking advantage of it.

Not only can we quickly access array values, but we can also change values at any specific location, usually faster than we can by performing the same operations on a list.

Because setting and getting specific values in a large data structure is so important, keep arrays in mind as a tool to help you get the best performance possible with your code.

Hash Tables

In the same way that arrays are sort of like lists, *hash tables* are sort of like *alists*, except that they also allow you to access arbitrary elements more quickly.

In fact, hash tables are so efficient that they can, at times, seem like magic. Think of the Babel fish in the *Hitchhiker's Guide to the Galaxy* trilogy—something so impossibly useful that it really has no business existing in the first place. That's why almost all modern languages now offer the hash table datatype.

Working with Hash Tables

Create a new hash table with the make-hash-table command:

```
> (make-hash-table)
#S(HASH-TABLE ...)
```

Like alists, hash tables store items using a lookup key and a value. We can retrieve an item from the hash table using the item's key with the gethash function:

```
> (defparameter x (make-hash-table))
#S(HASH-TABLE ...)
> (gethash 'yup x)
❶ NIL ;
❷ NIL
```

So far, our hash table remains empty. This means that when we look up any key in the hash table, such as 'yup in this example, we receive NIL as an answer ❶. Actually, we receive two NILs ❶❷—the gethash command returns multiple values, which you can do in Common Lisp (discussed in the next section). The first returned value is the actual value stored in the hash table, and the second indicates whether the key was found in the table (in this case, it wasn't).

Just as with arrays, we can once again combine a command used for referencing data elements—in this case, gethash—with the setf command in order to fill our table with data:

```
> (defparameter x (make-hash-table))
#S(HASH-TABLE ...)
❶ > (setf (gethash 'yup x) '25)
25
> (gethash 'yup x)
❷ 25 ;
❸ T
```

In this example, we've stored the value 25 in the hash table with a lookup key of yup ❶. Then, when we look up yup in the table, we get the answer of 25 ❷. We also get a second value of t ❸, which means, "Yes, I found the key in the table."

Remember when we discussed alists, we set up a data structure containing an order for coffee drinks? Here is that same data, but this time it's stored using a hash table:

```
> (defparameter *drink-order* (make-hash-table))
#S(HASH-TABLE ...)
> (setf (gethash 'bill *drink-order*) 'double-espresso)
DOUBLE-ESPRESSO
> (setf (gethash 'lisa *drink-order*) 'small-drip-coffee)
SMALL-DRIP-COFFEE
> (setf (gethash 'john *drink-order*) 'medium-latte)
MEDIUM-LATTE
```

Accessing the drink order for any person is now simple:

```
> (gethash 'lisa *drink-order*)
'small-drip-coffee ;
T
```

Returning Multiple Values

Common Lisp allows you to return more than one value as a result. Some of the core Common Lisp core functions do this, including the gethash function, as you've seen. Another commonly used function that does this is the round function, which rounds off a number:

```
> (round 2.4)
❶ 2 ;
❷ 0.4
```

Calling this function appropriately rounded our number to 2 ❶, but then it also generated a second value, which is the remainder of the rounding operation ❷. Both values are returned from this function call.

You can also create multiple values in your own code by using the values function. Here, for instance, we can write a foo function that returns two separate numbers, 3 and 7:

```
> (defun foo ()
    (values 3 7))
FOO
> (foo)
❶ 3 ;
❷ 7
```

Both of these values are printed out at the REPL ❶❷, just as with the round function. However, Lisp considers the first value to be more important, and it will always be used by default during follow-up calculations. For instance, we can perform an addition after calling foo, like this:

```
> (+ (foo) 5)
8
```

In this case, the addition operator just ignores the second value that foo returns.

However, sometimes you might need to use that additional returned value. You can do this by using the multiple-value-bind command:

```
> (multiple-value-bind (a b) (foo)
                       (* a b))
21
```

In this example, we've bound the variables a and b to both of the values returned by foo (3 and 7). Calling our function with multiple-value-bind lets us use the extra values returned from the function, which would otherwise be ignored.

You might be wondering whether you could just return a list from your function instead of using the multiple-value feature. The answer is, yes, you could. However, it's possible that using the multiple-value feature can lead to more optimized and cleaner code.

In this book, we will not be making much use of multiple values. In fact, more recent Lisp dialects, such as Arc and Clojure, do not support multiple values at all. Instead, they just return a list in the few cases where more than one value needs to be returned.

Hash Table Performance

As with arrays, accessing and modifying a value inside a hash table requires only a constant amount of time, no matter how many items your hash table contains. For instance, suppose we have a hash table with only 10 items in it. We access a value in the table, using a key, and find it takes on average 1 millisecond to do so. Now suppose that the hash table has 1,000,000 items in it. Because of how hash tables are designed, we could still expect it to take only about 1 millisecond to retrieve a value. In other words, no matter how big the table is, we can access items at a constant time of 1 millisecond.

Think of how incredible that is! Even if your hash table contained 1,000,000 items, the gethash function could take the key you gave it and determine in a constant amount of time exactly where your desired item could be found!

In this era of web-based programs backed by enormous amounts of data, the ability of hash tables to store large numbers of values with fast retrieval makes them indispensable. The efficient storage of key/value pairs is essential for most online storage systems. Even the latest tools for storing vast amounts of online data, like Google's BigTable or Amazon's S3, are built around the quick retrieval of values using keys, which makes them similar to hash tables.

However, you can't always expect hash tables to provide the best performance. Here's why:

Virtual memory paging and cache misses: As with arrays, large hash tables may cause your operating system to start paging virtual memory to your hard drive, thus degrading performance. Similarly, they can increase the number of cache misses within your CPU.

Hash collisions: Internally, hash tables use a special function called a *hash function*, which converts keys into numbers. Such a hash function can cause *hash collisions*. Basically, a hash collision happens when, by chance, two keys are converted by the hash function into the same number. In this case, the hash table will still behave correctly, but at a slightly degraded performance. In rare cases, certain types of keys can interact with a hash function to increase the number of collisions and impede an application's ability to perform lookups, degrading performance even more.

Inefficiency with small tables: With very small tables, the creation and lookup time required by hash tables can make them less inefficient than simpler structures, such as alists. The performance benefits of hash tables are noticeable only when they contain larger amounts of data in them.

Varying speed for operations: In Common Lisp, if you create a small hash table, and then fill it with values, you will find that occasionally, adding a new value will be unusually slow. This is because the `make-hash-table` function is designed to minimize the cost for creating small hash tables. However, as you start adding values to make the table big, Lisp will need to take extra time to allocate more memory so that the table can hold more items. These extra allocations will lead to occasional slow insertions into the table as it grows.

There is one final reason why hash tables are not always the best solution: They are simply not as Lispy as traditional Lisp structures built from cons cells. This means they can be harder to debug than cons cells, since they cannot be read and printed as naturally in the Lisp REPL. Therefore, a good rule of thumb is to stay away from arrays and hash tables as you conceive a new piece of code. Then, if performance ends up becoming an issue, and only then, judiciously modify the critical sections of your code to take advantage of arrays and hash tables to resolve any performance problems.

A Faster Grand Theft Wumpus Using Hash Tables

Let's look at a practical example of what hash tables can do for your code. There is a glaring inefficiency in our latest game, Grand Theft Wumpus, that we can now correct with hash tables.

Recall from the previous chapter that Grand Theft Wumpus uses lists of nodes and edges to represent the graph of the city. This means that in order to find connections to a given node, we must do a linear search through a list. This isn't a big deal in Grand Theft Wumpus, because Congestion City doesn't have a lot of intersections. But what if our city had a thousand nodes with a thousand edges? Let's time the `get-connected` function and see what kind of numbers we get:

```
> (setf *edge-num* 1000)
1000
> (setf *node-num* 1000)
1000
> (time (dotimes (i 100) (get-connected 1 (make-edge-list))))
Real time: 57.699303 sec.
Run time: 57.687607 sec.
Space: 39566832 Bytes
GC: 43, GC time: 0.120005 sec.
```

The `time` command is a Lisp utility that outputs all kinds of useful timing information about a chunk of code, and the `dotimes` function lets us run our code 100 times, building 100 cities. Using these commands, it took about a minute to run this code on my computer. Given how many gazillion instructions a CPU can crunch in a minute, this is absolutely horrifyingly bad performance.

To fix this problem, we'll replace our edge list for this code with a hash table so that the get-connected function will be able to find connections to a node in constant time. We'll also replace our visited list with a visited table, so the function can quickly tell whether a node has already been visited.

Here is the code that makes this happen, consisting of hashed versions of our previous functions:

```
❶ (defun hash-edges (edge-list)
❷   (let ((tab (make-hash-table)))
❸     (mapc (lambda (x)
             (let ((node (car x)))
❹               (push (cdr x) (gethash node tab))))
           edge-list)
❺     tab))
```

First, we need hash-edges, a function that converts our edge list into a hash table ❶. At the beginning of the function, we create a new hash table and name it tab ❷. Then, we iterate through the table with mapc ❸. Remember that mapc is just like mapcar, except that you use it in places where you care only about the side effects and don't care about generating a final list as a result.

For every node, we want the table to contain a list of nodes connected to it. Therefore, as we iterate through the list, we push a new neighbor onto the current list of neighbors for the current starting node ❹. We can use the push command on hash table values just as for regular Lisp variable values. This, again, makes use of the general variables system built into Common Lisp, which we'll discuss in "Handling Data in a Generic Way" on page 166.

You may be wondering why we don't need to deal with the case where there is no value yet for a node in the table. How can we push something into a value in the table if no value exists? Well, it turns out that because the gethash function returns NIL when a key is not found in the table, this code will simply push the new neighbor onto an empty list and stick a new record into the table where none was found before. In this way, the push command magically does the "right thing," no matter whether the node is new or old.

Finally, once our table is populated, we return it as a result ❺. It contains the same data as the original edge list. The difference is that we can now find the neighbors of any node in Congestion City at blazing speeds.

```
❶ (defun get-connected-hash (node edge-tab)
❷   (let ((visited (make-hash-table)))
     (labels ((traverse (node)
❸                (unless (gethash node visited)
❹                  (setf (gethash node visited) t)
❺                  (mapc (lambda (edge)
                          (traverse edge))
                        (gethash node edge-tab)))))
       (traverse node))
❻     visited))
```

Now we're ready to write get-connected-hash, which retrieves all the nodes connected to a starting node in Congestion City ❶. It is identical in behavior to get-connected, but is optimized through hash tables.

The first thing this function does is create a hash table of visited nodes ❷. Then we travel through the nodes of Congestion City, beginning with the starting node. Every time we visit a new node, we ask ourselves if we've visited it before. We can now answer this question very efficiently by looking up the current node in the visited table ❸. If the answer is no, we'll need to mark this node as visited ❹ and check all of its neighbors by mapcing through them—checking our edge table ❺. Finally, we return our visited table, which in the end will hold all nodes that are connected to the starting node ❻.

Now we can rerun our test with this new logic:

```
> (time (dotimes (i 100)
              (get-connected-hash 1 (hash-edges (make-edge-list)))))
Real time: 1.221269 sec.
Run time: 1.224076 sec.
Space: 33096264 Bytes
GC: 36, GC time: 0.10801 sec. :
```

As you can see, instead of taking a minute to calculate the connections in the graph, it now takes only one second to do the same thing! This is why you must know how to use hash tables.

Common Lisp Structures

A *structure* is an advanced datatype available in Common Lisp. Structures and their properties can be a useful way to represent data in your code.

Working with Structures

Structures can be used to represent objects with properties, as you might find in a typical object-oriented programming (OOP) language using the defstruct command, like so:

```
> (defstruct person
          name
          age
          waist-size
          favorite-color)
PERSON
```

According to the definition in this structure, a person has four properties (also called *slots* by Lispers): name, age, waist-size, and favorite-color.

Having defined this structure, we can create instances of a person using the make-person command, a special function that defstruct has automatically created for us:

```
> (defparameter *bob* (make-person :name "Bob"
                                    :age 35
                                    :waist-size 32
                                    :favorite-color "blue"))
*BOB*
```

Now when we enter *bob* into the REPL, we see our new person marked as a structure with the #S prefix. We also see that the structure is of type person, and the values of each of its properties (name, age, waist size, and favorite-color):

```
> *bob*
#S(PERSON :NAME "Bob" :AGE 35 :WAIST-SIZE 32 :FAVORITE-COLOR "blue")
```

We can determine Bob's age by calling another automatically created function, person-age:

```
> (person-age *bob*)
35
```

We can also use setf with these commands to change Bob's age. (Happy birthday, Bob!)

```
> (setf (person-age *bob*) 36)
36
```

The Lisp reader can also create a person directly from the printed representation of the person, another great example of the print/read symmetry in Lisp:

```
❶ > (defparameter *that-guy* #S(person :name "Bob" :age 35 :waist-size 32
   :favorite-color "blue"))
❷ > (person-age *that-guy*)
   35
```

Here, we're creating a new variable called *that-guy*, and we set its value using only the printed representation of the person ❶. This variable now has a real person structure in it, just as if we had used the make-person function ❷.

As you can see, defstruct is quite a powerful command that can be used to build special functions that make it easy to create instances of a new object and access its properties.

When to Use Structures

These days, many mainstream programmers believe that object orientation is a necessity when developing large and robust applications. Many Lispers, on the other hand, believe that it's possible to build high-quality software without taking a purely OOP approach.

Beginning with Chapter 14, we'll examine some of these alternate approaches, including higher-order functional programming and domain-specific language programming. The design of the Lisp language makes it much easier to take advantage of these alternate approaches than is possible with other, more object-oriented languages.

Regardless, even if you're not writing purely OOP-style software, structures and their properties can still prove to be a useful way to represent data in your code. For instance, instead of creating a person class with defstruct, we could do the same thing with a standard list and our own make-person function. After all, why bother with structures if we can just roll our own person using lists, like so:

```
> (defun make-person (name age waist-size favorite-color)
      (list name age waist-size favorite-color))
MAKE-PERSON
> (defun person-age (person)
      (cadr person))
PERSON-AGE
> (defparameter *bob* (make-person "bob" 35 32 "blue"))
*BOB*
> *bob*
❶ ("bob" 35 32 "blue")
> (person-age *bob*)
35
```

Although this approach will work, it has several downsides. First, in order to check a person's age or other properties, we would need to write a lot of error-prone functions that pull properties out of the list from the correct locations. Also, the printed version of our ad hoc object ❶ is very hard to understand. How do we know BOB is a person? Is Bob's age 35 or 32? Regular lists just don't lend themselves well to encoding objects with multiple properties.

Another problem with using lists to represent an object in the real world is that the properties of an object (like a person object) may change over time. Lists in Lisp work best when you are dealing with information that never changes once the list is created. When Bob turns 36, however, we need to change his age property.

Having part of a data structure change over time is called a *mutation* by computer scientists. It's easy to change the value of a specific property (mutate the property) in a structure created with defstruct, so these structures are very suitable for handling data that needs to be mutable. Therefore, it makes sense to store a person (or any other object that changes over time) in a structure. We will be discussing the issue of mutation in greater detail in Chapter 14.

NOTE *The* `defstruct` *facility is not the only tool that can be used to create objects in Common Lisp. For example, in the epilogue of the book, you'll see that Common Lisp's Common Lisp Object System (CLOS) allows you to build very sophisticated object-based systems. If you care to code with a strongly object-oriented mindset, you will probably find all the OOP language functionality you need in Common Lisp. Indeed, CLOS has many advanced object-oriented features that you won't find in many other places. Because of this, CLOS has often been used as a research tool for studying OOP ideas.*

Handling Data in a Generic Way

Common Lisp has many different datatypes available for writing elegant and efficient programs. But without some care, having so many datatypes can lead to ugly and repetitive code.

For example, suppose we want to add several groups of numbers, which are stored as both lists and arrays. Since lists and arrays behave differently, will we need to write two different addition functions—one for lists and the other for arrays? It would be great if we could write a single chunk of code to handle both cases without caring about how the numbers are stored.

Common Lisp has all the features we need to write such generic code, including generic library functions, type predicates, `defmethod`, and generic accessors. We can use these features to write code that works with many types of data—including built-in as well as custom types that we might create with `defstruct`—without superfluous repetition in our code.

Working with Sequences

The easiest way to write code that works with any type of argument is to hand the type-checking work to someone else. The Common Lisp libraries are packed with functions that can generically handle data of varying types in their arguments, the most commonly used of which are the *sequence functions*. The sequence functions work generically across the three main ways of sequencing objects in Lisp: lists, arrays, and strings.

You've already seen one of these sequence functions without even realizing it: the `length` function. You can use the `length` function to check for the length of all three sequence types:

```
> (length '(a b c))
3
> (length "blub")
4
> (length (make-array 5))
5
```

Without the generic length function, you would need to use three separate functions to determine the length of strings, arrays, and lists.

NOTE *Common Lisp has a specific function for checking the length of lists, called list-length. Because generic functions tend to require extra type-checking to determine the correct behavior, they can be slower to execute. The list-length function is useful for performance-sensitive code, but most Lispers prefer using the generic length function in regular code.*

Sequence Functions for Searching

Some sequence functions let you search sequences:

- find-if finds the first value that satisfies a predicate.
- count finds out how often a certain object appears in sequence.
- position tells you where an item is located.
- some and every tell you if some or every value in a sequence obeys a specific predicate.

Here are some examples:

```
❶ > (find-if #'numberp '(a b 5 d))
   5
❷ > (count #\s "mississippi")
   4
❸ > (position #\4 "2kewl4skewl")
   5
❹ > (some #'numberp '(a b 5 d))
   T
❺ > (every #'numberp '(a b 5 d))
   NIL
```

In these examples, we use find-if to find the first number in a sequence, which is the number 5 ❶. We use count to find out how many times the character s appears in "mississippi" ❷. We use position to find at what position the character 4 appears. In this case, it is in the fifth position, starting the count from zero ❸. We use some to see if any items in a sequence are numbers. Indeed, there is a number ❹. Finally, we use every to see if every item in the list is a number, which is not the case ❺.

Sequence Functions for Iterating Across a Sequence

One particularly useful generic sequence function is reduce. The reduce function allows you to iterate through a sequence and distill it down into a single result. Here, we use reduce to add together items in a list:

```
> (reduce #'+ '(3 4 6 5 2))
20
```

The sum of those numbers turns out to be 20. Here is a diagram that shows exactly what is happening in this example:

On the right side, shown in gray, is our list. On the left side, you can see the pairs of numbers that are fed into the plus (+) function and the intermediate results that are calculated. This shows that the plus function always receives a single intermediate result as well as the next number in the list as its arguments. The only exception to this is in the very first call to the plus function. Since no intermediate result exists when we start, the first time we call the plus function, we promote the number 3, which is at the start of the list, into our intermediate result column. Therefore, the first time the plus function is called, it actually receives *two items* straight off the top of the list.

Let's look at a slightly more complicated example, this time using our own reduction function. We're going to find the largest even number in the list:

```
❶ > (reduce (lambda (best item)
❷          (if (and (evenp item) (> item best))
❸              item
❹              best))
         '(7 4 6 5 2)
❺        :initial-value 0)
  6
```

Our reduction function, which we pass to reduce to distill down our answer from the list, has two arguments ❶. The first argument is the best value we've found so far—in other words, the largest even number we've found so far. The second argument is the next number from the list.

Our reduce function needs to return as a result the new best number. Therefore, if the latest number is better than the previous best ❷, we return it ❸. Otherwise, we return the previous best ❹.

Remember that the first number in the list we're reducing will be used as a starting value. If this is a problem, we can instead pass an explicit initial value to the reduce function by passing in a keyword parameter named :initial-value ❺.

Specifying an initial value for the reduce function is often necessary, or a bug can sneak into your code. In our example, it could allow an odd number at the front of the list to erroneously be deemed the best large even number. Let's see what happens if we leave out the initial value.

```
> (reduce (lambda (best item)
          (if (and (evenp item) (> item best))
              item
              best))
         '(7 4 6 5 2))
7
```

Yes, things go horribly, horribly wrong, as a result of not specifying an initial reduce value.

Another great benefit of the reduce function is that it is generic, as is true for all these sequence functions. This means that it can reduce lists, arrays, or strings in exactly the same way, and you can use reduce to write functions that are oblivious to the difference between these different sequence types.

Earlier, I mentioned that it would be convenient to be able to write a single function that could sum together numbers in lists or arrays equally well. Now we can write such a function:

```
> (defun sum (lst)
    (reduce #'+ lst))
SUM
> (sum '(1 2 3))
6
> (sum (make-array 5 :initial-contents '(1 2 3 4 5)))
15
> (sum "blablabla")
Error: The value #\b is not of type NUMBER.
```

sum is blissfully unaware of the difference between arrays and lists; it works on both. However, since addition doesn't make any sense for characters, the sum function returns an error when used on a string.

Another function that is useful for iterating across a sequence is the map function. This function is identical in behavior to mapcar. However, unlike mapcar, the map function works on all sequence types, not just lists. You specify the type of sequence to return from the mapping by passing an extra argument to the map function.

Here is an example of map:

```
❶ > (map 'list
       (lambda (x)
❷         (if (eq x #\s)
             #\S
             x))
       "this is a string")
❸ (#\t #\h #\i #\S #\  #\i #\S #\  #\a #\  #\S #\t #\r #\i #\n #\g)
```

In this example, we're turning every s character in a string to its uppercase version. The mapping function we pass into map simply checks if the current character is an s and returns the uppercase S if it is ❷.

The result of this calculation is a list of characters ❸. This is because we told the map function that we wanted a list as a result ❶. Had we asked for a string instead, a string would have been our result.

Two More Important Sequence Functions

The subseq function lets you pull a subsequence out of a larger sequence by specifying starting and ending points:

```
> (subseq "america" 2 6)
"eric"
```

As you can see, the word america contains the name eric, starting from the second character and ending at the sixth character.

The sort function lets you pass it an arbitrary function to use for the sorting. In this case, we're just using the less-than (<) function:

```
> (sort '(5 8 2 4 9 3 6) #'<)
(2 3 4 5 6 8 9)
```

There are many more sequence functions than we've discussed so far, but the examples in this chapter will get you off to a good start.

NOTE   *For a comprehensive list of sequence functions, and indeed all Common Lisp functions, visit the* Common Lisp Hyperspec *at* http://www.snipurl.com/rz3h0—*an exhaustive, but daunting, description of all Common Lisp has to offer.*

Creating Your Own Generic Functions with Type Predicates

Common Lisp, like virtually all other Lisps, is a dynamically typed language. This means that parameters or variables in your code can hold any type of data—symbols, strings, numbers, functions, or whatever else you want to place in them. In fact, the same parameter or variable can even hold different types of data at different times in a running program.

Therefore, it makes sense to have a bunch of functions that tell you whether a variable has a certain type of data in it. For instance, you can check whether you have a number with numberp:

```
> (numberp 5)
T
```

The type predicates you will probably use most frequently are arrayp, characterp, consp, functionp, hash-table-p, listp, stringp, and symbolp.

You can use type predicates to write functions that handle different types of data generically. Suppose we wanted to write a function that lets us add both numbers or lists. Here's one way we could write such a function:

```
> (defun add (a b)
    (cond ((and (numberp a) (numberp b)) (+ a b))
          ((and (listp a) (listp b)) (append a b))))
ADD
> (add 3 4)
7
> (add '(a b) '(c d))
(A B C D)
```

In this add function, we use predicates to see if the arguments passed in are numbers or lists, and then we act appropriately. If we aren't given two numbers or two lists, it simply returns nil.

Although you can write functions supporting multiple types of data using type predicates, most Lispers wouldn't write an add function this way, for the following reasons:

A single, monolithic function for all types: This is fine for just two types, but if we wanted to handle a dozen or more types, our function would quickly turn into a giant monstrosity.

Modifications required to accommodate new cases: We would need to change the add function whenever we want to support a new type, increasing the chance that we would break existing code. Ideally, we would like to handle each new situation by itself without touching already working code.

Hard to understand: It is hard to see exactly what the main cond statement is doing and if the types are all being routed to the right place.

Performance: The resulting function might be slow. For instance, a Lisp interpreter/compiler might be able to create faster code for appending two lists if it knew for sure that both items were lists when the appending happens. However, in our first attempt at the add function, the type of the two arguments is never really completely obvious. Our compiler would need a bit of smarts to be able to tell from the condition (and (listp a) (listp b)) that both variables are guaranteed to be lists. Life would be easier for the compiler if we explicitly stated the types of arguments for each type situation.

Because it is so useful to be able to have a single function that does different things when given certain datatypes, the Common Lisp command defmethod lets us define multiple versions of a function that each supports different types. When that function is called, Lisp checks the argument types at the time of the call and chooses the correct version of the function automatically. The proper term for having a compiler/interpreter choose among different versions of a function based on argument types is *type dispatching*.

Here's how we would write our add function using defmethod:

```
> (defmethod add ((a number) (b number))
    (+ a b))
ADD
> (defmethod add ((a list) (b list))
    (append a b))
ADD
> (add 3 4)
7
> (add '(a b) '(c d))
(A B C D)
```

As you can see, this version of the add function handles every type of situation with a separate function, and new cases can be added without modifying existing code. Overall, the code is much easier to understand. Also, the compiler can see the type of the parameters and may be able to write faster code using this knowledge.

The defmethod function is like defun, except that it allows us to write multiple functions with the same name. When using defmethod, we can explicitly state the type of each parameter in the function's argument list so that Lisp can use these type declarations to figure out the correct version of add for each situation.

If you're familiar with the world of OOP, the word *method* probably has a special meaning to you. Since this new command is called defmethod, does it have anything to do with OOP? In short, yes. This command can be used not only with Common Lisp's built-in types, but also with structures you've created with defstruct. The combination of defstruct and defmethod basically constitutes a simple object system.

Now we'll use this object system to write a game!

The Orc Battle Game

In the Orc Battle game, you're a knight surrounded by 12 monsters, engaged in a fight to the death. With your superior wits and your repertoire of swordfighting maneuvers, you must carefully strategize in your battle with orcs, hydras, and other nasty enemies. One wrong move and you may be unable to kill them all before being worn down by their superior numbers. Using defmethod and defstruct, let's dispatch some whoop ass on these vermin!

ORC BATTLE!

Global Variables for the Player and Monsters

We'll want to track three player stats: health, agility, and strength. When a player's health reaches zero, that player will die. Agility will control how many attacks a player can perform in a single round of battle, and strength will control the ferocity of the attacks. As the game progresses, each of these will change and affect gameplay and strategy in subtle ways.

```
(defparameter *player-health* nil)
(defparameter *player-agility* nil)
(defparameter *player-strength* nil)
```

We'll store our monsters in an array called *monsters*. This array will be *heterogeneous*, meaning it can contain different types of monsters, be they orcs, hydras, or anything else. We'll create our monster types with defstruct. Of course, we still need to figure out how to handle each type in the list in a meaningful way—that's where we'll use Lisp's generic features.

We'll also define a list of functions for building monsters that we'll store in the variable *monster-builders*. As we write the code for each type of monster, we'll create a function that builds a monster of each type. We'll then push each of these monster builders onto this list. Having all the builder functions in this list will make it easy for us to create random monsters at will for our game.

Finally, we'll create the variable *monster-num* to control how many opponents our knight must fight. Change this variable to increase (or decrease) the difficulty level of Orc Battle.

```
(defparameter *monsters* nil)
(defparameter *monster-builders* nil)
(defparameter *monster-num* 12)
```

Main Game Functions

Now we're ready to write our first real code for the game, starting with the big picture functions that drive the rest of the system.

First, we'll define a function called orc-battle. This function will initialize the monsters and start the game loop and, once the battle ends, it will determine the victor and print the appropriate ending message for the game. As you can see, orc-battle calls plenty of helper functions to do the actual work:

```
(defun orc-battle ()
❶  (init-monsters)
   (init-player)
❷  (game-loop)
❸  (when (player-dead)
     (princ "You have been killed. Game Over."))
❹  (when (monsters-dead)
     (princ "Congratulations! You have vanquished all of your foes.")))
```

At the top, we call the initialization functions for the monsters and the player ❶. Then we start the main game loop ❷. The game loop will keep running until either the player or the monsters are dead. We'll print a game-ending message depending on whether the player ❸ or monsters ❹ died.

Next, we'll create the function game-loop to handle the game loop. This function handles a round of the battle, and then calls itself recursively for the following round:

```
(defun game-loop ()
  (unless (or (player-dead) (monsters-dead))
❶    (show-player)
❷    (dotimes (k (1+ (truncate (/ (max 0 *player-agility*) 15))))
      (unless (monsters-dead)
        (show-monsters)
        (player-attack)))
    (fresh-line)
```

```
❸    (map 'list
          (lambda(m)
❹            (or (monster-dead m) (monster-attack m)))
          *monsters*)
❺    (game-loop)))
```

The game-loop function handles the repeated cycles of monster and player attacks. As long as both parties in the fight are still alive, the function will first show some information about the player in the REPL ❶.

Next, we allow the player to attack the monsters. The game-loop function uses the player's agility to modulate how many attacks can be launched in a single round of battle, using some fudge factors to transform the agility to a small, appropriate number ❷. When the game begins, the player will have three attacks per round. Later stages of battle could cause this number to drop to a single attack per round.

The calculated agility factor for our player attack loop ❷ is passed into the dotimes command, which takes a variable name and a number n, and runs a chunk of code n times:

```
> (dotimes (i 3)
      (fresh-line)
      (princ i)
      (princ ". Hatchoo!"))
0. Hatchoo!
1. Hatchoo!
2. Hatchoo!
```

The dotimes function is one of Common Lisp's looping commands (looping is covered in more detail in Chapter 10).

After the player has attacked, we allow the monsters to attack. We do this by iterating through our list of monsters with the map function ❸. Every type of monster has a special monster-attack command, which we'll call as long as the monster is still alive ❹.

Finally, the game-loop function calls itself recursively, so that the battle can continue until one side or the other has been vanquished ❺.

Player Management Functions

The functions we need for managing the player's attributes (health, agility, and strength) are very simple. Following are the functions we need to initialize players, to see if they've died, and to output their attributes:

```
(defun init-player ()
    (setf *player-health* 30)
    (setf *player-agility* 30)
    (setf *player-strength* 30))

(defun player-dead ()
    (<= *player-health* 0))
```

```
(defun show-player ()
  (fresh-line)
  (princ "You are a valiant knight with a health of ")
  (princ *player-health*)
  (princ ", an agility of ")
  (princ *player-agility*)
  (princ ", and a strength of ")
  (princ *player-strength*))
```

The player-attack function lets us manage a player's attack:

```
  (defun player-attack ()
    (fresh-line)
❶   (princ "Attack style: [s]tab [d]ouble swing [r]oundhouse:")
❷   (case (read)
❸    (s (monster-hit (pick-monster)
❹                    (+ 2 (randval (ash *player-strength* -1)))))
❺    (d (let ((x (randval (truncate (/ *player-strength* 6)))))
            (princ "Your double swing has a strength of ")
            (princ x)
            (fresh-line)
❻           (monster-hit (pick-monster) x)
            (unless (monsters-dead)
❼             (monster-hit (pick-monster) x))))
❽    (otherwise (dotimes (x (1+ (randval (truncate (/ *player-strength* 3)))))
                  (unless (monsters-dead)
❾                   (monster-hit (random-monster) 1))))))
```

First, this function prints out some different types of attacks from which the player can choose ❶. As you can see, the player is offered three possible attacks: a stab, a double swing, and a roundhouse swing. We read in the player's selection, and then handle each type of attack in a case statement ❷.

The stab attack is the most ferocious attack and can be delivered against a single foe. Since a stab is performed against a single enemy, we will first call the pick-monster function to let the player choose whom to attack ❸. The attack strength is calculated from the *player-strength*, using a random factor and some other little tweaks to generate a nice, but never too powerful, attack strength ❹. Once the player has chosen a monster to attack and the attack strength has been calculated, we call the monster-hit function to apply the attack ❺.

Unlike the stab attack, the double swing is weaker, but allows two enemies to be attacked at once. An additional benefit of the attack is that the knight can tell, as the swing begins, how strong it will be—information that can then be used to choose the best enemies to attack midswing. This extra feature of the double swing adds strategic depth to the game. Otherwise, the double-swing code ❺ is similar to the stab code, printing a message and allowing the player to choose whom to attack. In this case, however, two monsters can be chosen ❻❼.

The final attack, the roundhouse swing, is a wild, chaotic attack that does not discriminate among the enemies. We run through a dotimes loop based on the player's strength ❽ and then attack random foes multiple times. However, each attack is very weak, with a strength of only 1 ❾.

These attacks must be used correctly, at the right stages of a battle, in order to achieve victory. To add some randomness to the attacks in the player-attack function, we used the randval helper function to generate random numbers. It is defined as follows:

```
(defun randval (n)
  (1+ (random (max 1 n))))
```

The randval function returns a random number from one to *n*, while making sure that no matter how small *n* is, at least the number 1 will be returned. Using randval instead of just the random function for generating random numbers gives a reality check to the randomness of the game, since 0 doesn't make sense for some of the values we use in our calculations. For instance, even the weakest player or monster should always have an attack strength of at least 1.

The random function used by randval is the canonical random value function in Lisp. It can be used in several different ways, though most frequently it is used by passing in an integer *n* and receiving a random integer from 0 to *n*-1:

```
> (dotimes (i 10)
    (princ (random 5))
    (princ " "))
1 2 2 4 0 4 2 4 2 3
```

Helper Functions for Player Attacks

Our player-attack function needs two helper functions to do its job. First, it needs a random-monster function that picks a monster to target for the chaotic roundhouse attack, while ensuring that the chosen monster isn't already dead:

```
  (defun random-monster ()
❶   (let ((m (aref *monsters* (random (length *monsters*)))))
      (if (monster-dead m)
❷        (random-monster)
❸        m)))
```

The random-monster function first picks a random monster out of the array of monsters and stores it in the variable m ❶. Since we want to pick a living monster to attack, we recursively try the function again if we inadvertently picked a dead monster ❷. Otherwise, we return the chosen monster ❸.

The player-attack function also needs a function that allows the player to pick a monster to target for the nonrandom attacks. This is the job of the pick-monster function:

```
    (defun pick-monster ()
      (fresh-line)
❶    (princ "Monster #:")
❷    (let ((x (read)))
❸      (if (not (and (integerp x) (>= x 1) (<= x *monster-num*)))
            (progn (princ "That is not a valid monster number.")
                   (pick-monster))
❹          (let ((m (aref *monsters* (1- x))))
❺            (if (monster-dead m)
                (progn (princ "That monster is alread dead.")
                       (pick-monster))
❻                m)))))
```

In order to let the player pick a monster to attack, we first need to display a prompt ❶ and read in the player's choice ❷. Then we need to make sure the player chose an integer that isn't too big or too small ❸. If this has happened, we print a message and call pick-monster again to let the player choose again. Otherwise, we can safely place the chosen monster in the variable m ❹.

Another error the player could make is to attack a monster that is already dead. We check for this possibility next and, once again, allow the player to make another selection ❺. Otherwise, the player has successfully made a choice, and we return the selected monster as a result ❻.

Now let's work on our monsters.

Monster Management Functions

We'll use the init-monsters function to initialize all the bad guys stored in the *monsters* array. This function will randomly pick functions out of the *monster-builders* list and call them with funcall to build the monsters:

```
    (defun init-monsters ()
      (setf *monsters*
❶        (map 'vector
             (lambda (x)
❷               (funcall (nth (random (length *monster-builders*))
                              *monster-builders*)))
❸            (make-array *monster-num*))))
```

First, the init-monsters function builds an empty array to hold the monsters ❸. Then it maps across this array to fill it up ❶. In the lambda function, you can see how random monsters are created by funcalling random functions in our list of monster builders ❷.

Next, we need some simple functions for checking if the monsters are dead. Notice how we use the every command on the *monsters* array to see if the function monster-dead is true for every monster. This will tell us whether the entire monster population is dead.

```
(defun monster-dead (m)
  (<= (monster-health m) 0))

(defun monsters-dead ()
  (every #'monster-dead *monsters*))
```

We'll use the show-monsters function to display a listing of all the monsters. This function will, in turn, defer part of the work to another function, so it doesn't actually need to know a lot about the different monster types:

```
  (defun show-monsters ()
    (fresh-line)
    (princ "Your foes:")
❶  (let ((x 0))
❷    (map 'list
          (lambda (m)
              (fresh-line)
              (princ "   ")
❸            (princ (incf x))
              (princ ". ")
              (if (monster-dead m)
❹                (princ "**dead**")
                  (progn (princ "(Health=")
❺                        (princ (monster-health m))
                          (princ ") ")
❻                        (monster-show m))))
          *monsters*)))
```

Since our player will need to choose monsters with a number, we will maintain a count as we loop through monsters in our list, in the variable x ❶. Then we map through our monster list, calling a lambda function on each monster, which will print out some pretty text for each monster ❷. We use our x variable to print out the number for each monster in our numbered list ❸. As we do this, we use the incf function, which will increment x as we work through the list.

For dead monsters, we won't print much about them, just a message showing that they are dead ❹. For living monsters, we call generic monster functions, calculating the health ❺ and generating the monster description ❻ in a specialized way for each different type of foe.

The Monsters

So far, we haven't seen any functions that really give life to the monsters. Let's fix that.

First, we'll describe a generic monster.

The Generic Monster

As you would expect, orcs, hydras, and other bad guys all have one thing in common: a health meter that determines how many hits they can take before they die. We can capture this behavior in a monster structure:

```
(defstruct monster (health (randval 10)))
```

This use of the defstruct function takes advantage of a special feature: When we declare each slot in the structure (in this case, health) we can put parentheses around the name and add a default value for that slot. But more important, we can declare a form that will be evaluated when a new monster is created. Since this form calls randval, every monster will start the battle with a different, random, health.

Let's try creating some monsters:

```
> (make-monster)
#S(MONSTER :HEALTH 7)
> (make-monster)
#S(MONSTER :HEALTH 2)
> (make-monster)
#S(MONSTER :HEALTH 5)
```

We also need a function that takes away a monster's health when it's attacked. We'll have this function output a message explaining what happened, including a message to be displayed when the monster dies. However, instead of creating this function with defun, we'll use the generic defmethod, which will let us display special messages when the knight beats on particular monsters:

```
(defmethod monster-hit (m x)
❶   (decf (monster-health m) x)
    (if (monster-dead m)
       (progn (princ "You killed the ")
❷             (princ (type-of m))
              (princ "! "))
       (progn (princ "You hit the ")
❸             (princ (type-of m))
              (princ ", knocking off ")
              (princ x)
              (princ " health points! "))))
```

The decf function ❶ is a variant of setf that lets us subtract an amount from a variable. The type-of function lets monster-hit pretend it knows the type of the monster that was hit ❷ ❸. This function can be used to find the type of any Lisp value:

```
> (type-of 'foo)
SYMBOL
> (type-of 5)
```

```
INTEGER
> (type-of "foo")
ARRAY
> (type-of (make-monster))
MONSTER
```

Currently, the type of a monster will always be monster, but soon we'll have this value change for each monster type.

We can also use two more generic methods to create monsters: monster-show and monster-attack.

The monster-attack function doesn't actually do anything. This is because all our monster attacks will be so unique that there's no point in defining a generic attack. This function is simply a placeholder.

```
(defmethod monster-show (m)
  (princ "A fierce ")
  (princ (type-of m)))

(defmethod monster-attack (m))
```

Now that we have some generic monster code, we can finally create some actual bad guys!

The Wicked Orc

The orc is a simple foe. He can deliver a strong attack with his club, but otherwise he is pretty harmless. Every orc has a club with a unique attack level. Orcs are best ignored, unless there are orcs with an unusually powerful club attack that you want to cull from the herd at the beginning of a battle.

To create the orc, we define an orc datatype with defstruct. Here, we will use another advanced feature of defstruct to declare that the orc includes all the fields of monster.

By including the fields from our monster type in our orc type, the orc will be able to inherit the fields that apply to all monsters, such as the health field. This is similar to what you can accomplish in popular languages such as C++ or Java by defining a generic class and then creating other, more specialized, classes that inherit from this generic class.

Once the structure is declared, we push the make-orc function (automatically generated by the defstruct) onto our list of *monster-builders*:

```
(defstruct (orc (:include monster)) (club-level (randval 8)))
(push #'make-orc *monster-builders*)
```

NOTE   *Notice how powerful this approach is. We can create as many new monster types as we want, yet we'll never need to change our basic Orc Battle code. This is possible only in languages like Lisp, which are dynamically typed and support functions as first-class values. In statically typed programming languages, the main Orc Battle code would need some hardwired way of calling the constructor for each new type of monster. With first-class functions, we don't need to worry about this.*

Now let's specialize our monster-show and monster-attack functions for orcs. Notice these are defined in the same way as the earlier versions of these functions, except that we explicitly declare that these functions are orc-specific in the argument lists:

```
(defmethod monster-show ((m orc))
  (princ "A wicked orc with a level ")
❶ (princ (orc-club-level m))
  (princ " club"))

(defmethod monster-attack ((m orc))
❷ (let ((x (randval (orc-club-level m))))
     (princ "An orc swings his club at you and knocks off ")
     (princ x)
     (princ " of your health points. ")
     (decf *player-health* x)))
```

The one unique thing about our orc type is that each orc has an orc-club-level field. These orc-specific versions of monster-show and monster-attack take this field into account. In the monster-show function, we display this club level ❶, so that the player can gauge the danger posed by each orc.

In the monster-attack function, we use the level of the club to decide how badly the player is hit by the club ❷.

The Malicious Hydra

The hydra is a very nasty enemy. It will attack you with its many heads, which you'll need to chop off to defeat it. The hydra's special power is that it can grow a new head during each round of battle, which means you want to defeat it as early as possible.

```
(defstruct (hydra (:include monster)))
(push #'make-hydra *monster-builders*)

(defmethod monster-show ((m hydra))
  (princ "A malicious hydra with ")
❶ (princ (monster-health m))
  (princ " heads."))

(defmethod monster-hit ((m hydra) x)
❷ (decf (monster-health m) x)
  (if (monster-dead m)
      (princ "The corpse of the fully decapitated and decapacitated hydra
falls to the floor!")
❸     (progn (princ "You lop off ")
             (princ x)
             (princ " of the hydra's heads! "))))

(defmethod monster-attack ((m hydra))
  (let ((x (randval (ash (monster-health m) -1))))
    (princ "A hydra attacks you with ")
    (princ x)
    (princ " of its heads! It also grows back one more head! ")
❹   (incf (monster-health m))
    (decf *player-health* x)))
```

The code for handling the hydra is similar to the code for handling the orc. The main difference is that a hydra's health also acts as a stand-in for the number of hydra heads. In other words, a hydra with three health points will have three heads, as well. Therefore, when we write our hydra-specific monster-show function, we use the monster's health to print a pretty message about the number of heads on the hydra ❶.

Another difference between the orc and the hydra is that an orc doesn't do anything particularly interesting when it is hit by the player. Because of this, we didn't need to write a custom monster-hit function for the orc; the orc simply used the generic monster-hit function we created for a generic monster.

A hydra, on the other hand, does something interesting when it is hit: It loses heads! We therefore create a hydra-specific monster-hit function, where heads are removed with every blow, which amounts to lowering the hydra's health ❷. Also, we can now print a dramatic message about how the knight lopped off said heads ❸.

The hydra's monster-attack function is again similar to that for the orc. The one interesting difference is that we increment the health with every attack, so that the hydra grows a new head every turn ❹.

The Slimy Slime Mold

The slime mold is a unique monster. When it attacks you, it will wrap itself around your legs and immobilize you, letting the other bad guys finish you off. It can also squirt goo in your face. You must think quickly in battle to decide if it's better to finish the slime off early in order to maintain your agility, or ignore it to focus on more vicious foes first. (Remember that by lowering your agility, the slime mold will decrease the number of attacks you can deliver in later rounds of battle.)

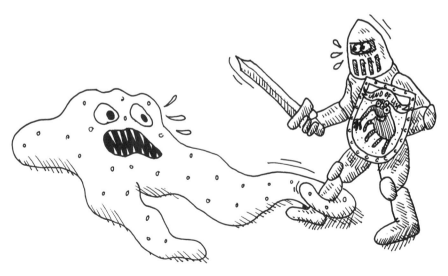

```
(defstruct (slime-mold (:include monster)) (sliminess (randval 5)))
(push #'make-slime-mold *monster-builders*)

(defmethod monster-show ((m slime-mold))
  (princ "A slime mold with a sliminess of ")
  (princ (slime-mold-sliminess m)))

(defmethod monster-attack ((m slime-mold))
❶  (let ((x (randval (slime-mold-sliminess m))))
       (princ "A slime mold wraps around your legs and decreases your agility
by ")
       (princ x)
       (princ "! ")
❷     (decf *player-agility* x)
❸     (when (zerop (random 2))
         (princ "It also squirts in your face, taking away a health point! ")
❹       (decf *player-health*))))
```

The `monster-attack` function for the slime mold must do some special things, which allow it to immobilize the player. First, it uses the slime mold's sliminess (which is generated when each slime mold is built) to generate a random attack against the player, stored in the variable x ❶. Unlike most other attacks in the game, this slime mold attack affects the agility of players, rather than their health ❷.

However, it would be pointless if the slime mold couldn't attack the player's health at least a little, or the battle could end awkwardly, with the player and slime mold frozen in place for all time. Therefore, the slime mold also has a superwimpy squirt attack that happens during half of all attacks ❸, but subtracts only a single health point from the player ❹.

The Cunning Brigand

The brigand is the smartest of all your foes. He can use his whip or slingshot and will try to neutralize your best assets. His attacks are not powerful, but they are a consistent two points for every round.

```
(defstruct (brigand (:include monster)))
(push #'make-brigand *monster-builders*)

(defmethod monster-attack ((m brigand))
❶  (let ((x (max *player-health* *player-agility* *player-strength*)))
❷    (cond ((= x *player-health*)
            (princ "A brigand hits you with his slingshot, taking off 2 health
points! ")
            (decf *player-health* 2))
```

```
❸            ((= x *player-agility*)
              (princ "A brigand catches your leg with his whip, taking off 2
  agility points! ")
              (decf *player-agility* 2))
❹            ((= x *player-strength*)
              (princ "A brigand cuts your arm with his whip, taking off 2
  strength points! ")
              (decf *player-strength* 2)))))
```

The first thing the wily brigand does when performing an attack is to look at the player's health, agility, and strength, and choose the max of those three as the focus of his attack ❶. If several of the attributes are equally large, the brigand will choose health over agility and agility over strength as the focus of attack. If health is the largest value, the player is hit with a slingshot ❷. If agility is the largest, the brigand will whip the player's leg ❸. If strength is the largest, the brigand will whip the player's arm ❹.

We have now completely defined all of our monsters for our game!

To Battle!

To start the game, call orc-battle from the REPL:

```
> (orc-battle)
You are a valiant knight with a health of 30, an agility of 30, and a strength
of 30
Your foes:
   1. (Health=10) A wicked orc with a level 5 club
   2. (Health=3) A malicious hydra with 3 heads.
   3. (Health=9) A fierce BRIGAND
   4. (Health=3) A malicious hydra with 3 heads.
   5. (Health=3) A wicked orc with a level 2 club
   6. (Health=7) A malicious hydra with 7 heads.
   7. (Health=6) A slime mold with a sliminess of 2
   8. (Health=5) A wicked orc with a level 2 club
   9. (Health=9) A fierce BRIGAND
  10. (Health=2) A wicked orc with a level 6 club
  11. (Health=7) A wicked orc with a level 4 club
  12. (Health=8) A slime mold with a sliminess of 2
```

That hydra with seven heads looks pretty gnarly—let's finish it off first with a stab:

```
Attack style: [s]tab [d]ouble swing [r]oundhouse:s
Monster #:6
The corpse of the fully decapitated and decapacitated hydra falls to the
floor!
Your foes:
   1. (Health=10) A wicked orc with a level 5 club
   2. (Health=3) A malicious hydra with 3 heads.
   3. (Health=9) A fierce BRIGAND
   4. (Health=3) A malicious hydra with 3 heads.
   5. (Health=3) A wicked orc with a level 2 club
   6. **dead**
   7. (Health=6) A slime mold with a sliminess of 2
   8. (Health=5) A wicked orc with a level 2 club
   9. (Health=9) A fierce BRIGAND
  10. (Health=2) A wicked orc with a level 6 club
  11. (Health=7) A wicked orc with a level 4 club
  12. (Health=8) A slime mold with a sliminess of 2
```

No other bad guy really stands out, so we'll try a roundhouse to bring down some of those health numbers overall:

```
Attack style: [s]tab [d]ouble swing [r]oundhouse:r
You hit the SLIME-MOLD, knocking off 1 health points! You hit the SLIME-MOLD,
knocking off 1 health points! You hit the ORC, knocking off 1 health points!
You lop off 1 of the hydra's heads! You lop off 1 of the hydra's heads! You
lop off 1 of the hydra's heads! You hit the ORC, knocking off 1 health points!
The corpse of the fully decapitated and decapacitated hydra falls to the
floor! You hit the ORC, knocking off 1 health points! You hit the ORC,
knocking off 1 health points! You hit the ORC, knocking off 1 health points!
```

```
Your foes:
    1. (Health=9) A wicked orc with a level 5 club
    2. (Health=2) A malicious hydra with 2 heads.
    3. (Health=9) A fierce BRIGAND
    4. **dead**
    5. (Health=2) A wicked orc with a level 2 club
    6. **dead**
    7. (Health=4) A slime mold with a sliminess of 2
    8. (Health=3) A wicked orc with a level 2 club
    9. (Health=9) A fierce BRIGAND
   10. (Health=2) A wicked orc with a level 6 club
   11. (Health=6) A wicked orc with a level 4 club
   12. (Health=8) A slime mold with a sliminess of 2
```

Great! That even killed one of the weaker enemies. Now, with full agility, we have three attacks per round. This means we should use our last attack to strategically take out some of the more powerful bad guys. Let's use the double swing:

```
Attack style: [s]tab [d]ouble swing [r]oundhouse:d
Your double swing has a strength of 3
Monster #:8
You killed the ORC!
Monster #:10
You killed the ORC!
An orc swings his club at you and knocks off 5 of your health points. A hydra
attacks you with 1 of its heads! It also grows back one more head! A brigand
catches your leg with his whip, taking off 2 agility points! An orc swings his
club at you and knocks off 1 of your health points. A slime mold wraps around
your legs and decreases your agility by 2! It also squirts in your face,
taking away a health point! A brigand cuts your arm with his whip, taking off
2 strength points! An orc swings his club at you and knocks off 1 of your
health points. A slime mold wraps around your legs and decreases your agility
by 1!
You are a valiant knight with a health of 21, an agility of 25, and a strength
of 28
Your foes:
    1. (Health=9) A wicked orc with a level 5 club
    2. (Health=3) A malicious hydra with 3 heads.
    3. (Health=9) A fierce BRIGAND
    4. **dead**
    5. (Health=2) A wicked orc with a level 2 club
    6. **dead**
    7. (Health=4) A slime mold with a sliminess of 2
    8. **dead**
    9. (Health=9) A fierce BRIGAND
   10. **dead**
   11. (Health=6) A wicked orc with a level 4 club
   12. (Health=8) A slime mold with a sliminess of 2
```

They got us pretty good, but we still have plenty of fight left. This battle isn't over yet!

As you can see, careful strategy is needed if you want to survive Orc Battle. I hope you enjoy this new game!

What You've Learned

In this chapter, we discussed the more advanced data structures in Common Lisp. We then used this to create a monster-fighting game. Along the way, you learned the following:

- Arrays are similar to lists, but allow you to access an item at a specific offset more efficiently.
- Hash tables are similar to alists, but let you look up the value associated with a key more efficiently.
- Using arrays and hash tables in the appropriate places will usually make your code much faster.
- The only true way to tell if changing a data structure or algorithm makes your program faster is to time your code with the time command.
- Common Lisp has generic functions that can be used against multiple datatypes. The most useful of these are sequence functions that can transparently handle lists, arrays, and strings.
- You can create objects with properties in list using the defstruct command.

SECTION III
LISP IS HACKING

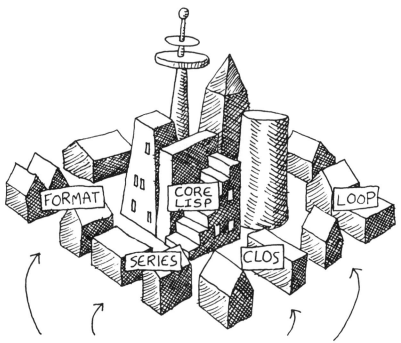

OUTLYING BOHEMIAN NEIGHBORHOODS
WHERE THE HACKERS LIVE

LOOP AND FORMAT: THE SEEDY UNDERBELLY OF LISP

Previously, we looked at the core of the Common Lisp language and admired its succinctness and elegance. However, there are also some darker, seedier parts of Lisp built around this core that have a certain charm of their own. They may lack the beauty of the Lisp core, but they easily make up for it with their power. These parts of the language are a real delight for any budding Lisp hacker.

The extensions we'll cover in this section, `loop` and `format`, place a strong emphasis on power over mathematical elegance. This has led to occasional controversy among Lisp programmers, some of whom question whether the power provided by these commands is worth the trade-off in elegance. These programmers believe that `loop` and `format` should be avoided when writing any serious code.

But there is one great reason to learn and use these commands: They embody the flexibility and extensibility of Lisp. Since Lisp is (arguably) the most flexible programming language available, hackers have been extending it with thousands of their own hacks for decades. `loop` and `format`, which are among the most successful of these extensions, had to be really spectacular to survive in the Darwinian battlefield.

10

LOOPING WITH
THE LOOP COMMAND

The loop and format commands are powerful and hacker-friendly. Though most of the functionality they offer is available elsewhere in the Lisp language, these highly specialized commands are worth learning if you like terse code. We'll look at loop in this chapter. The next chapter covers format.

The loop Macro

Any type of looping you would ever want to do inside a computer program can be accomplished with the loop macro. Here's a simple example:

```
> (loop for i
        below 5
        sum i)
```

This code adds together the natural numbers below 5, like this:

$$0 + 1 + 2 + 3 + 4 = 10$$

You can see that this `loop` command doesn't work in the way a proper Lisp command should. First of all, it's parenthetically challenged. Never before have we had seven tokens in a row without parentheses!

What makes it even less Lispy is that some of these extra tokens (`for`, `below`, and `sum`) appear to have special meanings. Recall from Chapter 3 that the first token in a form (the one immediately after the opening parenthesis) is typically what decides the basic behavior of the code, while the rest of the form contains parameters. Within the `loop` macro, several of these "magic tokens" fundamentally affect the `loop`'s behavior. Here's what they mean:

- `for` allows you to declare a variable (in this case, named `i`) that iterates through a range of values. By default, it will count through the integers starting at zero.
- `below` tells the `for` construct to halt when it reaches the specified value (in this case, `5`), excluding the value itself.
- `sum` adds together all values of a given expression (in this case, the expression is just `i`) and makes the `loop` return that number.

Some loop Tricks

The `loop` macro has a veritable cornucopia of special tokens that make just about any kind of behavior possible. Let's look at some of the possibilities.

Counting from a Starting Point to an Ending Point

By using from and to clauses, you can make the for construct count through any specific range of integers:

```
> (loop for i
        from 5
        to 10
      sum i)
45
```

Iterating Through Values in a List

In the following example, we iterate through values in a list using the in token:

```
> (loop for i
        in '(100 20 3)
      sum i)
123
```

doing Stuff in a Loop

The do token takes an arbitrary expression and executes it inside the loop:

```
> (loop for i
        below 5
      do (print i))
0
1
2
3
4
```

Doing Stuff Under Certain Conditions

The when token lets you run the following part of the loop only as needed:

```
> (loop for i
        below 10
      when (oddp i)
      sum i)
25
```

Notice that only the sum of the odd numbers is returned.

Breaking out of a Loop Early

The following loop uses several new tricks:

```
> (loop for i
       from 0
     do (print i)
     when (= i 5)
     return 'falafel)
0
1
2
3
4
5

FALAFEL
```

Notice that there's nothing in the for part of the loop that tells it to stop counting numbers—it goes from zero off to infinity. However, once we reach 5, the when clause triggers the loop to immediately return the value 'falafel.

Collecting a List of Values

The collect clause lets you return more than one item from the loop, in the form of a list. This command is useful when you need to modify each item in a list, as in the following example:

```
> (loop for i
     in '(2 3 4 5 6)
     collect (* i i))
(4 9 16 25 36)
```

Using Multiple for Clauses

It's possible for a loop macro to have more than one for clause. Consider the following example:

```
(loop for x below 10
      for y below 10
      collect (+ x y))
```

How many numbers do you think will be returned as a result? There are two possibilities: Either it increments x and y at the same time and returns a list of 10 items, or it iterates x and y in a nested fashion and returns 100 numbers. The answer is the former:

```
> (loop for x below 10
        for y below 10
        collect (+ x y))
(0 2 4 6 8 10 12 14 16 18)
```

As you can see, both numbers incremented at the same time between 0 and 9.

If there are multiple for clauses in a Common Lisp loop, each one will be checked, and the loop will stop when any one of the clauses runs out of values. This means that for clauses *do not* loop independently across multiple looping variables, so if you loop on two ranges of 10 values each, it will still just loop 10 times.

However, sometimes you want to generate the *Cartesian product* between multiple ranges. In other words, you want a loop to run once for every possible combination of two or more ranges. To accomplish this, you need to use nested loops for x and y:

```
> (loop for x below 10
        collect (loop for y below 10
                      collect (+ x y)))
((0 1 2 3 4 5 6 7 8 9) (1 2 3 4 5 6 7 8 9 10) (2 3 4 5 6 7 8 9 10 11)
 (3 4 5 6 7 8 9 10 11 12) (4 5 6 7 8 9 10 11 12 13) (5 6 7 8 9 10 11 12 13 14)
 (6 7 8 9 10 11 12 13 14 15) (7 8 9 10 11 12 13 14 15 16)
 (8 9 10 11 12 13 14 15 16 17) (9 10 11 12 13 14 15 16 17 18))
```

In this case, we've created 10 lists of 10 items each, looping for a total of 100 items.

Also, notice that using a for variable starting at zero, such as the i variable in the following example, provides a clean way to track the index number of items in a list:

```
> (loop for i
        from 0
        for day
        in '(monday tuesday wednesday thursday friday saturday sunday)
        collect (cons i day))
((0 . MONDAY) (1 . TUESDAY) (2 . WEDNESDAY) (3 . THURSDAY) (4 . FRIDAY) (5 .
SATURDAY) (6 . SUNDAY))
```

You might think we've covered every conceivable variation of looping at this point. If so, you are gravely mistaken. Behold! The Periodic Table of the Loop Macro!

Periodic Table of the Loop Macro

AN ASTERISK * MEANS A WORD CAN HAVE AN "ING" FORM (SO "SUM" AND "SUMMING" ARE BOTH LEGAL)

simple loop

```
(loop
  (princ
     "type something"
  (force-output)
  (read))
```

do*

```
(loop for i below 5
  do (print i))
```

NAMING & BREAKING OUT OF LOOPS

HASH TABLES

with ← VARIABLE

CREATE A LOCAL

```
(loop with x = (+ 1 2)
  repeat 5
  do (print x))
```

---

repeat

```
(loop repeat 5
  do (print
    "Prints five times"))
```

named

```
(loop named outer
    for i below 10
    do
  (progn
    (print "outer")
    (loop named inner
      for x below i
      do (print "**inner")
      when (= x 2)
      do
    (return-from outer
      'kicked-out-all-the-way))))
```

using

```
(defparameter salary
              (make-hash-table))
(setf (gethash 'bob salary) 80)
(setf (gethash 'john salary) 90)
(loop for person being each hash-key
of salary using (hash-value amt) do
(print (cons person amt)))
```

being

```
(defparameter salary
              (make-hash-table))
(setf (gethash 'bob salary) 80)
(setf (gethash 'john salary) 90)
(loop for person being each hash-key
of salary do (print person))
```

---

return

```
(loop for i below 10
  when (= i 5)
  return
    'leaving-early
  do (print i))
```

return-from

```
(loop named outer
    for i below 10
    do
  (progn
    (print "outer")
    (loop named inner
      for x below i
      do (print "**inner")
      when (= x 2)
      do
    (return-from outer
      'kicked-out-all-the-way))))
```

the ⟶ SAME

```
(defparameter salary
              (make-hash-table))
(setf (gethash 'bob salary) 80)
(setf (gethash 'john salary) 90)
(loop for person being the hash-keys
of salary do (print person))
```

each

```
(defparameter salary
              (make-hash-table))
(setf (gethash 'bob salary) 80)
(setf (gethash 'john salary) 90)
(loop for person being each hash-key
of salary do (print person))
```

---

initially

```
(loop initially
  (print
    'loop-begin)
  for x below 3
  do (print x))
```

while

```
(loop for i in '(0 2 4 555 6)
  while (evenp i)
  do (print i))
```

hash-keys SAME ⟶

```
(defparameter salary
              (make-hash-table))
(setf (gethash 'bob salary) 80)
(setf (gethash 'john salary) 90)
(loop for person being the hash-keys
of salary do (print person))
```

hash-key

```
(defparameter salary
              (make-hash-table))
(setf (gethash 'bob salary) 80)
(setf (gethash 'john salary) 90)
(loop for person being each hash-key
of salary do (print person))
```

---

finally

```
(loop for x below 3
  do (print x)
  finally
  (print 'loop-end))
```

until

```
(loop for i
    from 0
    do (print i)
    until (> i 3))
```

hash-values SAME ⟶

```
(defparameter salary
              (make-hash-table))
(setf (gethash 'bob salary) 80)
(setf (gethash 'john salary) 90)
(loop for amt being the hash-values
of salary do (print amt))
```

hash-value

```
(defparameter salary
              (make-hash-table))
(setf (gethash 'bob salary) 80)
(setf (gethash 'john salary) 90)
(loop for amt being each hash-value
of salary do (print amt))
```

BUILDING CONDITIONS

EXTRACTING A RESULT

LETS YOU CREATE LOCAL VARIABLES TO RETURN

if
```
(loop for i
    below 5
    if (oddp i)
    do (print i))
```

count*
```
(loop
    for i
    in '(1 1 1 1)
    count i)
```

for SAME
```
(loop for i
    from 0
    do (print i)
    when (= i 5)
    return
'zuchini)
```

as
```
(loop as x
    from 5
    to 10
    collect x)
```

when
```
(loop for i
    below 4
    when (oddp i)
    do (print i)
    do (print "yup"))
```

sum*
```
(loop
    for i below 5
    sum i)
```

in SAME
```
(loop
    for i
    in '(100 20 3)
    sum i)
```

on
```
(loop for x
    on '(1 3 5)
    do (print x))
```

across
```
(loop for i
    across
    #(100 20 3)
    sum i)
```

into
```
(loop for i
    in '(3 8 73 4 -5)
    minimize i
    into lowest
    maximize i
    into biggest
    finally
    (return
        (cons lowest
            biggest)))
```

unless
```
(loop for i
    below 4
    unless (oddp i)
    do (print i))
```

minimize*
```
(loop
    for i
    in '(3 2 1 2 3)
    minimize i)
```

FOR ARRAYS

by
```
(loop for i
    from 6
    to 8 by 2
    sum i)
```

from
```
(loop for i
    from 6
    to 8
    sum i)
```

to
```
(loop for i
    from 6
    to 8
    sum i)
```

always
```
(loop for i
    in '(0 2 4 6)
    always (evenp i))
```

and
```
(loop for x
    below 5
    when (= x 3)
    do (print "do this")
    and
    do (print
        "also do this")
    do (print
        "always do this"))
```

maximize*
```
(loop
    for i
    in '(1 2 3 2 1)
    maximize i)
```

CONTROL OF A FOR LOOP

INCREMENTS OF A FOR LOOP

CHECK COLLECTION FOR TRUTH OF A CONDITION

then
```
(loop repeat 5
    for x = 10.0
    then (/ x 2)
    collect x)
```

upfrom
```
(loop for i
    upfrom 6
    to 8
    sum i)
```

upto
```
(loop for i
    from 6
    upto 8
    sum i)
```

never
```
(loop for i
    in '(0 2 4 6)
    never (oddp i))
```

else
```
(loop for i
    below 5
    if (oddp i)
    do (print i)
    else
    do
    (print "w00t"))
```

append*
```
(loop for i
    below 5
    append
    (list 'z i))
```

downfrom
```
(loop for i
    downfrom 10
    to 7
    do (print i))
```

downto
```
(loop for i
    from 10
    downto 7
    do
    (print i))
```

thereis
```
(loop for i
    in '(0 2 4 555 6)
    thereis (oddp i))
```

end
```
(loop for i
    below 4
    when (oddp i)
    do (print i)
    end
    do (print "yup"))
```

nconc*
```
(loop for i
    below 5
    nconc
    (list 'z i))
```

Everything You Ever Wanted to Know About loop

The individual examples we've discussed so far give only the briefest hint of the full capabilities of loop. But fear not! You now have the world's first and only Periodic Table of the Loop Macro. Just tape it to your monitor, glue it to your wallet, or laser-etch it directly into your retina, and you'll be guaranteed to reach loop proficiency in no time!

Almost every legal command that can be used in a loop macro is covered by the periodic table. It shows how to manipulate hash tables and arrays, and perform special looping operations. Each square in the periodic table contains an example. If you run the example, you should be able to figure out the behavior of the given command.

Using loop to Evolve!

Let's create another game, making full use of loop. But this won't be a game that we play. Instead, it will be a game world that evolves as we watch it! We're going to create an environment of steppes and jungles, filled with animals running around, foraging, eating, and reproducing. And after a few million units of time, we'll see that they've evolved into different species!

NOTE *This example is adapted from A.K. Dewdney's article "Simulated evolution: wherein bugs learn to hunt bacteria," in the "Computer Recreations" column of* Scientific American *(May 1989: 138-141).*

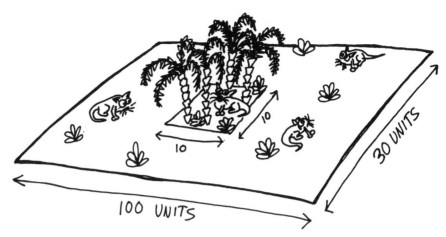

Our game world is extremely simple. It consists of a simple rectangular plane, with edges that wrap around to the opposite side. (Mathematically speaking, it has a toroidal topology.) Most of this world is covered in steppes, meaning that very few plants grow for the animals to eat. In the center of the world is a small jungle, where plants grow much faster. Our animals, who are herbivores, will forage this world in search for food.

Let's create some variables describing the extent of our world:

```
(defparameter *width* 100)
(defparameter *height* 30)
(defparameter *jungle* '(45 10 10 10))
(defparameter *plant-energy* 80)
```

We're giving the world a width of 100 units and a height of 30 units. Using these dimensions should make it easy to display the world in our Lisp REPL. The *jungle* list defines the rectangle in the world map that contains the jungle. The first two numbers in the list are the x- and y-coordinates of the jungle's top-left corner, and the last two numbers are its width and height. Finally, we give the amount of energy contained in each plant, which is set to 80. This means that if an animal finds a plant, it will gain 80 days' worth of food by eating it.

NOTE *If your terminal window isn't large enough to display the entire world, change the values of the *width* and *height* variables. Set the *width* variable to the width of your terminal window minus two, and the *height* variable to the height of your terminal window minus one.*

Growing Plants in Our World

As you might imagine, simulating evolution on a computer is a slow process. In order to see the creatures evolve, we need to simulate large stretches of time, which means we'll want our code for this project to be very efficient. As animals wander around our world, they will need to be able to check if there is a plant at a given x,y location. The most efficient way to enable this is to store all of our plants in a hash table, indexed based on each plant's x- and y-coordinates.

```
(defparameter *plants* (make-hash-table :test #'equal))
```

By default, a Common Lisp hash table uses eq when testing for the equality of keys. For this hash table, however, we're defining :test to use equal instead of eq, which will let us use cons pairs of x- and y-coordinates as keys. If you remember our rule of thumb for checking equality, cons pairs should be compared using equal. If we didn't make this change, every check for a key would fail, since two different cons cells, even with the same contents, test as being different when using eq.

Plants will grow randomly across the world, though a higher concentration of plants will grow in the jungle area than in the steppes. Let's write some functions to grow new plants:

```
(defun random-plant (left top width height)
❶   (let ((pos (cons (+ left (random width)) (+ top (random height)))))
❷     (setf (gethash pos *plants*) t)))

(defun add-plants ()
❸   (apply #'random-plant *jungle*)
❹   (random-plant 0 0 *width* *height*))
```

The random-plant function creates a new plant within a specified region of the world. It uses the random function to construct a random location and stores it in the local variable pos ❶. Then it uses setf to indicate the existence of the plant within the hash table ❷. The only item actually stored in the hash table is t. For this *plants* table, the keys of the table (the x,y position of each plant) are actually more than the values stored in the table.

It may seem a bit weird to go through the trouble of creating a hash table to do nothing more than store t in every slot. However, Common Lisp does not, by default, have a data structure designed for holding mathematical sets. In our game, we want to keep track of the set of all world positions that have a plant in them. It turns out that hash tables are a perfectly acceptable way of expressing this. You simply use each set item as a key and store t as the value. Indeed, doing this is a bit of a hack, but it is a reasonably simple and efficient hack. (Other Lisp dialects, such as Clojure, have a set data structure built right into them, making this hack unnecessary.)

Every day our simulation runs, the add-plants function will create two new plants: one in the jungle ❸ and one in the rest of the map ❹. Because the jungle is so small, it will have dense vegetation compared to the rest of the world.

Creating Animals

The plants in our world are very simple, but the animals are a bit more complicated. Because of this, we'll need to define a structure that stores the properties of each animal in our game:

```
(defstruct animal x y energy dir genes)
```

Let's take a look at each of these fields in detail.

Anatomy of an Animal

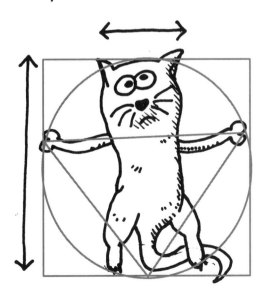

We need to track several properties for each animal. First, we need to know its x- and y-coordinates. This indicates where the animal is located on the world map.

Next, we need to know how much energy an animal has. This is a Darwinian game of survival, so if an animal can't forage enough food, it will starve and die. The energy field tracks how many days of energy an animal has remaining. It is crucial that an animal find more food before its energy supply is exhausted.

We also need to track which direction the animal is facing. This is important because an animal will walk to a neighboring square in the world map each day. The dir field will specify the direction of the animal's next x,y position as a number from 0 to 7:

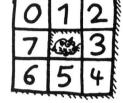

For example, an orientation of 0 would cause the animal to move up and to the left by the next day.

Finally, we need to track the animal's genes. Each animal has exactly eight genes, consisting of positive integers. These integers represent eight "slots," which encircle the animal as follows:

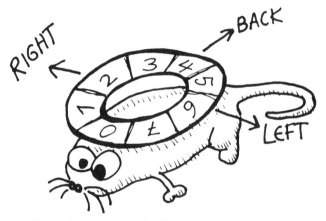

Every day, an animal will decide whether to continue facing the same direction as the day before or to turn and face a new direction. It will do this by consulting these eight slots and randomly choosing a new direction. The chance of a gene being chosen will be proportional to the number stored in the gene slot.

For example, an animal might have the following genes:

(1 1 10 1 1 1 1 1)

Let's represent these genes as a table, showing each slot number and how large of a value is stored in it:

In this example, an animal has a large number (10) stored in slot 2. Looking at our picture of the eight slots around the animal, you can see that slot 2 points to the right. Therefore,

Slot	Value
0	1
1	1
2	10
3	1
4	1
5	1
6	1
7	1

this animal will make a lot of right-hand turns and run in a circle. Of course, since the other slots still contain values larger than zero, the animal will occasionally move in another direction.

Let's create an *animals* variable, populated with a single starting animal. You can think of this animal as "Adam" (or "Eve", depending on what gender you prefer for our asexual animals).

```
(defparameter *animals*
    (list (make-animal :x      (ash *width* -1)
                       :y      (ash *height* -1)
                       :energy 1000
                       :dir    0
                       :genes  (loop repeat 8
                                     collecting (1+ (random 10))))))
```

We make the animal's starting point the center of the world by setting the x and y positions to half of the map's width and height, respectively. We set its initial energy to 1000, since it hasn't evolved much yet and we want it to have a fighting chance at survival. It starts off facing the upper left, with its dir field set to 0. For its genes, we just use random numbers.

Note that unlike the *plants* structure, which was a hash table, the *animals* structure is just a plain list (currently containing only a single member). This is because, for the core of our simulation, we never need to search our list of animals. Instead, we'll just be traversing *animals* once every simulated day, to let our critters do their daily activities. Lists already support efficient linear traversals, so using another, more complex data structure (such as a table) would have no significant effect on the performance of our simulation.

Handling Animal Motion

The move function accepts an animal as an argument and moves it, orthogonally or diagonally, based on the direction grid we have described:

```
(defun move (animal)
  (let ((dir (animal-dir animal))
❶      (x (animal-x animal))
❷      (y (animal-y animal)))
```

```
❸     (setf (animal-x animal) (mod (+ x
❹                                     (cond ((and (>= dir 2) (< dir 5)) 1)
❺                                           ((or (= dir 1) (= dir 5)) 0)
❻                                           (t -1))
                                      *width*)
                                   *width*))
❼     (setf (animal-y animal) (mod (+ y
                                      (cond ((and (>= dir 0) (< dir 3)) -1)
                                            ((and (>= dir 4) (< dir 7)) 1)
                                            (t 0))
                                      *height*)
                                   *height*))
      (decf (animal-energy animal)))))
```

The move function modifies the x and y fields, using the animal-x and animal-y accessors. As we've discussed, these are automatically generated through the defstruct macro, based on the field names. At the top of this function, we use the accessors to retrieve the x- and y-coordinates for the animal ❶❷. Then we use the same accessors to set the same values, with the aid of setf ❸❼.

To calculate the new x-coordinate, we use a cond command to first check if the direction is 2, 3, or 4 ❹. These are the directions the animal may face that point east in the world, so we want to add one to the x-coordinate. If the direction instead is 1 or 5, it means the animal is facing directly north or south ❺. In those cases, the x-coordinate shouldn't be changed. In all other cases, the animal is facing west and we need to subtract one ❻. The y-coordinate is adjusted in an analogous way ❼.

Since the world needs to wrap around at the edges, we do some extra math using the mod (remainder) function to calculate the modulus of the coordinates and enable wrapping across the map ❸❼. If an animal would have ended up with an x-coordinate of *width*, the mod function puts it back to zero, and it does the same for the y-coordinate and *height*. So, for example, if our function makes the animal move east until x equals 100, this will mean that (mod 100 *width*) equals zero, and the animal will have wrapped around back to the far west side of the game world.

The final thing the move function needs to do is decrease the amount of energy the animal possesses by one. Motion, after all, requires energy.

Handling Animal Turning

Next, we'll write the turn function. This function will use the animal's genes to decide if and how much it will turn on a given day.

```
(defun turn (animal)
❶   (let ((x (random (apply #'+ (animal-genes animal)))))
❷     (labels ((angle (genes x)
```

```
                     (let ((xnu (- x (car genes))))
❸                      (if (< xnu 0)
                           0
                           (1+ (angle (cdr genes) xnu))))))
                 (setf (animal-dir animal)
❹                    (mod (+ (animal-dir animal) (angle (animal-genes animal) x))
     8)))))
```

This function needs to make sure that the amount the animal turns is proportional to the gene number in the given slot. It does this by first summing the amount of all genes, and then picking a random number within that sum ❶. After that, it uses a recursive function named angle ❷, which traverses the genes and finds the gene that corresponds to the chosen number, based on the respective contributions of each gene to the sum. It subtracts the running count in the argument x from the number stored at the current gene ❷. If the running count has hit or exceeded zero, the function has reached the chosen number and stops recursing ❸. Finally, it adds the amount of turning to the current direction and, if needed, wraps the number around back to zero, once again by using mod ❹.

Handling Animal Eating

Eating is a simple process. We just need to check if there's a plant at the animal's current location, and if there is, consume it:

```
(defun eat (animal)
  (let ((pos (cons (animal-x animal) (animal-y animal))))
    (when (gethash pos *plants*)
      (incf (animal-energy animal) *plant-energy*)
      (remhash pos *plants*))))
```

The animal's energy is increased by the amount of energy that was being stored by the plant. We then remove the plant from the world using the remhash function.

Handling Animal Reproduction

Reproduction is usually the most interesting part in any animal simulation. We'll keep things simple by having our animals reproduce asexually, but it should still be interesting, because errors will creep into their genes as they get copied, causing mutations.

```
(defparameter *reproduction-energy* 200)

(defun reproduce (animal)
  (let ((e (animal-energy animal)))
❶    (when (>= e *reproduction-energy*)
❷      (setf (animal-energy animal) (ash e -1))
❸      (let ((animal-nu (copy-structure animal))
❹            (genes     (copy-list (animal-genes animal)))
            (mutation   (random 8)))
        (setf (nth mutation genes) (max 1 (+ (nth mutation genes) (random 3) -
1)))
        (setf (animal-genes animal-nu) genes)
        (push animal-nu *animals*)))))
```

It takes a healthy parent to produce healthy offspring, so our animals will reproduce only if they have at least 200 days' worth of energy ❶. We use the global constant *reproduction-energy* to decide what this cutoff number should be. If the animal decides to reproduce, it will lose half its energy to its child ❷.

To create the new animal, we simply copy the structure of the parent with the copy-structure function ❸. We need to be careful though, since copy-structure performs only a *shallow copy* of a structure. This means that if there are any fields in the structure that contain values that are more complicated than just numbers or symbols, the values in those fields will be shared with the parent. An animal's genes, which are stored in a list, represent the only such complex value in our animal structures. If we aren't careful, mutations in the genes of an animal would simultaneously affect all its parents and children. In order to avoid this, we need to create an explicit copy of our gene list using the copy-list function ❹.

Here is an example that shows what horrible things could happen if we just relied on the shallow copy from the copy-structure function:

```
  > (defparameter *parent* (make-animal :x 0
                                        :y 0
                                        :energy 0
                                        :dir 0
❶                                       :genes '(1 1 1 1 1 1 1 1)))
    *PARENT*
❷ > (defparameter *child* (copy-structure *parent*))
    *CHILD*
❸ > (setf (nth 2 (animal-genes *parent*)) 10)
    10
❹ > *parent*
    #S(ANIMAL :X 0 :Y 0 :ENERGY 0 :DIR 0 :GENES (1 1 10 1 1 1 1 1))
❺ > *child*
    #S(ANIMAL :X 0 :Y 0 :ENERGY 0 :DIR 0 :GENES (1 1 10 1 1 1 1 1))
```

Here, we've created a parent animal with all its genes set to 1 ❶. Next, we use copy-structure to create a child ❷. Then we set the third (second counting from zero) gene equal to 10 ❸. Our parent now looks correct ❹. Unfortunately, since we neglected to use copy-list to create a separate list of genes for the child, the child genes were also changed ❺ when the parent mutated. Any time you have data structures that go beyond simple atomic symbols or numbers, you need to be very careful when using setf so that these kinds of bugs don't creep into your code. In future chapters (especially Chapter 14), you'll learn how to avoid these issues by not using functions that mutate data directly, in the manner that setf does.

To mutate an animal in our reproduce function, we randomly pick one of its eight genes and place it in the mutation variable. Then we use setf to twiddle that value a bit, again using a random number. We did this twiddling on the following line:

```
(setf (nth mutation genes) (max 1 (+ (nth mutation genes) (random 3) -1)))
```

In this line, we're slightly changing a random slot in the gene list. The number of the slot is stored in the local variable mutation. We add a random number less than three to the value in this slot, and then subtract one from the total. This means the gene value will change plus or minus one, or stay the same. Since we don't want a gene value to be smaller than one, we use the max function to make sure it is at least one.

We then use push to insert this new critter into our global *animal* list, which adds it to the simulation.

Simulating a Day in Our World

Now that we have functions that handle every detail of an animal's routine, let's write one that simulates a day in our world.

```
(defun update-world ()
❶  (setf *animals* (remove-if (lambda (animal)
                                 (<= (animal-energy animal) 0))
                              *animals*))
❷  (mapc (lambda (animal)
            (turn animal)
            (move animal)
            (eat animal)
            (reproduce animal))
         *animals*)
❸  (add-plants))
```

First, this function removes all dead animals from the world ❶. (An animal is dead if its energy is less than or equal to zero.) Next, it maps across the list, handling each of the animal's possible daily activities: turning, moving, eating, and reproducing ❷. Since all these functions have side effects (they modify the individual animal structures directly, using setf), we use the mapc function, which does not waste time generating a result list from the mapping process.

Finally, we call the add-plants function ❸, which adds two new plants to the world every day (one in the jungle and one in the steppe). Since there are always new plants growing on the landscape, our simulated world should eventually reach an equilibrium, allowing a reasonably large population of animals to survive throughout the spans of time we simulate.

Drawing Our World

A simulated world isn't any fun unless we can actually see our critters running around, searching for food, reproducing, and dying. The draw-world function handles this by using the *animals* and *plants* data structures to draw a snapshot of the current world to the REPL.

```
(defun draw-world ()
❶  (loop for y
        below *height*
        do (progn (fresh-line)
                  (princ "|")
❷                 (loop for x
                        below *width*
```

```
❸                          do (princ (cond ((some (lambda (animal)
                                                     (and (= (animal-x animal) x)
                                                          (= (animal-y animal) y)))
                                                *animals*)
❹                                        #\M)
❺                                       ((gethash (cons x y) *plants*) #\*)
❻                                       (t #\space))))
❼                (princ "|"))))
```

First, the function uses a loop to iterate through each of the world's rows ❶. Every row starts with a new line (created with fresh-line) followed by a vertical bar, which shows us where the left edge of the world is. Next, we iterate across the columns of the current row ❷, checking for an animal at every location. We perform this check using the some function ❸, which lets us determine if at least one item in a list obeys a certain condition. In this case, the condition we're checking is whether there's an animal at the current x- and y-coordinates. If so, we draw the letter M at that spot ❹. (The capital letter M looks a little like an animal, if you use your imagination.)

Otherwise, we check for a plant, which we'll indicate with an asterisk (*) character ❺. And if there isn't a plant or an animal, we draw a space character ❻. Lastly, we draw another vertical bar to cap off the end of each line ❼.

Notice that in this function, we need to search through our entire *animals* list, which will cause a performance penalty. However, draw-world is not a core routine in our simulation. As you'll see shortly, the user interface for our game will allow us to run thousands of days of the simulation at a time, without drawing the world to the screen until the end. Since there's no need to draw the screen on every single day when we do this, the performance of draw-world has no impact on the overall performance of the simulation.

Creating a User Interface

Finally, we'll create a user interface function for our simulation, called evolution.

```
  (defun evolution ()
❶   (draw-world)
    (fresh-line)
❷   (let ((str (read-line)))
❸     (cond ((equal str "quit") ())
❹           (t (let ((x (parse-integer str :junk-allowed t)))
                (if x
❺                   (loop for i
                        below x
                        do (update-world)
                        if (zerop (mod i 1000))
                        do (princ #\.))
                    (update-world))
❻               (evolution)))))))
```

First, this function draws the world in the REPL ❶. Then it waits for the user to enter a command at the REPL using `read-line` ❷. If the user enters quit, the simulation ends ❸. Otherwise, it will attempt to parse the user's command using `parse-integer` ❹. We set `:junk-allowed` to `true` for `parse-integer`, which lets the interface accept a string even if it isn't a valid integer.

If the user enters a valid integer *n*, the program will run the simulation for *n* simulated days, using a loop ❺. It will also print a dot to the screen for every 1000 days, so the user can see that the computer hasn't frozen while running the simulation.

If the input isn't a valid integer, we run `update-world` to simulate one more day. Since `read-line` allows for an empty value, the user can just tap the ENTER key and watch the animals move around their world.

Finally, the evolution function recursively calls itself to redraw the world and await more user input ❻. Our simulation is now complete.

Let's Watch Some Evolution!

To start the simulation, execute `evolution` as follows:

```
> (evolution)




                                    M



```

Our world is currently empty, except for the Adam/Eve animal in the center. Hit ENTER a few times to cycle through a few days:

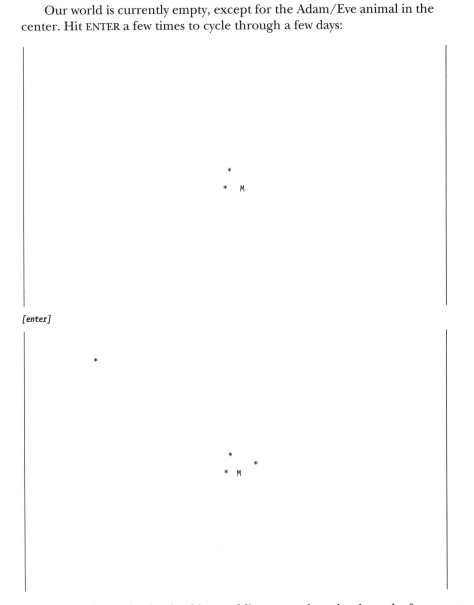

[enter]

Our under-evolved animal is stumbling around randomly, and a few plants are starting to grow.

Next, enter **100** to see what the world looks like after 100 days:

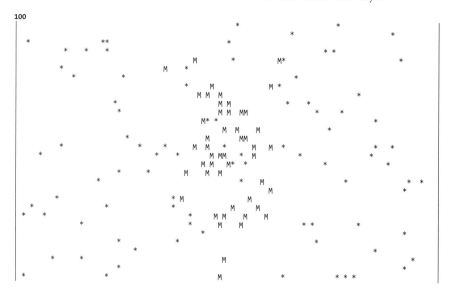

Our animal has already multiplied quite a bit, although this has less to do with the amount of food it has eaten than with the large amount of "starter energy" we gave it.

Now let's go all out and run the simulation for five million days! Since we're using CLISP, this will be kind of slow, and you may want to start it up in the evening and let it run overnight. With a higher-performance Lisp, such as SBCL, it could take only a couple of minutes.

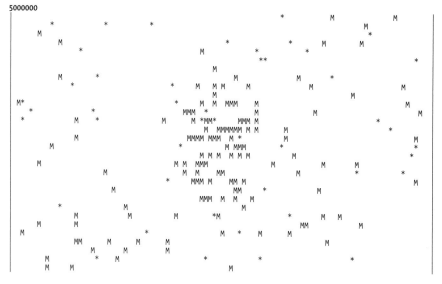

Our world doesn't look much different after five million days than it did after a hundred days. Of course, there are more animals, both traveling across the steppes and enjoying the lush vegetation of the jungle.

But appearances are deceptive. These animals are distinctly different from their early ancestors. If you observe them closely (by tapping ENTER), you'll see that some of the creatures move in straight lines and others just jitter around in a small area, never taking more than a single step in any direction. (As an exercise, you could tweak the code to use different letters for each animal, in order to make their motion even easier to observe.) You can see this contrast even more clearly by typing **quit** to exit the simulation, then checking the contents of the *animals* variable at the REPL:

```
>*animals*
#S(ANIMAL :X 6 :Y 24 :ENERGY 65 :DIR 3 :GENES (67 35 13 14 1 3 11 74))
 #S(ANIMAL :X 72 :Y 11 :ENERGY 78 :DIR 6 :GENES (68 36 13 12 2 4 11 72))
 #S(ANIMAL :X 16 :Y 26 :ENERGY 78 :DIR 0 :GENES (71 36 9 16 1 6 5 77))
 #S(ANIMAL :X 50 :Y 25 :ENERGY 76 :DIR 4 :GENES (2 2 7 5 21 208 33 9))
 #S(ANIMAL :X 53 :Y 13 :ENERGY 34 :DIR 4 :GENES (1 2 8 5 21 208 33 8))
 #S(ANIMAL :X 58 :Y 10 :ENERGY 66 :DIR 6 :GENES (5 2 7 2 22 206 29 3))
 #S(ANIMAL :X 74 :Y 3 :ENERGY 77 :DIR 0 :GENES (68 35 11 12 1 3 11 74))
 #S(ANIMAL :X 47 :Y 19 :ENERGY 47 :DIR 2 :GENES (5 1 8 4 21 207 30 3))
 #S(ANIMAL :X 27 :Y 22 :ENERGY 121 :DIR 1 :GENES (69 36 11 12 1 2 11 74))
 #S(ANIMAL :X 96 :Y 14 :ENERGY 78 :DIR 5 :GENES (71 37 9 17 2 5 5 77))
 #S(ANIMAL :X 44 :Y 19 :ENERGY 28 :DIR 1 :GENES (1 3 7 5 22 208 34 8))
 #S(ANIMAL :X 55 :Y 22 :ENERGY 18 :DIR 7 :GENES (1 3 8 5 22 208 34 7))
 #S(ANIMAL :X 52 :Y 10 :ENERGY 63 :DIR 0 :GENES (1 2 7 5 23 208 34 7))
 #S(ANIMAL :X 49 :Y 14 :ENERGY 104 :DIR 4 :GENES (4 1 9 2 22 203 28 1))
 #S(ANIMAL :X 39 :Y 23 :ENERGY 62 :DIR 7 :GENES (70 37 9 15 2 6 5 77))
 #S(ANIMAL :X 97 :Y 11 :ENERGY 48 :DIR 0 :GENES (69 36 13 12 2 5 12 72))
 ...
```

If you look closely at all the animals in the list, you'll notice that they have two distinct types of genomes. One group of animals has a high number toward the front of the list, which causes them to move mostly in a straight line. The other group has a large number toward the back of the list, which causes them to jitter about within a small area. There are no animals with a genome between those two extremes. Have we evolved two different species?

If you were to create a function that measured how far these evolved animals travel in a fixed amount of time, the histogram of the distance would appear as follows:

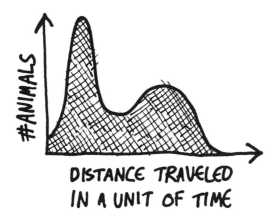

This is a clear bimodal distribution, showing that the behavior of these animals appears to fall into two populations. Think about the environment these animals live in, and try to reason why this bimodal distribution would evolve. We will discuss the solution to this conundrum next.

Explaining the Evolution

The solution to the evolution puzzle is pretty straightforward. There are two possible survival strategies an animal can adopt in this imaginary world:

- Focus on the rich food supply in the jungle. Any animal adopting this strategy needs to be conservative in its motion. It can't stray too far over time, or it might fall out of the jungle. Of course, these types of animals *do* need to evolve at least a bit of jittery motion, or they will never find any food at all. Let's call these conservative, jittery, jungle-dwelling animals the *elephant species*.

- Forage the sparse vegetation of the steppes. Here, the most critical trait for survival is to cover large distances. Such an animal needs to be open-minded, and must constantly migrate to new areas of the map to find food. (It can't travel in *too* straight a line however, or it may end up competing for resources with its own offspring.) This strategy requires a bit of naïve optimism, and can at times lead to doom. Let's call these liberally minded, risk-taking animals the *donkey species*.

Expanding the simulation to evolve the three branches of government is left as an exercise to the reader.

What You've Learned

In this chapter, we discussed the `loop` command in detail. Along the way, you learned the following:

- The `loop` command is a one-stop looping shop—it can do anything you need a `loop` to do.
- To count through numbers in a loop, use the `for` phrase.
- To count through items in a list within a loop, use the `for in` phrase.
- You can collect items inside a list and return them as a list with the `collect` phrase.
- Use the Periodic Table of the Loop Macro to find other useful phrases supported by `loop`.

11

PRINTING TEXT WITH THE FORMAT FUNCTION

Even in this modern era of programming, it's extremely important to be able to manipulate text, and Common Lisp has some of the fanciest text-printing functions available. Whether you need to manipulate XML, HTML, Linux configuration files, or any other data in a textual format, Lisp will make your work easy.

The most important advanced text printing function in Common Lisp is the format function, which is the subject of this chapter.

Anatomy of the format Function

Here is an example of the format function in use:

```
> (format t "Add onion rings for only ~$ dollars more!" 1.5)
Add onion rings for only 1.50 dollars more!
NIL
```

Let's take a look at what each part of this function means.

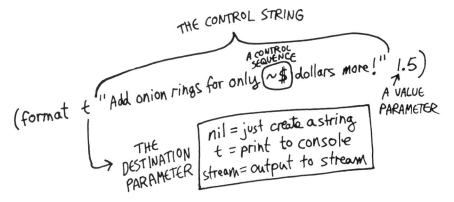

The Destination Parameter

The first parameter to the format function is the *destination* parameter, which tells format where to send the text it generates. Here are its possible values:

nil   Don't print anything; just return the value as a string.

t   Print the value to the console. In this case, the function just returns nil as a value (as in our example).

stream   Write the data to an output stream (covered in Chapter 12).

In the following example, we set the first parameter to nil so it simply returns the value as a string:

```
> (princ (reverse
      (format nil "Add onion rings for only ~$ dollars more!" 1.5)))
❶ !erom srallod 05.1 ylno rof sgnir noino ddA
❷ "!erom srallod 05.1 ylno rof sgnir noino ddA"
```

The resulting string value ("Add onion rings for only 1.50 dollars more!") is passed to the reverse function, and then that reversed string is printed to the screen with the princ command ❶.

In this example, the REPL will also print the value of the entered expression, along with the information output by the princ command. This is why you see the value displayed a second time ❷. For the remainder of this chapter, the examples will omit these values printed by the REPL, and show only the information explicitly printed by our code.

The Control String Parameter

The second parameter to the format function is a *control string*, which controls the text formatting. The format function's power lies in the control string. In our current example, the control string is "Add onion rings for only ~$ dollars more!".

By default, the text in this string is simply printed as output. However, you can place *control sequences* into this string to affect the format of the output, as described in the remainder of this chapter. Our current example contains the control sequence ~$, which indicates a *monetary floating-point* value. Every control sequence recognized by the format function begins with the tilde (~) character.

Value Parameters

The format parameters following the control string contain values, or the actual data to be displayed and formatted. As you'll see, the control string interacts with these parameters and controls their formatting.

Control Sequences for Printing Lisp Values

Any Lisp value can be printed with the print or prin1 command. To print a value for humans, without any delimiters, we can use the princ command:

```
> (prin1 "foo")
"foo"
> (princ "foo")
foo
```

We can use the ~s and ~a control sequences with format to produce the same behavior as prin1 and princ. When used with format, the ~s control sequence includes appropriate delimiters. The ~a shows the value, without delimiters, for humans to read:

```
> (format t "I am printing ~s in the middle of this sentence." "foo")
I am printing "foo" in the middle of this sentence.
> (format t "I am printing ~a in the middle of this sentence." "foo")
I am printing foo in the middle of this sentence.
```

We can adjust the behavior of these control sequences even further by entering parameters within the control sequence. For instance, we can place a number n in front of the a or s to indicate that the value should be *padded* with blank spaces on the right. The format command will then add spaces until the total width of the value is n.

For example, by writing ~10a in the following example, we add seven spaces to the right of foo, making the total width of the formatted value 10 characters:

```
> (format t "I am printing ~10a within ten spaces of room." "foo")
I am printing foo        within ten spaces of room.
```

We can also add spaces on the left side of the value by adding the @ symbol, as follows:

```
> (format t "I am printing ~10@a within ten spaces of room." "foo")
I am printing        foo within ten spaces of room.
```

In this case, the total width of the added spaces along with the value foo equals 10 characters.

Control sequences can accept more than just one parameter. In the preceding examples, we set only the first parameter, which controls the final width of the final formatted string. Let's look at an example that sets the second parameter of the ~a control sequence as well:

```
> (format t "I am printing ~10,3a within ten (or more) spaces of room." "foo")
I am printing foo          within ten (or more) spaces of room.
```

As you can see, additional parameters to a control sequence are separated with a comma. In this case, the second parameter is set to 3, which tells the format command to add spaces in groups of three (instead of just one at a time) until the goal width of 10 is reached. In this example, a total of nine spaces are added to the formatted value. This means it overshot our goal width of 10 (by design), leading instead to a total width of 12 (nine spaces plus the letters foo). Padding strings in multiples like this is not a commonly needed feature, so the second parameter to the ~a control sequence is rarely used.

Sometimes we need to control the exact number of spaces to add to our string, regardless of the length of the final value. We can do this by setting the third parameter in the ~a control sequence. For example, suppose we want to print exactly four spaces after the final formatted value. To set the third control sequence parameter equal to four, we place two commas in front of the parameter to indicate that the first two parameters are blank, then follow this with a 4:

```
> (format t "I am printing ~,,4a in the middle of this sentence." "foo")
I am printing foo     in the middle of this sentence.
```

Notice that there are exactly four extra spaces inserted in the results. Since the first and second parameters were not specified before the commas, their default values will be used.

The fourth control sequence parameter specifies which character will be used for padding. For example, in the following listing, we pad the printed value with four exclamation points:

```
> (format t "The word ~,,4,'!a feels very important." "foo")
The word foo!!!! feels very important.
```

These control sequence parameters can also be combined. For example, we can add the @ symbol to our code to indicate that the exclamation marks should appear in front of the value, like this:

```
> (format t "The word ~,,4,'!@a feels very important." "foo")
The word !!!!foo feels very important.
```

Now that you have an overview of format command control sequences, let's look at how to use them for formatting, beginning with numbers.

Control Sequences for Formatting Numbers

The format command has many options designed specifically for controlling the appearance of numbers. Let's look at some of the more useful ones.

Control Sequences for Formatting Integers

First, we can use format to display a number using a different base. For instance, we can display a number in hexadecimal (base-16) with the ~x control sequence:

```
> (format t "The number 1000 in hexadecimal is ~x" 1000)
The number 1000 in hexadecimal is 3E8
```

Similarly, we can display a number in binary (base-2) using the ~b control sequence:

```
> (format t "The number 1000 in binary is ~b" 1000)
The number 1000 in binary is 1111101000
```

We can even explicitly declare that a value will be displayed as a decimal (base-10) number, using the ~d control sequence:

```
> (format t "The number 1000 in decimal is ~d" 1000)
The number 1000 in decimal is 1000
```

In this case, we would have gotten the same result if we had just used the more generic ~a control sequence. The difference is that ~d supports special parameters and flags that are specific to printing decimal numbers. For example, we can place a colon inside the control sequence to enable commas as digit group separators:

```
> (format t "Numbers with commas in them are ~:d times better." 1000000)
Numbers with commas in them are 1,000,000 times better.
```

To control the width of the number, we can set the padding parameter, just as we did with the ~a and ~s control sequences:

```
> (format t "I am printing ~10d within ten spaces of room" 1000000)
I am printing    1000000 within ten spaces of room
```

To change the character used for padding, pass in the desired character (in this case, the *x* character) as the second parameter:

```
> (format t "I am printing ~10,'xd within ten spaces of room" 1000000)
I am printing xxx1000000 within ten spaces of room
```

Control Sequences for Formatting Floating-Point Numbers

Floating-point values are handled with the ~f control sequence. As with all of the previously discussed control sequences, we can change the value's display width by changing the first parameter. When used with floating-point numbers, the format command will automatically round the value to fit within the requested number of characters (including the decimal point):

```
> (format t "PI can be estimated as ~4f" 3.141593)
PI can be estimated as 3.14
```

As you can see, the final width of 3.14 is four characters wide, as specified by the control sequence.

The second parameter of the ~f control sequence controls the number of digits displayed after the decimal point. For example, if we pass 4 as the second parameter in the preceding example, we get the following output:

```
> (format t "PI can be estimated as ~,4f" 3.141593)
PI can be estimated as 3.1416
```

Note that Common Lisp actually includes the constant pi as part of the standard, so you could also rewrite the command like this:

```
> (format t "PI can be estimated as ~,4f" pi)
PI can be estimated as 3.1416
```

The third parameter of the ~f control sequence causes the number to be scaled by factors of ten. For example, we can pass 2 as the third parameter, which we can use to multiply a fraction by 10^2 to turn it into a percentage:

```
> (format t "Percentages are ~,,2f percent better than fractions" 0.77)
Percentages are 77.0 percent better than fractions
```

In addition to ~f, we can use the control sequence ~$, which is used for formatting currencies:

```
> (format t "I wish I had ~$ dollars in my bank account." 1000000.2)
I wish I had 1000000.20 dollars in my bank account.
```

You saw an example that used ~$ at the beginning of this chapter.

Printing Multiple Lines of Output

Common Lisp has two different commands for starting a new line during printing. The first, terpri, simply tells Lisp to terminate the current line and start a new one for printing subsequent output. For example, we can print two numbers on different lines like so:

```
> (progn (princ 22)
         (terpri)
```

```
        (princ 33))
22
33
```

We can also start a new line with `fresh-line`. This command will start a new line, but only if the cursor position in the REPL isn't already at the very front of a line. Let's look at some examples:

```
> (progn (princ 22)
         (fresh-line)
         (princ 33))
22
33
> (progn (princ 22)
         (fresh-line)
         (fresh-line)
         (princ 33))
22
33
```

As you can see, placing two `fresh-line` statements between the two `princ` calls resulted in Lisp printing only one line between the outputted numbers. The first `fresh-line` starts a new line; the second `fresh-line` is simply ignored.

Essentially, the `terpri` command says "start a new line," whereas the `fresh-line` command says "start a new line, *if needed.*" Any code using the `terpri` command needs to "know" what was printed before. Otherwise, unsightly empty lines may result. Since it's always better if different parts of a program know as little about each other as possible, most Lispers prefer using `fresh-line` over `terpri`, because it allows them to decouple the printing of one piece of data from the next.

The `format` command has two control sequences that are analogous to `terpri` and `fresh-line`:

~% causes a new line to be created in all cases (like `terpri`)

~& creates new lines only as needed (like `fresh-line`).

These examples illustrate this difference:

```
> (progn (format t "this is on one line ~%")
         (format t "~%this is on another line"))
this is on one line

this is on another line
> (progn (format t "this is on one line ~&")
         (format t "~&this is on another line"))
this is on one line
this is on another line
```

❶

As you can see, using an extra ~% prints an unsightly empty line ❶, and using ~& in the same places does not.

These two line-termination sequences can also have an additional parameter in front of them to indicate the number of new lines to be created. This is useful in cases where we want to use empty lines to space out our output. For example, the addition of 5 in the following example adds five empty lines to our output:

```
> (format t "this will print ~5%on two lines spread far apart")
this will print



on two lines spread far apart
```

Justifying Output

The format command also gives us a lot of control over text justification. Control sequences allow us to format tables, center text, and perform other useful justification feats.

To help you understand the various justification rules, we'll create a simple function that returns different animal names with varying character lengths:

```
> (defun random-animal ()
    (nth (random 5) '("dog" "tick" "tiger" "walrus" "kangaroo")))
RANDOM-ANIMAL
> (random-animal)
"walrus"
```

Now suppose we want to display a bunch of random animals in a table. We can do this by using the ~t control sequence. ~t can take a parameter that specifies the column position at which the formatted value should appear. For example, to have our table of animals appear in three columns at the fifth, fifteenth, and twenty-fifth character positions, we could create this table:

```
> (loop repeat 10
      do (format t "~5t~a ~15t~a ~25t~a~%"
                 (random-animal)
                 (random-animal)
                 (random-animal)))
    kangaroo  tick      dog
    dog       walrus    walrus
    walrus    tiger     tiger
    walrus    kangaroo  dog
    kangaroo  tiger     dog
    tiger     walrus    kangaroo
    tick      dog       tiger
    kangaroo  tick      kangaroo
    tiger     dog       walrus
    kangaroo  kangaroo  tick
```

Remember that a loop command with a repeat 10 clause executes the body of the loop 10 times. As you can see, use of the ~t control sequence caused the animals to be laid out in a neatly formatted table.

Now suppose we want all the animals be spaced equally apart on a single line. To do so, we can use the ~< and ~> control sequences, as follows:

```
> (loop repeat 10
        do (format t "~30<~a~;~a~;~a~>~%"
                    (random-animal)
                    (random-animal)
                    (random-animal)))
tick        tiger       tick
tick        tiger       dog
tick        dog         dog
kangaroo    kangaroo    tiger
tiger       tiger       kangaroo
walrus      kangaroo    dog
dog         dog         walrus
kangaroo    dog         walrus
walrus      dog         walrus
kangaroo    tiger       tick
```

Let's deconstruct this control string to understand how it works:

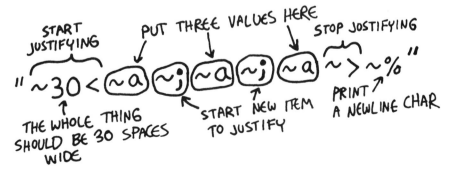

First, the ~30< tells the function that we're initiating a block of justified text. The parameter 30 indicates that the block should be 30 characters wide. Next, we have three ~a control sequences in a row, one for each animal. Each ~a is separated by ;, which tells format that we're starting a new value to be justified by ~<. (The ~; sequences indicate where extra spaces should be inserted to justify the values.) We then end the justified section with the ~> command sequence.

Because the equal spacing of the animals in each line doesn't guarantee that the columns created by printing multiple lines will be properly aligned, we add the :@ flag to our justification ~< command sequence. For example, we can create a single, neatly centered column as follows:

```
> (loop repeat 10 do (format t "~30:@<~a~>~%" (random-animal)))
          dog
         walrus
        kangaroo
          tick
          tick
         tiger
          dog
        kangaroo
        kangaroo
          dog
```

In the same way, we can use :@ with multiple justified values, centering them on the line with additional space at their left and right ends:

```
> (loop repeat 10
       do (format t "~30:@<~a~;~a~;~a~>~%"
                     (random-animal)
                     (random-animal)
                     (random-animal)))
   walrus      tick     tick
   walrus     tiger     tick
    tick       dog      tick
   walrus     tiger    tiger
  kangaroo     dog    kangaroo
   tiger    kangaroo   walrus
   tiger    kangaroo  kangaroo
  kangaroo   tiger     tick
    tick     tiger    walrus
   walrus    tiger     tick
```

This step brings us closer to having three neatly centered columns, but our columns are still a bit wavy because we're aligning the values within a single line, without telling format to arrange the values using three centered columns.

To produce neat columns, we'll still use the :@ flag, but we'll describe our rows using three separate 10-character justification sections:

```
> (loop repeat 10
       do (format t "~10:@<~a~>~10:@<~a~>~10:@<~a~>~%"
```

```
                      (random-animal)
                      (random-animal)
                      (random-animal)))
   tiger    kangaroo  kangaroo
kangaroo    kangaroo  walrus
   tick        tick   tick
   dog          dog   dog
   tiger        dog   walrus
   dog        tiger   kangaroo
walrus         dog    tick
   tick      walrus   kangaroo
   dog         tick   walrus
   tiger      tiger   tiger
```

At last, we have the nicely centered random animal columns of our dreams!

As you can see, the layout options for format are quite flexible. Since we often need to create complex lists and tables of data when debugging applications, these tricks are very helpful when you need to get a handle on your data, even with more complex programs.

Iterating Through Lists Using Control Sequences

The format function with its many control sequences is practically a programming language in its own right. (In fact, many Lispers would call it a *domain-specific language*, a concept we will revisit in Chapter 17.) And, like most programming languages, format can loop through data. It does this using the ~{ and ~} control sequences.

To achieve this looping, pass the format function a control string containing ~{ and ~}, and a list to iterate through. The part of the control string between the ~{ and ~} sequences is treated almost like the body of a loop. It will be executed a number of times, depending on the length of the list that follows it. The format function will iterate through this list, applying each of its items to the specified section of the control string.

For example, let's create a list of animals that we can use for testing:

```
> (defparameter *animals* (loop repeat 10 collect (random-animal)))
*ANIMALS*
> *animals*
("dog" "kangaroo" "walrus" "kangaroo" "kangaroo" "walrus" "kangaroo" "dog"
"tick" "tick")
```

Now we use the ~{ ~} control sequences to to loop through this list:

```
> (format t "~{I see a ~a! ~}" *animals*)
I see a dog! I see a kangaroo! I see a walrus! I see a kangaroo! I see a
kangaroo! I see a walrus! I see a kangaroo! I see a dog! I see a tick! I see a
tick!
```

To produce this loop, we simply pass the single variable *animals*, a list of items, to the format function. The control string iterates through the list, constructing the sentence "I see a ~a" for each member of *animals*.

A single iteration construct can also grab more than one item from the list, as in this example:

```
> (format t "~{I see a ~a... or was it a ~a?~%~}" *animals*)
I see a dog... or was it a kangaroo?
I see a walrus... or was it a kangaroo?
I see a kangaroo... or was it a walrus?
I see a kangaroo... or was it a dog?
I see a tick... or was it a tick?
```

Here, we have two ~a control sequences within a single looping construct. Each ~a pulls a single animal from the list, so two animals print for every iteration of the loop.

A Crazy Formatting Trick for Creating Pretty Tables of Data

Let's look at one last format example that uses some of the control sequences you've already seen, as well as some new ones. This example will illustrate how the varied control sequences can be combined for complex behavior.

```
> (format t "|~{~<|~%|~,33:;~2d ~>~}|" (loop for x below 100 collect x))
| 0  1  2  3  4  5  6  7  8  9 |
|10 11 12 13 14 15 16 17 18 19 |
|20 21 22 23 24 25 26 27 28 29 |
|30 31 32 33 34 35 36 37 38 39 |
|40 41 42 43 44 45 46 47 48 49 |
|50 51 52 53 54 55 56 57 58 59 |
|60 61 62 63 64 65 66 67 68 69 |
|70 71 72 73 74 75 76 77 78 79 |
|80 81 82 83 84 85 86 87 88 89 |
|90 91 92 93 94 95 96 97 98 99 |
```

To create this nicely formatted table of numbers, we first use the looping control sequences ~{ ~} to iterate through a list of numbers created by the loop command. Within the iteration, we place justification control sequences ~< ~>, which we've used earlier. In this case, we don't use them to justify our text, but instead use them to divide the resulting text into pieces. This is how we break our 100 numbers into nice clean rows of 10. We place the ~:; control sequence inside our justification control sequences ~< ~>, which causes text to be broken into pieces of equal length.

When used inside a justification, the control string preceding this sequence ~:; (which in this case happens to be |~%|) will be triggered only if the current cursor position is beyond a certain point, as specified by the second parameter, 33. In other words, we're telling the format function "Hey, once you have 33 characters' worth of text, start a fresh line."

The |~%| control string causes the line break and vertical bars to be printed. The number to be displayed is formatted using ~2d, which prints a left-justified number, two characters wide.

NOTE *For full details on every single control sequence, see the* Common Lisp HyperSpec *at* http://www.lispworks.com/documentation/HyperSpec/Front/index.htm.

Attack of the Robots!

Here, we look at a game so horrifying that it's sure to give you nightmares: Attack of the Robots! In this game, robots have taken over the world, and it's your job to destroy them. Though the plot may sound scary, the part of this game that will *really* give a Lisp programmer nightmares is the way it abuses the loop and format commands in order to squeeze a fully functional robot-fighting game into a *single page of code!* (This program uses the "crazy formatting trick" discussed in the previous section.)

I have annotated the code with some basic explanations. If you want to understand how the game works in detail, you'll need to review most of the information from the previous couple of chapters. Also, you can visit *http://landoflisp.com/* to download the source code for the game and read a more thorough explanation of the code.

To win the game, you need to strategically walk around the field to cause all robots to collide with each other. The movement keys are QWE/ASD/ZXC. These characters form a grid on the left side of your keyboard, letting you move up, down, left, right, as well as diagonally. You can also teleport with the T key.

Enjoy!

Play the classic game of Robots! All robots move towards the player. Robot collisions cause scrap that is deadly to other robots. Teleport as a last resort!

BY NAMING IT MAIN, WE CAN USE "RETURN FROM" TO EXIT EARLY

```
(defun robots ()
  (loop named main
        with directions = '((q . -65) (w . -64) (e . -63) (a . -1)
                            (d .  1) (z . 63) (x . 64) (c . 65))
        for pos = 544
        then (progn (format t "~%qwe/asd/zxc to move, (t)eleport, (l)eave:")
                    (force-output)
                    (let* ((c (read))
                           (d (assoc c directions)))
                      (cond (d (+ pos (cdr d)))
                            ((eq 't c) (random 1024))
                            ((eq 'l c) (return-from main 'bye))
                            (t pos))))
        for monsters = (loop repeat 10
                             collect (random 1024))
        then (loop for mpos in monsters
                   collect (if (> (count mpos monsters) 1)
                               mpos
                               (cdar (sort (loop for (k . d) in directions
                                                 for new-mpos = (+ mpos d)
                                                 collect (cons (+ (abs (- (mod new-mpos 64)
                                                                          (mod pos 64)))
                                                                  (abs (- (ash new-mpos -6)
                                                                          (ash pos -6))))
                                                               new-mpos))
                                           '<
                                           :key #'car))))
        when (loop for mpos in monsters
                   always (> (count mpos monsters) 1))
        return 'player-wins
        do (format t
                   "~%|~{~<|~%|~,65:;~A~>~}|"
                   (loop for p
                         below 1024
                         collect (cond ((member p monsters)
                                        (cond ((= p pos) (return-from main 'player-loses))
                                              ((> (count p monsters) 1) #\#)
                                              (t #\A)))
                                       ((= p pos)
                                        #\@)
                                       (t
                                        #\  ))))))
```

THESE ARE THE 8 OFFSETS WHEN THE GAME BOARD IS 64 WIDE

THE GAME BOARD IS 64 × 16 = 1024

(RANDOM 1024) PICKS A RANDOM SPOT

ASSOC PERFORMS A LOOKUP

PLAYER WANTS TO LEAVE GAME

CHANGE FOR MORE ROBOTS!!

THIS CALCULATES THE "MANHATTAN DISTANCE" TO THE PLAYER

CHECKS IF ALL MONSTERS ARE SCRAP

WE SORT LOCATIONS BASED ON DISTANCE TO PLAYER THEN CHOMP OFF THE CLOSEST

MORE THAN 1 ROBOT IN A SPOT MEANS THEY'RE SCRAP

BAD NEWS IF PLAYER IN SAME SPOT AS ROBOT

DON'T WORRY ABOUT THIS CRAZY FORMAT COMMAND YET

LOOP THROUGH BOARD POSITIONS

DRAW SCRAP FOR DOUBLED-UP ROBOTS

```
|    A                                          |
|                               A      A        |
|                           A                   |
|                                               |
|                          @            A       |
|                                               |
|              A               A                |
|     A  A             A                A       |
```

ROBOTS
PLAYER

```
| @   A  A   A           #A         A  A  AA   |
|                                               |
```

SCRAP DEADLY TO ROBOTS

What You've Learned

This chapter didn't really even come close to covering all of the features of the format function. However, it did provide an introduction, in which you learned the following:

- The first parameter of the format command determines whether the output is sent to the REPL, a stream, or returned as a string.
- The second parameter of the format command is a *control string* that lets you change the way your data is printed. The control string has a sophisticated syntax, acting almost like a programming language in its own right.
- The remaining format parameters are values that can be referenced from the control string to embed values into the formatted output.
- To embed a Lisp value into a formatted string, use the ~s or ~a control sequences.
- Many control sequences are available for printing and customizing the appearance of numbers.
- The format command also has complex looping abilities that can be used, for example, to format tables laid out in many different styles.

12

WORKING WITH STREAMS

Nearly every computer program you write will need to interact with the outside world at some point. Perhaps your program just needs to communicate with the user through the REPL, printing out information and capturing the user's input from the keyboard. Other programs you write may need to read or write files on a hard drive. Additionally, you may want to write programs that interact with other computers, either over a local network or the Internet. In Common Lisp, these kinds of interactions happen through streams.

Streams are data types in Common Lisp that allow you to take some external resource and make it look like just another simple piece of data you can manipulate with your code. The external resource could be a variety of things: a file on a disk, another computer on a network, or text in a console window on the screen. As you'll learn in this chapter, through the use of a stream, a Lisp program can interact with this outside resource just as easily as it might interact with a list or a hash table.

Types of Streams

When we communicate with an external resource from a Common Lisp program, we do so by using a stream. Different types of streams are available for different types of resources. Another factor is the direction of the stream—sometimes you will want to write data to a resource, and sometimes you will want to read data from a resource.

Streams by Type of Resource

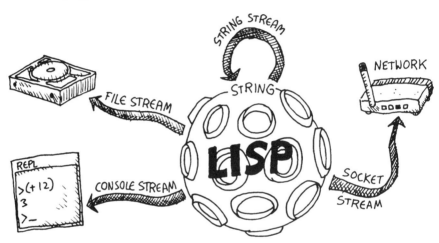

When organized by the type of resource on which they operate, the following are the most commonly used stream types:

Console streams   What we've been using so far when communicating with the REPL.

File streams   Let us read and write to files on our hard drive.

Socket streams   Let us communicate with other computers on a network.

String streams   Let us send and receive text from a Lisp string.

Of these stream types, string streams are the black sheep of the family. Rather than letting you communicate with the outside world, string streams allow you to manipulate strings in new and interesting ways.

Streams by Direction

When you write data to a resource, you use *output streams*. For reading data from a resource, you use *input streams*.

Output Streams

Output streams are used for tasks such as writing to the REPL, writing to a file, or sending information over a socket. At the most primitive level, you can do two things with an output stream:

- Check whether the stream is valid.
- Push a new item onto the stream.

As you can see, a stream is more restrictive than a true data structure in Lisp. For instance, a list supports all of the same features as a stream (we can push a new item onto a list with push and check if a list is valid with listp), and we also can do certain tasks with a list that we can't do with an output stream (such as changing items in the list with setf). But this limited functionality of streams actually makes them useful in many cases.

To see if we have a valid output stream, we can use the output-stream-p function. For example, the REPL has an output stream associated with it called *standard-output*. We can see if this is a valid output stream with the following code:

```
> (output-stream-p *standard-output*)
T
```

A Lisp character is one item that can be pushed onto an output stream using the basic command write-char. For example, to write the character #\x to the *standard-output* stream, we can run the following command:

```
> (write-char #\x *standard-output*)
xNIL
```

This code prints an *x* to the standard output (which, in this case, is the same as the REPL). Note that this function also returns nil, causing the *x* and the return value to be printed on the same line. As you saw in Chapter 6, this extra nil is just a side effect of running the code in the REPL. If we ran this command as part of a larger program, only the *x* would have printed out.

NOTE *In this chapter, we'll discuss only streams based on text characters. In Common Lisp, you can also create streams based on other data types. For instance, if you're working with binary data, you may want to send or receive raw bytes instead of characters. But for our purposes, manipulating textual data (and hence using streams that work with text characters) is the most convenient.*

Input Streams

Input streams are used for reading data. As with output streams, the actions that you can perform with an input stream are limited. At the most primitive level, you can do two things with an input stream:

- Check whether the stream is valid.
- Pop an item off of the stream.

We can see if we have a valid stream with the input-stream-p command. For instance, as with standard output, the REPL has an associated input stream called *standard-input*, which we can validate as follows:

```
> (input-stream-p *standard-input*)
T
```

We can pop an item off the stream with the read-char command. Since we're reading from the REPL, we need to type some characters and press ENTER to send the data into the standard input stream:

```
> (read-char *standard-input*)
123
#\1
```

As you can see, the 1 at the front of the stream was popped off and returned by read-char.

Working with Files

In addition to using streams to write to and read from the REPL, we can also use streams to write to and read from files.

You can create a file stream in Common Lisp in several ways. The best way is to use the with-open-file command. As you'll see shortly, this command contains special bug-prevention features that make it safer to use than other available file commands. The following example uses with-open-file to write the string "my data" to a file named data.txt:

```
> (with-open-file (❶my-stream "data.txt" :direction :output)
❷    (print "my data" my-stream))
```

In this example, the with-open-file command binds the output stream to the name my-stream ❶. This causes a file output stream to be created with the name my-stream. This stream will be available within the body of the with-open-file command (until the final closing bracket ❷), and any data we send to this stream will end up in the file named data.txt on the disk. The print command references my-stream as the destination for its output ❷. Therefore, after running this example, you should find a new file named data.txt in the folder from which you launched CLISP. This file has the text "my data" as its content.

Specifying :output as the direction for with-open-file creates an output stream. To make this an input stream instead, we could change the direction to :input, as follows:

```
> (with-open-file (my-stream "data.txt" :direction :input)
    (read my-stream))
"my data"
```

As you can see, this causes the data—the same data written to the file in the previous example—to be read in from the file.

As you learned in Chapter 6, the print and read commands can print and read any of the basic Common Lisp data types. This functionality makes it easy to use streams to store data from your programs to the hard drive. Here is a more complicated example that writes an association list (alist) to a file:

```
❶ > (let ((animal-noises '((dog . woof)
                           (cat . meow))))
❷     (with-open-file (my-stream "animal-noises.txt" :direction :output)
          (print animal-noises my-stream)))
   ((DOG . WOOF) (CAT . MEOW))
❸ > (with-open-file (my-stream "animal-noises.txt" :direction :input)
       (read my-stream))
   ((DOG . WOOF) (CAT . MEOW))
```

In this example, we're creating an association table of animals and the sounds they make. We create a new alist named animal-noises ❶. We put keys for dog and cat into this list. Now we can write this alist to a new file called animal-noises.txt ❷. Later, we can easily reconstitute this alist from the file ❸.

The with-open-file command can take keyword parameters that modify its behavior. For instance, you can tell the command what to do if a file with the given name already exists. In the following example, we'll display an error message using the :if-exists keyword parameter:

```
> (with-open-file (my-stream "data.txt" :direction :output :if-exists :error)
     (print "my data" my-stream))
*** - OPEN: file #P"/home/user/data.txt" already exists
```

Alternatively, you may simply want the existing file to be overwritten. In that case, set the :if-exists keyword parameter to :supersede, as follows:

```
> (with-open-file (my-stream "data.txt" :direction :output
                                        :if-exists :supersede)
     (print "my data" my-stream))
"my data"
```

The with-open-file command gives you a very succinct way to work with files. Unlike most programming languages, when using this command, you don't need to open and close files manually, and you don't need to worry about potentially messing up your files by failing to properly close them. (Actually, Common Lisp has lower-level commands for opening and closing files as well, but with-open-file packages them in a clean way that hides all the ugly details.)

The handwritten annotation in the diagram reads:

```
(with-open-file (s "data.txt" :direction :output)
   -s-  ← file handle is created and
            stream bound to it
   (print "my data" s)
   -s-  ← file handle is destroyed
)
```

body of with-open-file call

The main purpose of with-open-file is to acquire a file resource. It takes command of the file and assumes the responsibility of closing it. In fact, even if the code inside the with-open-file throws an ugly error that stops the program dead, with-open-file will still close the file properly to make sure this resource stays intact.

NOTE *Common Lisp has many commands that begin with with- that will safely allocate resources in this way. These with- commands, available in the core Lisp libraries, are built with Lisp's awesome macro system. You'll learn more about Lisp macros, and how to create your own with- commands, in Chapter 16.*

Working with Sockets

Now that we've used streams to communicate with the REPL and with files, let's see how we can use them to communicate with another computer.

If you want to write a program that can communicate with another computer elsewhere on a standard network (almost all networks nowadays use the TCP/IP protocol), you'll first need to create a socket. A *socket* is a mechanism for routing data over a computer network between programs running on different computers on that network.

Unfortunately, sockets didn't make it into the ANSI Common Lisp standard, which means there's no standard way of interacting with sockets at this time. However, every version of Common Lisp supports sockets, even if it doesn't follow any standard. Since we've been using CLISP as our Lisp of choice in this book, we'll consider only CLISP's socket commands.

NOTE *cl-sockets* (http://common-lisp.net/project/cl-sockets/) *and usocket* (http://common-lisp.net/project/usocket/) *are two attempts at adding a standard socket library to Common Lisp.*

Socket Addresses

Every socket within a network must have a *socket address*. This socket address has two components:

IP address   A number that uniquely identifies a computer on the network (typically shown as 4 bytes delimited by periods, such as 192.168.33.22).

Port number   Any programs that want to use the network must choose a unique port number that no other program on the same computer is already using.

The IP address and the port number combine to make up the socket address. Since the IP address is unique on a network and the port number is unique for a given computer, every socket address on a network is unique to a specific program running on a specific computer. Any messages running over the network (through chunks of data called *TCP packets*) will be labeled with a socket address to indicate their destination.

Once a computer receives a packet labeled with its IP address, the operating system will look at the port number in the socket address of the message to figure out which program should receive the message.

And how does the operating system know which program receives messages for a given port? It knows this because a program first must create a socket for that port in order to use it. In other words, a socket is simply a way for a computer program to tell the operating system, "Hey, if you get any messages on port 251, send them my way!"

Socket Connections

In order to actually send a message over a socket between two programs, we first need to follow some steps to initialize a *socket connection.* The first step in creating such a connection is to have one of the programs create a socket that starts in a listening state, waiting to see if other programs on the network want to start a communication. The computer with the socket in a listening state is called the *server.* Then the other program, called a *client*, creates a socket on its end and uses it to establish a connection with the server. If all goes well, these two programs can now transmit messages across the socket connection running between them.

But enough talk. Let's try connecting two programs right now to see the magic happen for ourselves!

Sending a Message over a Socket

First, open two copies of CLISP in two different console windows on your computer. We'll call one the client and one the server. (Or, if you have two computers on a network and know their IP addresses, you can create the two consoles on two separate machines, for the full network experience.)

NOTE   *You* must *use CLISP to get the socket code shown in this chapter to run.*

On the server, take control of a port by calling socket-server:

```
> (defparameter my-socket (socket-server 4321)) ;ON THE SERVER
MY-SOCKET
```

This command acquires port 4321 and binds a socket to it using the operating system. The socket is bound to the my-socket variable so that we can interact with it.

This command is somewhat dangerous, because the operating system is expecting us to give up the socket once we're finished with it. If we don't, no one will be able to use this socket anymore. In fact, if you make any mistakes during this socket exercise, you could mess up the socket at port 4321, and then you would need to switch to another port number until you restart your computer. (In the next chapter, you'll learn how to use the exception handling system in Common Lisp to work around these ugly problems.)

Next, let's make a stream from this socket (still on the server) that handles a connection from a single client:

```
> (defparameter my-stream (socket-accept my-socket)) ;ON THE SERVER
```

After running this command, the server will seem to lock up, and you won't be returned to the REPL prompt. Don't be alarmed—the socket-accept command is a *blocking operation*, which means the function won't exit until a client has connected.

Now switch over to your client CLISP and use the socket-connect command to connect to that socket on the server:

```
> (defparameter my-stream (socket-connect 4321 "127.0.0.1")) ;ON THE CLIENT
MY-STREAM
```

The IP address 127.0.0.1 is a special address that always points to the computer from which it's called. If you are using two different computers for this exercise, you should enter the actual IP address of your server.

After running this command, the server will unlock, and the value of the my-stream variable will be set. We now have a stream open in both copies of CLISP, and we can use it to communicate between them!

The stream CLISP has created here is called a *bidirectional* stream. This means it can act both as an input stream and an output stream, and we can use either set of commands on it to communicate in both directions. Let's send a cordial greeting between the client and the server.

Enter the following on the client:

```
> (print "Yo Server!" my-stream)
"Yo Server!"
```

And enter the following on the server:

```
> (read my-stream)
"Yo Server!"
```

Then, still on the server, enter this:

```
> (print "What up, Client!" my-stream)
"What up, Client!"
```

Back on the client, run this command:

```
> (read my-stream)
"What up, Client!"
```

Here's what your two CLISP windows should look like when you're finished:

```
conrad@conrad-inspiron-1420: ~
File  Edit  View  Terminal  Tabs  Help
Welcome to GNU CLISP 2.44.1 (2008-02-23) <http://clisp.cons.org/>

Copyright (c) Bruno Haible, Michael Stoll 1992, 1993
Copyright (c) Bruno Haible, Marcus Daniels 1994-1997
Copyright (c) Bruno Haible, Pierpaolo Bernardi, Sam Steingold 1998
Copyright (c) Bruno Haible, Sam Steingold 1999-2000
Copyright (c) Sam Steingold, Bruno Haible 2001-2008

Type :h and hit Enter for context help.

[1]> (defparameter my-socket (socket-server 4321))
MY-SOCKET
[2]> (defparameter my-stream (socket-accept my-socket))
MY-STREAM
[3]> (read my-stream)
"Yo Server!"
[4]> (print "What up, Client!" my-stream)
"What up, Client!"
[5]>
```

```
conrad@conrad-inspiron-1420: ~
File  Edit  View  Terminal  Tabs  Help
Welcome to GNU CLISP 2.44.1 (2008-02-23) <http://clisp.cons.org/>

Copyright (c) Bruno Haible, Michael Stoll 1992, 1993
Copyright (c) Bruno Haible, Marcus Daniels 1994-1997
Copyright (c) Bruno Haible, Pierpaolo Bernardi, Sam Steingold 1998
Copyright (c) Bruno Haible, Sam Steingold 1999-2000
Copyright (c) Sam Steingold, Bruno Haible 2001-2008

Type :h and hit Enter for context help.

[1]> (defparameter my-stream (socket-connect 4321 "127.0.0.1"))
MY-STREAM
[2]> (print "Yo Server!" my-stream)
"Yo Server!"
[3]> (read my-stream)
"What up, Client!"
[4]>
```

The message we sent across the socket was a Lisp string, but because of Lisp's elegant stream-handling capabilities, we could send almost any standard Lisp data structure in the same way, without any extra effort!

Tidying Up After Ourselves

It's crucial that we free up the resources we've created during this exercise. First, run the following command on *both* the client and the server to close the stream on both ends:

```
> (close my-stream)
T
```

Next, run `socket-server-close` on the server to free up the port and disconnect the socket from it. If you don't, port 4321 will be unusable until you reboot.

```
> (socket-server-close my-socket)
NIL
```

String Streams: The Oddball Type

Streams are usually used for communicating with the outside world from within a Lisp program. One exception to this is the string stream, which simply makes a string look like a stream. In the same way you can read or write to external resources with other types of streams, a string stream will let you read or write to a string.

You can create string streams with the `make-string-output-stream` and `make-string-input-stream` commands. Following is an example that uses `make-string-output-stream`:

```
> (defparameter foo (make-string-output-stream))
> (princ "This will go into foo. " foo)
> (princ "This will also go into foo. " foo)
> (get-output-stream-string foo)
"This will go into foo. This will also go into foo. "
```

You may be wondering why anyone would want to do this, since we can already directly manipulate strings in Lisp, without using streams. Actually, there are several good reasons for using string streams in this way. They are useful for debugging, as well as for creating complex strings efficiently.

Sending Streams to Functions

Using string streams allows us to use functions that require streams as parameters. This is great for debugging code that works with files or sockets, using only strings for the input and output of data.

For example, suppose we have a function `write-to-log` that writes log information to a stream. Usually, we would want to send the log information to a file stream, so it can be written to a file for safekeeping. However, if we want to debug the function, we may want to send it a string stream instead, so we can take a look at the data it writes and make sure it's correct. If we had hard-coded the `write-to-log` function to only write to a file, we wouldn't have this flexibility. This is why it makes sense to write functions to use the abstract concept of a stream whenever possible, instead of using other methods to access external resources.

Working with Long Strings

String streams can lead to better-performing code when dealing with very long strings. For instance, concatenating two strings together can be a costly operation—first, it requires a new block of memory to be allocated to hold both strings, and then the strings need to be copied into this new location. Because of this bottleneck, many programming languages use devices called *string builders* to avoid this overhead. In Lisp, we can get similar performance benefits by using string streams.

Reading and Debugging

Another reason for using string streams is that they can make our code easier to read and debug, especially when we use the with-output-to-string macro.

Here's an example of this command being used:

```
❶ > (with-output-to-string (*standard-output*)
❷     (princ "the sum of ")
      (princ 5)
      (princ " and ")
      (princ 2)
      (princ " is ")
      (princ (+ 2 5)))
❸ "the sum of 5 and 2 is 7"
```

The `with-output-to-string` macro ❶ will intercept any text that would otherwise be output to the console, REPL, or other output stream, and capture it as a string. In the preceding example, the output created by the `princ` functions ❷ within the body of the `with-output-to-string` call is redirected automatically into a string stream. Once the body of the `with-output-to-string` command has completed, the entire printed output that was put into the stream is returned as a result ❸.

You can also use the `with-output-to-string` macro to easily construct complex strings by "printing" each part, and then capturing the result as a string. This tends to be much more elegant and efficient than using the `concatenate` command.

NOTE   *Using `with-output-to-string` runs counter to the tenets of functional programming (discussed in Chapter 14). Some Lispers consider this function (and similar functions that intercept input or output intended for other destinations) to be an ugly hack. You'll see some disagreement in the Lisp community about whether the use of `with-output-to-string` is elegant or ugly.*

What You've Learned

This chapter described how to use streams to let your Lisp programs interact with outside resources. You learned the following:

- Different types of streams interact with different types of resources. These include *console streams, file streams, socket streams,* and *string streams.*

- Streams can be categorized based on their direction. *Output streams* let us write to a resource. *Input streams* let us read from a resource.

- Socket streams allow computer programs to communicate over a network. To establish a socket stream, we must first open sockets on both ends and open a socket connection between the programs.

- String streams allow us to use functions that require streams without linking to an outside resource, for debugging purposes. They also are useful for constructing complex strings efficiently and elegantly through the use of `with-output-to-string`.

13

LET'S CREATE A WEB SERVER!

In Chapter 6, you learned how to interact with a user by sending text to and from the REPL. However, when people talk about "interacting with a user" these days, they're usually referring to a user on the Web. In this chapter, you're going to learn how to interact with users on the Web by building a web server from scratch. Since communications over a network are error prone by their nature, you'll first learn how errors are handled in Lisp.

Error Handling in Common Lisp

Any time you're interacting with the outside world, as our web server will, unexpected things can happen. No matter how smart a modern computer network may be, it can never anticipate every possible exceptional situation. After all, even the smartest network can't recover from some fool tripping over the wrong cable.

Common Lisp has a very extensive set of features for dealing with unexpected exceptional situations in your code. This exception handling system is very flexible, and it can be used to do things that are impossible with exception systems in most other languages.

Signaling a Condition

If you're writing a function and something goes horribly wrong, a Lisp function can notify the Lisp environment that a problem has been encountered. This is done by *signaling a condition*. What sort of things could go wrong? Maybe a function tried to divide by zero. Or maybe a library function received a parameter of the wrong type. Or maybe a socket communication was interrupted because you tripped over your network cable.

If you want to signal a condition directly, you can do so with the error command. You would do this if a function you wrote detected a problem on its own—a problem so serious the program just could not continue normally. Using the error command will interrupt your running Lisp program, unless you intercept the error elsewhere to prevent an interruption. Let's signal a condition and print the message "foo" to describe the error:

```
> (error "foo")

*** - foo
The following restarts are available:
ABORT          :R1     Abort main loop
>
```

As you can see, signaling this condition causes Lisp to interrupt our program, print the message "foo," and show an error prompt at the REPL. (In CLISP, you can type :a at this point to abort the program and return to the normal REPL.)

Most of the time your program signals a condition, it will probably not be because you called error yourself. Instead, it will be because your program has a bug, or because you called a library function, and that function signals a condition. However, any time something prevents normal execution in your program, leading to a condition, your program will stop and show an error prompt such as in the preceding example.

Creating Custom Conditions

In our first example, we passed a string describing the condition to the error command. However, this text string just customizes the error message and doesn't lead to a different "type" of condition. Common Lisp also allows you to have various types of conditions that can be handled in different ways.

A more sophisticated way to signal conditions is to first define a custom condition using define-condition, as in the following example:

```
❶ (define-condition foo () ()
❷   (:report (lambda (condition stream)
❸            (princ "Stop FOOing around, numbskull!" stream))))
```

This is a typical example of creating a new type of condition, which we've named foo ❶. When this condition is signaled, we can supply a custom function that will be called to report the error. Here, we declare a lambda function for this purpose ❷. Within the lambda function, we print a custom message to report the error ❸.

Let's see what happens when we trigger this new condition:

```
> (error 'foo)

*** - Stop FOOing around, numbskull!
The following restarts are available:
ABORT          :R1      Abort main loop
>
```

As you can see, our custom message was printed. This technique allows the programmer to get a more meaningful error report, customized for the specific condition that was triggered.

Intercepting Conditions

When we create a condition with define-condition, it's given a name (such as foo). This name can be used by the higher-level parts of our program to intercept and handle that condition, so it won't stop the program's execution. We can do this with the handler-case command, as follows:

```
> (defun bad-function ()
     (error 'foo))
BAD-FUNCTION
❶ > (handler-case (bad-function)
❷      (foo () "somebody signaled foo!")
       (bar () "somebody signaled bar!"))
❸ "somebody signaled foo!"
```

The first thing we put inside a handler-case command is the piece of code that may signal conditions that we want to handle ❶.

In this example, the code we're watching is a call to bad-function. The rest of handler-case lets us specify actions to perform if a particular condition occurs ❷. When this code is run, bad-function signals the foo condition by calling (error 'foo). Usually, this would cause our program to be interrupted and lead to a error prompt at the REPL. However, our handler-case command intercepts the foo condition ❷. This means that the program can keep running without interruption, with the handler-case evaluating as "somebody signaled foo!" ❸.

Protecting Resources Against Unexpected Conditions

When an unexpected exception happens in a program, there is always a risk that it could bring down your program, or even cause damage to resources outside your program. Exceptions interrupt the regular flow of your code, and they may stop your code dead in its tracks, even while it's in the middle of a sensitive operation.

For instance, your program may be writing to a file or to a socket stream when an unexpected exception happens. In this case, it is critically important that your program has an opportunity to close the file/socket stream and free the file handle or socket; otherwise, that resource may become locked indefinitely. If such resources aren't cleaned up properly, the users may need to reboot their computer first before the resource becomes available again.

The unwind-protect command can help us to avoid these problems. With this command, we can tell the Lisp compiler, "This piece of code must run no matter what happens." Consider the following example:

```
❶ > (unwind-protect (/ 1 0)
❷                   (princ "I need to say 'flubyduby' matter what"))

*** - /: division by zero
The following restarts are available:
ABORT          :R1      Abort main loop
> :r1
I need to say 'flubyduby' matter what
>
```

Within the unwind-protect, we divide by 0, which signals a condition ❶. But even after we tell CLISP to abort, the program still prints its crucial message ❷.

We can usually avoid calling unwind-protect directly by relying on Common Lisp's "with-" macros; many of these call unwind-protect themselves, under the hood. In Chapter 16, we'll create our own macros to see how this is possible.

NOTE   *In the comic book epilogue at the end of the book, you'll learn about an additional feature of the Common Lisp signaling system called* restarts.

Writing a Web Server from Scratch

Now that you have a basic understanding of sockets (covered in Chapter 12) and error handling, you know enough to make a web server that can serve dynamic web pages written in Lisp. After all, why should Apache (the world's most popular web server) have all the fun?

How a Web Server Works

Hypertext Transfer Protocol, or HTTP, is the Internet protocol used for transferring web pages. It adds a layer on top of TCP/IP for requesting pages once a socket connection has been established. When a program running on a client computer (usually a web browser) sends a properly encoded request, the server will retrieve the requested page and send it over the socket stream in response.

NOTE *This web server is adapted from* http.lisp, *created by Ron Garret.*

For example, suppose the client is the Firefox web browser, and it asks for the page *lolcats.html.* The client's request might look like this:

```
GET /lolcats.html HTTP/1.1
Host: localhost:8080
User-Agent: Mozilla/5.0 (X11; U; Linux i686; en-US; rv:1.9.0.5)
Accept: text/html,application/xhtml+xml,application/xml;q=0.9,*/*;q=0.8
Accept-Language: en-us,en;q=0.5
Accept-Encoding: gzip,deflate
Accept-Charset: ISO-8859-1,utf-8;q=0.7,*;q=0.7
Keep-Alive: 300
Connection: keep-alive
```

For our web server, the most important part of this request is the first line. There we can see the type of request made (a GET request, which means we just want to look at a page without modifying it), and the name of the page requested (*lolcats.html*). This data sent to the server is called the *request header.* You'll see later that additional information can be sent to the server below the request header, in a *request body.*

NOTE *To readers from the distant future,* lolcats *was a viral Internet phenomenon from early in the third millennium. It involved pictures of cats with funny captions. If people of your time are no longer familiar with lolcats, it is of no great loss.*

In response, the server will send an HTML document that represents the web page over the socket stream. This is called the *response body*. Here is what a response body might look like:

```
❶ <html>
❷   <body>
❸     Sorry dudez, I don't have any LOLZ for you today :-(
    </body>
❹ </html>
```

An HTML document is wrapped in `html` opening ❶ and closing tags ❹. Within these tags, you can declare a body section ❷. In the body section, you can write a text message that will be displayed in the web browser as the body of the web page❸.

For a fully HTML-compliant web page, other items must exist in the document, such as a DOCTYPE declaration. However, our example will work just fine, and we can ignore these technical details for our simple demonstration.

A web server will typically also generate a *response header*. This header can give a web browser additional information about the document it has just received, such as whether it is in HTML or another format. However, the simplified web server we're going to create does not generate such a header and instead simply returns a body.

NOTE *Since we're using CLISP-specific socket commands, you must be running CLISP for the sample web server presented in this chapter to work.*

Request Parameters

Web forms are an essential element in powering websites. For instance, suppose we create a simple login form for a website.

userid	
password	
	Submit

After the visitor to our website hits the Submit button on this page, it will send a POST request back to the website. A POST request looks very similar to the GET request in the preceding example. However, a POST request usually carries the expectation that it may alter data on the server.

In our sample login form, we need to tell the server the user ID and password that the visitor to our site had entered into the text fields on this form. The values of these fields that are sent to the server as part of the POST request are called *request parameters*. They are sent within the POST request by appending them below the request header, in the area that makes up the request body.

This is what the POST request might look like for our login example:

```
POST /login.html HTTP/1.1
Host: www.mywebsite.com
User-Agent: Mozilla/5.0 (X11; U; Linux i686; en-US; rv:1.9.0.5)
Accept: text/html,application/xhtml+xml,application/xml;q=0.9,*/*;q=0.8
```

```
Accept-Language: en-us,en;q=0.5
Accept-Encoding: gzip,deflate
Accept-Charset: ISO-8859-1,utf-8;q=0.7,*;q=0.7
Keep-Alive: 300
Connection: keep-alive
Content-Length: 39
```

❶ `userid=foo&password=supersecretpassword`

The extra parameter in the header of this POST request, Content-Length, indicates the length of the parameter data at the bottom of the request. Specifically, Content-Length: 39 tells the server that the text containing the request parameters ❶ is 39 characters long.

Request Parameters for GET Requests

As we've discussed, the typical purpose of request parameters is to send web form data back to the server during a POST request. However, GET requests may also contain request parameters. Usually, with a GET request, we want to see what the parameters are in the URL of the request, whereas with a POST request, the parameters are hidden in the body of the request.

For instance, suppose you go to Google and search for "dogs." In this case, the follow-up page will have a URL that reads something like *http://www.google.com/search?q=dogs&hl=en&safe=off&*.... These values in the URL (such as the one stating that the [q]uery="dogs") are also request parameters.

The web server we're creating will need to give the server code access to both types of request parameters: the ones in the body of the request (as is common with POST requests) as well as the ones that appear in the URL (as is common with GET requests.)

Decoding the Values of Request Parameters

HTTP has a special way to represent the nonalphanumeric characters that a user might enter into a form, using *HTTP escape codes*. These escape codes let you have characters in the values of a request parameter that would not otherwise be available in the HTTP format. For instance, if a user enters **"foo?"**, it will appear in the request as **"foo%3F"**, since the question mark is represented with an escape code. Our web server will need to decode these escape characters, so the first function we'll write is decode-param:

```
❶ (defun http-char (c1 c2 &optional (default #\Space))
❷   (let ((code (parse-integer
                   (coerce (list c1 c2) 'string)
                   :radix 16
                   :junk-allowed t)))
      (if code
          (code-char code)
        default)))

  (defun decode-param (s)
❸   (labels ((f (lst)
               (when lst
```

```
                      (case (car lst)
                        (#\% (cons (http-char (cadr lst) (caddr lst))
                                   (f (cdddr lst))))
❹                       (#\+ (cons #\space (f (cdr lst))))
❺                       (otherwise (cons (car lst) (f (cdr lst)))))))))
❻        (coerce (f (coerce s 'list)) 'string)))
```

NOTE   *The HTTP escape codes we are discussing here are unrelated to the escape characters in
        Lisp strings we've discussed in other parts of this book.*

First, this function defines a local function named f ❸, which we'll use to
recursively process the characters. To make this recursion work, we need to
use coerce to turn the string into a list of characters ❻, and then pass this list
to f.

The f function checks the first character in the list to see if it's a percent
sign (%) or a plus sign (+). If it's a percent sign, we know that the next value
in the list is an ASCII code, represented as a hexadecimal number. (ASCII codes
are a standard set of numbers that correspond to text characters, shared among
many computer systems and applications.)

To decode this ASCII code, we've created a function named http-char ❶.
In this function, we use the parse-integer function to convert this string to an
integer ❷. In this case, we're using some keyword parameters on parse-integer:
the :radix parameter, which tells the function to parse a hexadecimal number,
and the :junk-allowed parameter, which tells it to just return nil when an invalid
number is given, rather than signaling an error.

We then use the code-char function to convert this integer (which holds
an ASCII code) into the actual character that the user entered.

As per the rules of HTTP encoding, if a value in a request parameter
contains a plus sign, it should be translated into a space character. We make
this conversion here ❹.

Any other character passes through the f function unchanged. However,
we still need to call f on the remainder of the list until all the characters have
been processed ❺.

Here are some examples of decode-param in action:

```
> (decode-param "foo")
"foo"
> (decode-param "foo%3F")
"foo?"
> (decode-param "foo+bar")
"foo bar"
```

Decoding Lists of Request Parameters

The next thing our server needs to do is to decode a list of parameters, which will
be given as name/value pairs in a string such as "name=bob&age=25&gender=male".
As we've discussed, URLs for web pages often contain such name/value pairs
at the end. As you can see, this string says that the person we're looking for
on the web page has a name of bob, an age of 25, and a gender of male.
These name/value pairs are separated by an ampersand (&). The structure

of these strings is equivalent to that of an association list (alist), so we'll store
these parameters as an alist using the following function:

```
(defun parse-params (s)
❶   (let* ((i1 (position #\= s))
          (i2 (position #\& s)))
❷     (cond (i1 (cons (cons (intern (string-upcase (subseq s 0 i1)))
❸                           (decode-param (subseq s (1+ i1) i2)))
❹                     (and i2 (parse-params (subseq s (1+ i2))))))
          ((equal s "") nil)
          (t s)))))
```

The parse-params function finds the first occurrence of an ampersand (&)
and equal sign (=) in the string, using the position function ❶. If a name/value
pair is found (we know this is true if an equal sign was found in the string and
is stored in i1), we use the intern function to convert the name into a Lisp
symbol ❷. We cons this name to the value of the parameter, which we decode
with our decode-param function ❸. Finally, we recursively call parse-params on
the remainder of the string ❹.

Let's give our new parse-params function a try:

```
> (parse-params "name=bob&age=25&gender=male")
((NAME . "bob") (AGE . "25") (GENDER . "male"))
```

Putting this data into an alist will allow our code to easily reference a specific variable whenever that's necessary.

NOTE   *Both* decode-param *and* parse-params *could achieve higher performance if they were
written using a tail call, as we'll discuss in Chapter 14.*

Parsing the Request Header

Next, we'll write a function to process the first line of the request header.
(This is the line that will look something like GET /lolcats.html HTTP/1.1).

The following parse-url function will process these strings:

```
(defun parse-url (s)
  (let* ((url (subseq s
                      (+ 2 (position #\space s))
❶                    (position #\space s :from-end t)))
❷        (x (position #\? url)))
    (if x
❸        (cons (subseq url 0 x) (parse-params (subseq url (1+ x))))
❹        (cons url '()))))
```

This function first uses the string's delimiting spaces to find and extract
the URL ❶. It then checks this URL for a question mark, which may indicate
that there are request parameters that need to be handled ❷. For instance,
if the URL is *lolcats.html?extra-funny=yes*, then the question mark lets us know
that there is a parameter named *extra-funny* in the URL. If such parameters
exist, we'll need to extract them, and then parse them using our parse-params

function ❸. If there aren't any request parameters, we just return the URL ❹. Note that this function skips over the request method (most often GET or POST). A fancier web server would extract this data point as well.

Let's try out our new URL extractor:

```
> (parse-url "GET /lolcats.html HTTP/1.1")
("lolcats.html")
> (parse-url "GET /lolcats.html?extra-funny=yes HTTP/1.1")
("lolcats.html" (EXTRA-FUNNY . "yes"))
```

Now that we can read the first line, we'll process the rest of the request. The following get-header function will convert the remaining lines of the request into a nice alist:

```
   (defun get-header (stream)
❶   (let* ((s (read-line stream))
            (h (let ((i (position #\: s)))
                 (when i
                   (cons (intern (string-upcase (subseq s 0 i)))
❷                         (subseq s (+ i 2)))))))
      (when h
❸       (cons h (get-header stream)))))
```

This function reads in a line from the stream ❶, converts it to a key/value pair based on the location of a colon ❷, and then recurses to convert additional lines in the header ❸. If it encounters a line that doesn't conform to a header line, it means we've reached the blank line at the end of the header and are finished. In this case, both i and h will be nil, and the function terminates.

The intern command used when generating the key above is a simple function that converts a string into a symbol. We could, instead, have used the read command for this purpose, as we have previously in this book. But remember that the flexibility of the read command also makes it a great target for hackers, who might try creating malformed headers to crack your web server. That's why it's wise to use the more limited, specific intern function to process this data sent over the Internet to our web server.

Testing get-header with a String Stream

Since the get-header function pulls its data directly from a socket stream, you might think we can't test it directly through the REPL. However, as you saw in the previous chapter, there are actually several different types of resources besides sockets that can be accessed through the stream interface in Common Lisp. Because of the common interface among streams, we can test our get-header function by passing it a string stream instead of a socket stream:

```
❶ > (get-header (make-string-input-stream "foo: 1
   bar: abc, 123

❷ "))
   ((FOO . "1") (BAR . "abc, 123"))
```

Using the make-string-input-stream function, we can create an input stream from a literal string. In this example, we're taking a string defining two keys (foo and bar) and ending it with an empty line, just like a typical HTTP header. Note that we have a single literal string from ❶ to ❷. Such strings are permitted in Common Lisp. As you can see, the get-header function appropriately pulled the two keys and their values out of this stream, in the same way it would pull these values out of a socket stream.

Using this trick, you can test functions that manipulate streams directly from the REPL. To do this, simply substitute string streams for other, more complicated stream types.

Parsing the Request Body

In a POST request, there will usually be parameters stored beneath the header, in an area known as the *request body* or *request content.* The following get-content-params function extracts these parameters:

```
   (defun get-content-params (stream header)
❶      (let ((length (cdr (assoc 'content-length header))))
❷        (when length
❸          (let ((content (make-string (parse-integer length))))
❹            (read-sequence content stream)
❺            (parse-params content)))))
```

First, this function searches the header for a value called content-length ❶, which tells us the length of the string that contains these content parameters. If content-length exists, then we know there are parameters to parse ❷. The function will then create a string with the given length using make-string ❸, and use read-sequence to fill that string with characters from the stream ❹. It then runs the result through our parse-params function to translate the parameters into our cleaned-up alist format ❺.

Our Grand Finale: The serve Function!

Now all the pieces are in place to write the heart of our web server: the serve function. Here it is in all its glory:

```
❶  (defun serve (request-handler)
❷    (let ((socket (socket-server 8080)))
❸      (unwind-protect
❹        (loop (with-open-stream (stream (socket-accept socket))
❺                (let* ((url    (parse-url (read-line stream)))
                       (path   (car url))
                       (header (get-header stream))
                       (params (append (cdr url)
                                       (get-content-params stream header)))
                       (*standard-output* stream))
❻                  (funcall request-handler path header params))))
        (socket-server-close socket)))))
```

The serve function takes a single parameter: request-handler ❶, which is supplied by the creator of a website that wants to use this web server. When the server receives a request over the network, it parses the request into clean Lisp data structures (using the functions we've discussed throughout this chapter), and then passes this request information to request-handler. The request-handler then displays the correct HTML.

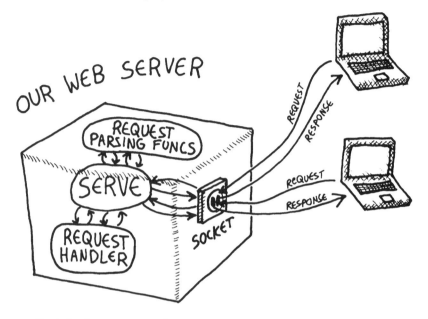

Let's look at our serve function in detail to see how it accomplishes this.

First, serve creates a socket bound to port 8080 ❷. This is one of several ports that is commonly used for serving web pages, especially when a site is still under development. (Port 80 is usually used for a production website/ web server.) We then call unwind-protect ❸, which ensures that no matter what happens as the server runs, socket-server-close will be called at some point to free the socket.

Next, we start the main web-serving loop. Within this loop, we open a stream for any client that accesses our server ❹. We then use the with-open-stream macro to guarantee that, no matter what, that stream will be properly closed. Now we're ready to read and parse the website request that the client has made to our server, using all of the reading and parsing functions we created ❺.

Finally, we call the request-handler function, passing in the request details ❻. Note how we redefine the *standard-output* dynamic variable beforehand. This means that the request handler can just write to standard output, and all the printed data will be redirected to the client stream automatically. As you learned in Chapter 12, capturing data from standard output allows us to minimize string concatenation. Also, it will make our request-handler function easier to debug, as you'll see shortly.

NOTE *One thing we did not do with our web server is prevent the web server from crashing if the request-handler triggers an exception. Instead, we simply guarantee that no resources are mangled in the case of an exception. We could easily add extra exception handling to keep the server ticking even if horrible exceptions occur. However, since our goal is to learn Lisp and develop games in a browser, it's better for us to know right away about any exceptions, even if that brings down our server.*

Building a Dynamic Website

To try out our shiny new web server, let's build a simple site that greets a visitor, using the dirt-simple function `hello-request-handler`:

```
(defun hello-request-handler (path header params)
  (if (equal path "greeting")
      (let ((name (assoc 'name params)))
        (if (not name)
            (princ "<html><form>What is your name?<input name='name' />
</form></html>")
            (format t "<html>Nice to meet you, ~a!</html>" (cdr name)))))
      (princ "Sorry... I don't know that page.")))
```

❶ (if (equal path "greeting")
❷   (let ((name (assoc 'name params)))
❸ </form></html>")
❹   (format t ...
❺   (princ "Sorry...

This `hello-request-handler` function supports only a single web page, called greeting. The first step in serving up this greeting page is to see if this page is indeed what the client requested ❶. If not, we print an apology to the user for not finding the specified page ❺. Otherwise, we check the request parameters to see if we know the user's name❷. If not, we ask the user to enter a username using a web form ❸. If we *do* know the user's name, we greet the visitor enthusiastically❹.

NOTE *We're taking a ton of shortcuts with our web server and this primitive website. For instance, any HTML sent to a client should be wrapped in a proper HTML skeleton, such as <html><body>...</body></html>. However, even then our page wouldn't be fully compliant with modern HTML standards. In addition, when a client requests a nonexistent page, the appropriate response is to display a 404 error page, not just print a polite apology. Luckily, web browsers are very forgiving about such shortcuts, and they will display our simplified responses anyway.*

Testing the Request Handler

Before we launch our new website, let's test our `hello-request-handler` in the REPL by first viewing a page about lolcats:

```
> (hello-request-handler "lolcats" '() '())
Sorry... I don't know that page.
```

Perfect. As you can see, when we ask our request handler for a page other than the greeting page, it just prints an apology. Now let's try viewing the correct greeting page:

```
> (hello-request-handler "greeting" '() '())
<html><form>What is your name?<input name='name' /></form></html>
```

Excellent! Our request handler has generated an HTML form asking the user for a username. Now let's pass in a parameter for the user's name, as if the form had been processed and sent to the server:

```
> (hello-request-handler "greeting" '() '((name . "Bob")))
<html>Nice to meet you, Bob!</html>
```

Because of the way we designed our web server, it's very simple to debug a request handler independently in the REPL. We were able to see that `hello-request-handler` generates the correct responses without actually firing up a web browser.

Launching the Website

Now that we know that our new website is functioning, let's launch it! But first, we need to make sure that all of the functions discussed in this chapter have been defined in an instance of CLISP. If you haven't been entering these functions into the REPL as you've been reading, you can just save them all into a file called *webserver.lisp*, and then load them with (load "webserve'").

Once you've defined your functions in the CLISP, start the server by entering the following into the REPL:

```
> (serve #'hello-request-handler)
```

That's it! Now you should be able to visit the site in a web browser:

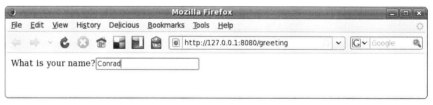

As you can see, when you visit our greeting page from a browser (using 127.0.0.1:8080, which will point to port 8080 on the same machine the web browser is running on), you are asked for your name. The server then shows a follow-up page, which greets you by name. This shows that our web server was able to parse out the name from the request parameters, and was able to pass the name to our `hello-request-handler` function.

We now have a fully functioning web server and request handling infrastructure. In future chapters, we'll use these tools to create an awesome, graphical, web-based game.

What You've Learned

In this chapter, you created a web server using Common Lisp, and learned the following along the way:

- You can signal conditions in Common Lisp with the error function. You can catch such errors with the `handle-case` command. If some code absolutely, positively needs to be called no matter what errors occur, you can place this code inside the `unwind-protect` command.

- A web server processes HTTP requests. The most common type of request is the GET request, used for viewing information. Another common type is a POST request, which is used when submitting web forms, for instance. You can tell the type of request, which page was requested, as well as other information, by looking at the *request header*. Both GET and POST requests may have request parameters, which can appear either at the end of the requested URL or at the bottom of the request in the *request body*.

SECTION IV: LISP IS SCIENCE

14

RAMPING LISP UP A NOTCH WITH FUNCTIONAL PROGRAMMING

As you've seen in the preceding chapters, Lisp makes it pretty easy to throw together some quick code and build some simple games in no time. However, Lisp's main claim to fame is as an academic tool, appropriate for tackling the most complicated scientific problems. The fact that it's also great for hacking is arguably just a side benefit.

In the rest of this book, we're going to focus on the scientific side of the language, exploring some advanced techniques to build a more sophisticated game that I hope will really blow your mind. It will do things you may never have thought would be possible in a computer program.

In this chapter, you're going to learn about the first advanced Lisp concept, called the *functional programming technique*. In the next chapter, we'll use this technique to build a simple dice wars game, as well as a crude artificially intelligent opponent to play against!

What Is Functional Programming?

We've already discussed the concept of functional programming a bit in earlier chapters. The glib answer is that functional programming is "a style of programming where we write all of our code using functions."

However, we mean something very specific when using the term *function* in this context—exactly the same thing that mathematicians mean when they use the word *function*. So, what do mathematicians mean when they use this word?

You probably already know the answer. Try to remember way, way back when you took pre-algebra. If you didn't fall asleep during that particular lesson, you might remember your teacher drawing something like this on the chalkboard:

This picture shows that a function has arguments that may go into it, called the *domain* of the function. The function then takes these arguments and returns a value. This value is said to fall within the *range* of the function.

NOTE *Some advanced Lispers will cringe when someone says that a function "returns a value." This is because Lisp derives from a something called the* lambda calculus, *which is a fundamental programming-like algebra developed back in the 1930s by Alonzo Church. In the lambda calculus, you "run" a program by performing substitution rules on the starting program to determine the result of a function. Hence, the result of a set of functions just sort of magically appears by performing substitutions; never does a function consciously "decide" to return a value.*

Because of this, Lisp purists prefer to say that a function "evaluates to a result." However, almost everyone else in the programming world likes to say that functions return a value. It's up to you to decide which way of thinking about functions feels the most natural.

Here are some important properties of mathematical functions that we'll want our Lisp functions to obey as well:

- The function always returns the same result, as long as the same arguments are passed into it. (This is often referred to as *referential transparency*.)
- The function never references variables that are defined outside the function, unless we are certain that these variables will remain constant.
- No variables are modified (or *mutated*, as functional programmers like to say) by the function.
- The purpose of the function is to do nothing other than to return a result.
- The function doesn't do anything that is visible to the outside world, such as pop up a dialog box on the screen or make your computer go "Bing!"
- The function doesn't take information from an outside source, such as the keyboard or the hard drive.

If we obey these rules whenever possible, we can say that our code is written in the *functional style*.

A great example of a true mathematical function is the sine function. Similarly, the sin function in Lisp (which calculates the mathematical sine) is a great example of a Lisp function that obeys the rules of the functional style:

```
> (sin 0.5)
0.47942555
```

The sin function always returns the same result, as long as you always pass the same argument (in this case, 0.5) into it. It doesn't do anything to interact with the outside world. Its entire purpose in life is to return the sine as a value. It obeys all the rules in the preceding list.

Clearly, it would be impossible to write *all* the code in a computer program in the functional style. For instance, one of the rules stipulates that the computer isn't allowed to go "Bing!"—who would want to use a computer if it didn't go "Bing!" once in a while?

Whenever a piece of code does something that is visible to the outside world, such as go "Bing!" or display a dialog box on the screen, we say that the code *causes a side effect.* Functional programmers think of such side effects as making your code "dirty."

The technical term for such dirty code that contains side effects is *imperative code.* The term *imperative* implies that the code is written in a "cookbook" style, where you basically say things like "first do this, and then do that." Like a cookbook, most lines in imperative code perform side effects, such as writing to the screen or modifying a global variable. Imperative code is the opposite of functional code.

This leads us to the central philosophy of functional programming. It states that you should break your program into two parts:

- The first, and biggest part, should be completely functional and free of side effects. This is the clean part of your program.

- The second, smaller part of your program is the part that has all the side effects, interacting with the user and the rest of the outside world. This code is dirty and should be kept as small as possible.

If a piece of code pops up a dialog box, for example, we deem it dirty and banish it to the imperative section of our code. Things like dialog boxes are not really math, and we shouldn't let them play with our math functions and other clean, functional code.

Anatomy of a Program Written in the Functional Style

Now that we've discussed how functional programming is done, let's write a simple program that follows this style. Since we want this program to be a typical example of most software, we should figure out what most software in the world actually does. So what do most programs in the world actually do? They keep track of widgets!

Here's our entire example program, written in the functional style:

```
;the clean, functional part
❶ (defun add-widget (database widget)
❷   (cons widget database))

;the dirty, nonfunctional part
❸ (defparameter *database* nil)

❹ (defun main-loop ()
❺   (loop (princ "Please enter the name of a new widget:")
❻         (setf *database* (add-widget *database* (read)))
          (format t "The database contains the following: ~a~%" *database*)))
```

As promised, it is split into two parts: the *clean part* and the *dirty part*. I did say that the clean part of the program should be much bigger than the dirty part. However, since this example is so short, the dirty part ended up a bit bigger. Usually, you can expect the clean part to be around 80 percent of the actual code.

NOTE   *Some programming languages are even more focused on functional programming than Lisp is. Haskell, for instance, has powerful features that let you write 99.9 percent of your code in a functional style. In the end, however, your program will still need to have some kind of side effect; otherwise, your code couldn't accomplish anything useful.*

So what does our example program do? Well, it basically does what most computer programs in the world are designed to do: It keeps track of widgets in a database!

The database in this example is very primitive. It's just a Lisp list, stored in the global variable *database*. Since the database is going to start off empty, we initialize this variable and set it to be empty ❸.

We can call the function main-loop to start tracking some widgets ❹. This function just starts an infinite loop, asking the user for a widget name ❺. Then, after it reads in the widget, it calls the add-widget function to add the new widget to the database ❻.

However, the add-widget function ❶ is in the clean part of the code. That means it's functional and isn't allowed to modify the *database* variable directly. Like all functional code, the add-widget function is allowed to do nothing more than return a new value. This means that the only way it can "add" a widget to a database is to return a brand-new database! It does this by simply taking the database passed to it and then consing the widget to the database to create a new database ❷. The new database is identical to the previous one, except that it now contains a new widget at the front of the list.

Think of how crazy this sounds on the face of it. Imagine that we're running an Oracle database server, containing millions of widgets:

Then, when we add a new widget, the database server accomplishes this by creating a brand-new replica of the previous database, which differs only in that a single new item has been added:

This would be horribly inefficient. However, in our widgets example, things are not as bad as they may first appear. It is true that the add-widgets function creates a new list of widgets every time it is called, and that repeated calls to this function would make the list longer and longer. However, since every new widget is simply added to the front of the list, it turns out that the tail end of the widget list is identical to the previous version of the list. Hence, the add-widget function can "cheat" whenever it creates a new list, by simply consing a single new widget to the front of the list, and then repurposing the old list as a tail to hold the rest of the items ❷. This allows the new list to be created in a way that is fast and also requires very little new memory to be allocated. In fact, the only new memory allocated by add-widget is a single new cons cell to link the new widget to the previous list.

This type of cheating when creating new data structures is a key technique that makes efficient functional programming possible. Furthermore, sharing of structures can be done safely, since one of the tenets of functional programming is to never modify old pieces of data.

So our `add-widget` function creates a new database for us with the additional item added to it. The `main-loop` function, in the dirty part of the code, sets the global *database* variable equal to this new database. In this way, we have indirectly modified the database in two steps:

1. The `add-widget` function, which is basically the brains of this program, generated an updated database for us.
2. The `main-loop` function, which was in charge of the dirty work, modified the global *database* variable to complete the operation.

This example program illustrates the basic layout of a Lisp program written in the functional style. Let's try out our new program to see it in action:

```
> (main-loop)
Please enter the name of a new widget: Frombulator
The database contains the following: (FROMBULATOR)
Please enter the name of a new widget: Double-Zingomat
The database contains the following: (DOUBLE-ZINGOMAT FROMBULATOR)
...
```

Remember that you can hit CTRL-C to exit the infinite loop in this example.

Higher-Order Programming

One common stumbling block for programmers learning to write programs in the functional style is that they find it hard to combine different chunks of code to perform a single action. This is called *code composition*. A programming language should make code composition easy. In other words, it should make it easy for you to take different pieces of code and use them together to solve a task. The most powerful tool for code composition when writing functional code is *higher-order programming*, which lets you use functions that accept other functions as parameters.

Let's look at an example to understand why code composition can be a challenge to a beginning functional programmer. Suppose we want to add two to every number in the following list:

```
> (defparameter *my-list* '(4 7 2 3))
*MY-LIST*
```

To do this, we will need to write code to traverse the list, as well as write code to add two to a number. These are the two tasks we need to compose.

Code Composition with Imperative Code

One possible naïve (and imperative) way to perform this task is to use a loop:

```
;For demonstration purposes only. A Lisper would not write code like this.
❶ > (loop for n below (length *my-list*)
❷       do (setf (nth n *my-list*) (+ (nth n *my-list*) 2)))
```

```
NIL
> *my-list*
(6 9 4 5)
```

Here, we're creating a variable n that counts through all the items in the list in a loop ❶. We then use setf to add two to the number at the location n in the list ❷. This is similar to the sort of code you might write if you were a C programmer. Although it's pretty ugly, there are positive things that can be said about it:

- Code structured like this is potentially very efficient. It's space-efficient, since we don't need to allocate any memory for storing a new list (we're just munging the old list to increase all the numbers in it by two). And it could also be very time-efficient, if we rewrote this loop to work on an array instead of a list. (Remember that finding the nth item in a list is slow.)

- Code written like this clearly composes the task of looping ❶ and the task of adding two to a number ❷. By putting our code for the addition inside the loop, we are composing these two activities to complete a more complicated goal: adding two to an entire list of numbers.

However, there are obvious downsides to the imperative approach:

- It destroys the original list. This is a problem if we use the *my-list* variable later, and miss the fact that this code has messed up the original values in this list. A Lisper would say that allowing the *my-list* variable to be modified willy-nilly makes this variable a piece of *hidden state* in the program. Bugs related to hidden state are common in programming languages that encourage imperative-style programming.

- We needed to create a variable n ❶ to keep track of our position in the list. This makes the code more bulky and also adds more places where bugs could lurk. There's always a risk that we give n a wrong value or use it incorrectly to access items from the list.

Using the Functional Style

Now let's see what happens if we rewrite this code in a functional style. Let's first write it as a beginning functional programmer might, without using higher-order programming:

```
❶ > (defun add-two (list)
     (when list
       (cons (+ 2 (car list)) (add-two (cdr list)))))
ADD-TWO
> (add-two '(4 7 2 3))
(6 9 4 5)
```

Here, we're creating a function add-two ❶, which adds two to the number at the front of the list and then calls itself recursively to build the tail of the list.

This code avoids many of the downsides from the imperative solution. It does not destroy the original list, and it does not require us to use a numeric index. Unfortunately, it also lacks one of the critical benefits of the imperative version: There is no longer a clear delineation between the code that adds two to items in the list and the code that traverses the list. These two activities are now deeply intertwined, which is the reason we needed to create a special function, add-two, to make this solution work. We have lost our ability to compose these two tasks in a clean way.

Higher-Order Programming to the Rescue

If we want to write code for this task in a functional style, but still allow our code to be composable, we'll need to make use of higher-order functions. Here is how an experienced Lisper would add two to every number in a list:

```
> (mapcar (lambda (x)
            (+ x 2))
          '(4 7 2 3))
(6 9 4 5)
```

Now we finally have a version of the code that is functional *and* allows us to compose the traversal code and the addition code. Here, the traversal is performed by the mapcar function, which is a higher-order function since it applies a supplied function to every member in a list. The addition is performed by a lambda function, which is responsible only for adding two to a number, and is oblivious to the fact that the numbers are in a list. This example shows that higher-order programming can let us write clearly delineated chunks of code and then compose them, without needing to break from the functional style.

Why Functional Programming Is Crazy

We already know one reason why functional programming is crazy: Functional programs can't really do anything, since they can't have *side effects*. As Simon Peyton Jones, a well-known functional programmer, likes to say, "All you can do without side effects is push a button and watch the box get hot for a while." (Which isn't technically true, since even the box getting hot is a side effect.)

We've seen that we can work around this limitation of functional programming by adding a dirty section to our programs, which is kept separate from the rest of the code and contains all our code that is imperative and not in the functional style. However, recall the problem with the functional style: It can cause code to be extremely inefficient.

Performance has always been a huge concern with functional programs. Having to write code that isn't allowed to mutate the value of existing variables, but only create new variables, can lead to a huge amount of memory copying and memory allocation, which can slow programs down to a crawl. One way to mitigate this copying and allocation is by using shared structures between different pieces of data in our programs.

Nonetheless, code written in the functional style has other properties that affect performance. For instance, functional code uses a lot of recursion, instead of looping. Using recursion causes the Lisp compiler/interpreter to put a lot of items on the program stack, which can be very slow.

Fortunately, functional programmers have developed optimization techniques that can solve the vast majority of performance problems. These include memoization, tail call optimization, lazy evaluation, and higher-order programming, which we'll cover in the next few chapters. Using these techniques and others, an experienced functional programmer can write code that is usually comparable in performance to code written in any other style.

However, some types of programs just can't be written in a purely functional way. For instance, you probably wouldn't write something like a full-on Oracle-style relational database system in a functional style. Yet, smaller, memory-resident database systems may be able to use purely functional techniques (an example is the HAppS-IxSet available to Haskell programmers at *http://happs.org/*). So there is really no hard limit as to when functional programming can be used.

Why Functional Programming Is Fantastic

Now that I've told you about all the headaches a functional programmer must endure, you may be wondering, "Why would anyone bother to program this way?" The answer is that functional programming has many enticing benefits that make up for these headaches.

Functional Programming Reduces Bugs

Bugs in computer programs usually happen because, under certain circumstances, the code behaves in ways the programmer didn't expect when the code was written. In functional programming, the behavior of your functions depends on one and only one thing: the arguments explicitly passed into the function. This makes it much easier for a programmer to appreciate all the circumstances a program could possibly encounter, including circumstances that could lead to errors.

Writing functions that depend on only their arguments for their behavior also makes bugs easy to duplicate. If you call a function with the same data passed in through its arguments, it should do the same exact thing every time. This is the property we called *referential transparency*.

Functional Programs Are More Compact

It turns out a lot of the work in run-of-the-mill computer programs involves creating, initializing, and updating variables. Functional programs don't do any of this. As we discussed earlier, functional programs make use of higher-order functions, which don't require us to create tons of temporary variables in our code, and that makes our code more compact.

Functional Code Is More Elegant

The biggest advantage of functional programming is that it brings all of computer programming back to the domain of mathematics. It wouldn't make sense for a math equation to pop up a dialog box or write to the hard drive. It can be argued that if we get our computer code back to this same level of purity, it will be far more elegant. Additionally, if our code is closer to the world of mathematics, we may be able to use tools in mathematics to write better computer code.

In fact, a lot of research continues to be done in using mathematical proofs to check for the correctness of functional computer programs. Although this research still isn't to the point where a practical programmer would use such techniques, they may be more common in the future. And, almost certainly, a functional programming style will be essential in making correctness proofs on your code possible.

What You've Learned

In this chapter, we discussed functional programming. Along the way, you learned the following:

- Programs written in the *functional style* always give the same result when they are given the same values in their arguments.

- Functional programs do not contain *side effects*. Their whole purpose in life is to just calculate a value to return.

- Programs that are not functional usually read like a cookbook, with statements like, "First do this, and then do that." This style of programming is called *imperative programming*.

- A good strategy for writing Lisp programs is to break them into a clean, functional part and a dirty, imperative part.

- Functional programs can be written quickly, are more compact, and tend to have fewer bugs, particularly in the hands of an experienced functional programmer.

15

DICE OF DOOM, A GAME WRITTEN IN THE FUNCTIONAL STYLE

Now we're finally ready to create a more sophisticated (and fun) computer program in the functional style. As we expand this program throughout the rest of this book, you'll learn about techniques for writing elegant functional code, while at the same time maintaining strong performance in your programs.

The Rules of Dice of Doom

Dice of Doom is a game in the same family as Risk, Dice Wars (*http://www
.gamedesign.jp/flash/dice/dice.html*), and KDice (*http://kdice.com/*). In the beginning, we're going to keep the rules of Dice of Doom mind-numbingly simple.
In later chapters, we'll expand the rules, until eventually we'll have a game
very similar to Dice Wars.

Here are the simplified rules we'll start with:

- Two players (named A and B) occupy spaces on a hexagonal grid. Each
  hexagon in the grid will have some six-sided dice on it, owned by the
  occupant.

- During a turn, a player can perform any number of moves, but must
  perform at least one move. If the player cannot move, the game ends.

- A move consists of attacking a neighboring hexagon owned by the
  opponent. The player must have more dice in her hexagon than the
  neighboring hexagon in order to attack. For now, all attacks will automatically lead to a win. In future variants, we'll actually roll the dice for a
  battle. But for now, the player with more dice just wins automatically.

- After winning a battle, the losing player's dice are removed from the
  board, and all but one of the winning player's dice are moved onto the
  newly won hexagon.

- After a player is finished making her moves, reinforcements are added to
  that player's dice armies. Reinforcements to the player's occupied hexagons
  are added one die at a time, starting from the upper-left corner, moving
  across and down. The maximum number of dice added as reinforcements
  is one less than the player took from the opponent in her completed turn.

- When a player can no longer take her turn, the game has ended. The
  player who occupies the most hexagons at this point is the winner. (A tie
  is also possible.)

A Sample Game of Dice of Doom

Since our implementation of Dice of Doom will include an AI player, we're
going to start with an extremely humble size for our game board. As you
probably know, AI code can be very computationally intensive. In our early,
very naive version of this game, any board larger than a 2-by-2 grid of hexagons would bring CLISP to its knees!

Here is a complete game, played on a puny 2-by-2 board:

At the beginning of the game, player A (indicated with black hexagons) possesses the top two hexagons, with three dice on each. Player B occupies the bottom row (indicated by the white hexagons), with three dice and one die, respectively. Player A attacks the lone die with one of his piles. After the attack, one of player A's dice remains behind, while the others move to the conquered spot. Then player A passes the turn.

Player B now attacks player A's two dice with a pile of three. Player B then passes. At this point, player B receives a single reinforcement die on her left hexagon. This is because she killed two of player A's dice. The reinforcements, as per the rules, consist of the number of dice killed, minus one.

Player A now attacks with three of his dice and passes. Also, he gets a reinforcement die.

Player B now has only one legal move, attacking two against one.

Player A now has the upper hand, killing all of player B's remaining dice. As you can see, player A is permitted to perform multiple attacks on his turn before passing. The game has ended with player A as the winner.

Implementing Dice of Doom, Version 1

Let's start coding this game in Lisp. As we discussed in the previous chapter, this game will contain both clean, functional code and dirty, imperative code. You'll be able to tell in which category a block of code fits by the "clean/functional" or "dirty/imperative" icon next to it.

Defining Some Global Variables

First, we'll create some global variables that define the basic parameters for our game:

```
❶ (defparameter *num-players* 2)
❷ (defparameter *max-dice* 3)
❸ (defparameter *board-size* 2)
❹ (defparameter *board-hexnum* (* *board-size* *board-size*))
```

We're stating that there will be two players ❶, that the maximum number of dice on a square is three ❷, and that the board will be 2-by-2 ❸. In later versions of Dice of Doom, we'll increase all of these parameters, to allow for a more challenging game.

Since it's useful to know the total number or hexagons there are at the current board size, we also define *board-hexnum* ❹. Note that even though the grid is made of hexagons, it is still basically a square grid, since the number of hexagons just equals the square of the side of the grid.

NOTE *In this chapter, every code sample has an associated icon to indicate whether it is made of dirty, imperative or clean, functional code. By the end of this chapter, you should be able to easily tell the difference and have some appreciation for the benefits of each style.*

Representing the Game Board

We're going to represent the game board using a simple list. The hexagons will be stored in this list, starting at the top left, and then moving across and down. For each hexagon, we'll store a list of two items: a number indicating the current occupant of the hexagon and another number indicating the number of dice at that location.

For instance, here is an example of a game board and the list that encodes it:

```
((0 3) (0 3) (1 3) (1 1))
```

Note that most Lisp programmers like to count starting at zero. Therefore, players A and B are represented with the numbers 0 and 1. This list indicates that player A has three dice on the first hexagon and three on the second. Player B has three dice on the third hexagon and one on the fourth.

When we create our AI player, it will need to be able to look at many hexagons on the board very quickly. Because of this, we're going to create a second representation of our board in the form of an array. Remember that checking a numeric location (for instance, hexagon 2) in a list requires the nth function, which is potentially slow. Arrays, on the other hand, will allow for very fast lookup at a specific location, even with very large board sizes.

The `board-array` function converts a board represented with a list to an array for us:

```
(defun board-array (lst)
  (make-array *board-hexnum* :initial-contents lst))
```

When the game begins, we'll start with a randomized board. Here's the function that creates a random board:

```
  (defun gen-board ()
❶   (board-array (loop for n below *board-hexnum*
❷                      collect (list (random *num-players*)
                                     (1+ (random *max-dice*))))))
```

This function is not in the functional style (as the icon indicates), since it will create a different, random result every time it is called. It generates the board as a list, but then converts the list to our speedier array format when it's done, using `board-array` ❶.

It generates random values using the Lisp function `random`. This function produces a different random integer every time, greater than or equal to zero, but smaller than the number passed to it. We use our `*num-players*` and `*max-dice*` global variables to generate random values for each hexagon ❷.

Let's try out the `gen-board` function:

```
> (gen-board)
#((0 3) (1 2) (1 3) (0 1))
```

Remember that the hash mark (#) indicates that we've created an array, not a list.

We'll name our players using letters (just A and B, until we start introducing more players). Here's a function that converts a player number into a letter:

```
(defun player-letter (n)
  (code-char (+ 97 n)))
```

The `code-char` function converts an ASCII code into the appropriate character. Let's call it for player 1 to see the result:

```
> (player-letter 1)
#\b
```

Finally, let's create a function that will take an encoded board and draw it in a pretty way on the screen. It will tilt the board in the same way as our drawings, so it's obvious which six hexagons neighbor any given hexagon.

```
    (defun draw-board (board)
❶    (loop for y below *board-size*
          do (progn (fresh-line)
❷                   (loop repeat (- *board-size* y)
                         do (princ " "))
❸                   (loop for x below *board-size*
❹                         for hex = (aref board (+ x (* *board-size* y)))
                          do (format t "~a-~a " (player-letter (first hex))
❺                                                (second hex))))))
```

Since the whole purpose of this draw-board function is to write stuff to the console, it's definitely not functional. Let's look at this function more closely.

The outer loop runs through all the rows of the board, stored in the variable y ❶. There are two inner loops. The first inner loop adds the indentation to the left side to give the board that tilted look ❷. The second inner loop loops through the columns, stored in the variable x ❸. It then uses x and y to calculate the appropriate hex number, and retrieves that hex from the board array using aref ❹. Finally, it prints the data in the hex ❺.

Here's the output of the draw-board function, as well as a drawing to compare it with:

```
> (draw-board #((0 3) (0 3) (1 3) (1 1)))
    a-3 a-3
   b-3 b-1
```

Decoupling Dice of Doom's Rules from the Rest of the Game

Now we're ready to write the code that takes care of the guts of our first Dice of Doom implementation. In writing this code, we're going to employ a powerful functional programming technique: a *function pipeline*. This means that our game is going to consist of a succession of functions that operate, one after another, on a big chunk of data, which will hold a representation of our game board, making modifications to the structure along the way. A function pipeline will allow us to build a game rule engine that's *100% decoupled from the rest of the game code*. To understand why this is so cool, let's first consider some of what's involved in writing a board game with a smart AI player.

For one thing, any computer implementation of a board game will need code that handles the human player's moves. This part of the code will need to know the rules of the board game and make sure the human player's move is legal before letting it happen.

We'll also need to write the AI code. And in order for the AI player to pick a move, it needs to know all the rules of the board game.

Notice something? Both of these separate parts of our game engine need to understand the rules of the game! Clearly, what we want to do is break our game code into three big pieces:

- The handling of the human's moves
- The AI player
- The rule engine

One piece handles the player's moves. Another is the code for the AI player. Both of these then talk to some code that understand the rules, sort of a "rule engine." Is this kind of design possible?

In a traditional, imperative programming style, it would be very difficult to write a program like this. Most imperative game engines duplicate the code that "understands the rules," because of the complexity of writing fully decoupled components in an imperative language. The reason for this is that a board game requires a lot of context—every move is dependent on what moves preceded it. This means that every time the AI module or player-handling module needs to check the rules, it must tell the "rule code" the current context in detail. Both would need to tell the rule code that "It's player so-and-so's turn and the game board looks like such-and-such." Without this information, the rule code can't tell whether or not a move is legal.

Passing around this context requires tons of tedious bookkeeping code everywhere, is error-prone, and is inefficient. It's inefficient because, with a naive design, the player-handling code may check the legality of moves the AI code had already explored and found legal.

Using functional programming, however, we can decouple these three concerns entirely in our program. We will be able to do this without book-keeping code and in a way that avoids duplication any legality calculations. We will accomplish this by encoding our rule code in a lazy game tree!

NOTE   *The basic approach we're using—programming a game in the functional style using a lazy game tree and a function pipeline—is described in the classic paper "Why Functional Programming Matters" by John Hughes* (http://www.scribd.com/doc/26902/whyfp/).

In this chapter, we'll be creating a game tree that is not yet lazy. You'll need to wait until Chapter 18 to understand lazy programming and what a lazy game tree will look like. That's also when you'll be able to fully appreciate how cool this architectural design really is.

Generating a Game Tree

The entire rule set for our game is encoded in the following master function:

```
❶ (defun game-tree (board player spare-dice first-move)
❷    (list player
           board
❸          (add-passing-move board
                             player
                             spare-dice
                             first-move
❹                           (attacking-moves board player spare-dice))))
```

The game-tree function builds a tree of all possible moves, given a certain starting configuration. This function will be called only a single time at the beginning of the game. It will then recursively build a tree of all possible moves for the game, down to the final winning positions. The other parts of our game will then elegantly traverse this tree in order to conform to the rules of the game.

In order to calculate the legal possible moves of the game tree from a given context, the function needs four pieces of data passed to it as arguments ❶:

- What the board looks like
- The current player

- How many dice have been captured by the player in the player's current turn, which is needed to calculate any future reinforcements, as per our rules
- Whether the current move is the first move for the current player, because a player can't pass a turn without first making at least one move

As the game-tree function creates the tree, it will put information about the current board and current player at every branch ❷. The subbranches will then hold all the legal follow-up moves from the current branch:

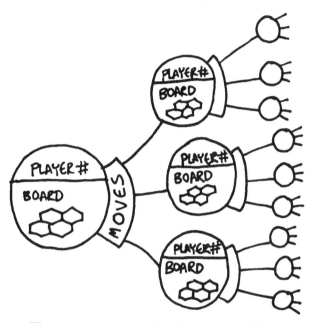

There are two types of legal moves possible for players: attack a hexagon or pass their turn to the next player (assuming they've already attacked at least once already). The passing move is added to the list of legal moves through the add-passing-move function ❸. The attacking moves are added to the list through the attacking-moves function ❹. Let's look at these functions next.

Calculating Passing Moves

Here is the function that adds the passing moves to the game tree:

```
❶ (defun add-passing-move (board player spare-dice first-move moves)
❷   (if first-move
❸       moves
❹       (cons (list nil
❺                   (game-tree (add-new-dice board player (1- spare-dice))
❻                              (mod (1+ player) *num-players*)
                               0
                               t))
             moves)))
```

The job of this function is to add a passing move to the tally of moves, if passing is permitted. The current list of moves is passed in to this function ❶, and then the function will return the expanded list of moves. If the move is the first move in a player's turn ❷, no passing is allowed, and we just return the unaltered list ❸. Otherwise, we add a new move to the list.

Every move in our game tree consists of two parts:

- The first part is a description of the move. Since we're just passing in this move, we'll set the description to nil ❹.

- The second part of the move is an entirely new game tree, which holds the entire universe of moves that exists after this move has been performed. We create this by recursively calling game-tree again ❺. Since this is the end of the player's turn, the player may receive dice as reinforcements. So, we update the board sent to this new game-tree call with the add-new-dice function ❺.

Of course, we also will need to change the current player, since a new person's turn is now starting. We do this by adding one to the current player number and taking the modulus of the result, with the total number of players as the denominator ❻. Changing a player in this fancy way will allow the code to work, even when we increase the number of players in the game in future versions.

Calculating Attacking Moves

Here is the function that adds the possible attacking moves to the game tree:

```
    (defun attacking-moves (board cur-player spare-dice)
❶   (labels ((player (pos)
                (car (aref board pos)))
❷            (dice (pos)
                (cadr (aref board pos))))
❸      (mapcan (lambda (src)
❹              (when (eq (player src) cur-player)
❺                (mapcan (lambda (dst)
                          (when (and (not (eq (player dst) cur-player))
❻                                    (> (dice src) (dice dst)))
                            (list
❼      (list (list src dst)
❽            (game-tree (board-attack board cur-player src dst (dice src))
                        cur-player
                        (+ spare-dice (dice dst))
                        nil)))))
❾                        (neighbors src))))
              (loop for n below *board-hexnum*
                    collect n))))
```

The attacking-moves function is a bit more complicated than the add-passing-move function. It's responsible for scanning the current game board and figuring out what moves the current player is legally allowed to perform.

Since it must spend a lot of time figuring out who the player is on a given hexagon, we first write a convenience function called player that returns the player for a given board position ❶. We write a similar function to get the number of dice on a given hexagon ❷.

Next, we need to scan the board top to bottom and find out which squares the current player occupies. For each occupied square, there may be one or more legal attacks starting at that position. Since the number of attacks from any hexagon may vary, we use mapcan to scan the board ❸. Remember that mapcan lets each hexagon we scan return its results as a list. Then mapcan concatenates these lists together. This way, any scanned hexagon can contribute zero to *n* moves to the list.

Within the lambda function used by the mapcan, which gets called for every hexagon, we first want to check whether the current player occupies this hexagon ❹. Then we want to check all of its neighbors to see if any of them present a viable attack. We do this with another mapcan ❺. We'll figure out the neighbors to this hexagon by using the neighbors function, which we'll write shortly ❾.

How do we decide if a hexagon can be an attack destination? Well, it must be a hexagon we don't already own, plus (as per the rules) the source hexagon needs to have more dice than the destination hexagon ❻. If we have found a legal attack move, we then describe the move ❼. The description is simply a list of the source position and the destination position. We then (as with passing moves) recursively generate another game tree that describes what happens if the move is executed ❽.

Finding the Neighbors

Next, let's create the function that calculates the neighboring hexagons to a given hexagon:

```
    (defun neighbors (pos)
      (let ((up (- pos *board-size*))
            (down (+ pos *board-size*)))
❶      (loop for p in (append (list up down)
❷                             (unless (zerop (mod pos *board-size*))
                                (list (1- up) (1- pos)))
❸                             (unless (zerop (mod (1+ pos) *board-size*))
                                (list (1+ pos) (1+ down))))
❹                when (and (>= p 0) (< p *board-hexnum*))
                  collect p)))
```

Every hexagon on the board may have up to six neighbors, or fewer, if the hexagon is on an edge of the board. We build up a list of possible neighbors in a loop ❶, and then collect the ones with position numbers that aren't off the edge of the board ❹. Also, since our position numbers wrap from row to row, we need to make sure we don't look to the left if we're on the left edge of the board ❷ or look to the right if we're on the right edge of the board ❸.

This function is marked clean (it is in the functional style), but nonetheless contains a loop. Usually, looping goes against the tenets of functional programming. However, many Lispers consider it kosher to use a loop in functional code if all it does is collect some values, since it really isn't mutating any values or producing any other side effects. So, we will allow ourselves to use such loops in the functional-style part of this game.

Let's try out our neighbors function:

```
> (neighbors 2)
(0 3)
```

2×2 BOARD

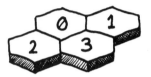

As you can see, it correctly tells us that hexagon 2 neighbors hexagons 0 and 3.

Attacking

Now let's write our board-attack function:

```
  (defun board-attack (board player src dst dice)
❶   (board-array (loop for pos
❷                      for hex across board
❸                      collect (cond ((eq pos src) (list player 1))
❹                                    ((eq pos dst) (list player (1- dice)))
❺                                    (t hex)))))
```

This is a function that figures out what happens if the hexagon src attacks the hexagon dst. It works by looping across the board, keeping track of the current position ❶ and the contents in the hexagon at that position ❷. If the current hexagon is the source hexagon, we just place a single die in that place; as per our rules, a single die is left behind after an attack ❸. If the current hexagon is the destination position, we place the remaining dice there, subtracting the one left behind ❹. In other cases, we just collect the very same hex ❺.

Let's try out our board-attack function:

```
> (board-attack #((0 3) (0 3) (1 3) (1 1)) 0 1 3 3)
#((0 3) (0 1) (1 3) (0 2))
```

As you can see, attacking from hexagon 1 to 3 causes board-attack to properly update the game board, so that one die remains on the old square and two are on the new, conquered square.

NOTE   *Many of the functions in this chapter have inefficiencies to keep things simple. We'll fix many of these in future versions of the game.*

Reinforcements

To add the reinforcements to the board, we need to scan across the game board, find occupied spots that can accommodate another die, and add the die there. Of course, the number of reinforcements is limited based on how many opponent dice the player captured in the last turn. Because of this, we'll need to keep a running tally of how many reinforcement dice remain.

The most obvious way to track the remaining dice would be to have a remaining-dice variable, and decrement this every time a die is placed. However, having a die that is decremented (mutated) would not be in line with the functional style.

Therefore, instead, we're going to write our add-new-dice function using a local recursive function, which will also maintain this running count of dice. Here is this add-new-dice function:

```
    (defun add-new-dice (board player spare-dice)
❶     (labels ((f (lst n)
❷               (cond ((null lst) nil)
❸                     ((zerop n) lst)
                      (t (let ((cur-player (caar lst))
                               (cur-dice (cadar lst)))
❹                          (if (and (eq cur-player player) (< cur-dice *max-dice*))
                               (cons (list cur-player (1+ cur-dice))
❺                                    (f (cdr lst) (1- n)))
❻                              (cons (car lst) (f (cdr lst) n)))))))))
❼       (board-array (f (coerce board 'list) spare-dice))))
```

The first thing add-new-dice does is define a local function named f ❶. This function will be our list-eater that goes through the hexagons of the board and spits out a new list that includes the reinforcements. Since our board is actually stored in an array for efficiency reasons, we convert our array into a list with the coerce function before calling f ❼.

Inside the function f, we must consider three situations:

- That we're at the end of the board. In this case, the reinforced board will also be completed, so we just return nil ❷.

- That we're out of spare-dice to add to add as reinforcements. In this case, the rest of the board will just be the same as before, so we can just return the remainder of the list as the new board ❸.

- Neither of the preceding situations. In all other cases, we need to analyze the current hexagon and decide whether a reinforcement should be added in it. We check whether the current player occupies that hexagon and whether we have less than the maximum number of dice on that square ❹. If this is the case, we add a new die on the hexagon and call f against the rest of the board, recursively ❺. Otherwise, we leave the current hexagon unchanged and proceed by recursively calling f against the rest of the board ❻.

Let try adding reinforcements to a board:

```
> (add-new-dice #((0 1) (1 3) (0 2) (1 1)) 0 2)
#((0 2) (1 3) (0 3) (1 1))
```

As you can see, add-new-dice properly placed two reinforcement dice for player A (player 0).

Trying Out Our New game-tree Function

We have now written all the code needed to create a comprehensive game tree of our simplified version of Dice of Doom. But be careful! A game tree of most board games is excruciatingly large. Even on a 2-by-2 board, our game may consist of hundreds of possible moves. You'll want to call the game-tree function only on a game board that is near the end of play, or you'll be watching helplessly as the CLISP REPL prints out a humongous tree showing all the possible ways in which a game may progress.

Here is a safe board position for you to try out:

```
> (game-tree #((0 1) (1 1) (0 2) (1 1)) 0 0 t)
❶ (0
❷  #((0 1)(1 1) (0 2) (1 1))
❸  (((2 3)(0
           #((0 1) (1 1) (0 1) (0 1))
❹          ((NIL(1
                 #((0 1) (1 1) (0 1) (0 1))
                 NIL)))))))
```

The game tree first lists the current player number ❶, the layout of the board ❷, and then the legal moves for that context. For the initial board position, at the beginning of player A's turn, there is only one possible move: The player can move from hexagon 2 to hexagon 3, capturing player B's die in that spot ❸. After that, the player can pass. Player B now has no move available. Since this player's game tree has no available moves listed ❹, the game has ended, with a win for player A.

Playing Dice of Doom Against Another Human

Now that we've completely captured the universe of Dice of Doom in our comprehensive game-tree function, it's simple to create a human versus human version of this game. All we need to do is create some functions that travel down the game tree as players choose their moves.

The Main Loop

Here is the function that travels down the game tree, allowing two humans to play Dice of Doom:

```
    (defun play-vs-human (tree)
❶     (print-info tree)
❷     (if (caddr tree)
❸         (play-vs-human (handle-human tree))
❹       (announce-winner (cadr tree))))
```

This function, play-vs-human, is the main loop of our game. It accepts a tree describing the starting position of the board.

First, it calls a function named print-info, which will draw the board on the screen, along with other helpful information about the current state of the game ❶. Next, we need to check if any follow-up moves exist. These follow-up moves would be listed starting at the caddr position of the game tree ❷.

If follow-up moves are available, we call the function handle-human, which will interact with the current player to help him pick his new move. This handle-human function will then return the subbranch of the tree that represents the player's choice. We can then recursively pass this subbranch into play-vs-human to proceed with the game ❸.

If no follow-up moves are available, the game has officially ended. We then call the announce-winner function, which, appropriately, will announce the winner ❹.

Giving Information About the State of the Game

Here is the print-info function, which describes the status of the current node in the game tree:

```
    (defun print-info (tree)
      (fresh-line)
❶     (format t "current player = ~a" (player-letter (car tree)))
❷     (draw-board (cadr tree)))
```

This function displays two important pieces of information on the REPL. First, it shows who the current player is ❶. Then it prints out a pretty version of the game board with the draw-board function ❷.

Handling Input from Human Players

Next is the function that lets humans choose their next move. It displays a very helpful, numbered menu of all currently available moves for the player to choose from.

```
    (defun handle-human (tree)
      (fresh-line)
      (princ "choose your move:")
      (let ((moves (caddr tree)))
❶      (loop for move in moves
❷            for n from 1
              do (let ((action (car move)))
                   (fresh-line)
❸                  (format t "~a. " n)
❹                  (if action
❺                      (format t "~a -> ~a" (car action) (cadr action))
❻                      (princ "end turn"))))
        (fresh-line)
❼      (cadr (nth (1- (read)) moves)))))
```

To display the list of available moves, we use a loop that traverses all the available moves and prints a description about each one ❶. This loop is not functional, since it prints stuff on the screen for the player to read. We print a counting number in front of each move ❸ using the variable n, which counts from 1 inside our loop ❷.

Each move has an action value associated with it. If the action is non-nil ❹, then the action is an attack, where the action value describes the source and destination hexagons of the attack. We print such attacking action using the format command ❺.

We use an empty action value to represent the passing move. In that case, we just princ "end turn" to describe this move ❻.

After the available moves have been displayed, we use read to read in the player's choice. With the nth function, we can then select that branch of the game tree and return it from our handle-human function ❼.

Determining the Winner

The task of announcing the winner can be nicely broken into a *clean/functional* and a *dirty/imperative* part.

The clean part concerns the task of calculating the winning player. We want to calculate this in a way that can handle more than just two players, since our game will allow for more in the future. Also, the function must be cognizant of possible ties.

To accomplish this, we'll write a function called winners that returns a list of one or more players who captured the maximum number of hexagons at the end of the game. If there is a tie, it will simply return all the players who share first place, in terms of the total count of occupied spaces for all players. With this design, the function will work for *any number of players* and will elegantly handle ties. This is what the winners function looks like:

```
  (defun winners (board)
❶   (let* ((tally (loop for hex across board
                        collect (car hex)))
           (totals (mapcar (lambda (player)
❷                            (cons player (count player tally)))
❸                          (remove-duplicates tally)))
❹           (best (apply #'max (mapcar #'cdr totals))))
❺      (mapcar #'car
❻          (remove-if (lambda (x)
                         (not (eq (cdr x) best)))
                       totals))))
```

We calculate the winner for a given ending board position in four steps.

- First, we build up a tally of who occupies each hexagon on the board ❶. With the across loop construct, we can traverse the array of the ending board directly and collect the occupier of each hexagon.

- Second, we need to count the total number of squares each player has captured, using this tally. The totals variable will be an alist of player->spaces pairs. We build this alist by finding all players who have at least one entry in the tally with remove-duplicates ❸. We can map across this and then create a count for each occupier ❷.

- Third, we want to find what the maximum number of occupied hexagons for a single player is. We do this by stripping the counts from our alist by mapping cdr across the list ❹. We then apply max to this list to find the largest number of occupied spaces for a single player.

- Finally, we need create a list of all the "best" players. We do this by stripping out all but the best from our totals using the remove-if function ❻. We then just pull out the player numbers for the best players by mapping car across the list of bests ❺.

Next, let's write the dirty announce-winner function:

```
  (defun announce-winner (board)
    (fresh-line)
❶   (let ((w (winners board)))
❷     (if (> (length w) 1)
❸       (format t "The game is a tie between ~a" (mapcar #'player-letter w))
❹       (format t "The winner is ~a" (player-letter (car w))))))
```

This function is rather simple. First, we calculate the winners by calling our earlier function ❶. Then we check if there is more than one winner ❷ (a tie). For ties, we print a special message ❸. Otherwise, we just announce a single winner ❹.

Trying Out the Human vs. Human Version of Dice of Doom

We now have a completely playable game of dice of doom. Here is an example game from start to finish:

```
> (play-vs-human (game-tree (gen-board) 0 0 t))
current player = a
    b-2 b-2
  a-2 b-1
choose your move:
1. 2 -> 3
1
current player = a
    b-2 b-2
  a-1 a-1
choose your move:
1. end turn
1
current player = b
    b-2 b-2
  a-1 a-1
choose your move:
1. 0 -> 2
2. 0 -> 3
3. 1 -> 3
1
current player = b
    b-1 b-2
  b-1 a-1
choose your move:
1. end turn
2. 1 -> 3
1
current player = a
    b-1 b-2
  b-1 a-1
The winner is b
```

Creating an Intelligent Computer Opponent

As we discussed when we were designing the game tree code for Dice of Doom, having a separate game tree generator makes it easy to add an AI player to a game engine. In fact, we're now going to add a computer player that can play an absolutely perfect game with only 23 additional lines of code!

So how does an AI player decide to make a move? We'll use the following strategy:

1. Look at each available move.
2. Give a point rating to the board position resulting from each move.
3. Pick the move with the maximum point rating.

This sounds like a simple plan, but there is one step in this algorithm that's pretty tricky: calculating the best point rating for a given board position.

If a move leads immediately to a win, it's easy to give a point rating to that move—any winning move clearly deserves a very high point rating. However, most moves in a game cannot lead to an immediate win. In those cases, in order to determine if the result of a set of moves deserves a good point rating, we need to figure out what the opponent player will do in response.

But how will we know what the opponent player will decide to do? If we're not careful, we'll end up in an ugly impasse where we say, "He thinks that I think that he thinks that I think . . ." in order to calculate a meaningful point value for a given board position. How do we account for the opponent's behavior without giving ourselves a headache?

The Minimax Algorithm

It turns out that for a two-player board game, a simple method exists to model what an opponent will do. We simply accept the truism "What is good for my opponent is bad for me." This means we can use the following approach to model a move for the opponent:

1. Look at each available move.
2. Give a point rating to the board position resulting from each move.
3. Pick the move with the minimum point rating.

This algorithm for estimating what an opponent will do is identical to the one used for the primary player, except that in step 3, we pick the move with the *minimum* instead of *maximum* rating. The benefit of this approach, called the *minimax algorithm*, is that we use the same point ratings when working out the opponent's moves that we use for the primary AI player, but then just tweak the third step a little to adjust.

This is crucial: It turns out that if we can avoid calculating separate ratings for ourselves as for our opponent in the game, then searching down the game tree for good moves becomes dramatically easier and faster.

NOTE *The basic minimax algorithm works only in two-player games. When three or more players are involved in a game, we can't really say that "What is good for my opponent is bad for me" is completely true any more. This is because an additional truism becomes important: "The enemy of my enemy is my friend." This means that some of my opponents may, at times, act as a friend by making moves that harm a common enemy, while not affecting me directly. We'll discuss this issue more in Chapter 20.*

Turning Minimax into Actual Code

Now we're ready to put the minimax idea into practice, like so:

```
  (defun rate-position (tree player)
    (let ((moves (caddr tree)))
❶    (if moves
        (apply (if (eq (car tree) player)
❷                #'max
❸                #'min)
❹             (get-ratings tree player))
❺      (let ((w (winners (cadr tree))))
          (if (member player w)
❻            (/ 1 (length w))
❼            0)))))
```

The rate-position function generates a numeric point rating for a given branch of the game tree. In order to do this, we first need to figure out if there are any moves available from the given position ❶ (that is, the current move is not an ending move in the game).

If moves are available, we'll need to look at all the subsequent moves to decide how to rate the current position. We accomplish this by calling get-ratings ❹, a function that will return the point rating of each follow-up move. As per minimax, we will then pick either the best (max) ❷ or worst (min) ❸ rating of all the follow-up moves, depending on whether the move being rated is for the AI player or its opponent.

If, on the other hand, there are no follow-up moves, we'll need to check who the winner is for the current board position ❺. If the player isn't among the winners of this position, we can give the position the minimum rating of 0 ❼. Otherwise, we'll divide one by the number of winners to determine our rating ❻. By doing this, we also give a meaningful rating for ties. If the player is the sole winner, the rating, using this formula, will be the maximum value of 1. For a two-player tie, the rating will be a sensible 0.5.

Here is what the get-ratings function looks like:

```
(defun get-ratings (tree player)
  (mapcar (lambda (move)
            (rate-position (cadr move) player))
          (caddr tree)))
```

This function simply maps rate-position across each available follow-up move for the given branch of the tree.

Creating a Game Loop with an AI Player

Earlier, we wrote a function called handle-human that interacted with a human to decide on a move in the game. Here is an analogous function, handle-computer, that interacts with our AI player to choose a move:

```
(defun handle-computer (tree)
❶  (let ((ratings (get-ratings tree (car tree))))
❷    (cadr (nth (position (apply #'max ratings) ratings) (caddr tree)))))
```

This handle-computer function is quite straightforward. First, we get the ratings of each available move ❶. Then we pick the move that is rated the highest ❷.

Finally, let's create a function that handles the main loop for playing against the computer. This one is analogous to our earlier play-vs-human function:

```
(defun play-vs-computer (tree)
❶  (print-info tree)
❷  (cond ((null (caddr tree)) (announce-winner (cadr tree)))
❸        ((zerop (car tree)) (play-vs-computer (handle-human tree)))
❹        (t (play-vs-computer (handle-computer tree)))))
```

As with the play-vs-human function, play-vs-computer first prints out information about the current state of the game ❶. If no more moves are available, it then calls the announce-winner function ❷.

Next, we need to check who the current player is. By convention, we'll have the human be player A (player 0). If the player number is 0, we call our old handle-human function to let the human decide on her move ❸. Otherwise, we treat the player as an AI player and use the handle-computer function to decide on a move ❹.

We have now written a fully functional AI engine for Dice of Doom!

Playing Our First Human vs. Computer Game

The following is an example game playing against the computer AI. The computer plays an optimal game and wins.

```
> (play-vs-computer (game-tree (gen-board) 0 0 t))
current player = a
    a-3 b-3
  a-2 b-2
choose your move:
1. 0 -> 3
1
current player = a
    a-1 b-3
  a-2 a-2
choose your move:
1. end turn
1
current player = b
    a-2 b-3
  a-2 a-2
current player = b
    b-2 b-1
  a-2 a-2
current player = a
    b-3 b-1
  a-2 a-2
choose your move:
1. 3 -> 1
1
current player = a
    b-3 a-1
  a-2 a-1
choose your move:
1. end turn
1
current player = b
    b-3 a-1
  a-2 a-1
current player = b
    b-1 a-1
  b-2 a-1
```

```
current player = b
    b-1 a-1
  b-1 b-1
current player = a
    b-2 a-1
  b-2 b-1
The winner is b
```

Making Dice of Doom Faster

The functional programming style can lead to slow code, at least in the hands of a novice programmer. We used the functional style to develop the core of Dice of Doom. Hence, this first version of our game is excruciatingly inefficient. We had to limit our game to a 2-by-2 board to make it playable. But now we can increase our board size to 3-by-3, as we optimize our game engine.

Let's increase the parameters controlling the board size to make this happen. You may not want to play a game at this new size until you've implemented all the optimizations throughout the rest of this chapter, unless you are an extremely patient person and don't mind having the computer take minutes building the initial game tree and deciding on moves.

```
(defparameter *board-size* 3)
(defparameter *board-hexnum* (* *board-size* *board-size*))
```

There, we've upgraded the board size to 3 by 3.

The rest of this chapter covers some important techniques for optimizing functional code. These techniques apply to all programs written in the functional style, which includes Dice of Doom. In later chapters, we'll add other optimizations. Eventually, we'll be able to play against an AI player on much more spacious boards, while still having elegant code written in the functional style.

Closures

Before we start optimizing Dice of Doom, there is an important Lisp programming concept we need to discuss: *closures*. Closures are extra bits of data from the outside world that are captured whenever a lambda function is created. To understand the hows and whys of capturing variables in a closure, consider the following example:

```
> (defparameter *foo* (lambda ()
❶                         5))
*FOO*
❷ > (funcall *FOO*)
5
```

In this example, we're creating a new, unnamed function ❶, and then setting *foo* equal to this function. Next, we call this function using the funcall command ❷. As you would expect, the value returned from this function is 5. All the lambda function does is return this number.

Next, consider this more interesting example:

```
❶ > (defparameter *foo* (let ((x 5))
                          (lambda ()
❷                          x)))
   *FOO*
```

This version of foo is exactly the same as the previous version of *foo*, except that we first declare a local variable x ❶, which is set to 5. Then, in the body of the lambda, we return x ❷. So, what do you think will happen if we call this new version of *foo*?

The reason this is a tough question is that x is declared as a "local" variable. However; x (apparently) no longer exists once we call *foo*, since we're already long past the point where we're evaluating the body of the let expression.

Let's try it out and see what happens:

```
> (funcall *foo*)
5
```

Holy cow! Somehow the lambda expression we created remembered what x was at the time it was created. The variable x, which we previously thought of as a local variable, has somehow managed to live on past the block in which it was created!

When we first covered let expressions in Chapter 2, you learned that advanced Lispers prefer to call variables created with a let expression *lexical variables*. Now you can see why: A variable created in this way does not need to be local, if it is captured in a closure, by using the variable in a lambda expression.

To understand how closures work, remember that Lisp uses garbage collection. In fact, it was the first language to have this feature. Garbage collection means that you never have to "free" variables (as you do in C programming). The Lisp compiler/interpreter is smart enough to know when variables are no longer in use and destroys them automatically.

Garbage collection will happen at some arbitrary future time after you've exited a let expression. Periodically, Lisp will search its memory for items that are no longer referenced anywhere and can therefore be safely destroyed. If Lisp notices that a variable defined in a let is no longer used by anything, it will destroy that variable.

However, if you create a lambda expression within the let expression (as we did in the previously), it's possible for those variables to live on, being referenced from within the lambda expression. In that case, the garbage collector will leave those variables alone. Basically, you've created variables that are permanent—at least as long as the lambda expression doesn't fall out of use and get garbage collected.

You can do a lot of cool things using closures. They're often used for caching small pieces of information between uses of a function. For instance, here a function that remembers what line number is currently being printed:

```
❶ > (let ((line-number 0))
❷     (defun my-print (x)
❸       (print line-number)
         (print x)
❹       (incf line-number)
             nil))
  MY-PRINT
  > (my-print "this")
  0
  "this"
  nil
  > (my-print "is")
  1
  "is"
  nil
  > (my-print "a")
  2
  "a"
  nil
  > (my-print "test")
  3
  "test"
  nil
```

In order to keep track of the line number, we first create a lexical variable named line-number ❶. Next, we declare our my-print function using defun ❷, in the body of the let. This command will create a lambda function behind the scenes, therefore letting us also generate a closure.

Within the body of the my-print function, we can then print the line-number ❸, and even mutate it using incf ❹. (incf just adds one to a variable.) Because the line-number variable is captured in the closure, it can "live on" between calls to my-print, allowing us to count line numbers.

Memoization

The first optimization we're going to perform is called *memoization*. This technique makes use of closures. Memoization works only for functions written in the functional style. As you know, the behavior of a function in the functional style depends only on the arguments passed into it. Also, the only action of a function in the functional style is to calculate a value to return to the caller.

This suggests an obvious optimization: What if we remember the arguments and result of each call of this function? Then, if the function ever gets called again with the same arguments, we won't need to recalculate the result. Instead, we can simply return the precalculated result.

Several functions in Dice of Doom can benefit from memoization.

Memoizing the neighbors Function

Let's start with the `neighbors` function, which lets us know which hexagons on the board can be attacked from a given location:

```
> (neighbors 0)
(3 1 4)
```

What `neighbors` is telling us is that if we want to attack other hexagons on the board from hexagon 0, we can reach only hexagon 3, 1, or 4 (based on our new 3-by-3 board size).

As you may remember, the `neighbors` function needed to do all kinds of ugly checking for the edges of the board, since hexagons along the edges are limited in the hexagons they can attack. However, since the shape of the board never changes mid-game, these numbers never change for a given board position. This makes `neighbors` a perfect candidate for memoization! Here is the code that accomplishes this:

```
❶ (let ((old-neighbors (symbol-function 'neighbors))
❷       (previous (make-hash-table)))
❸   (defun neighbors (pos)
❹     (or (gethash pos previous)
❺         (setf (gethash pos previous) (funcall old-neighbors pos)))))
```

Let's dissect this code to make sense of what's happening. First, we save the old version of the `neighbors` function in a local variable named old-neighbors ❶. The `symbol-function` command simply retrieves the function bound to a symbol. Using `symbol-function` here allows us to retain access to the old value of `neighbors`, even if we define a new function with the same name, as we'll do shortly.

Next, we define a local variable previous ❷, which will hold all previous arguments and results the function has ever seen. This can be represented as a hash table, where the arguments are the hash key and the results are the values.

Now we define a new `neighbors` function that will override the old definition of `neighbors` ❸. This new definition will add memoization to the old version of the function. Then we look up the argument pos in the hash table and return it, if available ❹. Otherwise, we call the old definition of the function (that's why we needed to create the old-neighbors lexical variable) and add this new argument/result pair to the hash table ❺. Since `setf` returns the value being set, this command will also cause this newly calculated result to be returned to the caller of `neighbors`.

NOTE   *Be careful not to declare the memoized version of the* neighbors *function more than once, without also redeclaring the original version of the function. Otherwise, the* neighbors *function will be wrapped in multiple unsightly layers of memoization, since there are no checks if the memoization has already been done.*

Memoizing the Game Tree

The biggest payoff by far for memoization in our program will be in the game-tree function. This makes sense, if you think about how a board game works. Very often, you can get the same board positions in a board game by performing the same moves in a slightly different order. In our naive version of the game-tree function, every different move sequence leads to a completely different branch in the game tree that we need to build in a totally repetitive and inefficient way.

In the memoized version of the game-tree code, the function can say to itself, "Hey, I've seen that board position before!" and can then share branches of the game tree. Here is a memoized version of game-tree that does this:

❶
```
(let ((old-game-tree (symbol-function 'game-tree))
      (previous (make-hash-table :test #'equalp)))
  (defun game-tree (&rest rest)
    (or (gethash rest previous)
        (setf (gethash rest previous) (apply old-game-tree rest)))))
```

As you can see, this memoization is virtually identical to the one we used for the neighbors function. The only difference is that we're setting the hash table to use equalp instead of eql (the default) for the test on the key ❶.

This is because the key (that is, the arguments to game-tree) contains the game board, in the form of an array. If we change the test function to be equalp, then Lisp will check every hexagon on the board and make sure it matches before using a previous calculation.

Memoizing the rate-position Function

Another function that will benefit greatly from memoization is the rate-position function. Here it is, memoized:

❶
❷
❸
❹
❺
```
(let ((old-rate-position (symbol-function 'rate-position))
      (previous (make-hash-table)))
  (defun rate-position (tree player)
    (let ((tab (gethash player previous)))
      (unless tab
        (setf tab (setf (gethash player previous) (make-hash-table))))
      (or (gethash tree tab)
          (setf (gethash tree tab)
                (funcall old-rate-position tree player))))))
```

We need to do something a bit special for the memoization on this function to work correctly, because of the tree argument passed into rate-position. The game tree is potentially huge, so we need to make sure we never compare a game tree object with equal (or a similar comparison function that is slow with large lists). Instead, we want to compare it with eql. Because of this, we handle the memoization of each of the two parameters to rate-position (tree and player) separately. We accomplish this by having nested hash tables.

First, we create an outer hash table with the default eql test ❶. Then, we define a tab variable that looks up one of our variables (player) in the outer hash table ❷, to retrieve an inner hash table. If tab is not found in the outer hash table ❸, we'll create a new, empty inner hash table, storing it in the outer hash table with the same key ❹. The rest of the function is similar to our previous examples, except that we're now using our inner hash table, with the tree argument as a key ❺.

This memoization will bring us a step closer to having larger, and more fun, boards for Dice of Doom.

NOTE   *You use memoization for optimizing the performance of code written in the functional style. However, memoization code is not, in itself, written in the functional style. It cannot be, since it requires you to maintain and update a table of previous calls to the target function.*

Tail Call Optimization

The next technique we're going to use to optimize our functional program is called *tail call optimization*. To understand this concept, let's study a simple function that calculates the length of a list:

```
> (defun my-length (lst)
❶    (if lst
❷       (1+ (my-length (cdr lst)))
❸       0))
MY-LENGTH
> (my-length '(fie foh fum))
3
```

The my-length function should be pretty easy for you to understand at this point. First, it checks if the list is empty ❶. If not, it recursively calls itself against the tail of the list and adds one to the total, using the 1+ function ❷. If the list is empty, the function just returns 0 ❸.

It turns out that this function is actually quite inefficient. We can easily see this by trying to use it against a really big list:

```
> (defparameter *biglist* (loop for i below 100000 collect 'x))
*BIGLIST*
> (my-length *biglist*)

*** - Program stack overflow. RESET
```

Calling this function in CLISP actually causes the program to crash! (Other Common Lisp compilers/interpreters may do better, depending on whether the compiler writers use any special tricks to anticipate this common pitfall in Lisp code.)

This happens because of the 1+ function. It tells Lisp, "*First*, figure out the length of the shorter list, *then* call 1+ on the result."

The problem is that each time we call my-length recursively, Lisp must remember that we need to add one to the result later on, once the length of the tail of the list has been figured out. Since the list is 100,000 items long, it must remember this 99,999 times before it can perform a single addition! The CLISP interpreter places a reminder for all of these additions on the program stack, which eventually overflows, crashing the program.

So how do we avoid this problem? We do it by rewriting our my-length function like so:

```
> (defun my-length (lst)
❶     (labels ((f (lst acc)
❷                (if lst
❸                    (f (cdr lst) (1+ acc))
❹                    acc)))
❺       (f lst 0)))
MY-LENGTH
> (my-length '(fie foh fum))
3
```

Here, we define a local function f ❶ that will act as our list-eater. This function takes an extra parameter, often called an *accumulator*, here shortened to acc ❶. This acc argument keeps a running count of how many items in the list we have previously encountered. When we initially call the function f, we set acc to 0 ❺.

By making this accumulator available, it means that when f calls itself recursively ❸, it now longer needs to add one to the result. Instead, it just adds one to the accumulator. Once we reach the end of the list (lst is nil ❷), then acc will equal the total number of items in the list, so we can just return it ❹.

What is important here is that *the very last thing* the function f does, in the case where more items are on the list, is call itself recursively ❸. (The additional line in the if statement ❹ doesn't count, since that part won't be called if the expression evaluates to true.) When a function in Lisp calls itself (or another function) as its very last action, we call this action a *tail call*. A smart Lisp compiler, when seeing a tail call, can then say to itself, "Hey, since I don't need to do anything more after calling f again, I can just go straight to f, without needing to put the current program context on the stack."

This is actually similar to performing a GOTO in BASIC or a longjmp in C++. In all of these cases, we just "forget" where we came from, which is very fast and doesn't thrash the stack. However, in the case of a tail call in Lisp, it is also perfectly safe. Anyone who has used GOTO or longjmp knows they're anything but safe!

Notice that there are two different definitions for lst that exist in the preceding example code. One is an argument to the my-length function, and the other is an argument to the function f ❶. The values of these two lst arguments will deviate as the program runs and f is called recursively. However, within the function f, the version in its own argument list will take precedence. This process of hiding one variable with another through precedence is called *variable shadowing.*

NOTE *I used variable shadowing in the my-length function so it would be impossible for me to accidentally use the "wrong list" when writing the code inside of function f. Other programmers dislike this technique, since having similarly named variables with different values can lead to confusion. You'll need to decide which of these arguments is most convincing to you and whether you'll use variable shadowing in your own code.*

Support for Tail Calls in Common Lisp

Unfortunately, you can't be 100 percent sure in Common Lisp that a compiler/interpreter will perform tail call optimizations. It is not required by the ANSI Common Lisp standard. (The situation is actually different in the Scheme dialect, since Scheme has a strict requirement for tail call optimization.)

However, most Common Lisp compilers support this feature, although CLISP requires some extra cajoling to make tail call optimization work for some functions, including our example function. The reason for this is that tail calls can actually lead to performance problems themselves, in some esoteric cases. Also, when we debug a program, it's nice to be able to look at the full call stack; tail call optimizations will prevent this, since, by their nature, they will minimize the information available on the stack.

Here's the extra step we need to take to get CLISP to tail call optimize the my-length function:

```
(compile 'my-length)
```

Calling this function will tell CLISP to run the my-length function through its full compiler, which includes a tail code optimization step. Now we can run my-length against our jumbo-sized list!

```
> (my-length *biglist*)
100000
```

Tail Call Optimization in Dice of Doom

One function in our game that could definitely benefit from tail call optimization is the add-new-dice function. Here's the fully optimized version:

```
(defun add-new-dice (board player spare-dice)
❶   (labels ((f (lst n acc)
               (cond ((zerop n) (append (reverse acc) lst))
❷                    ((null lst) (reverse acc))
                     (t (let ((cur-player (caar lst))
                              (cur-dice (cadar lst)))
```

```
                         (if (and (eq cur-player player)
                                  (< cur-dice *max-dice*))
                             (f (cdr lst)
                                (1- n)
                                (cons (list cur-player (1+ cur-dice)) acc))
                             (f (cdr lst) n (cons (car lst) acc)))))))))
        (board-array (f (coerce board 'list) spare-dice ())))))
```

As before, we're performing the list-eating in a function called f ❶, which also has an accumulator. However, this time the acc variable will contain a *list* of newly updated hexagons with extra dice. We can now call f in tail call positions in two places ❸❹, where we cons new hexagons to the acc variable.

Once we've processed the whole list of hexagons on the board, we can just return acc. However, since we've consed stuff to acc as we went along the list, acc will actually be reversed. Therefore, we need to perform an extra call to reverse at the very end ❷.

We have now explored some basic techniques for optimizing computer programs written in the functional style.

A Sample Game on the 3-by-3 Board

Now let's enjoy the fruits of our labor. The following is a full game against the AI player on a 3-by-3 board. As you can see, on an evenly matched starting board, the computer is now practically unbeatable.

```
> (play-vs-computer (game-tree (gen-board) 0 0 t))
current player = a
      b-1 a-2 a-3
    a-1 b-1 b-2
  b-2 a-2 b-3
choose your move:
1. 1 -> 4
2. 1 -> 0
3. 2 -> 5
4. 7 -> 4
3
current player = a
      b-1 a-2 a-1
    a-1 b-1 a-2
  b-2 a-2 b-3
choose your move:
1. end turn
2. 1 -> 4
3. 1 -> 0
4. 5 -> 4
5. 7 -> 4
1
current player = b
      b-1 a-3 a-1
    a-1 b-1 a-2
  b-2 a-2 b-3
```

```
current player = b
      b-1 a-3 a-1
    b-1 b-1 a-2
  b-1 a-2 b-3
current player = a
      b-1 a-3 a-1
    b-1 b-1 a-2
  b-1 a-2 b-3
choose your move:
1. 1 -> 4
2. 1 -> 0
3. 5 -> 4
4. 7 -> 4
5. 7 -> 3
6. 7 -> 6
1
current player = a
      b-1 a-1 a-1
    b-1 a-2 a-2
  b-1 a-2 b-3
choose your move:
1. end turn
2. 4 -> 0
3. 4 -> 3
4. 7 -> 3
5. 7 -> 6
1
current player = b
      b-1 a-1 a-1
    b-1 a-2 a-2
  b-1 a-2 b-3
current player = b
      b-1 a-1 a-1
    b-1 a-2 b-2
  b-1 a-2 b-1
current player = a
      b-2 a-1 a-1
    b-1 a-2 b-2
  b-1 a-2 b-1
choose your move:
1. 4 -> 3
2. 4 -> 8
3. 7 -> 3
4. 7 -> 6
5. 7 -> 8
2
current player = a
      b-2 a-1 a-1
    b-1 a-1 b-2
  b-1 a-2 a-1
choose your move:
1. end turn
2. 7 -> 3
3. 7 -> 6
1
```

```
current player = b
     b-2 a-1 a-1
   b-1 a-1 b-2
 b-1 a-2 a-1
current player = b
     b-1 b-1 a-1
   b-1 a-1 b-2
 b-1 a-2 a-1
current player = a
     b-1 b-1 a-1
   b-1 a-1 b-2
 b-1 a-2 a-1
choose your move:
1. 7 -> 3
2. 7 -> 6
1
current player = a
     b-1 b-1 a-1
   a-1 a-1 b-2
 b-1 a-1 a-1
choose your move:
1. end turn
1
current player = b
     b-1 b-1 a-1
   a-1 a-1 b-2
 b-1 a-1 a-1
current player = b
     b-1 b-1 b-1
   a-1 a-1 b-1
 b-1 a-1 a-1
current player = a
     b-1 b-1 b-1
   a-1 a-1 b-1
 b-1 a-1 a-1
The winner is b
```

What You've Learned

In this chapter, we used our knowledge of functional programming to develop a board game with AI. Along the way you learned the following:

- Functional programming techniques allow you to write a game program with a "rule engine" that is separate from the rest of the code. You accomplish this by using *function pipelining* and building a *game tree* that is independently traversed by other parts of your game code as the game progresses.

- You can create an AI player for a two-player game using the *minimax algorithm*. This algorithm is based on the truism "What is good for my enemy is bad for me." It allows you to efficiently rate positions in a two-player board game.

- Lexical variables (which we've been calling *local* variables) can live on past the form in which they were created if they are referenced by a lambda expression. Capturing variables in this way is called *creating a closure.*

- Functional programs can be optimized using *memoization*, which requires you to cache previous results calculated by a function.

- You can also improve functional programs by using *tail call optimizations,* which allow you to make sure the call stack isn't abused. You do this by controlling which function appears in the tail call (final) position of your list-eater functions.

16

THE MAGIC OF LISP MACROS

Macro programming allows you to mess around inside your Lisp compiler/interpreter to turn Lisp into your own custom programming language. When faced with a difficult programming challenge, many experienced Lispers will first ask themselves, "What programming language could I use to make this problem easy to solve?" Then they'll use macros to convert Lisp into *that* language!

No other programming language possesses such a simple and comprehensive macro system. One can even argue that it would be impossible to add this feature to other programming languages, for a simple reason: The Lisp languages are the only ones in which computer code and program data are made out of the same "stuff." As discussed many times in this book, the fundamental structures for storing data in Lisp are symbols, numbers, and lists, which are made of cons cells. Similarly, the code of a Lisp program is made out of these same basic building blocks. As you'll see in this chapter, this symmetry between code and data in Lisp is the magic that makes the Lisp macro system possible.

NOTE *You may have heard that other programming languages, such as C++, also have a feature called macros. For instance, in the C++ language, you would create these using the #define directive. However, these are not the same thing! Lisp macros work in an entirely different and far more sophisticated way.*

A Simple Lisp Macro

Sometimes when you're writing a computer program, you get a feeling of *déjà vu*. I'm sure you know this feeling. You're typing away at your computer, and you suddenly realize, "Hey, this is the third time this week I've written this same fragment of code!"

Suppose, for example, that your program needs a special add function:

```
(defun add (a b)
❶   (let ((x (+ a b)))
      (format t "The sum is ~a" x)
      x))
```

This function adds together two numbers and prints out the sum on the REPL as a side effect. You might find this function useful in a program during debugging:

```
> (add 2 3)
The sum is 5
5
```

This add function seems straightforward, but its code has an annoyance: Why do you need so many parentheses to declare your variable x ❶? The let command requires so many parentheses that when you need only a single variable, the code ends up looking especially ludicrous.

The parentheses required by let are an example of the kind of *visual noise* a programmer must deal with almost every day. However, you can't just write a regular function to hide those parentheses, because the let command can do things a regular Lisp function can't support. The let command is a *special form*. It's a core part of the language and has special powers beyond those of a standard Lisp function.

Macros let us get rid of the superfluous parentheses. Let's create a new macro named let1:

```
❶ (defmacro let1 (var val &body body)
    `(let ((,var ,val))
       ,@body))
```

As you can see, the definition of a macro looks similar to the definition of a function. However, instead of using defun, we use defmacro to define it. Like a function, it has a name (in this case, let1) and arguments passed to it ❶.

Once we've defined the macro let1, it can be used just like let, except that it works with fewer parentheses:

```
> (let ((foo (+ 2 3)))
    (* foo foo))
25
> (let1 foo (+ 2 3)
    (* foo foo))
25
```

Macro Expansion

Although a macro definition looks very similar to a function definition, a macro is actually very different from a function. To understand why, imagine your Lisp is actually a cute little blob, merrily running your Lisp programs.

This blob understands only standard Lisp code. If it were to see our let1 command, it would have no idea what to do.

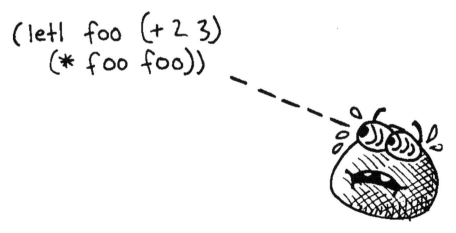

Now imagine that we have a magic wand that transforms the appearance of our code *just before* Lisp gets a peek at it. In our example, it will transform let1 into a regular let, so Lisp will stay happy.

This magic wand is called *macro expansion*. This is a special transformation that your code is put through before the core of the Lisp interpreter/compiler gets to see it. The job of the macro expander is to find any macros in your code (such as our let1 macro) and to convert them into regular Lisp code.

This means a macro is run at *a different time* than a function is run. A regular Lisp function runs when you execute a program that contains the function. This is called *runtime*. A macro, on the other hand, runs before the program does, when the program is read and compiled by your Lisp environment. This is called *macro expansion time*.

Now that we've discussed the basic thinking behind Lisp macros, let's take a closer look at how let1 was defined.

How Macros Are Transformed

When we define a new macro with the defmacro command, we're basically teaching the Lisp macro expansion system a new transformation that it can use to translate code before running a program. The macro receives raw source code in its arguments, in the form of Lisp expressions. Its job is to help the macro expander transform this raw code into standard Lisp code that keeps the Lisp blob happy.

Let's take a closer look at how our let1 macro gets transformed. Here is its definition once again:

❶
```
(defmacro let1 (var val &body body)
  `(let ((,var ,val))
     ,@body))
```

The first line of this defmacro call ❶ tells the macro expander, "Hey, if you see a form in code that begins with let1, here's what you need to do to transform it into standard Lisp." A macro defined with defmacro may also have arguments passed into it, which will contain the raw source code found inside the macro when the macro is used. The let1 macro has three such arguments passed into it: var, val, and body ❶. So what do these three arguments represent?

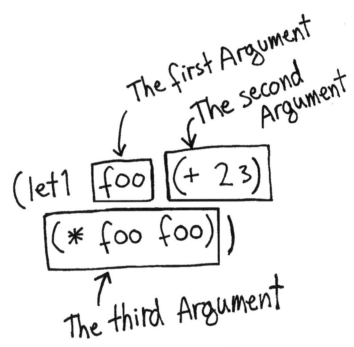

As you can see, when we use let1, we'll end up having three different expressions inside it, which are the arguments to the let1 macro:

var   The first argument is the name of the variable we're defining. This name will be available within our macro using the argument named var. In this example, it will equal the symbol foo.

val   The second expression holds the code that determines the value of the variable. In our macro, this is the second argument, val. It will equal the list (+ 2 3).

body   The third expression inside a let1 call is the body code, which makes use of the new variable that's created (in this case, foo). It will be available in the macro through the argument named body.

Since the let command is allowed to have multiple statements in its body, we will want to mirror this behavior in the let1 macro. This is why, in the def-macro command defining let1, the final body argument has the special keyword &body in front of it. This tells the macro expander "Give me all remaining expressions in the macro in a list." Because of this, the body argument in our let1 example is actually ((* foo foo))—a nested list. In this example, we put only a single statement inside let1.

Now that you've seen what the values to the arguments of our let1 macro are, let's see how the macro uses this information to transform the let1 into a standard let that the Lisp compiler can understand. The easiest way to transform source code in Lisp is to use backquote syntax. (If you don't remember how to use backquotes, please see "How Quasiquoting Works" on page 73.) With backquotes, we can build the code for a proper let command using code passed to let1. Here's our let1 macro again for reference:

```
(defmacro let1 (var val &body body)
❶  `(let ((,var ,val))
❷     ,@body))
```

As you can see, the let1 macro returns a backquoted list starting with the symbol let ❶, followed by the variable name and value, placed in a proper nested list, which Lisp's let command requires. The commas cause the actual variable name and value to be plopped in at these locations. Finally, we place the body code from the let1 in the analogous place in the let command ❷.

The body argument is inserted into the transformed code using the splicing comma (,@). To understand why the body needs to be handled in this special way, consider the following use of our let1 macro:

```
> (let1 foo (+ 2 3)
    (princ "Lisp is awesome!")
    (* foo foo))
Lisp is awesome!
25
```

In this case, we've put more than one thing inside the body of our let. Remember that the let command includes an implicit progn command, and it can have multiple Lisp instructions inside. Our new let1 macro allows for this as well by placing the special &body marker in front of the body argument, causing all remaining syntax expressions to be passed into let1 as a list. So, in the preceding example, the body argument contains the code ((princ "Lisp is awesome!") (* foo foo)).

Using the Simple Macro

Now that we've written our let1 macro, let's rewrite our custom add function in a cleaner way:

```
(defun add (a b)
  (let1 x (+ a b)
    (format t "The sum is ~a" x)
    x))
```

Isn't this much easier on the eyes?

We can use the macroexpand command to see code generated by a macro. Simply pass the macro's code to macroexpand, like this:

```
> (macroexpand '(let1 foo (+ 2 3)
                  (* foo foo)))
❶ (LET ((FOO (+ 2 3))) (* FOO FOO)) ;
❷ T
```

You can now see the raw code generated by let1 ❶. The T at the end ❷ just means macroexpand was handed a valid macro that it was able to expand.

As your macros become more complex, you'll find that macroexpand is a valuable tool in testing and debugging their structure.

More Complex Macros

Let's suppose you need a custom my-length command. This is a classic list-eating function that will count the length of a list. We'll write it in the proper "tail call optimized" style (discussed in Chapter 14), where the recursive function call is in the tail position. Here's the code:

```
  (defun my-length (lst)
❶   (labels ((f (lst acc)
❷             (if lst
❸               (f (cdr lst) (1+ acc))
                acc)))
      (f lst 0)))
```

As you can see, this function has tons of repetitive stuff, once again giving us that dreaded feeling of *déjà vu*. There are two repetitive patterns in this function:

- As in other list-eater functions, we have the annoying check to see if the list is empty ❷ and the associated use of cdr ❸.
- We did all this verbose work to create a local function f ❶.

Let's write some macros that make this function (and other functions with the same repetition) more pithy.

A Macro for Splitting Lists

First, let's create a split macro. It will let us write cleaner list-eater functions, such as our my-length function.

List-eaters always check if the list is empty. If it isn't, they take apart the list using car and/or cdr, and then perform operations on the head and/or tail of the list. The split macro does this for us. Here's what it looks like when we use the finished split macro:

```
❶ > (split '(2 3)
❷     (format t "This can be split into ~a and ~a." head tail)
       (format t "This cannot be split."))
   This can be split into 2 and (3).
❸ > (split '()
       (format t "This can be split into ~a and ~a." head tail)
❹     (format t "This cannot be split."))
   This cannot be split.
```

The first argument of the split macro is a list you want to split into a head and a tail ❶. If this is possible, the next expression in the split macro will be called ❷. As a bonus, our split macro automatically creates two variables for us, named head and tail. This way, we don't always need to call car and cdr inside list-eating functions. If the list is empty ❸, we call the expression at the end ❹.

Let's look at the code for the split macro. Note that this initial version of the macro contains some bugs we'll discuss shortly:

```
   ;Warning! Contains Bugs!
❶ (defmacro split (val yes no)
❷   `(if ,val
❸      (let ((head (car ,val))
❹            (tail (cdr ,val)))
❺        ,yes)
❻      ,no))
```

Our split macro requires three (and only three) expressions as arguments ❶. This means when we use this macro, we'll always need exactly three items.

The code that needs to be generated by split is pretty straightforward. First, we have an if that checks if the list is empty ❷. If it is, we break apart the list and stick it into our two local variables, head ❸ and tail ❹. Then we put in the code that handles the "yes, we can split the list" case ❺. If we can't split the list, we call the no case ❻. Note that in the no case, we don't have access to the head/tail variables, since they aren't created if the list can't be split.

With this new `split` macro, we can clean up our `my-length` macro a bit:

```
(defun my-length (lst)
  (labels ((f (lst acc)
             (split lst
               (f tail (1+ acc))
               acc)))
    (f lst 0)))
```

❶

Notice how we now make use of the `tail` variable created by `split`, simplifying our code ❶. Macros that automatically generate variables like this are called *anaphoric macros*.

However, we are not yet finished with our `split` macro. Although it basically works, it contains some subtle bugs that we need to address.

Avoiding Repeated Execution in Macros

One common bug that can happen in a macro is incorrect repeated execution of code. In fact, our current version of the `split` macro contains this flaw. Here is an example that clearly shows the problem:

❶
```
> (split (progn (princ "Lisp rocks!")
               '(2 3))
        (format t "This can be split into ~a and ~a." head tail)
        (format t "This cannot be split."))
Lisp rocks!Lisp rocks!Lisp rocks!This can be split into 2 and (3).
```

In this use of `split`, the statement "Lisp rocks!" was printed three times, even though it appears only once in the original code. How is this possible?

Remember that the arguments passed into a macro consist of raw source code. This means the `val` argument passed into `split` contains the raw code of the `progn` statement ❶, including the raw code for the `princ` statement within it. Since we reference `val` three times inside the `split` macro, it causes the `princ` statement to be executed three times.

We can verify this by running this example through `macroexpand`:

```
> (macroexpand '(split (progn (princ "Lisp rocks!")
                              '(2 3))
                       (format t "This can be split into ~a and ~a." head tail)
                       (format t "This cannot be split.")))
```
❶   `(IF (PROGN (PRINC "Lisp rocks!") '(2 3))`
`    (LET`
❷   `     ((HEAD (CAR (PROGN (PRINC "Lisp rocks!") '(2 3))))`
❸   `      (TAIL (CDR (PROGN (PRINC "Lisp rocks!") '(2 3)))))`
`     (FORMAT T "This can be split into ~a and ~a." HEAD TAIL))`
`    (FORMAT T "This cannot be split.")) ;`
`T`

As you can see, the princ statement appears three times **❶❷❸**. This causes unexpected behavior and is inefficient, since we're repeatedly running the same code unnecessarily.

If you give this problem some thought, the solution isn't too hard to figure out. We simply need to create a local variable inside the split macro, like this:

```
;Warning! Still contains a bug!
(defmacro split (val yes no)
  `(let1 x ,val
     (if x
       (let ((head (car x))
             (tail (cdr x)))
         ,yes)
       ,no)))
```

Note that we made use of let1 in this new version of split. As this shows, it is perfectly okay to use macros inside *other* macros.

Now if we rerun our previous example, we can see that split behaves correctly, princing the statement only once:

```
> (split (progn (princ "Lisp rocks!")
                '(2 3))
    (format t "This can be split into ~a and ~a." head tail)
    (format t "This cannot be split."))
Lisp rocks!This can be split into 2 and (3).
```

Unfortunately, this new version of the split macro introduces *yet another* bug. Let's tackle this new bug next.

Avoiding Variable Capture

To see the bug in our newest version of split, try running the following:

```
> (let1 x 100❶
    (split '(2 3)
      (+ x head)
      nil))
*** - +: (2 3) is not a number
```

Can you tell what happened? We just created a variable x inside the new version of our split macro! Here's what the call to split looks like if we macroexpand it:

```
> (macroexpand '(split '(2 3)
                   (+ x head)
                   nil))
❷ (LET ((X '(2 3)))
    (IF X (LET ((HEAD (CAR X)) (TAIL (CDR X))) (+ X HEAD)) NIL)) ;
  T
```

Notice how the expanded version of split contains a definition of x ❷. This blocks the competing definition in our troublesome example ❶. In this scenario, the split macro accidentally *captured* the variable x and overwrote it in an unexpected way. How can we avoid this problem?

One simple solution would be to not create a variable x in the macro, but to instead use a variable with some insane long name like xqweopfjsadlkjgh. Then we could feel pretty confident the variable used inside the macro will never clash with a variable inside the code that uses it. If fact, there is a Common Lisp function called gensym whose job it is to generate crazy variable names exactly for this purpose:

```
> (gensym)
#:G8695
```

The gensym function will create a unique variable name for you that is guaranteed never to clash with any other variable name in your code. You may notice that it also has a special prefix (#:) that differentiates it from other names. Common Lisp handles these gensym-based names as a special case and will stop you from using the name of a gensym variable directly.

Now let's use the gensym function inside our split macro to protect the macro from causing variable capture:

```
;This function is finally safe to use
  (defmacro split (val yes no)
❶   (let1 g (gensym)
❷     `(let1 ,g ,val
        (if ,g
          (let ((head (car ,g))
                (tail (cdr ,g)))
            ,yes)
          ,no)))))
```

In the first line of our revised macro, we define a variable g that contains the gensym name ❶. It's very important to notice that there is *not* a backquote at the front of this line. This means that this line of code is run at *macro expand time*, not *runtime*, and it is perfectly fine to define the variable g at this point. The let1 on the next line, however, has a backquote in front of it ❷. This line will be run at runtime, so we don't want to use a hardcoded variable in this spot. In this new version, we instead use the unique gensym name stored in g.

Now every time the split macro is used, a unique name is generated to hold the internal value. We can test this by running some examples through macroexpand:

```
> (macroexpand '(split '(2 3)
                   (+ x head)
                   nil))
(LET ((❶#:G8627 '(2 3))) (IF #:G8627 (LET ((HEAD (CAR #:G8627)) (TAIL (CDR
#:G8627))) (+ X HEAD)) NIL)) ;
T
> (macroexpand '(split '(2 3)
```

```
        (+ x head)
        nil))
(LET (((❷)#:G8628 '(2 3))) (IF #:G8628 (LET ((HEAD (CAR #:G8628)) (TAIL (CDR
#:G8628)))) (+ X HEAD)) NIL)) ;
T
```

Notice how a differently named local variable was created in both instances ❶❷. This guarantees that the variable name will not only be unique within your code, but will also be unique if the split macro is ever used multiple times in a nested fashion. We have now created a fully debugged version of our split macro.

Just because it is now bug-free does not mean that it is free of variable capture. Note that the macro still defines the variables head and tail. If you used this function in other code in which head or tail had an alternate meaning, your code would fail! However, in the case of head and tail, the capture is on purpose. In this situation, the variable capture is a *feature*, not a bug—it is an anaphoric macro. As we've discussed, this means that it makes named variables or functions available that we can use in the body of the macro.

A Recursion Macro

Let's take another look at our improved my-length macro:

```
(defun my-length (lst)
  (labels ((f (lst acc)
             (split lst
               (f tail (1+ acc))
               acc)))
    (f lst 0)))
```

As we discussed, there is an additional repetitive pattern in this code: The creation of a local function f. Let's write another macro that gets rid of this additional visual noise: recurse. Here's an example of the recurse macro in use:

```
❶ > (recurse (n 9)
❷     (fresh-line)
❸     (if (zerop n)
❹       (princ "lift-off!")
❺       (progn (princ n)
❻               (self (1- n)))))
9
8
7
6
5
4
3
2
1
lift-off!
```

The first parameter into the recurse macro is a list of variables and their starting values ❶. In this case, we're declaring only one variable (n) and setting its starting value to 9. The rest of the lines in the macro make up the body of the recursive function.

The first thing we do in the body is start a fresh line ❷. Then we check if n has reached zero yet ❸. If it has, we print "lift-off!" ❹. Otherwise, we print the current number ❺ and call the function again, recursively. Like our split macro, the recurse macro is anaphoric. In the case of recurse, it makes a function named self available, which we call when we're ready to perform a recursion ❻. We also subtract one from n at this point to lower the countdown number.

Now that we've seen how recurse should work, let's write this recurse macro. In order to process the list of arguments and starting values, it's useful for us to have a function that can group items into a list of pairs. Here is a function, pairs, that accomplishes this:

```
> (defun pairs (lst)
❶    (labels ((f (lst acc)
❷              (split lst
❸                (if tail
❹                  (f (cdr tail) (cons (cons head (car tail)) acc))
❺                  (reverse acc))
❻                (reverse acc))))
       (f lst nil)))
PAIRS
> (pairs '(a b c d e f))
((A . B) (C . D) (E . F))
```

The pairs function is a tail-call-optimized list-eater, which, ironically, has its own local function f ❶. (Shortly, we won't need to declare such a function anymore.) It uses split to break an item off the list ❷. However, since it needs to process two items (a pair) from the list at once, we need to run an additional check to see if the tail is empty ❸. If there are no items in the list ❻ (or only one item left ❺), we return our accumulated values. Otherwise, we recursively process the rest of the list, with a new pair of items placed into the accumulator ❹.

Now we're finally ready to write the recurse macro:

```
(defmacro recurse (vars &body body)
❶    (let1 p (pairs vars)
❷      `(labels ((self ,(mapcar #'car p)
                 ,@body))
❸        (self ,@(mapcar #'cdr p)))))
```

As you can see, it simply transforms the recursion into a traditional local function. First, it uses our new pairs function to take apart the variable names and starting values, and puts the result into p ❶. Then it defines a local function simply named self. The variable names for self are the odd-numbered items from p ❷. Since we want self to be accessible, anaphorically, from inside the macro, we use a plain name instead of a gensym name for this function. At the bottom of the macro, we then simply call self, passing in all the starting values ❸.

Now that we've created the recurse macro, let's once again clean up our my-length function using this new language construct:

```
(defun my-length (lst)
  (recurse (lst lst
            acc 0)
           (split lst
             (f tail (1+ acc))
             acc)))
```

As you can see, there is very little repetition or visual noise in this version of our my-length function.

Now you can appreciate how helpful macros can be when trying to write clean, succinct code. However, a liberal use of macros will also require you to bear some costs that you need to be aware of. We'll look at the potential downsides to macros next.

Macros: Dangers and Alternatives

Macros allow us to write code that generates other code, making the Lisp languages a wonderful tool for metaprogramming and prototyping new language ideas. But, at some level, macros are just a sleight of hand: They let you trick the Lisp compiler/interpreter into accepting your own customized language constructs and treating them like standard Lisp. They are indeed a powerful tool in a programmer's tool chest, but they are not as elegant as some of the other programming tools you've encountered in this book.

The main drawback of macros is that they can make it hard for other programmers to understand your code. After all, if you're creating your own language dialect, other programmers won't be familiar with it. Even your future self—say, in a year or two—may have a hard time understanding the structure of your code if you've made heavy use of macros. Because of this, experienced Lispers will do their best to use alternate techniques to macro programming whenever possible. Often, a beginning Lisper will write a macro in situations that could be addressed in other, cleaner ways.

For instance, it's fun to see how we were able to clean up our my-length function by adding a couple of macros named split and recurse. However, in the previous two chapters, you learned about another tool, functional programming, which can also be used to clean up list-eater functions. One powerful function often used by functional programmers is reduce. It is a higher-order function that accepts a function and a list, and will call the function once for every value in the list. Here is the my-length function rewritten to use the powerful reduce function, rather than macros:

```
(defun my-length (lst)
❶  (reduce (lambda (x i)
❷             (1+ x))
❸          lst
❹          :initial-value 0))
```

As you can see, this new version of my-length easily blows away our previous version. It is shorter, and it doesn't rely on any of the nonstandard macros that we created.

The first argument to reduce holds our *reduction function* ❶. Its job is to keep track of, and update, an accumulated value, here named x. This variable x will hold the current accumulated value, which in this case will be the length of the list so far. This means we can simply add one to x to update it to its new value ❷. Since the reduction function will be called once for every item in the list, it will, in the end, generate the length of the list. (The reduction function also receives, as an argument, the current item in the list, here given as the variable i. However, we do not need it for calculating the list's length.) The next item passed to reduce is the list we want to reduce ❸. Finally, since the accumulated length we're calculating should have an initial value of zero, we indicate this by setting the :initial-value keyword argument to zero ❹.

Clearly, there are other scenarios where the list-eater macros we've created in this chapter are still useful. There are many cases where the reduce function could not be so easily used. So in the end, there are still many situations where creating your own Lisp dialect is exactly the right solution to a problem, as you'll see in the next chapter.

What You've Learned

This chapter covered macro programming. You've learned the following:

- Macros let you write code that writes code. With macros, you can create your own programming language and convert it to standard Lisp just before the compiler can get a peek at it.

- Macros allow you to get rid of that feeling of *déjà vu* when writing your code, in situations when nothing else can do so.

- You must be careful when writing macros so that they don't lead to unintentional, repeated execution of code.

- You need to be careful to avoid unintended *variable capture* in macros. You can avoid this by using gensym names.

- If variables created by a macro are exposed on purpose, as a feature of the macro, the macro is called an *anaphoric macro*.

- Macro programming is a very powerful technique. However, try to use functional programming instead to solve a problem whenever possible. Macros should always be a last resort.

17

DOMAIN-SPECIFIC LANGUAGES

One of the best reasons for using macros is to perform *domain-specific language (DSL)* programming. DSL
programming is an advanced macro programming
technique that allows us to solve difficult programming
problems by drastically changing the structure and
appearance of Lisp code to optimize it for a specialized
purpose. Although macros are not strictly necessary for
doing DSL programming, by writing a set of macros,
you can easily create a DSL in Lisp.

What Is a Domain?

According to the 2000 US Census, the average family in the United States
had 1.86 children. Since no individual family has exactly 1.86 children, it is
obvious that no particular family is truly perfectly average. In the same way,
there is no such thing as an average computer program. Every program is
designed to solve a specific problem, and every area of human inquiry, or

domain, has its own idiosyncratic requirements that influence programs that solve problems in the given area. With DSLs, we enhance the core of our programming language to take these domain-specific requirements into account, potentially making our resulting code easier to write and understand.

Let's take a look at some specific domains and create some DSLs that let us easily work within these domains using Lisp. In this chapter, we'll create two different DSLs. First, we'll create a DSL for writing *scalable vector graphics (SVG)* files. Then we'll write a DSL for creating commands in a text adventure—we're finally going to upgrade our Wizard's Adventure Game from Chapters 5 and 6 to make it fully playable!

Writing SVG Files

The SVG format is a file format for drawing graphics. In this format, you specify objects like circles and polygons, and then pass them to a compatible computer program to view. Because the SVG format specifies a drawing using pure math functions instead of raw pixels, it is easy for a program to render an SVG image at any size, making images in this format easily scalable.

The SVG format is currently receiving a lot of attention from web developers. All modern browsers (excluding Microsoft Internet Explorer) support SVG natively. Recently, Google released a set of libraries called SVG Web that adds decent support for SVG, even in Internet Explorer. This allows SVG to work in more than 90 percent of current web browsers. Finally, SVG has become a practical and efficient option for drawing graphics on websites.

The SVG format is built on top of the XML format. Here is an example of what a complete SVG file looks like:

```
<svg xmlns="http://www.w3.org/2000/svg">
  <circle cx="50"
          cy="50"
          r="50"
          style="fill:rgb(255,0,0);stroke:rgb(155,0,0)">
  </circle>
  <circle cx="100"
          cy="100"
          r="50"
          style="fill:rgb(0,0,255);stroke:rgb(0,0,155)">
  </circle>
</svg>
```

Simply copy this text and place it in a file named *example.svg* (or download this file from *http://landoflisp.com/*). Then you can open the file from the Firefox web browser (the Safari, Chrome, and Opera web browsers should also work).

Here is what you should see, with a red and blue circle:

Now, let's write some macros and functions to let us create a picture like this directly in Common Lisp!

Creating XML and HTML with the tag Macro

The XML data format (just like the HTML data format) consists primarily of nested tags:

```
❶ <mytag>
      <inner_tag>
      </inner_tag>
❷ </mytag>
```

Every tag ❶ also has a matching closing tag ❷. The closing tag has the same name, but with a slash preceding it. Additionally, tags may contain attributes:

```
<mytag color="BLUE" height="9"></mytag>
```

In this example, we create a tag named mytag that has the attribute of being blue and has a height of 9.

Writing a Macro Helper Function

Often, when writing a macro to perform a task, you'll find a lot of what your macro needs to do can be handled by a function instead. Because of this, it is often prudent to first write a helper function that does most of what the macro needs to do. Then you write the macro, keeping it as simple as possible by leveraging the helper function. This is what we're going to do as we write a macro to create XML-style tags in Lisp.

Here is our helper function, called print-tag, which prints a single opening (or closing) tag:

```
  (defun print-tag (name alst closingp)
❶   (princ #\<)
❷   (when closingp
      (princ #\/))
❸   (princ (string-downcase name))
❹   (mapc (lambda (att)
❺          (format t " ~a=\"~a\"" (string-downcase (car att)) (cdr att)))
        alst)
❻   (princ #\>))
```

First, the print-tag function prints an opening angle bracket ❶. Since this is only a character, we use the literal character syntax by prefixing the bracket with #\. Then we check the predicate closingp ❷. If it is true, the tag needs to have a slash in front of it to make it a closing tag. Then we print the name of the tag, converted to lowercase with the string-downcase function ❸. Next, we iterate through all the attributes in the alst of attributes ❹ and print out each attribute/value pair ❺. Finally, we end by putting in a closing angle bracket ❻.

The following is an example use of the print-tag function. Since it is a plain function and not a macro, it's easy to debug in the REPL. This is another reason why helper functions are a good idea when creating macros.

```
> (print-tag 'mytag '((color . blue) (height . 9)) nil)
<mytag color="BLUE" height="9">
```

As you can see, this function does a fine job of printing an XML tag. However, it would be a real chore if all tags had to be created in this way. That's why we're going to write the tag macro next.

Creating the tag Macro

The tag macro we'll create has been adopted from the macro of the same name in Paul Graham's Arc Lisp dialect. It improves on the print-tag function in several crucial ways, all of which could not be remedied without having a macro:

- Tags always come in pairs. However, if we want to nest tags, a function would not be able to print tags that surround the tags printed inside it. This is because it requires us to execute code before and after nested tags are evaluated. This is possible in a macro, but not a function.

- Tag names and attribute names usually do not need to change in a dynamic way. Because of this, it's redundant to need to prefix tag names with a single quote. In other words, tag names should by default be treated as if they were in data mode.

- Unlike tag names, it's very desirable for the values of attributes to be dynamically generated. Our macro will have a syntax that places the attribute values into code mode so we can execute Lisp code to populate these values.

Ideally, this is how we would like the tag macro to work, when we use it in the REPL:

```
> (tag mytag (color 'blue height (+ 4 5)))
<mytag color="BLUE" height="9"></mytag>
```

Notice that the tag name and attribute list no longer need quotes in front of them. Additionally, it is now easy to calculate an attribute dynamically with Lisp code. In this case, we're calculating that the height is 4 plus 5.

Here's the macro that accomplishes this task:

```
(defmacro tag (name atts &body body)
❶   `(progn (print-tag ',name
❷                 (list ,@(mapcar (lambda (x)
❸                                   `(cons ',(car x) ,(cdr x)))
❹                                 (pairs atts)))
                  nil)
❺           ,@body
❻           (print-tag ',name nil t)))
```

As you would expect, the macro first calls print-tag to generate the opening tag ❶. This is a bit tricky when we generate the alist of attributes for print-tag, since we want the values for the attributes to be in code mode. We accomplish this by wrapping the attributes using list ❷. Then we mapcar through the attributes, which we've paired with the pairs function ❹. (Remember that we created the pairs function toward the end of the previous chapter.) For each attribute pair, we generate a code fragment in the list that consists of cons, without a quotation mark in front of the value of the attribute, so that we can dynamically calculate it ❸.

Next, we put all the code nested inside our tag macro, so that it is called after the opening tag ❺. Finally we create a closing tag ❻.

To make more sense of how this macro handles the attribute list, let's pass the output from our example to macroexpand:

```
> (macroexpand '(tag mytag (color 'blue height (+ 4 5))))
(PROGN (PRINT-TAG 'MYTAG
❶                 (LIST (CONS 'COLOR 'BLUE)
❷                       (CONS 'HEIGHT (+ 4 5)))
                  NIL)
       (PRINT-TAG 'MYTAG NIL T)) ;
T
```

Looking at the macro expansion, it should be clear how the tag macro builds the attribute list to pass to print-tag ❶ and how it allows us to dynamically generate attribute values, such as the height attribute ❷.

Here is another example of this macro in use, now with two inner tags:

```
> (tag mytag (color 'blue size 'big)
      (tag first_inner_tag ())
      (tag second_inner_tag ()))
❶ <mytag color="BLUE" size="BIG">
  <first_inner_tag></first_inner_tag>
  <second_inner_tag></second_inner_tag>
</mytag>
```

Notice how it correctly surrounds the inner, nested tags with proper XML opening and closing tags. Note also that I have added line breaks and indentation to the output ❶ for clarity. The actual output of the tag function always prints on a single line, without line breaks or indentation.

Using the tag Macro to Generate HTML

The tag macro can be used for generating XML *or* HTML. For instance, we could do the following to generate a "Hello World" HTML document:

```
> (tag html ()
      (tag body ()
          (princ "Hello World!")))
<html><body>Hello World!</body></html>
```

Since HTML uses predefined tags (unlike XML, where the tags can have any name), we could write simple macros for specific HTML tags that make them even easier to write HTML in Lisp. For instance, here are some simple html and body macros:

```
(defmacro html (&body body)
  `(tag html ()
        ,@body))
```

```
(defmacro body (&body body)
  `(tag body ()
       ,@body))
```

Now we could write our "Hello World" HTML example even more elegantly:

```
> (html
    (body
      (princ "Hello World!")))
<html><body>Hello World!</body></html>
```

However, we want to use the tag macro to create SVG drawings instead. So let's expand our DSL for the SVG domain.

Creating SVG-Specific Macros and Functions

First, let's write the svg macro, which embodies an entire SVG image. Here it is:

```
(defmacro svg (&body body)
❶  `(tag svg (xmlns "http://www.w3.org/2000/svg"
❷             "xmlns:xlink" "http://www.w3.org/1999/xlink")
       ,@body))
```

The svg macro is built on top of the tag macro. SVG images, for our purposes, require two special attributes to be created:

- The xmlns attribute tells the SVG viewer (in our case, the Firefox web browser) where it can find the proper documentation for the SVG format ❶.

- The second attribute enables hyperlinks inside the picture ❷. We'll be using this hyperlinking feature in more advanced examples, starting in the next chapter.

To draw pictures, we'll need to manipulate colors. To keep things simple, we're just going to represent colors as RGB triples stored in a list. For instance, the color (255 0 0) is bright red.

Often, it is useful to generate lighter or darker variants of a particular color. The following brightness function does this for us:

```
(defun brightness (col amt)
  (mapcar (lambda (x)
            (min 255 (max 0 (+ x amt))))
          col))
```

If you pass bright red into this function and set the brightness to negative 100, you can see that it will generate a darker red:

```
> (brightness '(255 0 0) -100)
(155 0 0)
```

Next, let's create a function that sets the style of an SVG picture element:

```
(defun svg-style (color)
  (format nil
❶         "~{fill:rgb(~a,~a,~a);stroke:rgb(~a,~a,~a)~}"
          (append color
❷                 (brightness color -100))))
```

The svg-style function accepts a color, and then sets the fill and stroke (outline) of a picture element ❶. By using our brightness function, we can make the outline a darker variant of the fill ❷. This way, we need to specify only a single color for every element in our pictures, while maintaining a pleasing appearance.

Now, let's create a function to draw a circle. Since we won't need to nest other SVG tags inside a circle, there is no need to write a macro for drawing circles—a function suffices.

```
(defun circle (center radius color)
❶  (tag circle (cx (car center)
❷               cy (cdr center)
❸               r radius
❹               style (svg-style color))))
```

We'll want to set the center, radius, and color of each circle. The center needs to be assigned to the cx ❶ and cy ❷ SVG attributes of the circle. The radius is put in the r attribute ❸. We set the style of our circle with our svg-style function ❹.

We are now ready to draw the simple SVG picture of two circles shown earlier, using our new DSL! Here's how we do it:

```
> (svg (circle '(50 . 50) 50 '(255 0 0))
       (circle '(100 . 100) 50 '(0 0 255)))
<svg xmlns="http://www.w3.org/2000/svg" xmlns:xlink="http://www.w3.org/1999/
xlink"><circle cx="50" cy="50" r="50"
style="fill:rgb(255,0,0);stroke:rgb(155,0,0)"></circle><circle cx="100"
cy="100" r="50" style="fill:rgb(0,0,255);stroke:rgb(0,0,155)"></circle></svg>
```

We now have a functional SVG DSL. Let's add some more functionality to our DSL so we can appreciate the power a DSL can give to our programs.

Building a More Complicated SVG Example

Let's add a new function to our SVG DSL that makes it easy to draw an arbitrary polygon:

```
(defun polygon (points color)
❶  (tag polygon (points (format nil
❷                 "~{~a,~a ~}"
❸                 (mapcan (lambda (tp)
```

```
            (list (car tp) (cdr tp)))
          points))
  style (svg-style color)))))
```

An SVG polygon stores all the points of the polygon in the `points` attribute ❶. We construct the list of points by using a `format` statement, which contains the `~{ ~}` control strings ❷. Remember from Chapter 11 that these control strings let us iterate through a list inside the `format` function. In this case, we're iterating through the list of points. We then flatten the list of point pairs using `mapcan` ❸, which you may remember is the same as using a `mapcar` followed by an append.

In this example, we're going to draw some random walks. A *random walk* is a graph of what you would get if you decide, at each moment in time, to flip a coin and then move either up or down a step. Random walks are very similar in behavior to stocks in the stock market. They are often used as a starting point for financial modeling. Here is a function that generates a random walk:

```
(defun random-walk (value length)
  (unless (zerop length)
    (cons value
❶       (random-walk (if (zerop (random 2))
                         (1- value)
                         (1+ value))
                     (1- length)))))
```

This function builds a list of numbers, starting with the `value` parameter. Then it increases or decreases this value randomly. We choose which direction to move using the `random` function ❶. (Note that, in order to keep it simple, this function isn't tail call optimized, since the `cons` happens after the recursive call.)

Here's an example of how we can use the `random-walk` function:

```
> (random-walk 100 10)
(100 101 102 101 100 101 102 103 102 103)
```

Now let's use our SVG DSL to draw a slew of random walks in a picture:

```
(with-open-file (*standard-output* "random_walk.svg"
                 :direction :output
❶                :if-exists :supersede)
❷  (svg (loop repeat 10
❸        do (polygon (append '((0 . 200))
                            (loop for x
                                  for y in (random-walk 100 400)
                                  collect (cons x y))
❹                           '((400 . 200)))
                     (loop repeat 3
❺                          collect (random 256)))))))
```

Since the amount of data created in this example is quite huge, we're dumping the data straight to a file (named *random_walk.svg*), instead of printing it to the REPL. We do this by redirecting the *standard-output* dynamic variable ❶, a technique introduced in Chapter 12. Notice how we can mix Lisp code freely with our DSL commands. For instance, we can loop right inside the SVG macro to generate 10 polygons at once ❷.

To make the graph pretty, we're going to fill in the area under each graph line with a color. To do this, we'll represent each line using a polygon, with the base line along the bottom of the graph (with a y-coordinate of 200) included as points to close the shape:

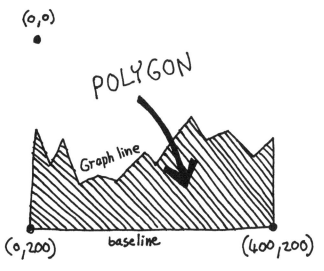

This is why we add points for the bottom-left ❸ and bottom-right ❹ corner as we create each polygon. For even more fun, we also randomize the color of each graph line ❺.

Here is an example of some random graphs generated by this very simple DSL code:

Now that you've seen how easily you can write XML, HTML, and SVG DSLs in Lisp, let's create an entirely different kind of DSL—one that will let us build custom game commands for our Wizard's Adventure Game from Chapters 5 and 6!

Creating Custom Game Commands for Wizard's Adventure Game

If you remember, when we last encountered the game starring our wizard and apprentice in Chapters 5 and 6, we could walk around the world and pick up objects. However, we couldn't really perform any other interesting or fun actions. To make a game fun, it should include special actions that can be performed with certain objects and/or at certain locations in the game. We need frogs that can be kissed, dragons that can be fought, and perhaps even maidens that can be rescued!

Creating these kinds of interesting activities in the game poses a unique challenge. On the one hand, there are clearly many similarities between such different game actions. For instance, most of them will require us to have an object in our possession. On the other hand, they all need to have *unique and idiosyncratic properties* (enabled through command-specific Lisp code) or the game becomes boring. As you'll see, a DSL can help you add many such unique commands to your game.

To run the code from here until the end of this chapter, we're going to use all the game code from Chapters 5 and 6. Just put the code from those chapters into a file named *wizards_game.lisp* (or download *wizards_game.lisp* from *http://landoflisp.com/*). As soon as the game is loaded, you can type game commands like look directly in the CLISP REPL. Alternatively, you can use the game-repl command we created in Chapter 6 to get a more polished game experience. Remember that the quit command will take you out of the game REPL.

Here's what you do to load the game code from the REPL and start running game commands:

```
> (load "wizards_game.lisp")
;; Loading file wizards_game.lisp ...
;; Loaded file wizards_game.lisp
T
```

```
> (look)
(YOU ARE IN THE ATTIC. THERE IS A GIANT WELDING TORCH IN THE CORNER. THERE IS
A LADDER GOING DOWNSTAIRS FROM HERE.)
> (game-repl)
look
You are in the living-room. A wizard is snoring loudly on the couch. There is
a door going west from here. There is a ladder going upstairs
from here. You see a whiskey on the floor. You see a bucket on the floor.
quit
```

Creating New Game Commands by Hand

So what should our game DSL look like? The only way to really know is to first
create some commands by hand. Then we can see if there are any common
patterns between different commands that we can use as the basis of our DSL.

A Command for Welding

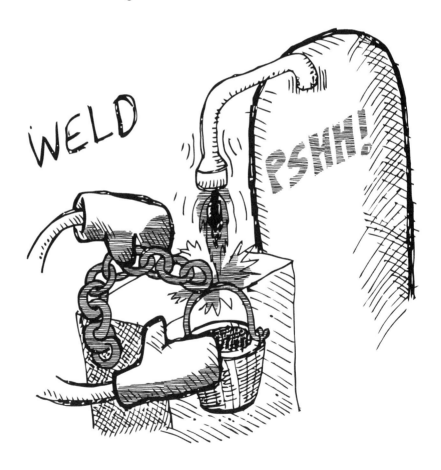

In the attic of the wizard's house is a welding machine. Let's allow the players to weld the chain to the bucket if they bring those items to that location. Here's the code to make this happen:

```
❶ (defun have (object)
    (member object (inventory)))

❷ (defparameter *chain-welded* nil)

❸ (defun weld (subject object)
❹   (if (and (eq *location* 'attic)
            (eq subject 'chain)
            (eq object 'bucket)
            (have 'chain)
            (have 'bucket)
            (not *chain-welded*))
❺      (progn (setf *chain-welded* t)
              '(the chain is now securely welded to the bucket.))
❻      '(you cannot weld like that.)))
```

First, we need an easy way of checking whether the player is currently carrying an object, using the have function ❶. Remember that we created a command for checking what the player is carrying, named inventory. If an object is a member of the inventory, it means the player must "have" that object.

Next, our program needs some way of keeping track of whether or not the chain and bucket are welded together, since there will be actions later in the game that are possible only once this welding has happened. For this purpose, we create a global, dynamic variable named *chain-welded* ❷.

Finally, we need to create the welding command itself ❸. Welding is possible only if a slew of conditions are met ❹:

- You must be in the attic.
- You must have chain and bucket as the subject and object of the welding command.
- You must be carrying the chain and bucket with you.
- The chain and bucket can't already be welded together.

If these conditions are met, we set our *chain-welded* variable to true ❺ and print a message indicating this success. If any of the conditions fail, we indicate that the welding was unsuccessful ❻.

Let's try the command in the CLISP REPL:

```
> (weld 'chain 'bucket)
(YOU CANNOT WELD LIKE THAT.)
```

Well, that's exactly the right response. After all, we're not in the attic, and we aren't carrying the right objects. So far, so good.

Next, let's try our new command in our fancy game-repl:

```
> (game-repl)
weld chain bucket
I do not know that command.
quit
```

What? Why doesn't it "know" that command? The answer is simple: Our game-repl has some basic protections against running unauthorized commands. To remedy this, we need to add weld to our list of permitted commands:

```
> (pushnew 'weld *allowed-commands*)
(WELD LOOK WALK PICKUP INVENTORY)
> (game-repl)
weld chain bucket
You cannot weld like that.
```

By using the pushnew command, the weld function is added only to the allowed commands if it wasn't already present in that list. Problem solved!

A Command for Dunking

In the wizard's garden, there is a well. Let's create a command that lets the player dunk the bucket in the well to fill it with water:

```
❶ (setf *bucket-filled* nil)

❷ (defun dunk (subject object)
❸   (if (and (eq *location* 'garden)
            (eq subject 'bucket)
            (eq object 'well)
            (have 'bucket)
```

```
      *chain-welded*)
   (progn (setf *bucket-filled* 't)
          '(the bucket is now full of water))
  '(you cannot dunk like that.)))
```

❹ `(pushnew 'dunk *allowed-commands*)`

As with our `weld` command, we first need a variable to keep track of whether the bucket has been filled yet ❶. Next, we need a `dunk` function ❷. Notice how, with dunking, we once again have a long list of conditions that need to be met before we can successfully complete the action ❸. Some of these are similar to those we needed for our welding command. For instance, dunking also requires the player to be in a specific location with the correct object. Other conditions are dunking-specific, such as the fact that the player needs to have a welded chain before being able to dunk. Finally, we need to push the `dunk` function onto our list of allowed actions ❹.

The game-action Macro

Now that we've created two custom game actions for our game, it's obvious that the `weld` and `dunk` commands are very similar in some ways. However, as in our SVG library, each game command needs to contain a certain amount of dynamic logic in it, to customize the behavior of the command. Let's write a game-action macro that addresses these issues. It will make it much easier to create new game commands.

```
❶ (defmacro game-action (command subj obj place &body body)
❷   `(progn (defun ,command (subject object)
❸          (if (and (eq *location* ',place)
                    (eq subject ',subj)
```

```
                          (eq object ',obj)
❹                         (have ',subj))
❺                    ,@body
❻                 '(i cant ,command like that.)))
❼              (pushnew ',command *allowed-commands*)))
```

This game-action macro embodies the common pattern between our dunk and weld commands. The parameters to game-action are the name of the command, the two objects involved in the action, the place it needs to occur, and some arbitrary additional code in the body parameter that lets us add custom logic to the command ❶.

The main job of the game-action macro is to define a new function for a command ❷. It may be surprising to you that a macro can do something as powerful as define a new function on its own, but there is nothing to stop it from doing this. I hope this example shows you just how flexible and mind-bending the Common Lisp macro system can be.

Since all game actions for this game require the location, subject, and object, we can take care of some of the conditions directly within this macro ❸. However, we're going to leave other conditions open for each specific command. Notice, for example, that the subject of the game sentence needs to be owned by the player ❹, but the object does not. This makes sense, since there are many actions that can be performed, such as "throw rock dragon," where the object of the sentence (dragon) does *not* need to be in the player's inventory.

Once the basic macro-level conditions have been met, we will defer the rest of the logic to the level of the individual command ❺. If the conditions were *not* met, we print an error message, customized with the name of the current command ❻. Finally, we pushnew the command into the list of allowed commands for our fancy game-repl ❼.

One thing we do *not* do in this macro is define or set any global variables. If a game command needs to define a *chain-welded* or *bucket-filled* global variable, it must do this itself. This makes sense, since there is clearly no guarantee that there will be a one-to-one relationship between state variables for our game and particular commands. For instance, some commands may be permitted multiple times, making the state unnecessary. Or an action may depend on multiple state variables. Having this kind of variation in the commands is what makes them unique and fun.

With this macro, we now have a simple DSL for creating new game actions! Essentially, this command gives us our own programming language, specialized for the domain of creating game commands. Let's rewrite our previous weld and dunk commands using our new game command programming language:

```
(defparameter *chain-welded* nil)

(game-action weld chain bucket attic
          (if (and (have 'bucket) (not *chain-welded*))
              (progn (setf *chain-welded* 't)
                     '(the chain is now securely welded to the bucket.))
```

```
                '(you do not have a bucket.)))

(setf *bucket-filled* nil)

(game-action dunk bucket well garden
             (if *chain-welded*
                 (progn (setf *bucket-filled* 't)
                        '(the bucket is now full of water))
                 '(the water level is too low to reach.)))
```

As you can see, these commands have become much easier on the eyes. Notice how weld checks for ownership of the bucket, whereas dunk does not need to check for ownership of the well.

To further illustrate the value of using macros to implement our game command DSL, let's implement a more complicated game command, splash:

```
(game-action splash bucket wizard living-room
   (cond ((not *bucket-filled*) '(the bucket has nothing in it.))
         ((have 'frog) '(the wizard awakens and sees that you stole his frog.
                         he is so upset he banishes you to the
                         netherworlds- you lose! the end.))
         (t '(the wizard awakens from his slumber and greets you warmly.
              he hands you the magic low-carb donut- you win! the end.))))
```

For this command, there are three distinct scenarios that might happen:

- The bucket is empty.
- Your bucket is full, but you stole the frog. In that case, you lose.
- Your bucket is full and you didn't steal the frog. You win!

With our game-action macro, we can support many action commands, each with special idiosyncratic behavior. Still, we are able to avoid unnecessary repetition.

NOTE *The game-action command exposes the subject and object variables within the body of the macro. This allows game commands to access this information, but it might also cause a name collision if the code that creates the game-action commands also has variables named subject and object. As an exercise, try modifying the game-action macro so that the subject and object variables are replaced by gensym names, as discussed in Chapter 16.*

Let's Try the Completed Wizard's Adventure Game!

Here is a sample run through of the Wizard's Adventure Game that shows off some of the rich functionality we've put into this game. Play the game yourself and see if you can win the magic donut!

> (game-repl)
look
You are in the living-room. There is a wizard snoring loudly on the couch.
There is a door going west from here. There is a ladder going upstairs from
here. You see a whiskey on the floor. You see a bucket on the floor.
pickup bucket
You are now carrying the bucket
pickup whiskey
You are now carrying the whiskey
inventory
Items- whiskey bucket
walk upstairs
You are in the attic. There is a giant welding torch in the corner. There is a
ladder going downstairs from here.
walk east
You cannot go that way.
walk downstairs
You are in the living-room. A wizard is snoring loudly on the couch. There is
a door going west from here. There is a ladder going upstairs from here.
walk west
You are in a beautiful garden. There is a well in front of you. There is a
door going east from here. You see a frog on the floor. You see
a chain on the floor.
dunk bucket well
The water level is too low to reach.

```
pickup chain
You are now carrying the chain
walk east
You are in the living-room. A wizard is snoring loudly on the couch. There is
a door going west from here. There is a ladder going upstairs
from here.
splash bucket wizard
The bucket has nothing in it.
```

What You've Learned

This chapter demonstrated how to create DSLs in Lisp. You learned the
following:

- When you need to do some weird programming for a very specific
  domain, Macros are a great solution. With them, you can create your
  own DSL.

- Often, it makes sense to first write a helper function for a macro (like
  print-tag), and then write a macro (like tag) to add improvements that
  only a macro can provide. These improvements usually involve being
  able to access the code with a clearer, and often safer, syntax.

- You can mix DSLs with regular Lisp code, which gives you a lot of power.

- DSLs are useful when you need to write very specific code—whether it's
  code for a web page, code that draws a picture, or code that builds special
  game commands.

18

LAZY PROGRAMMING

In Chapter 14, you learned that your programs can be simpler and cleaner when built with clean, math-like functions. These functions always return the same result, which depends solely on the arguments passed into them. When you rely only on these types of functions, you are using the *functional programming style.*

However, when we used the functional programming style to create the Dice of Doom game in Chapter 15, a problem became evident: If your functions rely entirely on the arguments passed into them, the stuff that you need to pass into them often becomes *huge.*

In the Dice of Doom game, we pass around the game-tree variable, which holds all the possible future states of the game board. This is a truly massive structure, even on a measly 3-by-3 board! So while the game's current design makes our code very simple and elegant, it doesn't appear to scale well to larger game boards, which would have exponentially larger game trees. The only way we could conceivably maintain our elegant code while allowing more complex games on larger boards is to make our program smart enough not to look at every conceivable move right from the start of the game. Is this possible? Yes, it is possible, using a feature called *lazy evaluation*. In this chapter, we'll employ lazy evaluation to create an improved version of Dice of Doom.

Adding Lazy Evaluation to Lisp

With lazy evaluation, we can still create our entire game tree in a single place in our code—at the beginning of our game. However, we use some clever tricks so that some branches of our game tree are hidden in clouds:

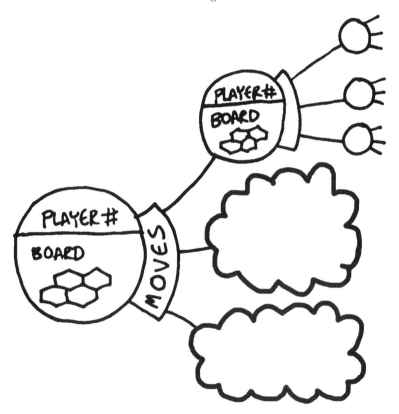

The branches of the game tree are still declared right from the start. However, we don't bother doing all the actual calculations for the branches in clouds, as we would do when we create a "real" branch. This is the *lazy* part of lazy evaluation.

Instead, we wait to see if anyone "looks" at a cloudy branch. The moment this happens, POOF!, we create a real branch of our game tree at that spot:

This means that these branches in the game tree are created only if some part of the code happens to look at them. If the player never chooses a particular move in the game, and the AI never decides to contemplate it, our program will lazily avoid the calculations needed to figure out what the given branch actually looks like.

Some languages, such as Haskell and Clojure Lisp, contain support for lazy evaluation as part of the core of the language. In fact, Clojure encourages its use and clearly demonstrates how useful it is for functional programming. However, the ANSI Common Lisp standard does not contain any similar feature for such lazy evaluation. Fortunately, with Common Lisp's powerful macro system, we can easily add this feature to the language ourselves!

Creating the lazy and force Commands

The most basic commands for lazy evaluation we're going to create are lazy and force. The lazy command will be a wrapper you can put around a piece of code, telling Lisp that you would like the code to be evaluated in a lazy way, like this:

```
> (lazy (+ 1 2))
#<FUNCTION ...>
```

As you can see, the computer *does not* try to calculate the value of 1 plus 2. Instead, it simply returns a function. To get the actual result of the calculation, we must call our other basic lazy evaluation command on a lazy value:

```
> (force (lazy (+ 1 2)))
3
```

The important thing is that the calculation was performed, but not when the lazy value was created—only when it was forced. To see that this is the case, let's look at a more complex example:

```
❶ > (defun add (a b)
      (princ "I am adding now")
      (+ a b))
  ADD
❷ > (defparameter *foo* (lazy (add 1 2)))
  *FOO*
❸ > (force *foo*)
❹ I am adding now
  3
```

Here, we've created our own add function, which, as a side effect, prints a message to the console showing when the addition is happening ❶. Next, we lazily add two numbers with our function and store the result in the variable *foo* ❷. So far, we know the addition hasn't actually happened, since the message "I am adding now" has not yet appeared.

Then we force our variable ❸. By forcing the value, the calculation is actually performed, and the result of 3 is returned. You can see that the addition took place when we forced the lazy value, since our message was also printed in the console ❹.

Here is the code for a simple implementation of lazy:

```
❶ (defmacro lazy (&body body)
❷   (let ((forced (gensym))
          (value (gensym)))
❸     `(let ((,forced nil)
❹          (,value nil))
❺        (lambda ()
❻          (unless ,forced
❼            (setf ,value (progn ,@body))
❽            (setf ,forced t))
❾          ,value)))))
```

We implement lazy by declaring a macro ❶. This macro will require two variables in the code it generates. We need to declare these as gensym names ❷, as discussed in Chapter 16. Next, we begin generating the code that the macro will output ❸ (note the backquote at the beginning of this line).

At the top of the code generated by the macro is a declaration for two local variables, using the gensym names we created ❸. The first variable tells us whether this lazy value has been forced yet ❸. If it is nil, the value can hide in a cloud. If the variable is true, the value is no longer hidden in a cloud, because it has been forced.

Once the value has been calculated through a call to force, we store the resulting value in another variable, though initially this value isn't used and is set to nil ❹. When our lazy macro is called, we want it to return a function, which can be called at a later time to force our lazy value to return a result. Therefore, we declare a lambda function next ❺.

Remember that any local variables declared outside this lambda function will be captured by the function as a closure. This means that the local variables above ❸❹ will persist between subsequent calls of the lambda function. Why does this matter? Well, once the cloud goes POOF!, we have completed all the work to calculate a value, and we don't want to do it again when the lazy value is forced and checked again multiple times in the future. We can avoid this by remembering the value after the first force here ❹ between calls.

When our lazy value is forced (by calling the lambda function we created), the first question we must ask ourselves is whether it has been forced already or is still hidden behind the cloud ❻. For a value that has not yet been forced, we go POOF! and perform the lazy calculation ❼, and save it as our value. We also mark it as having been forced ❽. Now the cloud has been destroyed.

Once the cloud is gone, we can simply return our calculated value ❾. This may have been just calculated, or it may already exist from a previous call to force.

Unlike the (admittedly mind-bending) code for the lazy macro, the force function is super-simple. All it does is call the lambda function created by lazy:

```
(defun force (lazy-value)
  (funcall lazy-value))
```

We now have a fully functional set of primitive lazy evaluation commands. Many different types of sophisticated tools could be built on top of these simple lazy and force commands.

Creating a Lazy Lists Library

We will now employ our new commands to build a library for *lazy lists,* based loosely on their implementation in Clojure. (In Clojure, lazy lists are referred to as *lazy sequences.*)

Since the fundamental command for working with Lisp lists is the cons command, you shouldn't be surprised that the first command we create for working with lazy lists is the lazy-cons command:

```
(defmacro lazy-cons (a d)
  `(lazy (cons ,a ,d)))
```

This macro emulates the behavior of cons, except that the result is wrapped in the lazy macro. To accompany lazy-cons, we'll also create lazy-car and lazy-cdr commands:

```
(defun lazy-car (x)
  (car (force x)))
```

```
(defun lazy-cdr (x)
  (cdr (force x)))
```

All these functions do is force the lazy value and then call car and cdr, respectively. Let's try using these new commands:

```
❶ > (defparameter *foo* (lazy-cons 4 7))
  *FOO*
❷ > (lazy-car *foo*)
  4
❸ > (lazy-cdr *foo*)
  7
```

As you can see, we can use lazy-cons exactly as we would use cons ❶. Then we can take apart a lazy cons in the same way we would take apart a cons ❷❸.

So far, it looks like our lazy list functions aren't any different from the standard cons, car, and cdr functions. However, we can actually use them to perform some pretty amazing feats. Consider, for instance, the following definition:

```
(defparameter *integers*
❶  (labels ((f (n)
❷            (lazy-cons n (f (1+ n)))))
      (f 1)))
```

Here, we've used the lazy-cons command to declare something impossible: a variable that holds a list of all positive integers! We do this by creating a local function f ❶, which we then call recursively to build an infinite chain of lazy-conses, using an ever-increasing number n ❷. Once we've declared this seemingly impossible *integers* variable, we can use it just as you might expect:

```
> (lazy-car *integers*)
1
> (lazy-car (lazy-cdr *integers*))
2
> (lazy-car (lazy-cdr (lazy-cdr *integers*)))
3
```

As long as we stick to using only our lazy- commands, we can pull whatever we want out of our infinite list of integers, forcing more and more numbers from *integers* on an as-needed basis.

Since not all lists are infinite (as is the list of positive integers), we'll also need to have a concept of a lazy-nil to terminate a list. Similarly, we need a lazy-null function that we can use to check if we've reached the end of a list, just as the null function can be used to check for the end of a regular list.

```
(defun lazy-nil ()
  (lazy nil))

(defun lazy-null (x)
  (not (force x)))
```

Now that we have all the basic building blocks for working with lazy lists, let's create some useful functions for our library.

Converting Between Regular Lists and Lazy Lists

One obvious thing we would want to be able to do is convert a regular list into a lazy list. The make-lazy function allows us to do this:

```
(defun make-lazy (lst)
❶  (lazy (when lst
❷          (cons (car lst) (make-lazy (cdr lst))))))
```

As the `make-lazy` function clearly shows, writing lazy list library functions is sort of like writing zen koans. The only way to understand them is to stare at them for a long time. The English language doesn't have appropriate words for clearly explaining functions like `make-lazy`.

In broad terms, `make-lazy` uses recursion to travel across the list ❷, and then wraps each cons in a call to the `lazy` macro ❶. However, to get the full meaning of this function (and the other remaining functions in our lazy library), you'll just have to try to think carefully about what `lazy` and `force` really mean, and meditate a bit over each function. Luckily, once our little lazy list library is complete, it will hide most of the strangeness of lazy evaluation.

Just as we wrote the `make-lazy` function to convert regular lists to lazy lists, we can create some functions to do the reverse—convert lazy lists into regular ones. The `take` and `take-all` functions allow us to do this.

```
❶ (defun take (n lst)
    (unless (or (zerop n) (lazy-null lst))
      (cons (lazy-car lst) (take (1- n) (lazy-cdr lst)))))

❷ (defun take-all (lst)
    (unless (lazy-null lst)
      (cons (lazy-car lst) (take-all (lazy-cdr lst)))))
```

The reason we want two different commands for going from lazy to regular lists is that, unlike regular lists, lazy lists can be infinite. Therefore, it is useful to have an additional command that lets us take just a specified number of items from the list. The `take` function accepts an extra argument n that indicates just how many values we want to take ❶. If we just want all values, we can call the `take-all` function ❷. Of course, this function cannot be used on infinite lists—taking all items from an infinite list would lead to an infinite loop.

Let's try out our new lazy list conversion functions:

```
❶ > (take 10 *integers*)
  (1 2 3 4 5 6 7 8 9 10)
❷ > (take 10 (make-lazy '(q w e r t y u i o p a s d f)))
  (Q W E R T Y U I O P)
  > (take-all (make-lazy '(q w e r t y u i o p a s d f)))
❸ (Q W E R T Y U I O P A S D F)
```

As you would expect, if we take the first 10 integers off the list of all positive integers, we just get the numbers 1 through 10 as a result ❶. The `take` function can also be used on a finite list we've created by calling `make-lazy` ❷. However, if a list is finite, we can use the simpler `take-all` function and just get a regular list of all items in the lazy list ❸.

Mapping and Searching Across Lazy Lists

We also want to be able to map and search across lazy lists. Here are some functions to allow that:

```
(defun lazy-mapcar (fun lst)
  (lazy (unless (lazy-null lst)
          (cons (funcall fun (lazy-car lst))
                (lazy-mapcar fun (lazy-cdr lst))))))

(defun lazy-mapcan (fun lst)
  (labels ((f (lst-cur)
            (if (lazy-null lst-cur)
                (force (lazy-mapcan fun (lazy-cdr lst)))
                (cons (lazy-car lst-cur) (lazy (f (lazy-cdr lst-cur)))))))
    (lazy (unless (lazy-null lst)
            (f (funcall fun (lazy-car lst)))))))

(defun lazy-find-if (fun lst)
  (unless (lazy-null lst)
    (let ((x (lazy-car lst)))
      (if (funcall fun x)
          x
          (lazy-find-if fun (lazy-cdr lst))))))

(defun lazy-nth (n lst)
  (if (zerop n)
      (lazy-car lst)
      (lazy-nth (1- n) (lazy-cdr lst))))
```

These functions are analogous to the functions mapcar, mapcan, find-if, and nth. The only difference is that they accept and return lazy lists. This means that instead of using null, car, and cdr, they use the lazy versions of these functions (lazy-null, lazy-car, and lazy-cdr) that we just created.

Using these functions is pretty straightforward:

```
❶ > (take 10 (lazy-mapcar #'sqrt *integers*))
   (1 1.4142135 1.7320508 2 2.236068 2.4494898
    2.6457512 2.828427 3 3.1622777)
❷ > (take 10 (lazy-mapcan (lambda (x)
                            (if (evenp x)
❸                              (make-lazy (list x))
❹                              (lazy-nil)))
                          *integers*))
   (2 4 6 8 10 12 14 16 18 20)
❺ > (lazy-find-if #'oddp (make-lazy '(2 4 6 7 8 10)))
   7
❻ > (lazy-nth 4 (make-lazy '(a b c d e f g)))
   E
```

Calling `lazy-mapcar` to map the square root function across the positive integers gives us a lazy list of the square roots of the positive integers. The first 10 are shown ❶. Next, we call `lazy-mapcan` ❷ and check if each positive integer is even. If it is, we return a lazy list of the numbers ❸. If it isn't, we return the lazy empty list ❹. The result is that we've filtered out all the even numbers from our lazy list of integers. We can use `lazy-find-if` to find the first odd number in a lazy list ❺. In this case, the number was 7. Finally, we can use `lazy-nth` to pick a number out of a specific location in a lazy list ❻.

We have now written an entire, if rather simple, lazy list library. Place all the functions we've written so far in this chapter in a file named *lazy.lisp* (or simply download that file from *http://landoflisp.com/*).

Now, you're going to see that lazy lists allow us to greatly boost the power of our Dice of Doom game engine!

Dice of Doom, Version 2

In Chapter 15, we created the first version of our Dice of Doom game. We are now going to modify some of the functions from that version. To proceed, place the code from that chapter into a file named *dice_of_doom_v1.lisp* so that we can reference it in this new version (or just download that file from *http://landoflisp.com/*).

To use our previous Dice of Doom and our new lazy list library, run the following in the REPL:

```
> (load "dice_of_doom_v1.lisp")
> (load "lazy.lisp")
```

Next, we're going to increase the size of our board to a more roomy 4-by-4:

```
> (defparameter *board-size* 4)
> (defparameter *board-hexnum* (* *board-size* *board-size*))
```

To allow the game to run at a reasonable speed at this larger size, we'll make the list of moves at each branch of our game tree a lazy list, instead of just a regular list. By simply converting this one structure in our game from a regular list to a lazy list, the entire game tree will become lazy as a result. To accomplish this, we now need to redefine some of the functions from the first version of our game to use our new lazy list functions.

First, let's make some small modifications to the functions that calculate the attacking and passing moves possible from a given board position:

```
(defun add-passing-move (board player spare-dice first-move moves)
  (if first-move
      moves
❶     (lazy-cons (list nil
                       (game-tree (add-new-dice board player
                                                (1- spare-dice))
                                  (mod (1+ player) *num-players*)
```

```
                                 0
                                 t))
                  moves)))

     (defun attacking-moves (board cur-player spare-dice)
       (labels ((player (pos)
                  (car (aref board pos)))
                (dice (pos)
                  (cadr (aref board pos))))
❷       (lazy-mapcan
          (lambda (src)
            (if (eq (player src) cur-player)
❸               (lazy-mapcan
                  (lambda (dst)
                    (if (and (not (eq (player dst)
                                      cur-player))
                             (> (dice src) (dice dst)))
❹                       (make-lazy
                          (list (list (list src dst)
                                      (game-tree (board-attack board
                                                               cur-player
                                                               src
                                                               dst
                                                               (dice src))
                                                 cur-player
                                                 (+ spare-dice (dice dst))
                                                 nil))))
❺                       (lazy-nil)))
❻                 (make-lazy (neighbors src)))
❼               (lazy-nil)))
❽         (make-lazy (loop for n below *board-hexnum*
                           collect n)))))
```

As you can see, the add-passing-move function needs only one small change. Since the list of moves is now a lazy list, we use lazy-cons to add a passing move to the top of the list of possible moves ❶.

The attacking-moves function requires a few more changes. First, since it now needs to return a lazy list, we use lazy-mapcan in lieu of mapcan in two places as the moves are calculated ❷❸. The lazy-mapcan function also requires the lists created inside it to be lazy, which we accomplish with the make-lazy function ❹❻. Also, any place we returned nil we now instead return a lazy-nil ❺❼. Finally, we also make the list of calculated board positions lazy ❽, since it is fed into the outer lazy-mapcan.

Next, let's make similar changes to two of the functions that deal with human players:

```
(defun handle-human (tree)
  (fresh-line)
  (princ "choose your move:")
  (let ((moves (caddr tree)))
    (labels ((print-moves (moves n)
❶              (unless (lazy-null moves)
```

```
❷                              (let* ((move (lazy-car moves))
                                      (action (car move)))
                                 (fresh-line)
                                 (format t "~a. " n)
                                 (if action
                                     (format t "~a -> ~a" (car action) (cadr action))
                                     (princ "end turn"))))
❸                              (print-moves (lazy-cdr moves) (1+ n)))))))
                  (print-moves moves 1))
             (fresh-line)
❹           (cadr (lazy-nth (1- (read)) moves)))))

    (defun play-vs-human (tree)
      (print-info tree)
❺     (if (not (lazy-null (caddr tree)))
          (play-vs-human (handle-human tree))
          (announce-winner (cadr tree))))
```

In the handle-human function, we have a local function print-moves, which is a list-eater function across the list of moves. We modify it to use our lazy commands when checking for the end of the list ❶, taking a move off the front of the list ❷, and recursing across the tail of the list ❸. Finally, we modify handle-human to use lazy-nth to pick a move after the human chooses it from the list of options ❹.

In the play-vs-human function, we make just a single pinpoint change. In order to determine whether we've reached the end of a game, we need to check whether the list of subsequent possible moves is empty, and then announce the winner. We simply use lazy-null to check if the lazy list of moves is empty ❺.

With these simple changes in place, you can play Dice of Doom against another human on much larger board sizes, since no move in the tree is realized unless one of the players decides to make it. On our larger, 4-by-4 board, enter the following to start a game (just as for version 1 of our game):

```
> (play-vs-human (game-tree (gen-board) 0 0 t))
current player = a
        a-1 a-3 a-1 b-2
      b-3 a-3 a-3 a-1
    a-3 a-3 b-1 a-2
  b-3 a-3 a-1 a-3 .
choose your move:
1. 5 -> 10
2. 6 -> 10
3. 9 -> 10
4. 11 -> 10
5. 15 -> 10
```

Version 1 would screech to a halt the moment this command was executed. This is because it would need to generate the entirety of the game tree, *for every possible move of the whole game*, before the game would even start playing.

With our lazy version of Dice of Doom, the game starts instantly!

Making Our AI Work on Larger Game Boards

Next, we're going to adjust our game AI functions to use the new lazy list library when processing moves. Along the way, we will make some additional improvements to the AI code.

Trimming the Game Tree

In version 1 of Dice of Doom, our AI code was, in certain ways, extremely powerful. This is because, at every decision point, the AI player would look at *every possible future board position* to choose the absolute best next move. In this way, it could play a perfect game of Dice of Doom, winning every game that was winnable.

However, such a design does not scale to larger boards. This is because it becomes impossible to contemplate every single possible future move once there are too many. In fact, the whole point of our new lazy game tree is to avoid contemplating every possible move. Therefore, we need a way to tell the computer, "Consider only this many moves, and no more." In other words, we want to be able tell it to look only two, three, or four moves ahead, and then stop looking any further.

The functional programming style of Dice of Doom allows us to do this in a very elegant but nonobvious way.

The *obvious* solution to the problem would be to modify the get-ratings and rate-position from version 1 to have a new argument called search-depth. Then we could ask ourselves at every call of those functions, "Have we reached the maximum search depth we want?"

The problem with this approach is that it gunks up those functions with extra, confusing code. In fact, the way we evaluate board positions is theoretically a separate issue from how deep we wish to search. As programmers like to say, these issues are *orthogonal*, and it would be best if we could write separate functions to deal with each of these issues independently.

In fact, with our new lazy game tree, it is possible to write a separate function that is solely responsible for "trimming" the search tree and is completely independent from the main AI code that contemplates and rates possible moves.

Here is the function that trims our tree:

```
❶ (defun limit-tree-depth (tree depth)
    (list (car tree)
      (cadr tree)
❷    (if (zerop depth)
❸        (lazy-nil)
        (lazy-mapcar (lambda (move)
                        (list (car move)
❹                            (limit-tree-depth (cadr move) (1- depth))))
                (caddr tree)))))
```

This is a pretty simple function that takes just two arguments: a lazy tree and the depth to which we wish to trim it ❶. As a result, it just outputs a new game tree, calling itself recursively, decrementing the depth for each level it travels into the tree ❹. Once this depth reaches zero ❷, we know we're at the level that we want to trim, and we set the lazy list of moves to the empty list ❸.

Now all we need to do is call our new limit-tree-depth function before doing our AI rating calculations. We do this by tweaking our handle-computer function a bit:

```
(defparameter *ai-level* 4)

(defun handle-computer (tree)
❶  (let ((ratings (get-ratings (limit-tree-depth tree *ai-level*)
                                (car tree))))
    (cadr (lazy-nth (position (apply #'max ratings) ratings)
❷                   (caddr tree)))))
```

Before calling get-ratings to get a rating for every next available move, we transform our game tree into our trimmed game tree ❶. All of our AI code can now run on the trimmed tree, completely oblivious to the fact that a larger game tree exists or that there are deeper moves it isn't including in its calculations. With this technique, we have managed to decouple the code that limits the AI search depth from the algorithm that actually evaluates board positions. One other small modification is to use lazy-nth when picking a move out of the lazy list of moves ❷.

NOTE *The limit-tree-depth function uses a pretty crude method for trimming our tree: It simply trims all tree branches beyond a certain depth. For most board games, doing this is an optimal way of trimming the game tree. However, Dice of Doom has the uncommon property that multiple moves in a row are allowed for each player. It would probably be more optimal if limit-tree-depth took into account how many times we've switched players as a criterion for trimming a branch. But our simpler version works well enough.*

At this point, we should also make a pinpoint change to play-vs-computer:

```
(defun play-vs-computer (tree)
  (print-info tree)
❶ (cond ((lazy-null (caddr tree)) (announce-winner (cadr tree)))
        ((zerop (car tree)) (play-vs-computer (handle-human tree)))
        (t (play-vs-computer (handle-computer tree))))))
```

Here, we just added a lazy-null to check for the end of the lazy list of moves in a single spot ❶.

Now let's look at another trick that will improve the power of our AI code.

Applying Heuristics

By trimming our game tree, we've fundamentally changed our AI player. Without trimming, the AI player was able to play a perfect game at all times. By trimming the tree, however, it is possible for the AI to "miss something," since it is no longer contemplating every possible future move. In version 2 of Dice of Doom, the computer player will no longer be able to play a perfect game—just a "pretty good" game is possible.

Basically, we've exchanged the AI's ability to play a perfect game for much better performance. In the process, we've turned the AI code from something precise that can be analyzed by mathematics into something that is "squishier" and far less precise. As computer scientists would say, we have now entered into the realm of *heuristics.*

In computer science, heuristics are programming techniques that are imperfect, but allow us to get good results very quickly. Broadly speaking, any technique that is fast but not guaranteed to work 100 percent of the time is a heuristic. When we write code that uses heuristics (as our Dice of Doom AI engine now does), it is often worthwhile to use some creative thinking and to "play around" with the code in different ways.

Basically, since we're already given up on our goal of a perfect solution and are now using imprecise techniques, it's possible that tweaking the knobs on the heuristic code in different ways could dramatically improve our results. And indeed, it turns out that there is a simple change we can make to our Dice of Doom AI heuristics that will significantly improve the AI player's game.

Winning by a Lot vs. Winning by a Little

In version 1 of our Dice of Doom code, the AI player had no reason to ever worry about its margin of victory. All it cared about was that when the game ended, it had ownership of at least one more territory of the board than its opponent, which meant it had won.

However, now that we're using imprecise heuristics in our AI code, it matters *a lot* how large the lead is at any point in the game. A heuristic rule for this situation is "If I am totally whomping my opponent in the game, it is pretty unlikely he/she will be able to recover, even if I look only a few moves ahead."

Remember that a minimax algorithm (as we're using in our AI) assigns a point score to every final leaf branch in the tree. In version 1 of our game, this score was either 0 or 1, or sometimes 1/2 when the game ended in a tie. In version 2, these are not truly "final leaves" in the tree, but simply leaves in our much smaller trimmed tree. In this situation, it would be much better if our leaf point scores had a larger range of values, so that we can tell which moves lead to a game we're winning by "a lot" and which moves lead to a game we're winning by only "a little."

Let's write a score-board function that uses some more complex heuristics to score the board position at a leaf:

```
   (defun score-board (board player)
❶    (loop for hex across board
           for pos from 0
❷         sum (if (eq (car hex) player)
❸              (if (threatened pos board)
❹                  1
❺                2)
❻           -1)))
```

The score-board function loops ❶ across all of the hexes of the board and builds a running total of points for each hex using the sum directive of the loop macro. If the player we're scoring owns the current hex ❷, we want to add positive points to the total ❹❺.

To decide exactly how many points to add to the total for an occupied hex, we make another heuristic observation: Hexes that neighbor a stronger opponent aren't quite as valuable as hexes without strong neighbors. We'll call a hex that neighbors an enemy hex that has more dice on it a *threatened hex*. For hexes that are threatened ❸, we'll add only 1 point to the point total ❹. For hexes that are unthreatened, we'll add 2 points ❺. Finally, for each hex owned by an opposing player, we'll subtract 1 point from the total ❻.

Again, the important thing to realize is that score-board is a heuristic function, and there is no truly right or wrong way to generate such a score. Instead of adding 2 points for unthreatened hexes, we could just as easily have added 1.5 points. In developing this example, I ran some simulations playing various opponents using different versions of the score-board function, and this version ended up working reasonably well. Developing heuristics is not an exact science.

Here is the function that determines whether a given hex is threatened:

```lisp
(defun threatened (pos board)
❶  (let* ((hex (aref board pos))
         (player (car hex))
         (dice (cadr hex)))
❷    (loop for n in (neighbors pos)
❸         do (let* ((nhex (aref board n))
                    (nplayer (car nhex))
                    (ndice (cadr nhex)))
❹             (when (and (not (eq player nplayer)) (> ndice dice))
❺               (return t))))))
```

First, we get the hex in question and figure out who the occupying player is, and how many dice that player has ❶. Then we loop through all the neighboring squares for the current position ❷. After that, we find out the player and dice count for each of the neighbors ❸. As soon as we find a neighboring hex owned by an opponent with a larger dice count (a threatening neighbor) ❹, we can return true ❺. Calling return in this way causes the loop to stop early with true as a result.

Now that we have completed our score-board and threatened functions, we're ready to write our improved get-ratings and rate-position functions:

```lisp
(defun get-ratings (tree player)
❶  (take-all (lazy-mapcar (lambda (move)
                           (rate-position (cadr move) player))
                         (caddr tree))))

(defun rate-position (tree player)
  (let ((moves (caddr tree)))
❷    (if (not (lazy-null moves))
      (apply (if (eq (car tree) player)
               #'max
             #'min)
             (get-ratings tree player))
❸      (score-board (cadr tree) player))))
```

As you can see, we've updated a couple lines of code ❶❷ to be compatible with our new lazy game tree. Notice that any game positions that lack follow-up moves (that is, leaves) now cause our new score-board function to be called ❸.

Now that we have a fully working heuristic AI player that can play on larger game boards, let's try it out. As usual, all moves for player B in the following example are being automatically calculated by the AI algorithm:

```lisp
> (play-vs-computer (game-tree (gen-board) 0 0 t))
current player = a
      a-1 b-2 b-1 a-3
    b-3 a-1 a-3 a-3
   b-3 b-2 b-2 b-2
  a-3 a-3 a-2 a-2
```

```
choose your move:
1. 3 -> 2
2. 6 -> 2
3. 6 -> 10
4. 6 -> 1
5. 6 -> 11
6. 7 -> 11
7. 7 -> 2
8. 13 -> 9
3
current player = a
        a-1 b-2 b-1 a-3
      b-3 a-1 a-1 a-3
    b-3 b-2 a-2 b-2
  a-3 a-3 a-2 a-2
choose your move:
1. end turn
2. 3 -> 2
3. 7 -> 11
4. 7 -> 2
5. 13 -> 9
1
current player = b
        a-2 b-2 b-1 a-3
      b-3 a-1 a-1 a-3
    b-3 b-2 a-2 b-2
  a-3 a-3 a-2 a-2
current player = b
        a-2 b-1 b-1 a-3
      b-3 b-1 a-1 a-3
    b-3 b-2 a-2 b-2
  a-3 a-3 a-2 a-2
current player = b
        b-2 b-1 b-1 a-3
      b-1 b-1 a-1 a-3
    b-3 b-2 a-2 b-2
  a-3 a-3 a-2 a-2
current player = b
        b-2 b-1 b-1 a-3
      b-1 b-1 b-1 a-3
    b-3 b-2 a-2 b-1
  a-3 a-3 a-2 a-2
current player = a
        b-3 b-2 b-2 a-3
      b-1 b-1 b-1 a-3
    b-3 b-2 a-2 b-1
  a-3 a-3 a-2 a-2
```

```
choose your move:
1. 3 -> 2
2. 7 -> 11
3. 7 -> 2
4. 7 -> 6
5. 10 -> 6
6. 10 -> 5
7. 10 -> 11
8. 13 -> 9
9. 15 -> 11
...
```

With these changes in place, the AI player will win around 65 to 70 percent of all games (depending on the board size and AI level) when pitted against a player that chooses only random moves. This is actually a very good result. Our simple gen-board function often creates very lopsided starting positions, so many of the remaining 30 percent of the games are simply unwinnable for the computer.

Alpha Beta Pruning

Let's add one final improvement to version 2 of our Dice of Doom AI.

Alpha-beta pruning is a well-known optimization of the minimax algorithm that improves performance by skipping over some branches (*pruning* those branches) if it is certain that they will not impact the final minimax evaluation.

When would a branch in the game tree be unable to impact the final result? In order to understand how alpha-beta pruning works, look at the following picture, showing the game tree for a simple 2-by-2 board:

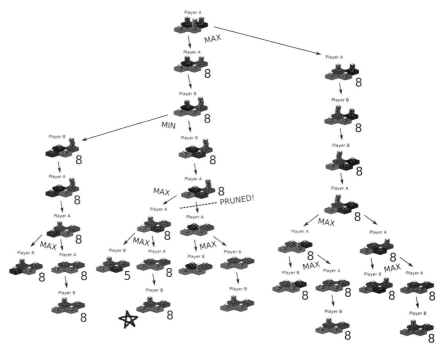

At the top of this picture is the starting position of the game. The arrows point to possible moves. Above each board it states which player (A or B) currently is making a move.

The picture also shows the results of a minimax analysis of the game tree. On the bottom right of each board, you can see a number showing how our latest get-ratings function (with the new score-board logic) would rate that position. For leaf nodes (the boards along the very bottom), this number is calculated through score-board. For branch nodes, the number is calculated based on the minimax algorithm.

Every position in the game tree that allows a choice of moves is marked either as a MAX node or MIN node. Since the analysis in the picture is based on finding the best move for player A, all places allowing choices for player A are marked as MAX. All positions allowing choices for player B are marked as MIN. As you can see from the picture, this game is pretty unexciting, and there is only one position where player B actually has a choice of moves. In other words, only one MIN node exists in the game tree.

Working left to right, the minimax algorithm travels, depth first, exploring all the way down to the leaves. This is called a *depth-first search*. (We're assuming no trimming is occurring, with *ai-level* set very high.) Then it chooses either the maximum or minimum scores for any nodes that have more than one branch.

When it does this, the first (left) branch of the MIN node in the picture ends up with a score of 8. If the AI engine now dips into the right branch, it really only cares what it finds there as long as the score remains below 8. After all, the minimum of 8 and any larger number larger than 8 will still be 8, making such large numbers irrelevant to the eventual outcome of the calculation.

As soon as the AI finds a node in the right branch that has a score of 8 (marked with a star in the picture), it knows the rest of the right branch is irrelevant and can be pruned away from our calculations. This means the minimax algorithm has no need to look at the branch in the tree marked with the dotted line in the picture.

This is a simple example, showing alpha-beta pruning in action. In the game tree shown in the picture, this pruning leads to only modest savings, since just a small number of the total nodes can be pruned. However, with larger game trees, the savings from alpha-beta pruning are typically immense, constituting a majority of the nodes in the game tree.

We're going to take some liberties in how we implement alpha-beta pruning in our game to keep things simple. First, an alpha-beta pruning algorithm usually will pass around two variables called, naturally, alpha and beta.

This is because it's possible to write code that handles both the MAX nodes and MIN nodes at once by switching alpha and beta between the high and low limits. In our example, we're going to use the variables upper-limit and lower-limit instead, indicating the highest and lowest values we care about as we traverse the game tree. As a cost, there will be some repetitive-looking code for handling the MAX and MIN cases. However, thinking of alpha-beta pruning in terms of upper-limit and lower-limit makes the code a bit easier to understand.

Another compromise we're making is that we're not decoupling the pruning code from the minimax code. Remember that with the trimming code, we wrote an independent function named limit-tree-depth, which separated the act of trimming from the rest of the AI code. We could use a similar approach for separating the alpha-beta pruning code as well, creating a function that can transform the game tree into a pruned version on its own. However, doing this is a bit more involved, because the alpha-beta pruning code must have access to intermediate minimax calculations. For a more advanced AI engine, this would be a good idea. For our simple engine, we will just add our alpha-beta pruning check directly inside our minimax functions.

So let's get started. First, we'll rewrite our get-ratings function as two new functions: ab-get-ratings-max and ab-get-ratings-min.

Remember that the get-ratings function was responsible for calculating the best score out of multiple available moves from a single-board arrangement. Now, however, we want it to stop early in its evaluation of moves once it decides it has found a move that's "as good as is possible." Determining whether it has reached this point is subtly different depending on whether the node in question is a MAX move (a move of the current player) or a MIN move (a move for the opponent).

Let's look at the version responsible for MAX nodes first:

```
❶ (defun ab-get-ratings-max (tree player upper-limit lower-limit)
    (labels ((f (moves lower-limit)
              (unless (lazy-null moves)
❷               (let ((x (ab-rate-position (cadr (lazy-car moves))
                                           player
                                           upper-limit
                                           lower-limit)))
❸                 (if (>= x upper-limit)
❹                     (list x)
❺                     (cons x (f (lazy-cdr moves) (max x lower-limit)))))))))
      (f (caddr tree) lower-limit)))
```

We're now passing in an extra upper-limit and lower-limit argument into ab-get-ratings-max ❶. This function won't actually ever check the lower-limit argument directly, since it is concerned only with finding the maximum rating possible from the given location in the tree. However, it will pass this value on to child branches, which may contain MIN nodes that *do* care about the lower limit.

When we rate the next branch of the tree ❷ (by calling ab-rate-position, which we'll write shortly), we save the result as x. If x is greater than or equal to our upper-limit ❸, we know we got a result as good as we can hope for, and can just return the latest rating as a final value in our list ❹.

If x isn't large enough, we need to keep looking at the remaining branches ❺. Note that x will become the new lower-limit if it's larger than the previous lower-limit.

Next, let's look at the ab-get-ratings-min function:

```
(defun ab-get-ratings-min (tree player upper-limit lower-limit)
  (labels ((f (moves upper-limit)
            (unless (lazy-null moves)
              (let ((x (ab-rate-position (cadr (lazy-car moves))
                                         player
                                         upper-limit
                                         lower-limit)))
                (if (<= x lower-limit)
                    (list x)
                    (cons x (f (lazy-cdr moves) (min x upper-limit)))))))))
    (f (caddr tree) upper-limit)))
```

The ab-get-ratings-min function is basically identical to the ab-get-ratings-max function, except the roles of the upper and lower limits are flipped. Based on the repetitiveness of these two functions, you could probably imagine how the ab-get-ratings-max and ab-get-ratings-min functions could be combined into a single function. As mentioned earlier, with that approach, rather than upper-limit and lower-limit, you would use the more generic terms alpha and beta, as these will differ based on whether the node is a MAX node or a MIN node.

Next, we need to tweak rate-position, the function that rates a single-board arrangement:

```
(defun ab-rate-position (tree player upper-limit lower-limit)
  (let ((moves (caddr tree)))
    (if (not (lazy-null moves))
❶      (if (eq (car tree) player)
❷          (apply #'max (ab-get-ratings-max tree
                                            player
                                            upper-limit
                                            lower-limit))
❸          (apply #'min (ab-get-ratings-min tree
                                            player
                                            upper-limit
                                            lower-limit)))
        (score-board (cadr tree) player))))
```

In our new ab-rate-position, we check if this node in the game tree is a move for us or a move for an opponent ❶. If it's a move for us, then it's a MAX node, and we want to dispatch to ab-get-ratings-max ❷. If it's the opponent's turn, we instead dispatch to ab-get-ratings-min ❸. Otherwise, ab-rate-positon is the same as our previous rate-position function.

To complete our support for alpha-beta pruning, we need to modify one more function: the handle-computer function that kicks off our minimax calculations:

```
(defun handle-computer (tree)
❶  (let ((ratings (ab-get-ratings-max (limit-tree-depth tree *ai-level*)
                                      (car tree)
❷                                     most-positive-fixnum
❸                                     most-negative-fixnum)))
    (cadr (lazy-nth (position (apply #'max ratings) ratings) (caddr tree)))))
```

This function starts off the minimax calculation by calling ab-get-ratings-max ❶, since the first move most definitely belongs to the target player and therefore is a MAX node.

When we call this function, we'll need to pass in our starting upper-limit and lower-limit. Since we're at the very beginning of our minimax searching, we'll want to set these to be as large and as small as possible. Ideally, we would want them to be *positive infinity* and *negative infinity*. Although many Lisp environments contain support for such concepts, they are not part of the ANSI Common Lisp standard. However, the standard does define most-positive-fixnum and most-negative-fixnum, which are very large positive and negative numbers, making them perfectly suited for our purposes. Hence, we pass these into ab-get-ratings-max to start off our limits ❷❸.

If we wanted to squeeze out a tad more efficiency from our AI engine, we could, instead, set the upper-limit and lower-limit to be the maximum and minimum values from our score-board function. That would slightly improve the amount of pruning that is possible. However, the score-board function may return a different range of scores based on the size of the board. and it might have other dependencies if we decide to optimize board scoring even more in the future. Therefore, it is best for the time being if we set our limits to nigh infinity for the start of our minimax calculations so we don't need to worry about this.

As a final reward for once again improving the performance of our AI, let's increase the size of the board to use a 5-by-5 game field. With our new lazy, trimmed, and pruned AI algorithms, we should be able to handle this larger board without a sweat:

```
(defparameter *board-size* 5)
(defparameter *board-hexnum* (* *board-size* *board-size*))
```

NOTE *Remember that we used memoization for some of our earlier functions. If you have already played some games in this chapter on a 4-by-4 board, one function in particular, the neighbors function, may return results based on this old board size. This is only an issue if you've already played a game on the 4-by-4 board without restarting your Lisp in the interim. To fix this, simply rerun the definition of the neighbors function in dice_of_doom_v1.lisp from the REPL (including the memoized revision at the bottom of the file) to clear any cached results.*

Here's what our game looks like now:

```
> (play-vs-computer (game-tree (gen-board) 0 0 t))
current player = a
        a-2 b-2 a-1 b-2 b-2
      a-1 b-2 b-3 b-3 a-3
    a-1 b-2 a-3 b-1 b-2
  b-1 b-3 a-2 b-2 a-1
b-3 b-1 b-1 a-3 b-3
choose your move:
1. 9 -> 13
2. 9 -> 4
3. 9 -> 14
4. 12 -> 13
5. 17 -> 22
6. 23 -> 18
7. 23 -> 22
3
current player = a
        a-2 b-2 a-1 b-2 b-2
      a-1 b-2 b-3 b-3 a-1
    a-1 b-2 a-3 b-1 a-2
  b-1 b-3 a-2 b-2 a-1
b-3 b-1 b-1 a-3 b-3
```

```
choose your move:
1. end turn
2. 12 -> 13
3. 14 -> 13
4. 14 -> 15
5. 17 -> 22
6. 23 -> 18
7. 23 -> 22
1
current player = b
        a-3 b-2 a-1 b-2 b-2
      a-1 b-2 b-3 b-3 a-1
    a-1 b-2 a-3 b-1 a-2
  b-1 b-3 a-2 b-2 a-1
  b-3 b-1 b-1 a-3 b-3
current player = b
        a-3 b-1 a-1 b-2 b-2
      b-1 b-2 b-3 b-3 a-1
    a-1 b-2 a-3 b-1 a-2
  b-1 b-3 a-2 b-2 a-1
  b-3 b-1 b-1 a-3 b-3
current player = b
        a-3 b-1 b-1 b-1 b-2
      b-1 b-2 b-3 b-3 a-1
    a-1 b-2 a-3 b-1 a-2
  b-1 b-3 a-2 b-2 a-1
  b-3 b-1 b-1 a-3 b-3
current player = b
        a-3 b-1 b-1 b-1 b-1
      b-1 b-2 b-3 b-3 b-1
    a-1 b-2 a-3 b-1 a-2
  b-1 b-3 a-2 b-2 a-1
  b-3 b-1 b-1 a-3 b-3
current player = b
        a-3 b-1 b-1 b-1 b-1
      b-1 b-1 b-3 b-3 b-1
    b-1 b-2 a-3 b-1 a-2
  b-1 b-3 a-2 b-2 a-1
  b-3 b-1 b-1 a-3 b-3
current player = b
        a-3 b-1 b-1 b-1 b-1
      b-1 b-1 b-3 b-3 b-1
    b-1 b-2 a-3 b-1 a-2
  b-1 b-1 b-2 b-2 a-1
  b-3 b-1 b-1 a-3 b-3
current player = b
        a-3 b-1 b-1 b-1 b-1
      b-1 b-1 b-3 b-3 b-1
    b-1 b-2 a-3 b-1 a-2
  b-1 b-1 b-2 b-2 b-2
  b-3 b-1 b-1 a-3 b-1
```

```
current player = a
        a-3 b-2 b-2 b-2 b-2
      b-2 b-2 b-3 b-3 b-1
    b-1 b-2 a-3 b-1 a-2
  b-1 b-1 b-2 b-2 b-2
b-3 b-1 b-1 a-3 b-1
choose your move:
1. 0 -> 4
2. 0 -> 1
3. 0 -> 5
4. 12 -> 13
5. 14 -> 10
6. 14 -> 9
7. 14 -> 13
8. 14 -> 15
9. 23 -> 18
10. 23 -> 17
11. 23 -> 22
12. 23 -> 24
```

At this point, our REPL game interface is becoming really impractical for such a large game field. We'll be addressing that next.

What You've Learned

In this chapter, we made the computer player for our Dice of Doom game much more sophisticated. We implementing the game tree using lazy lists, and applied several optimization techniques to limit the number of board positions that are searched by the AI engine. Along the way, you learned the following:

- *Lazy programming* allows you to work with very large (and even infinite) data structures and do so efficiently.

- Once you have a lazy macro and a force function, you can use them to build more sophisticated lazy operations, including building a lazy list library.

- Heuristics are imperfect algorithms that can be used to improve the performance of your code, with some creative thinking. In our example, we made some heuristic changes to how we score leaf nodes.

- Once we converted Dice of Doom to use a lazy tree, we were able to elegantly trim the game tree in order to limit how deep the AI thinks when contemplating its moves.

- Alpha-beta pruning lets us improve performance even more, by pruning branches that have no way of impacting the final scores on the moves being considered by the AI.

19

CREATING A GRAPHICAL, WEB-BASED VERSION OF DICE OF DOOM

In the previous chapter, we created a second version of Dice of Doom to play on larger game boards. It has become quite difficult to understand the board and make moves using our crude console interface. Certainly, Dice of Doom would be infinitely better if we had a pretty graphical game board that allowed us to simply click where we wanted to make our moves. Well, I have good news for you . . .

In this chapter, we'll put together a lot of code from earlier chapters to transform Dice of Doom into a full-featured, graphical game you can play right inside a web browser!

Drawing the Game Board Using the SVG Format

We've already written a primitive web server in Chapter 13. Also, we've covered how to draw SVG graphics with a DSL in Chapter 17. Lucky for us, the new HTML5 standard includes features that make it possible to embed SVG pictures directly inside a standard HTML document. In this way, we'll be able to use our simple little web server to serve up some fully interactive vector graphics. You'll be amazed at how easy it is to do this.

NOTE   *At the time this book was written, the only web browser to support inline SVG within HTML was Firefox 3.7 Alpha. Use this, or a more recent release of Firefox with our new version of Dice of Doom. If you're having problems, try navigating to the about:config page in the Firefox address bar, and set the html5.enable configuration setting to true. This will allow Firefox to use the latest HTML5 settings.*

Also, remember that our web server library is not pure ANSI Common Lisp, and makes use of some CLISP-specific extensions. This means it requires CLISP to function.

First, we'll need to pull in code from various other chapters to get ready. In the previous chapter, we created version 2 of our Dice of Doom engine. Place all the code from that chapter in a file named *dice_of_doom_v2.lisp*. You should also already have created a file named *webserver.lisp* from Chapter 13. (These files are all freely available from *http://landoflisp.com/*.)

Let's load in these files:

```
> (load "dice_of_doom_v2.lisp")
> (load "webserver.lisp")
```

For our SVG support, we'll also need the SVG-rendering code from Chapters 16 and 17. Place those functions in *svg.lisp*. (This file is also available from *http://landoflisp.com/*.) For reference, the functions we'll need are let1, split, pairs, print-tag, tag, svg, brightness, svg-style, and polygon. Load this file next:

```
> (load "svg.lisp")
```

Now let's write some code that can draw a pretty version of our game board using SVG. First, we'll want to define some constants that control the various dimensions needed to draw the board:

```
  (defparameter *board-width* 900)
  (defparameter *board-height* 500)
❶ (defparameter *board-scale* 64)
❷ (defparameter *top-offset* 3)
❸ (defparameter *dice-scale* 40)
❹ (defparameter *dot-size* 0.05)
```

The board width and height will be 900-by-500 pixels, which is a good size for playing a game in a browser on most people's computer screens. The board scale ❶ represents half the width of a single hex on the screen in pixels. The *top-offset* variable ❷ tells us we want three extra hex heights of free space above the base of the board. We'll need this because a hex with lot of dice on it will have its dice sticking out, upward, and we need room for these dice to be visible on the screen. The *dice-scale* variable ❸ tells us that a single die will be about 40 pixels tall and wide on the screen. Finally, we set *dot-size* to 0.05, which tells us that each dot will be about 0.05 times the size of a die ❹.

Drawing a Die

Now we're ready to write a function that can draw a die. Note that we won't use bitmaps or anything like that to draw. Instead, we're drawing a die "the hard way," by rendering it directly out of raw SVG polygons. Here's the code:

```
❶ (defun draw-die-svg (x y col)
❷   (labels ((calc-pt (pt)
                (cons (+ x (* *dice-scale* (car pt)))
                      (+ y (* *dice-scale* (cdr pt))))))
❸         (f (pol col)
                (polygon (mapcar #'calc-pt pol) col)))
❹       (f '((0 . -1) (-0.6 . -0.75) (0 . -0.5) (0.6 . -0.75))
           (brightness col 40))
        (f '((0 . -0.5) (-0.6 . -0.75) (-0.6 . 0) (0 . 0.25))
           col)
        (f '((0 . -0.5) (0.6 . -0.75) (0.6 . 0) (0 . 0.25))
           (brightness col -40))
❺       (mapc (lambda (x y)
                (polygon (mapcar (lambda (xx yy)
                                   (calc-pt (cons (+ x (* xx *dot-size*))
                                                  (+ y (* yy *dot-size*)))))
                         '(-1 -1 1 1)
                         '(-1 1 1 -1))
                 '(255 255 255)))
❻       '(-0.05 0.125 0.3 -0.3 -0.125 0.05 0.2 0.2 0.45 0.45 -0.45 -0.2)
        '(-0.875 -0.80 -0.725 -0.775 -0.70 -0.625
          -0.35 -0.05 -0.45 -0.15 -0.45 -0.05)))))
```

To draw a die, we need to pass in three arguments ❶. The first two are the x and y position at which the die should appear in the SVG picture. The third is the color we want the die to be. This function will take some liberties with that color and modify it as needed to give the die a little shading.

Anything we draw in this function will need to be rendered in a scaled fashion, based on the *dice-scale* constant we defined. Therefore, we first define a local function calc-pt that scales a point for us ❷. Since we'll need to draw several scaled polygons, let's also create a convenience function, f, that runs calc-pt against all points in a polygon and then draws it by calling the polygon function ❸.

A die in our picture will have three visible faces: the top face, the front face, and the right face. We draw these by calling our function f three times starting here ❹ and using some hard-coded coordinates for the three faces.

The last thing we need to do is draw the little dots on the faces of the die. We do this by mapcing ❺ the coordinates for the dots ❻ against a lambda function that can render a dot. This lambda function uses the *dot-size* variable to scale down a square-shaped polygon that represents each dot on the die face. We could write more sophisticated code to draw circular and/or elliptical dots, but the dots are so small that squares look just fine.

Let's try drawing a die at x=50 and y=50 with an RGB red (255 0 0) color:

```
> (svg 100 100 (draw-die-svg 50 50 '(255 0 0)))
<svg xmlns="http://www.w3.org/2000/svg" xmlns:xlink="http://www.w3.org/1999/
xlink" height="100" width="100"><polygon points="50,10 26.0,20.0 50,30.0
74.0,20.0 " style="fill:rgb(255,40,40);stroke:rgb(155,0,0)"></polygon><polygon
points="50,30.0 26.0,20.0 26.0,50 50,60.0 "
style="fill:rgb(255,0,0);stroke:rgb(155,0,0)"></polygon><polygon
points="50,30.0 74.0,20.0 74.0,50 50,60.0 "
style="fill:rgb(215,0,0);stroke:rgb(115,0,0)"></polygon><polygon
points="46.0,13.0 46.0,17.0 50.0,17.0 50.0,13.0 "
style="fill:rgb(255,255,255);stroke:rgb(155,155,155)"></polygon><polygon
points="53.0,16.0 53.0,20.0 57.0,20.0 57.0,16.0 "
style="fill:rgb(255,255,255);stroke:rgb(155,155,155)"></polygon><polygon
points="60.0,18.999998 60.0,23.0 64.0,23.0 64.0,18.999998 "
style="fill:rgb(255,255,255);stroke:rgb(155,155,155)"></polygon><polygon
points="36.0,17.0 36.0,21.000002 40.0,21.000002 40.0,17.0 "
style="fill:rgb(255,255,255);stroke:rgb(155,155,155)"></polygon><polygon
points="43.0,20.0 43.0,24.0 47.0,24.0 47.0,20.0 "
style="fill:rgb(255,255,255);stroke:rgb(155,155,155)"></polygon><polygon
points="50.0,23.0 50.0,27.0 54.0,27.0 54.0,23.0 "
style="fill:rgb(255,255,255);stroke:rgb(155,155,155)"></polygon><polygon
points="56.0,34.0 56.0,38.0 60.0,38.0 60.0,34.0 "
style="fill:rgb(255,255,255);stroke:rgb(155,155,155)"></polygon><polygon
points="56.0,46.0 56.0,50.0 60.0,50.0 60.0,46.0 "
style="fill:rgb(255,255,255);stroke:rgb(155,155,155)"></polygon><polygon
points="66.0,30.0 66.0,34.0 70.0,34.0 70.0,30.0 "
style="fill:rgb(255,255,255);stroke:rgb(155,155,155)"></polygon><polygon
points="66.0,42.0 66.0,46.0 70.0,46.0 70.0,42.0 "
style="fill:rgb(255,255,255);stroke:rgb(155,155,155)"></polygon><polygon
points="30.0,30.0 30.0,34.0 34.0,34.0 34.0,30.0 "
style="fill:rgb(255,255,255);stroke:rgb(155,155,155)"></polygon><polygon
points="40.0,46.0 40.0,50.0 44.0,50.0 44.0,46.0 "
style="fill:rgb(255,255,255);stroke:rgb(155,155,155)"></polygon></svg>
```

If you want to see what the final die looks like, just save this gobbledygook to a file named *die.svg*. Then load the result in Firefox, where you should see the following picture (shown at a blown-up size):

Drawing a Tile

Next, let's write the function to draw an entire hex tile, including the base and the dice on the tile:

```
(defun draw-tile-svg (x y pos hex xx yy col chosen-tile)
❶  (loop for z below 2
❷        do (polygon (mapcar (lambda (pt)
                               (cons (+ xx (* *board-scale* (car pt)))
                                     (+ yy (* *board-scale*
                                              (+ (cdr pt) (* (- 1 z) 0.1))))))
❸                     '((-1 . -0.2) (0 . -0.5) (1 . -0.2)
                         (1 . 0.2) (0 . 0.5) (-1 . 0.2)))
❹                   (if (eql pos chosen-tile)
                       (brightness col 100)
                       col)))
❺  (loop for z below (second hex)
❻        do (draw-die-svg (+ xx
                            (* *dice-scale*
                               0.3
❼                              (if (oddp (+ x y z))
                                   -0.3
                                   0.3)))
                          (- yy (* *dice-scale* z 0.8)) col)))
```

This function takes in a lot of parameters, because a lot of information is encoded in a single tile of the board. You'll learn the precise meaning of each of these parameters when we draw the board in the next section.

First, our `draw-tile-svg` function draws the base. To give the base a mild 3D look, we'll draw it twice, with one level stacked on top of the other. Here ❶ is the loop that draws the two bases. Within that loop, we need to draw a hexagonal polygon ❷. We map a scaling function across the coordinates so that they are scaled to our *board-scale* variable. Here ❸ you can see the six points of a hexagon in perspective encoded using decimal notation. The color of the base will be brightened slightly if it has been chosen by the player to perform a move. We do this by increasing the brightness of the tile when creating our polygons ❹.

After we've finished drawing the tile base, we need to draw the dice that reside on the tile. We do this by looping across the number of dice ❺ and then calling our `draw-die-svg` function ❻. When calculating the x and y positions of the dice, we need to perform a bit of scaling math. The most interesting piece of this math is that we shift the dice a bit to the left or right, depending on whether the sum of the x-, y-, and z-coordinates for a given die is odd or even ❼. This makes the stacks look a little imperfect and will give the stacked dice for the complete board a pleasing, natural appearance.

Now let's call our function to draw a finished tile and see how it looks. Again, just copy the output from this command to a file named something like *tile.svg*.

```
> (svg 300 300 (draw-tile-svg 0 0 0 '(0 3) 100 150 '(255 0 0) nil))
<svg xmlns="http://www.w3.org/2000/svg" xmlns:xlink="http://www.w3.org/1999/
xlink" height="300" width="300"><polygon points="36,143.6 100,124.4 164,143.6
164,169.2 100,188.4 36,169.2 " style="fill:rgb(255,0,0);stroke:rgb(155,0,0)">
...
```

Here's what you should see when looking at the file in Firefox:

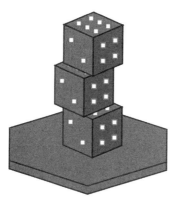

Drawing the Board

Now we're ready to write a function that draws an entire game board as an SVG. It will be very similar to our `draw-board` function, which we've been using to draw the board to the console. It fulfills the same role, but simply outputs the result as SVG data.

```
(defparameter *die-colors* '((255 63 63) (63 63 255)))

❶ (defun draw-board-svg (board chosen-tile legal-tiles)
❷   (loop for y below *board-size*
❸       do (loop for x below *board-size*
❹               for pos = (+ x (* *board-size* y))
                for hex = (aref board pos)
                for xx = (* *board-scale* (+ (* 2 x) (- *board-size* y)))
                for yy = (* *board-scale* (+ (* y 0.7) *top-offset*))
                for col = (brightness (nth (first hex) *die-colors*)
                                       (* -15 (- *board-size* y)))
❺               do (if (member pos legal-tiles)
                       (tag g ()
❻                        (tag a ("xlink:href" (make-game-link pos))
❼                          (draw-tile-svg x y pos hex xx yy col chosen-tile)))
                       (draw-tile-svg x y pos hex xx yy col chosen-tile)))))

(defun make-game-link (pos)
  (format nil "/game.html?chosen=~a" pos))
```

The draw-board-svg function takes the board as an argument, but also
requires two other arguments that will be important for using the picture as
the front end of the user interface for our game ❶. One argument is chosen-
tile, which indicates a tile that the player has clicked with the mouse. We're
going to color that tile a bit lighter, so the player can tell that the computer
has recognized the selection. Another argument is legal-tiles, which indicates
which tiles the player can legally click next.

It so happens that SVG pictures have a feature for web links, which works
just like the <a href="..."> hyperlinks in regular HTML. If a tile is a legal tile
for the player's next move, we'll wrap the SVG for that tile in such a link, making
it clickable. Having the legal-tiles parameter lets us know which tiles we want
to be clickable.

The draw-board-svg function consists of a couple of nested loops that loop
through the y ❷ and x ❸ coordinates of the tile board. For each tile, we then
define a ton of local variables (using the facility for local variables in the loop
macro introduced in Chapter 10). First, we declare pos ❹, which indicates the
position of current tile in the hex array. Then we fetch that hex. Next, we calculate the pixel coordinates for the tiles, in the variables xx and yy. As you can
see, the math for these coordinates gets a bit tricky, since the board is drawn
in perspective on the screen.

The final local variable we define is col, which will hold the color of the
tile and dice in the current spot. We do this by using a list of die colors, which
currently holds the colors red (for player A) and blue (for player B). We also
darken the color a bit based on the y-coordinate using the brightness function
(discussed in Chapter 17). This darkens the rows in the back a bit, adding to
the 3D appearance of our SVG game board.

If the current tile is a member of the legal tiles ❺, we're going to wrap it
in a web link, as mentioned previously. In SVG, this is done with a tag in the
form <a xlink:href="...">, which we create here ❻. Notice that we also wrap

each tile in a <g> tag, which tells the SVG renderer to treat the polygons in this tile as a group. To figure out the actual URL we want to link to, we call the make-game-link function. This function builds an appropriate URL. You'll understand the format of the URL better once we start writing the code that handles the web server for our game.

Finally, we're ready to call our draw-tile function ❼. There are two different versions of the call in our code: one for the hyperlinked version and one for the nonlinked version.

Phew! Now we can finally draw a full game board dynamically, using the SVG format:

```
> (svg *board-width* *board-height* (draw-board-svg (gen-board) nil nil))
<svg xmlns="http://www.w3.org/2000/svg" xmlns:xlink="http://www.w3.org/1999/
xlink" height="500" width="900"><polygon points="256,185.6 320,166.4 384,185.6
384,211.2 320,230.4 256,211.2 "
...
```

If you save the output to *board.svg* and load it in Firefox, here is what you should see:

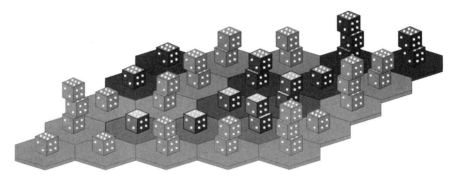

Building the Web Server Interface

Now that we've completed the graphical side of Dice of Doom version 3, we're ready to write the side that interfaces with the web server.

Writing Our Web Request Handler

The central function for our web server handling is called dod-request-handler. It is the function that we can pass to the serve command in our web server library, and it is responsible for handling all the web requests coming from the web browser. Here is the code for dod-request-handler:

```
(defparameter *cur-game-tree* nil)
(defparameter *from-tile* nil)

(defun dod-request-handler (path header params)
❶  (if (equal path "game.html")
❷      (progn (princ "<!doctype html>")
```

```
❸                (tag center ()
                  (princ "Welcome to DICE OF DOOM!")
                  (tag br ())
❹                 (let ((chosen (assoc 'chosen params)))
❺                   (when (or (not *cur-game-tree*) (not chosen))
                      (setf chosen nil)
❻                     (web-initialize))
                    (cond ((lazy-null (caddr *cur-game-tree*))
❼                          (web-announce-winner (cadr *cur-game-tree*)))
                          ((zerop (car *cur-game-tree*))
❽                          (web-handle-human
                            (when chosen
                                  (read-from-string (cdr chosen)))))
❾                         (t (web-handle-computer))))
                    (tag br ())
❿                   (draw-dod-page *cur-game-tree* *from-tile*)))
          (princ "Sorry... I don't know that page."))))
```

First, this function checks whether the current page being fetched from the web server is game.html ❶. This is the page where our game will reside on the web server. At the top of the page, we specify the doctype ❷. When done in this way, it tells the web browser to expect an HTML5-encoded web page. Then we put in some simple HTML to center the page and print a welcome message ❸.

The params passed from the web server library may contain an important value named chosen, which we fetch using this line ❹. If there is no chosen tile, or if the game tree is currently empty ❺, it means the player must be starting a brand-new game. If that's the case, we will call a function named web-initialize ❻.

Next, we need to find out whether the game has ended. We can tell this by checking if the list of moves is empty (which, as you might remember, is stored in the caddr location of the tree). In that case, we'll announce a winner ❼.

Following that, we need to see if the current player is player zero, which means the player is the human player. In that case, we'll call the function web-handle-human ❽ to build the rest of the HTML data in the body of the page. We also use the read-from-string function to pull the number of the chosen tile from the chosen parameter, if it exists.

In all other cases, we know we're dealing with a computer player and hand over control to web-handle-computer ❾ to build the rest of the HTML.

Lastly, the dod-request-handler function needs to call the draw-dod-page function to draw the game board, which we do here ❿.

Limitations of Our Game Web Server

The limitations of our game web server are quite significant. First of all, for simplicity's sake, the dod-request-handler function makes absolutely no effort to try to determine from whom the web request is coming. It behaves as if all game interactions were coming from a single player, and therefore isn't a true multiplayer server for Dice of Doom. If multiple players were to try to play different games at the same time, the dod-request-handler would get confused and *bad things* would happen.

It would not be too difficult to expand dod-request-handler into a true web server for multiple, parallel games. To do this, we would need to pull session information out of the header data it receives as an argument from the web server, and then all variables it references (such as *cur-game-tree*, for instance) would need to live in a hash table, using the session information as a key. This way, each player would have her own game tree, and our engine could then serve multiple games in parallel. The implementation of such a multigame version of the dod-request-handler is "an exercise for the reader."

Another limitation of dod-request-handler is that it reads information from the URL using the read-from-string function. As you've learned in earlier chapters, this function can be compromised to run arbitrary code in the hands of an experienced (and evil) Lisper.

Initializing a New Game

Here is the web-initialize function, which initializes our game engine to start a brand-new game of Dice of Doom:

```
(defun web-initialize ()
  (setf *from-tile* nil)
❶ (setf *cur-game-tree* (game-tree (gen-board) 0 0 t)))
```

As you can see, it generates a random game board, builds a tree from it, and then stores the result in the global *cur-game-tree* variable ❶.

Announcing a Winner

Here is the function that announces the winner within the web browser:

```
(defun web-announce-winner (board)
  (fresh-line)
  (let ((w (winners board)))
    (if (> (length w) 1)
        (format t "The game is a tie between ~a" (mapcar #'player-letter w))
        (format t "The winner is ~a" (player-letter (car w)))))
❶ (tag a (href "game.html")
    (princ " play again")))
```

It is exactly the same as our previous announce-winner function, except that it now includes some extra code at the end to build a web link ❶, which will allow us to conveniently start a brand-new game, since the current game has ended.

Handling the Human Player

The web-handle-human function is responsible for creating the HTML and doing the bookkeeping when the player taking the current turn is the human player.

```
(defun web-handle-human (pos)
❶  (cond ((not pos) (princ "Please choose a hex to move from:"))
        ((eq pos 'pass) (setf *cur-game-tree*
                          (cadr (lazy-car (caddr *cur-game-tree*)))))
❷        (princ "Your reinforcements have been placed.")
         (tag a (href (make-game-link nil))
           (princ "continue")))
❸        ((not *from-tile*) (setf *from-tile* pos)
                          (princ "Now choose a destination:"))
❹        ((eq pos *from-tile*) (setf *from-tile* nil)
                          (princ "Move cancelled."))
❺        (t (setf *cur-game-tree*
              (cadr (lazy-find-if (lambda (move)
                                    (equal (car move)
                                           (list *from-tile* pos)))
                          (caddr *cur-game-tree*))))
           (setf *from-tile* nil)
           (princ "You may now ")
❻         (tag a (href (make-game-link 'pass))
              (princ "pass"))
           (princ " or make another move:"))))
```

The recent choices the human has made dictate what this function will do. The web-handle-human function knows the human's choices by referencing the most recently chosen position, which derives from a variable passed as a parameter through the web request. It also can reference the *from-tile* global variable, which tells it which tile the player initially chose to use as a starting location for a move. It needs both of these values, since a move has both a source location and a destination location.

If the player has not yet chosen a location, we want to print a message requesting that the player choose a hex ❶. If the player chose to pass, we want to print a message saying that player's reinforcements have been placed ❷. (Remember that reinforcements are placed right after someone passes.)

Next, we check if the *from-tile* variable is nil. If this is the case, it means the player has not yet chosen a starting location for a dice attack. If it's nil, we can set *from-tile* equal to the location that was just selected ❸, as well as ask the player to select a destination.

If the currently selected location is the same as the *from-tile* variable, it means a tile was selected twice. This must mean the player has changed his mind and wants to undo his selection. Therefore, we will set *from-tile* to nil and print a cancellation message ❹.

In all other cases, it means the player has selected two valid locations for the start and end of an attack. We can now advance the *cur-game-tree* to point to the appropriate next tree inside the lazy list of available moves ❺. We want to print a message, allowing the player to pass ❻ or make yet another attack.

We have now completed the code our game server will use to interact with the human player. Next, let's write a function to handle the computer player.

Handling the Computer Player

Handling the web interface for our computer player is pretty simple. After all, computer players don't need any fancy user interface stuff to know what's going on in the game. All the web stuff that happens when the computer is making moves is there solely for the benefit of the human player. Here is the web-handle-computer code that renders the HTML in the web interface as the AI player makes a move:

```
(defun web-handle-computer ()
❶  (setf *cur-game-tree* (handle-computer *cur-game-tree*))
❷  (princ "The computer has moved. ")
❸  (tag script ()
     (princ
       "window.setTimeout('window.location=\"game.html?chosen=NIL\"',5000)")))
```

All this function does is call our previous handle-computer function, which will return the next branch that the computer has selected in the game tree. We use this to update our *cur-game-tree* variable ❶. Next, we print a message to state that the player has moved ❷. The last part of the function is a clever little gimmick to spice up our web interface a bit. It puts a smidgen of JavaScript in the HTML of the web page ❸, which forces the web browser to automatically load a new web page in five seconds. This means that as the computer AI player makes its moves, we get to see everything happen in a crude animation!

Drawing the SVG Game Board from Within the HTML

We have only one more function to write to complete version 3 of Dice of Doom: the draw-dod-page function. This function interfaces our page game server code with the SVG code that draws our board.

```
(defun draw-dod-page (tree selected-tile)
  (svg *board-width*
       *board-height*
       (draw-board-svg (cadr tree)
                       selected-tile
❶                     (take-all (if selected-tile
                                     (lazy-mapcar
❷                                     (lambda (move)
                                        (when (eql (caar move)
❸                                                  selected-tile)
❹                                         (cadar move)))
                                      (caddr tree))
❺                                   (lazy-mapcar #'caar (caddr tree))))))))
```

The most complicated part of this function is the code that determines which tiles on the board are legal tiles for the player to click ❶. If the player has already selected a tile, we want to find all moves ❷ where the starting position for the move matches the selected tile ❸ and return the destination position for the given move ❹. If the player hasn't selected a tile yet, we just want to return all the legal starting positions ❺.

We have now completed our fully graphical version of Dice of Doom. Let's play!

Playing Version 3 of Dice of Doom

First, we need to start up our web server. Simply serve up our dod-request-handler, and we're ready to go:

```
> (serve #'dod-request-handler)
```

Now move over to Firefox and go to *http://localhost:8080/game.html*. You should see our game in your browser:

Welcome to DICE OF DOOM!

Please choose a hex to move from:

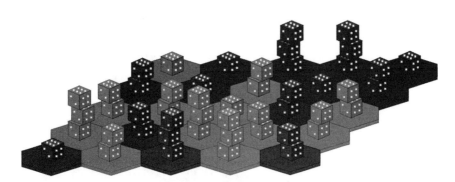

When you click a tile, it is highlighted:

Welcome to DICE OF DOOM!

Now choose a destination:

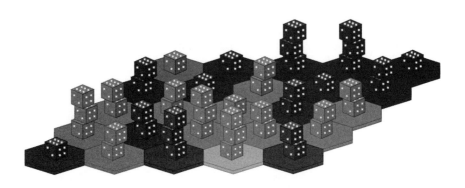

Now you can select a tile to attack. In this example, we'll choose the stack of two dice to the right of the selected stack:

Welcome to DICE OF DOOM!

You may now pass or make another move:

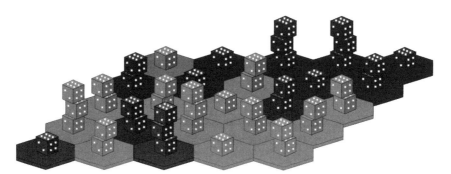

Next, let's pass our turn by clicking the **pass** web link. This will cause the reinforcement dice to be placed (in this case, only a single additional die in the upper-left corner):

Welcome to DICE OF DOOM!

Your reinforcements have been placed.continue

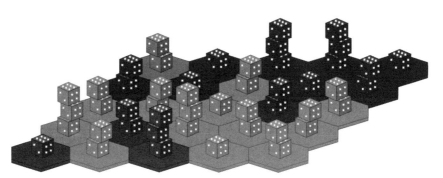

If you now hit **continue**, you will see the game cycle automatically through the moves for the computer player, in a similar fashion. It will keep going on like this until there is a winner for the game. You can always start a new game by just going back to the original *game.html* URL.

This is much nicer than the crude console interface we've been using so far! But there are still a few, final improvements we're going to make to pep up Dice of Doom. We'll be covering those in the next (and final chapter) of this book.

What You've Learned

In this chapter, we discussed how you can generate interactive graphics in a web browser from a Lisp program. Along the way, you learned the following:

- You can create a graphical version of Dice Of Doom by rendering the board using the SVG format.

- The HTML5 standard supports inline SVG images. You can use this to create an interactive, web-based version of your game.

- The simple web server used for our example has several limitations. For example, our game cannot be played by multiple players. However, the request handler could be expanded to allow for multiple, parallel games.

20

MAKING DICE OF DOOM
MORE FUN

It's now time to create a final version of Dice of Doom.
Version 4 of our game will be much more fun to play
than our earlier versions.

Although you probably were not aware of it, we made some major compromises in the rules for our game to make it easier to program. In this chapter, we will allow more players, add rolling of the dice, and implement a few
more changes to make Dice of Doom a much more interesting game.

Increasing the Number of Players

To begin, put all the code from the previous chapter in a file named
dice_of_doom_v3.lisp (also available from the companion website), and
then execute the following command:

```
> (load "dice_of_doom_v3.lisp")
```

The first change we're going to make is to increase the number of players from two to four. Three of these will be AI opponents, played by the computer. Because of how we've written our code so far, this requires very little extra code:

```
(defparameter *num-players* 4)
(defparameter *die-colors* '((255 63 63) (63 63 255) (63 255 63)
                             (255 63 255)))
```

First, we simply change our *num-players* variable to 4. Then we need to indicate additional die colors for our new players. The colors for the four players will be red, blue, green, and purple.

It turns out that the AI we've created so far already works just fine in a four-player game.

Our AI game engine will use what is called a "paranoid strategy." This means that the AI players will always assume that every other player (including the human) has no other goal but to—how should I put this?—screw them over personally. This isn't a bad strategy to use; however, a game with more than two players opens up new possibilities. For instance, losing players could gang up on a winning player to improve their odds. Our game AI isn't smart enough to form such packs of cooperation, but it's good enough.

Now that we've already tweaked some constants to increase the number of players, let's tweak a couple more:

```
(defparameter *max-dice* 5)
(defparameter *ai-level* 2)
```

Here, we're increasing the maximum number of dice on a hex tile from three to five, and decreasing the level of our AI from four to two. With the new rules described in this chapter, we'll need to dumb down our AI a bit to make sure it stays zippy. Since there are now four competing players, the AI actually doesn't need to be so smart to challenge the human opponent.

Rolling the Dice

I'm sure you've probably noticed one obvious flaw in our game so far: Despite the fact that it is called Dice of Doom, it actually is completely devoid of any randomness! The dice are never rolled, and the larger stack will always automatically win, which makes for a pretty lame dice game. Now we're finally going to rectify this flaw.

In this version of the game, during an attack, both piles of dice are rolled, and whoever rolls the highest number wins the battle. Ties are a victory for the defender. If the attacker loses, that player must surrender all dice from the attacking hex except one.

In the lingo of AI programming, this means we will add *chance nodes* to our game tree. The way we're going to implement this is pretty simple.

Building Chance Nodes

Every move in our lazy list of moves up to now has always had exactly two items in it: a description of the move (a list of the source and destination of the attack, or `nil` for a passing move) and the new node of the game tree for when the move has been taken. Now we're simply going to add a third item to a move, which contains the game tree for an unsuccessful attack. This means that each move in our move list will double as a chance node, with two possible follow-up nodes for the next game tree, depending on whether an attack is successful.

Let's update our attacking-moves function to add this extra item to the move so that each move acts as a chance node.

```
(defun attacking-moves (board cur-player spare-dice)
  (labels ((player (pos)
                (car (aref board pos)))
           (dice (pos)
                (cadr (aref board pos))))
    (lazy-mapcan (lambda (src)
                   (if (eq (player src) cur-player)
                       (lazy-mapcan
                         (lambda (dst)
                           (if (and (not (eq (player dst) cur-player))
                                    (> (dice src) 1))
                               (make-lazy (list (list (list src dst)
        (game-tree (board-attack board cur-player src dst (dice src))
                   cur-player
                   (+ spare-dice (dice dst))
                   nil)
❶      (game-tree (board-attack-fail board cur-player src dst (dice src))
                   cur-player
                   (+ spare-dice (dice dst))
                   nil))))
                               (lazy-nil)))
                         (make-lazy (neighbors src)))
                       (lazy-nil)))
                 (make-lazy (loop for n below *board-hexnum*
                              collect n)))))
```

The only thing new in this updated version of attacking-moves is right here ❶, where we add a third item as we create a new move in the game tree. The board in this alternate branch of our chance node is constructed by calling the function board-attack-fail, which we will write next.

The board-attack-fail function does exactly what you would expect: It takes a board and returns a board that has all dice but one removed from the hex from which a failed attack originated.

```
(defun board-attack-fail (board player src dst dice)
  (board-array (loop for pos from 0
                     for hex across board
                     collect (if (eq pos src)
```

```
❶                            (list player 1)
❷                         hex))))
```

Here, we simply loop over the board and return each hex unmodified ❷, unless it happens to be the source hex for the attack. In that case, we remove all dice from that hex but one ❶.

Doing the Actual Dice Rolling

Next, we need to write some functions to actually roll the dice. Here is a function that rolls a pile of dice:

```
(defun roll-dice (dice-num)
❶   (let ((total (loop repeat dice-num
                       sum (1+ (random 6)))))
      (fresh-line)
❷    (format t "On ~a dice rolled ~a. " dice-num total)
❸    total))
```

First, it calculates a total count of a pile of rolled dice by looping once for each die. For each die, it generates a random number from 1 to 6. Then it stores the total sum in the total variable ❶. Next, the roll-dice function prints a descriptive message about the roll ❷. Finally, it returns the total ❸.

Since we're never going to roll a pile of dice in isolation, let's create another function that pits two piles of dice against each other:

```
(defun roll-against (src-dice dst-dice)
  (> (roll-dice src-dice) (roll-dice dst-dice)))
```

This simply calls roll-dice twice and compares the total of the two rolls. We'll want to use this function as we travel along our game tree to pick either the winning or losing move as a turn is chosen by either the human or the computer.

Calling the Dice Rolling Code from Our Game Engine

In the context of our game engine, rolling dice simply means picking either the winning or losing branch of the chance node after the human or computer has chosen a move. This action is performed by the pick-chance-branch function:

```
❶ (defun pick-chance-branch (board move)
    (labels ((dice (pos)
               (cadr (aref board pos))))
      (let ((path (car move)))
❷      (if (or (null path) (roll-against (dice (car path))
                                          (dice (cadr path))))
❸          (cadr move)
❹          (caddr move)))))
```

This function takes the current board and also the move that contains the chance node that needs to be resolved ❶. When the path inside the move is not null, we call roll-against with a count of dice in the source and destination hexes along the path of attack ❷. We check for a null path because that means the move was a "pass," which doesn't require any dice rolling.

If the dice roll for the attack is successful, we remove the first child tree from the chance node within the move ❸. If the attack is unsuccessful, we return the second child of the chance node ❹.

Now we need to make sure that the pick-chance-branch function is called when the human or computer chooses a move. First, let's take care of the human:

```
(defun handle-human (tree)
  (fresh-line)
  (princ "choose your move:")
  (let ((moves (caddr tree)))
    (labels ((print-moves (moves n)
                (unless (lazy-null moves)
                  (let* ((move (lazy-car moves))
                         (action (car move)))
                    (fresh-line)
                    (format t "~a. " n)
                    (if action
                      (format t "~a -> ~a" (car action) (cadr action))
                      (princ "end turn")))
                  (print-moves (lazy-cdr moves) (1+ n)))))
      (print-moves moves 1))
    (fresh-line)
    (pick-chance-branch (cadr tree) (lazy-nth (1- (read)) moves))))
```
❶

All we've done here is to add a call to pick-chance-branch at the end of our previous handle-human function, at the point we need to return the child branch of the game tree that holds the next state of the game ❶.

We update the handle-computer function in the same way:

```
(defun handle-computer (tree)
  (let ((ratings (get-ratings (limit-tree-depth tree *ai-level*) (car tree))))
    (pick-chance-branch
      (cadr tree)
      (lazy-nth (position (apply #'max ratings) ratings) (caddr tree)))))
```
❶

Again, we've simply added a call to pick-chance-branch at the end of the function ❶.

It is now possible to play our updated Dice of Doom game. However, at this point, the computer player will play a very poor game, because the AI does not yet understand that the chance nodes exist. It will simply assume that every attack will always be successful, making it much too foolhardy to play a decent game. We need to improve our AI so that it takes into account the rolling of the dice as it makes its decisions.

Updating the AI

For the AI to be able to deal with the dice rolls that are now important to our game, it must know a little something about the statistics of dice rolls. The following table gives it the needed statistical information:

```
(defparameter *dice-odds* #(#(0.84 0.97 1.0 1.0)
                            #(0.44 0.78 0.94 0.99)
                            #(0.15 0.45 0.74 0.91)
                            #(0.04 0.19 0.46 0.72)
                            #(0.01 0.06 0.22 0.46))))
```

This table contains the odds of winning for each possible pairing of dice in our game. The columns represent the attacking dice, starting with one die. The rows represent the destination dice, starting with two dice (the minimum dice needed for an attack).

This table tells us, for instance, that a roll of two attacking dice against one defending die has an 84 percent chance of winning. Four attacking dice against three defending dice have a 74 percent chance of winning.

If you remember, the core function in our AI code is the get-ratings function, which gives a point score to the list of possible follow-up moves. We need to modify how it calculates the score of each possible move to take the odds of success of the dice roll into account. We are now going to make use of our *dice-odds* table, as well as the point scores of the successful or failed outcomes of each attack, to interpolate a combined score for each available move:

```
(defun get-ratings (tree player)
  (let ((board (cadr tree)))
    (labels ((dice (pos)
               (cadr (aref board pos))))
      (take-all (lazy-mapcar
                 (lambda (move)
                   (let ((path (car move)))
                     (if path
                         (let* ((src (car path))
                                (dst (cadr path))
❶                               (odds (aref (aref *dice-odds*
                                                  (1- (dice dst)))
                                            (- (dice src) 2))))
❷                           (+ (* odds (rate-position (cadr move) player))
❸                              (* (- 1 odds) (rate-position (caddr move)
                                                            player))))
                         (rate-position (cadr move) player))))
                 (caddr tree))))))
```

In our updated get-ratings function, we look up the odds of each attack succeeding from our table ❶. Then we multiply the odds with the rating for the winning child tree ❷. Additionally, we add in the odds of losing the attack (one minus the odds of winning) multiplied by the rating for the losing board position ❸. We now have an updated get-ratings function that understands chance nodes and accounts for them appropriately when generating the score for a move.

For our game AI to be fully compatible with chance nodes, we need to make one additional small change. Our tree-trimming function needs to know about the two branches of the chance node within each move, so it can properly trim both the winning and losing alternatives for each move:

```
(defun limit-tree-depth (tree depth)
  (list (car tree)
        (cadr tree)
        (if (zerop depth)
            (lazy-nil)
          (lazy-mapcar (lambda (move)
                         (cons (car move)
❶                               (mapcar (lambda (x)
                                         (limit-tree-depth x (1- depth)))
                                       (cdr move))))
                       (caddr tree)))))
```

We mapcar ❶ across the tail of each move, so trimming is performed on both branches of any chance nodes.

NOTE   *Version 4 of Dice of Doom will not have alpha-beta pruning. Performing proper alpha-beta pruning in the presence of chance nodes is very complex.*

Improving the Dice of Doom Reinforcement Rules

Until now, the number of reinforcements at the end of a player's turn always equals the number of captured opponent dice, minus one. This reinforcement rule guaranteed that the total number of dice in a game always decreases, so that the game was certain to eventually terminate, and the game tree was always finite in size.

However, since version 2, our game tree has been a lazy tree, so it is perfectly fine if the tree is infinite. Remember that one of the main benefits of lazy evaluation is that you can have data structures that are infinite in size.

Therefore, we are now going to adjust our reinforcement rules to make our game strategically more interesting.

According to our new rules, the number of reinforcement dice will equal the number of tiles in the player's largest contiguous territory. This adds a lot of strategic depth, because the players must constantly decide whether to risk connecting their territories, or perhaps even to sacrifice smaller, nonviable territories by sending them on suicide missions.

In order to implement this new reinforcement rule, let's first define the function get-connected, which returns a list of tiles that are owned by the current player and are connected as a cluster of neighbors to the target tile:

```
(defun get-connected (board player pos)
❶  (labels ((check-pos (pos visited)
               (if (and (eq (car (aref board pos)) player)
                        (not (member pos visited)))
                  (check-neighbors (neighbors pos) (cons pos visited))
                 visited))
❷           (check-neighbors (lst visited)
               (if lst
                  (check-neighbors (cdr lst) (check-pos (car lst) visited))
                 visited)))
❸    (check-pos pos '()))))
```

This function uses the same algorithm for finding connected tiles as we used for calculating connectedness in our Grand Theft Wumpus game in Chapter 8. We traverse through the hexes and their neighbors recursively, while maintaining a visited list.

The get-connected function accomplishes this by defining two recursive local functions. The check-pos function ❶ checks a single position and appends any new neighbors accessible from that location to the visited list. The check-neighbors function ❷ checks an entire list of neighbors, similarly appending new neighbors to the visited list. These two functions call each other recursively until all neighbors in a cluster are found. To start off this recursive calculation, we call the check-pos function with the target position and an initially empty visited list ❸.

We can now find clusters. However, to find the *largest* cluster, we need the largest-cluster-size function:

```
(defun largest-cluster-size (board player)
❶  (labels ((f (pos visited best)
❷             (if (< pos *board-hexnum*)
                  (if (and (eq (car (aref board pos)) player)
❸                          (not (member pos visited)))
❹                     (let* ((cluster (get-connected board player pos))
                             (size (length cluster)))
❺                        (if (> size best)
❻                           (f (1+ pos) (append cluster visited) size)
❼                          (f (1+ pos) (append cluster visited) best)))
                     (f (1+ pos) visited best))
                 best)))
      (f 0 '() 0)))
```

This function defines a local function f, which we'll use to check every position on the board, while maintaining both a list of previously visited nodes and the size of the largest, best cluster found so far ❶.

As long as the current position number is less than the total number of spots on the board ❷, we continue to check tiles. If the current tile to be checked belongs to the player and also has not yet been visited ❸, we'll call get-connected to retrieve the cluster of hexes reachable from this spot ❹. Then, if the size of the cluster is larger than the best found so far ❺, we make this the new best size in our recursive call ❻. Otherwise, we proceed by calling f while keeping the previous best size ❼. (The best variable at this point will hold the best value found so far from previous iterations.) No matter what happens, however, the pos variable is incremented with every recursive call to f, so that we eventually cover the whole board.

Finally, we need to update add-new-dice to make use of our new rule for choosing the number of reinforcements:

```
❶ (defun add-new-dice (board player spare-dice)
     (labels ((f (lst n)
                 (cond ((zerop n) lst)
                       ((null lst) nil)
                       (t (let ((cur-player (caar lst))
                                (cur-dice (cadar lst)))
                            (if (and (eq cur-player player) (< cur-dice *max-dice*))
                                (cons (list cur-player (1+ cur-dice))
                                      (f (cdr lst) (1- n)))
                                (cons (car lst) (f (cdr lst) n))))))))
       (board-array (f (coerce board 'list)
❷                      (largest-cluster-size board player)))))
```

As you can see, the add-new-dice function still receives spare-dice as an argument for compatibility with our old code ❶, but now this argument is simply ignored. Instead, the number of reinforcements added to the board depends on the size of the largest cluster ❷. Otherwise, the add-new-dice is identical to our previous version.

This is all the code we need to enable the new reinforcement rules. Note that, due to the design of our code, the AI player has full access to the game tree. Since the game tree now contains all of this new reinforcement data, the AI will automatically adapt its playing strategy to take into account the new reinforcement rules!

Conclusion

We've gone through quite a long trip as we've created the Dice of Doom game, employing an immense number of different programming techniques along the way. We've taken even more trips with all the other games in this book. Thanks for taking this journey with me through the world of Lisp programming!

I suggest that you take a moment to enjoy the fruits of your labor and play a few games of the fourth and final version of Dice of Doom. Again, all you need to do is serve up the Dice of Doom request handler through our web server:

```
> (serve #'dod-request-handler)
```

Now you can play Dice of Doom in Firefox (again, at the address *localhost:8080/game.html*) as it is meant to be played, with four players and all the new rules we've added in this chapter.

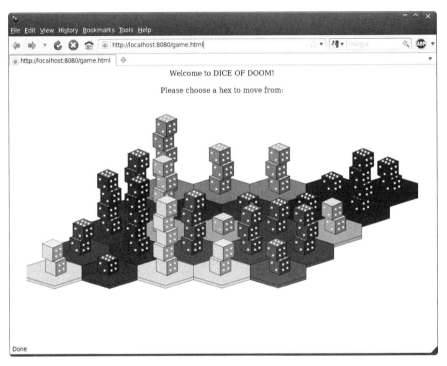

Good luck with all your Dice of Doom battles and all your future Lisp programming!

EPILOGUE

Now that you've worked your way through this book, here is one final reward: A story about the technologies behind the entire Lisp family of programming languages, set in the not-too-distant future . . .

THIS NIGHT AT THE SECRET PUB THE PROGRAMMERS HAD A SPECIAL GUEST: SIMON THE SYSADMIN...

...YEAH, THEY'VE BEEN INCREASING SECURITY ALL ALONG THE EAST COAST...

HE NOW DROVE HONEY TRUCKS FOR THE INSECTOIDS. BECAUSE OF THIS, HE HAD A TRAVEL PERMIT AND COULD TALK OF DISTANT PLACES...

BROOKLYN HAS BEEN REPLACED ENTIRELY BY NECTAR PROCESSING FACILITIES...

AS THE MUGS BECAME EMPTIER, HIS TALES BECAME TALLER...

UNTIL, FINALLY...

YOU KNOW, I'VE HEARD STORIES OF THIS LONG FORGOTTEN PLACE... JUST A MYTH REALLY... WHERE THEY HAVE PROGRAMMING WEAPONS SO POWERFUL, THEY CAN DEFEAT *ANY* BUG...

THEY CALL IT "THE LAND OF LISP." IT'S SUPPOSED TO BE ON A PLANET SOMEWHERE NEAR ALPHA CENTAURI. THE BEINGS THERE USED TO BE OUR FRIENDS, BUT WE LOST CONTACT WITH THEM OVER THE YEARS.

BECAUSE OF HIS ROCKET'S TINY SIZE, DOUG FLEW UNSEEN PAST THE GIANT AND WICKED BUG SHIPS.

HE STEERED HIS WAY TO ALPHA CENTAURI.

UNTIL, EVENTUALLY, HE REACHED A PLANET EXACTLY WHERE SIMON HAD PREDICTED IT WOULD BE!

HOLY COW!

FUNCTIONAL GUILD CRUISER

Lisp Dialect Common Lisp

Synopsis

Functional programming is a mathematical approach to programming that was pioneered by the creators of Lisp. Functional programming places certain restrictions on the programmer, but it can lead to very elegant code. When using functional programming, every variable that is used by a given function must be one of the following:

- A parameter passed into that function
- A local variable created within that function
- A constant

    Also, functional programming doesn't allow a function to have *side effects*. This means a function can't write to the disk, print messages on the screen, or do anything other than return a result. The goal is to write most of a program using "functional code," while retaining a teensy bit of code that does any dirty, nonfunctional stuff that is still needed.

How It Kills Bugs

Writing code in a functional style guarantees that a function does only one thing (returns a value) and is dependent on one only thing (the parameters passed to it). This makes it very easy to debug. No matter how many times you run a function, as long as you're passing it the same data, you will always get the same result.

Example

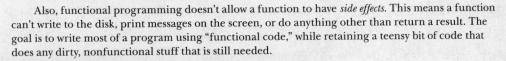

❶ (defun unique-letters (name)
    (concatenate 'string
              "Hello "
              (coerce (remove-duplicates name) 'string)))

❷ (defun ask-and-respond ()
    (princ "What is your name?")
    (princ (unique-letters (read-line))))

Explanation

If you enter this code into the Lisp REPL and execute (ask-and-respond), you will be asked for your name, and then greeted by your name but with all duplicate letters removed. All the hard work in this function is handled by unique-letters, which is written in a functional style ❶. The dirty work of interacting with the user, which can't be written in a purely functional way, is handled by ask-and-respond ❷.

Weakness

The main weakness of functional programming is that some side effects are almost always necessary for a program to actually *do* something. This means you can't write a useful program that has the entirety of its code written in the functional style. At least a small amount of code will be nonfunctional.

    Functional programming is discussed in Chapter 14.

MACRO GUILD MELEE FIGHTERS

Lisp Dialect   Common Lisp

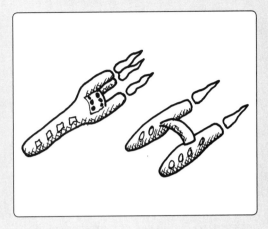

Synopsis

True macros are one of Lisp's most unique and amazing features. In fact, the reason Lispers put up with all those annoying parentheses in their code is that those parentheses enable the awesome Lisp macro system.

True macros allow you to add new functionality to Lisp in a very fundamental way. Experienced Lispers can use macros to make their Lisp compiler/interpreter do their bidding cleanly and elegantly.

How It Kills Bugs

By using macros, an experienced Lisper can minimize code duplication, and better tailor the underlying language to the problem at hand. This leads to cleaner code and fewer bugs.

Example

```
(defmacro three-way-if (expr a b &rest c)
  (let ((val (gensym)))
     `(let ((,val ,expr))
        (cond ((and (numberp ,val) (zerop ,val)) ,a)
❶
❷             (,val ,@c)
❸             (t ,b)))))
```

Explanation

Lisp macros are so powerful that you can actually write your own if-then command! The code shown here creates a macro called three-way-if that has three branches: one for a nil value ❶, one for a numerical zero value ❷, and one for everything else ❸. For most purposes, a function like this might seem stupid, but if you ever want to write a program that constantly needs to distinguish zeros from nils (or needs to handle some other domain-specific headache), you'll make your life much easier by writing a macro.

Weakness

Since Lisp macros are so powerful, there is always the danger of programmers abusing them. Overuse of macros can make it hard for other programmers to understand your code.

Macros are discussed in Chapter 16.

RESTART GUILD ARMORED FIGHTER

Lisp Dialect   Common Lisp

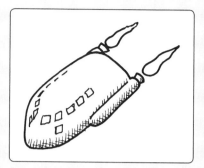

Synopsis

Proper exception handling is extremely difficult. There are really only two good approaches: Don't handle exceptions at all and just let your program die when one occurs, or handle every single exception in the most direct and specific way possible. But is it truly possible to handle every potential exception in your code? If your write Common Lisp code, it's possible to get extremely close to this ideal goal.

For example, suppose you write a function that raises the prices on a list of widgets. But then, while the function is processing one of the widgets in the list, there's a memory allocation error. You can't prepare for this type of error ahead of time, since it could happen anywhere in a program. This makes it impossible to address using traditional exception handling methods.

Even if a function lower in the call stack catches and resolves the source of the exception, the program still faces an unsolvable problem: Some of the widget prices have been raised, while others have not. Common Lisp, however, has a mechanism for addressing this problem, called *restarts*.

In a language that supports restarts, the function that raises the widget prices can make the proclamation, "Hey everybody! If something bad happens while I'm working on my widgets, just use my restart (called try-again) when it's safe for me to finish my work!" Another function, lower in the call tree, can now handle the error, and then call try-again to ensure that the widget prices won't become corrupt. This allows the function to finish raising widget prices at the exact point of failure.

In fact, if you have a program that can't afford to shut down (a web server, for example), you can still handle a surprising number of extreme exceptions in Common Lisp without ending the program. Even if the program encounters a truly exceptional exception, it can simply divert control back to the REPL. The programmer can then fix the cause of the exception, access a list of available restarts, and continue running the program on the spot.

How It Kills Bugs

By using restarts and the Lisp REPL, a bug can be fixed in a running program, allowing you to "hot script" long-running applications with only a negligible interruption.

Example

```
(defun raise-widget-prices (widgets)
  (when widgets
❶       (loop (restart-case  (progn (raise-price (car widgets))
❷                                   (return))
❸             (try-again () (princ "trying again"))))
❹         (raise-widget-prices (cdr widgets)))))
```

Explanation

This is an implementation of a function that raises prices on a list of widgets. The actual work of raising the price of a single widget is done by the raise-price function ❶. The call to this function is protected by wrapping it in a loop and the restart-case command, which declares a restart called try-again ❸. If the price can be raised without problems, the raise-price function will complete normally, the loop is interrupted with a return ❷, and the next item in the list of widgets is processed. On the other hand, if an error occurs while raising the price on a widget, another function (or the programmer) can attempt to fix the problem and call the try-again restart to retry the widget at the point of failure ❸, which leads to another cycle through the loop ❶. The function can then continue down the rest of the list, raising the prices on the remaining widgets ❹.

By using restarts, your code can offer multiple alternative follow-up options for coping with an exception, so that even the most exceptional exceptions can be handled appropriately.

Weakness

Even though Common Lisp has one of the most advanced exception handling systems in existence, it is still difficult to handle every exception appropriately in your code. However, restarts give you the unique ability to fix a running program and allow it to continue operating, which is usually not possible in other languages.

Restarts are discussed in Chapter 14.

GENERIC SETTER GUILD SUPPLY SHIP

Lisp Dialect Common Lisp

Synopsis

To modify the value of a variable in Common Lisp, you use setf. However, this command also has an amazing special power: Instead of a variable name, you can pass it a complex Lisp expression that retrieves a value. It can then turn that expression "inside out" and use it to modify that value, rather than simply retrieve it. These types of expressions are called *generic setters*.

Many commands besides setf also support generic setters. Using this feature, most types of data structures can get by without any specific "setting" functions of their own.

How It Kills Bugs

When you have a complicated, nested data structure, it's often easier to understand code that retrieves data from a specific location than it is to understand code that sets a value at the same location. If you want to set a value at a specific location in a complicated structure, you usually need to work backward through the structure to figure out how to change it. But with generic setters, you can let Lisp handle the hard code for you. Having simpler code is a great way to fight bugs.

Explanation

The example creates a variable named foo, which holds a list of three items ❶. The second item in the list is an empty hash table. Then it adds a key named my-key with a value of 77 to the table inside foo all at once, by putting a complex expression into setf that "gets at" this location ❷.

Example

❶ `(defparameter foo (list 1 (make-hash-table) 3))`

❷ `(setf (gethash 'my-key (nth foo 1)) 77)`

Weakness

By mutating an existing data structure, generic setters cause a side effect, which violates one of the tenets of functional programming. This means they can't be used when programming in a purely functional style.

Generic setters are discussed in Chapter 9.

DSL GUILD HOT RODS

Lisp Dialect   Common Lisp

Synopsis

Because Lisp has such a simple syntax (everything is delimited with parentheses), it is easy to use it to build your own custom programming language, designed for a specific domain. Such *domain-specific languages* (*DSLs*) tend to make heavy use of the Lisp macro system. They represent an extreme form of macro programming, transforming Lisp into a completely new programming language.

Explanation

This is an example of code that uses a DSL to build an HTML page. In this case, the page displays "Hello **World**" in a browser, with the second word rendered in bold. The `html` and `body` commands (macros created for the HTML library in Chapter 16) generate opening and closing tags that will contain the body of the page ❶. Then it calls the regular Lisp function `princ` to generate the text. The second word is wrapped in another custom DSL command, `bold` ❷, which generates opening and closing bold tags around the specified text.

Example

```
❶ (html (body (princ "Hello ")
❷            (bold (princ "World!"))))
```

Weakness

Since DSLs are programming languages you create all by yourself, you can definitely shoot yourself in the foot if you aren't careful. It's easy to create code in a language that is impossible for others (and perhaps even you) to understand.

Chapter 17 discusses DSLs, including the DSL that allows you to write HTML directly inside your Lisp code, as shown in this example.

CLOS Guild Battleship

Lisp Dialect   Common Lisp

Synopsis

Common Lisp has the most sophisticated object-oriented programming framework of any major programming language, called the *Common Lisp Object System* (*CLOS*). It is customizable at a fundamental level using the *Metaobject Protocol* (*MOP*). There's really nothing like it anywhere else in programming. It lets you create incredibly complex software without losing control over the code.

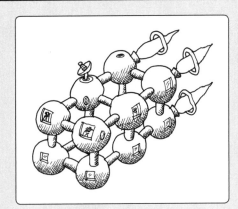

How It Kills Bugs

Object-oriented programing (*OOP*) is a commonly used technique for keeping bugs under control. By writing code in an object-oriented style, you can *decouple* different parts of your code. When you decouple code, you break your code into logical components, which can be tested independently.

The basic concepts behind object-oriented programming in Common Lisp are discussed in Chapter 9. For detailed information on the design of CLOS, I recommend reading the CLOS papers compiled at *http://www.dreamsongs .com/CLOS.html*.

Example 1: Wrapping Code Around Methods

```
❶ (defclass widget ()
      ((color :accessor widget-color
              :initarg :color)))

❷ (defmethod describe-widget ((w widget))
      (format t "this is a ~a widget" (widget-color w)))

❸ (defmethod describe-widget :before ((w widget))
      (add-to-log "Somebody is checking on a widget"))
```

Explanation

For this example, imagine we run a company that sells widgets, and we need some object-oriented Lisp code to help keep track of them. First, we need to create a new CLOS class (called `widget`) with `defclass` ❶. It has one property (or *slot*, in Lisp lingo) describing the widget's color. Next, we declare a `describe-widget`, which prints out a description of the widget ❷. By convention, a function designed to operate on a specific type of object is called a *method*. In this case, the `describe-widget` is considered a method of the `widget` object.

Now suppose we want to write an entry to a log file every time a user checks on a widget. Using the CLOS, we can declare one or more *before methods* that will automatically be called before the main `describe-widget` method is executed ❸.

If we didn't have before methods available, we would need to dirty up our main widget code to add logging, like so:

```
❶ (defmethod describe-widget ((w widget))
❷   (add-to-log "Somebody is checking on a widget")
     (format t "this is a ~a widget" (widget-color w)))
```

continued

Here, we've added the command for logging ❷ right in the middle of the describe-widget method ❶. This code is a lot uglier, because writing to logs has nothing intrinsically to do with describing a widget. The logging in this version is also tightly coupled to the main code, which means we can no longer test the widget code independently from the debugging code. Using the before method leads to cleaner, more decoupled code.

Explanation

This example demontrates *multiple dispatch*, a powerful technique for writing methods that are chosen based on the types of their parameters.

The example begins by creating a color class ❶ and also defines three derived classes: red, green, and blue ❷. Then we declare a mix method, which will tell us what happens if we mix any two colors. By default, when we mix two colors, it just says, "I don't know what color that makes" ❸. However, using multiple dispatch, *we can define more versions* of the mix method. For instance, we can declare a version that mixes blue and yellow ❹, and another version for yellow and red ❺. Here's what happens when we call these methods with different colors:

Example 2: Multiple Dispatch

```
❶ (defclass color () ())
❷ (defclass red (color) ())
  (defclass blue (color) ())
  (defclass yellow (color) ())

❸ (defmethod mix ((c1 color) (c2 color))
     "I don't know what color that makes")

❹ (defmethod mix ((c1 blue) (c2 yellow))
     "you made green!")

❺ (defmethod mix ((c1 yellow) (c2 red))
     "you made orange!")
```

```
> (mix (make-instance 'red) (make-instance 'blue))
"I don't know what color that makes"
> (mix (make-instance 'yellow) (make-instance 'red))
"you made orange!"
```

The important thing to note about the example is that in order to figure out which mix method to call in a given situation, the CLOS needs to take into account both of the objects passed into the method. It is *dispatching* to a specific implementation of the method based on the types of *multiple* objects. This is a feature that is not available in traditional object-oriented languages, such as Java or C++.

Weakness

Opinions vary widely in the Lisp community as to how large a role object-oriented techniques should play in programming. The critics of this style complain that object-oriented techniques force data to be hidden away in lot of disparate places by requiring them to live inside many different objects. Having data located in disparate places can make programs difficult to understand, especially if that data changes over time. Therefore, many Lispers prefer to use functional techniques over object-oriented techniques, though the two can often be used together with some care. Nonetheless, there are still many domains in which object-oriented techniques are invaluable, such as in user interface programming or simulation programming.

THE CONTINUATION GUILD ROCKET PODS

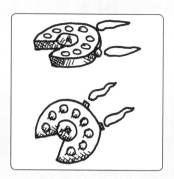

Lisp Dialect   Scheme (limited support in Common Lisp with *continuation-passing style*, or through the use of special libraries)

Synopsis

In the 1970s, a special dialect of Lisp was created that featured a particularly powerful programming feature called *continuations*. Basically, continuations let you put "time travel" into your code. This allows you to do things like run programs backward, sideways, or in other crazy ways. For instance, it's great for implementing advanced programming techniques, such as *nondeterministic programming*. In nondeterministic programming, you write code that offers the computer multiple choices for what to do next. If one choice isn't satisfactory, the computer can "roll back time" with continuations to try a different path.

How It Kills Bugs

There are many situations where having time travel in your code can make the code easier to understand. The classic example is in a web server. Often, a person must visit several pages on a web page in order to perform a single action. With a continuation-aware web server, you can write code that pretends these pages were visited all at the same time, making your code a lot less buggy. Later on, the web server uses continuations to break your code into several parts (by using the time-travel abilities of continuations), taking care of all the ugly details of handling a multipage web action.

Example

```
(define continuation null)

❶ (define (foo n)
❷    (* (call-with-current-continuation
           (lambda (c)
❸            (set! continuation c)
             (+ n 1)))
❹       2))
```

NOTE   *This example is in the Scheme Lisp dialect and won't run in Common Lisp.*

Explanation

In the example, we create a simple function called foo ❶, which adds one to a number, and then doubles it. For instance, running (foo 7) will return 16. However, inside the function, there is a call to call-with-current-continuation ❷, which captures the state of the function before the doubling step. It saves this "moment in time" in the variable continuation ❸. The current state of the running program is captured at this line ❷. Everything that happens *after* the continuation was captured will then be executed if we call the captured continuation. The only part of the foo command that happens after the continuation was captured is the multiplication by two ❹. Consequently, the variable continuation is now a time machine that we can use to jump into this past moment to switch out the number we want to double with another one. So, if we were to now call (continuation 100), it would return 200 (which is 100 doubled). We have traveled backward in time!

Weakness

Continuations are such an awesome feature that they don't really have a downside. The only real problem they present is for creators of programming languages. True continuations are technically difficult to put into a programming language, so few languages support them. Scheme happens to be one of them. To learn more about continuation-based web servers, see "Implementation and Use of the PLT Scheme Web Server"by Shriram Krishnamurthi, et al.

AND SO THE SEVEN GUILDS OF LISP, EACH OF THEM MASTERS OF THEIR OWN BUG FIGHTING WEAPON UNIQUE TO LISP, UNDERTOOK THE WEEK-LONG JOURNEY BACK TO PLANET EARTH. THERE, THEY CONFRONTED THE INSECTOID ARMY...
ATTACK!
BLING!
RATATAT!
RATATAT!
WHOOSH!
ZOOM!
ZOOM!
ZOOM!

BREVITY GUILD MICRO FIGHTER

Lisp Dialect Arc Lisp (indirectly available in Common Lisp using custom macros)

Synopsis

Lisp allows you to write code that is incredibly concise but doesn't look like your cat walked over your keyboard. (I'm looking at you, Perl!) This is possible because of the various features we've already mentioned, such as macros, functional programming, and Lisp's dynamic typing system.

There is one Lisp dialect, however, that takes this idea to the extreme: Arc. In fact, code brevity is the primary design goal for this language. Paul Graham, the designer of Arc, analyzed large amounts of computer code in an attempt to figure out which primitive commands are needed to write code that is as concise as possible, while keeping the code readable.

How It Kills Bugs

With Arc, the goal is to write programs that are short. It is designed to let you say what you want to say in the most concise way possible, leaving no place for bugs to hide.

Example

```
❶  (accum a
❷    (for n 1 1000
❸      (unless (some [is 0 (mod n _)] (range 2 (- n 1)))
❹        a.n)))
```

NOTE *This example is in the Arc Lisp dialect and won't run in Common Lisp.*

Explanation

This example creates a list of all prime numbers between 1 and 1000, using the naïve method of checking for smaller numbers that divide evenly into the current loop value.

The accum function creates a local function named a, which is used to collect any primes that are found ❶. We iterate through the integers with a for loop ❷, checking for smaller numbers that divide evenly into the current value of i ❸. If none are are found, i is added to the list of primes ❹, by calling the function a with this new number. The brackets, [ ], are a shortcut for creating a lambda function with one parameter, which is accessed with the underscore character.

Weakness

Finding an optimally concise set of commands is difficult. With too many commands available, your code can become hard to understand, since it's difficult to remember what each function does. With too few commands, programs can get too bulky. Arc Lisp tries to find a happy medium, although there's still room for alternative language designs optimized for code brevity.

Chapter 16 demonstrates how to use macros to make your code concise, and many other examples of Lisp's powers of brevity are shown in the chapters following that discussion.

MULTICORE GUILD FORMATION FIGHTERS

Lisp Dialect   Clojure Lisp (available in
Common Lisp with the CL-STM extension)

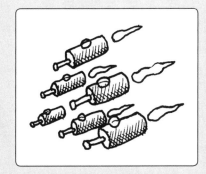

Synopsis

Now that most computers have multiple cores, there is a lot
of interest in finding elegant ways to write multicore/multi-
threaded code. One popular approach is to use functional
data structures along with a *software transactional memory*
system.

   Using software transactional memory, you can share
complex data structures between several threads, with a
guarantee that no thread will see inconsistent information in the data, even if it tries to read shared data while
another thread is attempting to write to it.

How It Fights Bugs

Multithreaded code tends to be very buggy. By using software transactional memory, you can greatly
increase your odds of writing bug-free multithreaded software.

Explanation

In this example, we define
two bank accounts called
checking and savings ❶, with
a total amount of $300
between them. We then
define a transfer-to-savings
function, which can be called
to move money from the
checking account to the savings
account ❷.
   Because this function
contains a dosync block,
Clojure will make sure these
two alter operations ❸ happen at the same moment in time. Of course, both values aren't really
altered at the exact same point in time, but the language makes sure it will appear to happen simultaneously. If another thread were to read these two accounts at the same time, also within a dosync
block, it would see exactly $300 in the combined accounts, no matter how many times either thread
checks these values.

Example

```
❶ (def checking (ref 100))
  (def savings (ref 200))

❷ (defn transfer-to-savings [n]
❸     (dosync (alter checking - n)
              (alter savings + n)))
```

NOTE   *This example is in the Clojure Lisp dialect and won't
run in Common Lisp.*

Weakness

Software transactional memory carries a performance penalty that cancels out some of the performance gains that come with using multiple CPU cores. However, as the number of CPU cores
increases, this penalty is less of an issue.

THE LAZY GUILD FRIGATE

Lisp Dialect

Clojure (available in Common Lisp with the Series library, CLAZY library, or custom macros)

Synopsis

A lazy programming language will perform a calculation *only* if the compiler determines it is absolutely necessary to produce a visible result. Clojure is the most popular Lisp dialect to include lazy programming as a primary feature. However, limited forms of lazy programming are common in all Lisp dialects.

How It Kills Bugs

Lazy languages let you create infinitely big data structures (as long as you don't try to use *all* of the data), which allows more of your code to be formulated as transformations of large data structures. In general, it is easier to debug data structures than it is to debug algorithms. Algorithms involve steps that unfold over time, and to understand them, you usually need to watch them as they execute. Data, on the other hand, exists independently of time, which means you can find bugs in a data structure just by looking at it.

Example

(take 20❶ (filter even?❷ (iterate inc 0)❸))

NOTE   *This example is in the Clojure Lisp dialect and won't run in Common Lisp.*

Explanation

This code returns the first 20 even positive integers. To do this, it first creates an infinite list of all positive integers ❸, using the iterate function to create a list of integers starting at zero. Then it filters out the even numbers ❷. Finally, it takes the first 20 numbers from that result ❶. Until the final take command, the data structures being operated on are theoretically infinite. However, since Clojure is a lazy language, it instantiates these data structures only on an as-needed basis. This means that only the first 20 such numbers are ever generated. (And even then, they are generated only if we actually use the final value somehow, such as printing it to the screen.)

Weakness

Since a lazy programming language chooses the order in which your code is run, it can lead to debugging headaches if you try to trace your code as it is running.

Chapter 18 discusses lazy programming.

INDEX

Symbols & Numbers

&body keyword, 344

* (asterisk), in variable names, 23

board-scale variable, 406

dice-scale variable, 403

from-tile variable, 411

num-players variable, 418

print-circle variable, 111

standard-output variable, 364

top-offset variable, 403

@ (at), in control sequence parameters, 223

` (backquote), 344

for enabling switching from data to code mode, 73

\ (backslash), for escaped characters, 35

: (colon), for keyword parameters, 81, 122

:@ flag, for columns in tables, 230–231

:if-exists keyword parameter, 243

:initial-value keyword parameter, 168

:junk-allowed parameter, 260

:pretty parameter, 117

:radix parameter, 260

:test keyword parameter, 141

to use equal, 204

. (dot), for representing cons cells, 39

" (double quotes), for strings, 35

= (equal sign) function, 65

(hash mark), for array, 154

#\newline, 89

#\space, 89

#\tab, 89

#' (function) operator, 75

#S prefix, for structures, 164

< (less-than) function, with sort, 170

() parentheses

for calling commands and functions, 22, 24

empty lists, 25

symmetry of nil and, 49–52

for list of declared variables in let, 28

for organizing code into lists, 33

' (single quote), as data indicator, 37

~ (tilde), for control sequences, 223

~& control sequence, 227

~< control sequence, 229

~> control sequence, 229

~:; control sequence, 232

~{ control sequence, 231

~} control sequence, 231

~$ control sequence, 223, 226

~% control sequence, 227–228

~a control sequence, 223–224

~b control sequence, 225

~d control sequence, 225

~f control sequence, 226

~t control sequence, 228–229

~x control sequence, 225

| (vertical pipe), for case-sensitive symbols, 89

404 error page, 265

A

ab-get-ratings-max function, 395–396

ab-get-ratings-min function, 395–396

ab-rate-position function, 397

academic research, 8

accum function, 459

accumulator, 332

~a control sequence, 223–224

across in loop macro, 201, 320

add-cops function, 140, 141–142
add function, predicates in, 171
add-new-dice function, 316–317, 333–334, 425
add-passing-move function, 312, 384–385
add-plants function, 204, 212
add-two function, 299–300
add-widget function, 296–297, 298
AI (artificial intelligence), 8
alists. *See* association lists (alists)
Allegro Common Lisp, 18
alpha beta pruning, 393–400
    and chance nodes, 423
alphanumericp function, 117
always in loop macro, 201
Amazon S3, 160
anaphoric macros, 347
and in loop macro, 201
and operator, 58
announce-winner function, 320
ANSI Common Lisp (CL), 15–16, 17–18. *See also* Common Lisp (CL)
append function, 75, 76, 143
append in loop macro, 201
apply function, 76
apt-get install clisp, 18
ARC assembly, 5
Arc Lisp dialect, 17, 359, 459
aref function, 154
    and performance, 156
arrayp function, 170
arrays, 153–157
    vs. lists, 156–157
    for monsters, 173
    sequence functions for, 166
    sum function for, 169
artificial intelligence (AI), 8
ASCII code, 260
    code-char function to convert, 308
ash (arithmetic shift) function, 25–26
as in loop macro, 201
assemblers, 5
assembly languages, 5
assoc function, 71, 83, 112
association lists (alists), 111–112, 141
    attributes for print-tag, 359
    of known nodes, 146
    nested, 142

for nodes in city, 142
for scenery description, 70–71
web request parameters in, 261
writing to file, 243
asterisk (*), in variable names, 23
at (@), in control sequence parameters, 223
at-loc-p function, 78
attacking-moves function, 313–314, 385, 419
Attack of the Robots! game, 233–234
Autocode, 5

B
backquote (`), 344
    for enabling switching from data to code mode, 73
backslash (\), for escaped characters, 35
~b control sequence, 225
being in loop macro, 200
below in loop macro, 196
bidirectional stream, 247
bigger function, 27
binary, number display as, 225
binary search, 23, 26
blocking operation, 247
board-array function, 308
board-attack-fail function, 419–420
board-attack function, 315–316
board-scale variable, 406
&body keyword, 344
Boolean values, manipulating, 58
branching, 56–57
    with case form, 57–58
breaking out of loop, 198
brevity of code, 459
brightness function, 361
bug fighters
    Clojure Lisp, 461
    comic book, 429–463
    Common Lisp Object System (CLOS), 451
    continuations, 454
    domain-specific language, 450
    exception handling, 444–445
    functional programming, 441
    generic setters, 447
    lazy evaluation, 462
    macros, 443

bugs, functional programming to
reduce, 301
by in loop macro, 201

C

C++ language, 9, 10, 32
    #define directive, 340
cached results, clearing, 398
cache misses, performance
        impact, 160
cadadar function, 42
cadadr function, 42
cadr function, 40–41
calc-pt function, 403
capitalized text, converting all
        caps to, 97
capturing console output, 123
car function, 40–41, 75
case form, branching with, 57–58
case-insensitivity, of symbols, 33
case of text, adjusting, 97
case-sensitive symbols, 89
cdr function, 40, 143–144
cells, retrieving item from first slot, 40
centered columns, 230
chain of cons cells, 40, 108
chance nodes, in game tree, 418–420
characterp function, 170
characters
    comparison, 65
    literal, 89
    for padding numbers, 225
char-downcase function, 99
char-equal function, 65
charge function, 151
char-upcase function, 99
chosen-tile parameter, 407
Church, Alonzo, 293
circle function, 362
circular lists, 110–111
CISC (complex instruction set
        computer), 8
city.dot.png picture, 145
CL (Common Lisp), 15, 17–18. *See
        also* Lisp
    basics, 441
    tail call optimization support, 333
client, for socket connection, 246

CLISP, 18–19
    installing, 18
    printing of circular lists, 111
    shutting down, 19
    starting, 19
Clojure Lisp, 17, 461
    and lazy evaluation, 377, 462
    lazy sequences, 380
CLOS (Common Lisp Object
        System), 166, 451
closingp predicate, 358
closing tag in XML, 358
closures, 326–328, 379
Clozure CL, 18
cl-sockets, 245
clusters, finding in Dice of Doom,
        424–425
cmd variable, 95
CMUCL, 18
COBOL, 8
code
    brevity, 459
    vs. data, 35–37
    symmetry between data and,
        91–92
code-char function, 260, 308
code composition, 298
code mode, 35, 36
    backquote (`) for enabling
        switching to, 73
coerce function, 98, 260
collect clause in loop, 137, 198
colon (:), for keyword parameters,
        81, 122
color
    for dice, 407
    manipulating, 361
columns in table, centered, 230
comic book, 4
    bug fighters, 429–463
    on functional programming,
        269–287
command-line interface, 85
    printing to screen, 86–87
commands, adding to permitted
        list, 368
Common Lisp (CL), 15, 17–18. *See
        also* Lisp
    basics, 441
    tail call optimization support, 333

Common Lisp HyperSpec, 170
    on control sequences, 233
Common Lisp Object System
        (CLOS), 166, 451
communication, with other network
        computers, 245
comparison, 62–65
    eql for numbers and
        characters, 65
    of symbols, 63
compiler, 5
    versions of function for, 172
complex instruction set computer
        (CISC), 8
computation, delayed, 124
computer, as game opponent,
        321–326
concatenate command, 95
cond command, 56, 208
conditions, tricks with, 58–62
Congestion City, 131, 132. *See also*
        Grand Theft Wumpus
        game
    building final edges, 139–142
    defining edges, 135–142
    drawing map, 145–149
        from partial knowledge,
        146–148
    nodes for, 142–144
    preventing islands, 137–139
    walking around town, 148–149
connect-all-islands function, 139
connect-edge-list function, 140
connect-with-bridges function, 139
Conrad's Rule of Thumb for
        Comparing Stuff, 62–63
cons cells, 37, 38, 107
    in nested lists, 42
conses, eq for comparing, 63
cons function, 38–40
consing, 39
console output, capturing, 123
console streams, 238
consp function, 170
constants, for game board
        dimensions, 402
continuations, 454
control sequences, 222–223
    Common Lisp HyperSpec on, 233
    for formatting numbers, 225–226

iterating through lists with,
        231–232
    for new lines, 227–228
control string parameter, for format
        function, 222–223
copy-list function, 211
copy-structure function, problems
        from, 211
count function, 167
counting from starting point to
        ending point, 197
count in loop macro, 201
currencies, formatting, 226

D

data
    vs. code, 35–37
    generic process for handling,
        166–172
    symmetry between code and, 91–92
    tree-like, 113
data mode, 35, 37
    backquote (`) for enabling
        switching to, 73
data structures, self-referential, 111
~d control sequence, 225
dead animals, in evolving
        environment, 212
dead monsters, checking for, 179
Debian-based Linux machine,
        CLISP on, 18
debugging
    in functional programming, 441
    string streams and, 250–251
decf function, 180
decimal number, value
        displayed as, 225
decimal point, and number type, 34
declaration, of function, 29
decode-param function, 259–260
default, code mode as, 36
define-condition function, 254–255
defmacro command, 341, 342–344
defmethod command, 171–172, 180
defparameter command, 23, 24, 135
defstruct command, 163, 164, 172,
        173, 180, 208
    for brigand, 185–186
    for hydra, 183

to include monster type fields, 181
for slime mold, 185
defun command, 25, 27
defvar command, 24
delayed computation, 124
deprecated function, 117
depth-first search, 394
describe-location function, 71
describe-objects function, 78
describe-obj function, 78
describe-path function, 72–73
describe-paths function, 73–74, 75, 77
destination parameter, for format
    function, 222
Dewdney, A.K., "Simulated evolution;
    wherein bugs learn to hunt
    bacteria," 202
Dice of Doom game, 303–336
    attacking, 315–316
    calculating attacking moves,
        313–314
    calculating passing moves,
        312–313
    computer opponent, 321–326
        game loop with AI player,
            324–325
        minimax algorithm, 323
        minimax algorithm code,
            323–324
    decoupling rules from rest of
        game, 309–310
    finding neighbors, 314–315
    game board, 307–309
        3-by-3 sample game, 334–336
        5-by-5, 398–400
        constants for dimensions, 402
        using SVG format, 402–408
    generating game tree, 311–312
    new game-tree function, 317–318
    performance improvement,
        326–336
    playing against another human,
        318–321
        input from human players, 319
        main loop, 318
        state of game information,
            318–319
        winner determination,
            319–320

playing first human vs. computer
    game, 325–326
reinforcements, 316–317
rules, 304
sample game, 304–306
tail call optimization, 333–334
version 1, 306–321
    global variables, 306–307
version 2, 384–386
    alpha beta pruning, 393–400
    lazy lists for game tree, 384
    score-board function, 390
    starting game on 4-by-4
        board, 386
    winning by a lot vs. winning by
        a little, 389–393
version 3 (web-based), 401
    announcing winner, 410
    drawing die, 403–405
    drawing tile, 405–406
    game board, 406–408
    game board in HTML, 412
    handling computer player, 412
    handling human player,
        410–411
    initializing new game, 410
    playing, 413–414
    web server interface, 408–412
version 4
    calling dice rolling code from
        game engine, 420–421
    improving reinforcement
        rules, 423–425
    increasing number of players,
        417–418
    rolling dice, 418–423
    updaing AI, 422–423
dice_of_doom.v2.lisp file, 402
dice-scale variable, 403
digit-char-p function, 116
digraph command (Graphviz), 115
direct-edges function, 138
directed graph, 124
dirty code, 294, 296
dividing by zero, 53
division function, 34
DOCTYPE declaration, 258
dod-request-handler function, 408–409
domain, explained, 355–356

domain of function, 292

domain-specific language (DSL), 231, 355, 450. *See also* macros

dot (.), for representing cons cells, 39

dot->png function, 123

dotimes function, 161, 175

DOT information generation, 115–120

    edges conversion, 119

    labels for graph nodes, 117–118

    node identifiers conversion, 116–117

    for nodes, 118

    turning DOT file into picture, 120–123

dot-name function, 116

do token, 197, 200

dotted lists, 108–109

double quotes ("), for strings, 35

downfrom in loop macro, 201

downto in loop macro, 201

draw-board function, 309

draw-board-svg function, 407

draw-city function, 145

draw-die-svg function, 403

draw-dod-page function, 409, 412

draw-known-city function, 147, 149

draw-tile-svg function, 405

draw-world function, 212–213

DSL (domain-specific language), 231, 355, 450. *See also* macros

dunk function, 368–369, 371

dynamic variable, 24

dynamic website, 265–267

    testing request handler, 265–266

E

each in loop macro, 200

earmuffs, 23

eat function, 209

edge-pair function, 136, 139

edges, 72

    of Congestion City, 135–142

    converting to descriptions, 74–76

    converting to DOT format, 119

    erasing duplicate, 126

    replacing list with hash table, 162

edges->dot function, 119

edges-to-alist function, 139, 141

EDSAC Initial Orders, 5

else in loop macro, 201

Emacs Lisp, 17

empty lists (), 39

    as false value, 50–51

    other expressions as disguises for, 51–52

end in loop macro, 201

energy, in plants, 203

eq function, 33, 57, 63

eql function, 65, 331

equal function, 63, 331

equalp function, 65, 330

= (equal sign) function, 65

error command, 254

escaped characters, in strings, 35

eval command, 92

    danger of, 101

    improving, 96

every function, 167, 179

evolution function, 213–214

evolving environment game, 202–218

    animals, 205–212

        anatomy, 205–207

        eating process, 209

        energy, 206

        motion, 207–208

        properties, 206

        reproduction, 210–212

        starting point, 207

        tracking genes, 206

        turn function, 208–209

    bimodal distribution in, 217–218

    drawing world, 212–213

    plants

        energy, 203

        growth, 204

    simulating day, 212

    starting simulation, 214–218

    user interface, 213–214

exception handling, 95, 253–256, 444–445

    custom conditions, 254–255

    intercepting conditions, 255

    resources protected against unexpected conditions, 255–256

    signaling condition, 254

    for web server, 265

exponent, 36

expressive language, 10
expt function, 34, 36

F

false value, empty list () as, 50–51
~f control sequence, 226
files
 streams to write and read, 242–243
 writing information to, 121
file streams, 238
finally in loop macro, 200
find-empty-node function, 144–145
find-if function, 61, 167
find-island function, 139
find-islands function, 139
Firefox, for Dice of Doom game,
 413–414
Firefox 3.7 alpha, for SVG
 support, 402
first-class values, functions as, 104
flet function, 29
 for local function definition, 95
floating-point numbers, 34
 control sequences for
  formatting, 226
force command, 378–380
for in loop macro, 196, 201
format function, 193. *See also* printing
 anatomy, 221–223
 control string parameter, 222–223
 destination parameter, 222
 and text justification, 228
formatting numbers, control
 sequences for, 225–226
forms, 36
 nested, 36
FORTRAN, 5
freeing of variables, 327
fresh-line command, 227
from in loop macro, 201
from-tile variable, 411
funcall function, 178, 327
functional programming, 54, 71, 441
 anatomy of program, 295–298
 benefits, 301–302
 comic book, 269–287
 higher-order, 105
 and loops, 315
 problems from, 375–376

reduce function, 352–353
side effects, 294, 300–301
using, 299–300
what it is, 292–295
function operator, shorthand for, 75
functionp function, 170
function pipeline, 309
functions
 calling in Lisp, 22
 call to itself, 30
 comprehensive list of
  sequence, 170
 creating with lambda, 103–105
 deprecated, 117
 generic, 116
 higher-order, 75
 names available in defined
  functions, 29–30
 namespaces for, 75
 nullary, 120
 parentheses for, 22
 sending string streams to, 249

G

game-action macro, 369–371
game board
 AI adjustments for larger, 387–400
 for Dice of Doom, 307–309
  3-by-3 sample game, 334–336
  5-by-5, 398–400
  constants for dimensions, 402
  using SVG format, 402–408
game-eval function
 approved list of commands for, 101
 limiting commands called, 96
game-loop function, 174–175
game-print function, 96–99
game-read function, 94–95
game-repl function, 93–94, 365
games. *See also* Dice of Doom game;
  evolving environment game;
  Grand Theft Wumpus
  game; Orc Battle game;
  Wizard's Adventure Game
 Attack of the Robots! game,
  233–234
 Guess-My-Number, 21–23
 loading code from REPL, 365–366
 winning by a lot vs. winning by a
  little, 389–393

game tree
    branches hidden in clouds,
        376–377
    chance nodes in, 418–420
    generating, 311–312
    memoizing, 330
    trimming, 387–389
game-tree function, 311, 317–318
garbage collection, 9, 327
Garret, Ron, 257
gen-board function, 308
generalized reference, 155
generic functions, 116
    creating with type predicates,
        170–172
generic setters, 154–156, 447
gensym function, 349
get-connected function, 138, 161, 162,
        424, 425
get-connected-hash function, 163
get-content-params function, 263
gethash function, 155, 158, 160, 162
get-header function, 262
    testing, with string stream,
        262–263
get-ratings function, 324, 391, 422
    new versions, 395
GET request, 257
    request parameters for, 259
global functions, defining, 25–28
global variables
    changing value, 27
    defining, 23–24
    in look function, 80
    macros and, 370
    for player and monsters, 173–174
    setting inside conditional
        branch, 54
Google BigTable, 160
Graham, Paul, 17
    Arc Lisp dialect, 359
Grand Theft Wumpus game. *See also*
        Congestion City
    basics, 131–135
    clues, 142
    drawing map, 145–149
        from partial knowledge,
            146–148

with hash tables, 161–163
    initializing new game, 144–145
    playing game, 149–151
    police roadblocks, 139
graph->dot function, 124
graphs
    creating, 114–124
    creating picture of, 123–124
    directed, 124
    labels for nodes, 117–118
    undirected, 124–127
    visualizing, 114
graph utilities, loading, 135
graph-util.lisp file, 127
Graphviz, 114–124
Graphviz DOT file
    edges conversion, 119
    for graph drawing library,
        115–120
    labels for graph nodes, 117–118
    node identifiers conversion,
        116–117
    for nodes, 118
    turning DOT file into picture,
        120–123
guess-my-number function, 25–27
Guess-My-Number game, 21–23
Guile Scheme, 17

H

hackers
    and dangerous commands, 101
    and read command, 262
handle-computer function, 324, 388,
        397, 412, 421
handle-direction function, 148
handle-human function, 319,
        385–386, 421
handle-new-place function, 149
handler-case function, 254
hash collisions, 160
hash-edges function, 162
hash-key in loop macro, 200
hash-keys in loop macro, 200
hash mark (#), for array, 154
hash-table-p function, 170

hash tables, 155, 157–163
    Grand Theft Wumpus game
        with, 161–163
    inefficiency for small tables, 160
    performance, 160–161
    for plants, 204
    returning multiple values,
        159–160
hash-value in loop macro, 200
hash-values in loop macro, 200
Haskell, 17, 296
    and lazy evaluation, 377
have function, 367
health meter, for monsters, 180
hello-request-handler function, 265
heuristics, 389
hexadecimal, number display as, 225
Hickey, Rich, 17
hidden state, 299
hierarchical data, 113
higher-order functions, 75
higher-order programming, 105,
        298–300
homoiconic programming code, 91
HTML5 standard, 402
HTML code, 97
    embedding SVG pictures, 402
    page skeleton, 265
    tag macro to generate, 360–361
html tags, 258
HTTP (Hypertext Transfer
        Protocol), 256
http-char function, 260
HTTP escape codes, 259
http.lisp file, 257
Hughes, John, "Why Functional
        Programming Matters," 310
Hunt the Wumpus, 129
hyperlinks, in SVG image, 361
Hypertext Transfer Protocol
        (HTTP), 256

I

if command, 50, 52–54
:if-exists keyword parameter, 243
if in loop macro, 201
imperative code, 294
    code composition with, 298–299

imperative game engine, 310
implicit progn, 55
incf function, 179
indentation of code, 28
infinite loop
    getting out of, 93
    preventing, 111
infinity, positive and negative, 397
Information Processing Language, 5
in in loop macro, 201
initially in loop macro, 200
:initial-value keyword parameter, 168
init-monsters function, 178
input-stream-p command, 240
input streams, 238, 240–241
installing CLISP, 18
instruction set of processor, 5
integers, 34
    control sequences for
        formatting, 225
intern command, 262
interpreter, 5
    versions of function for, 172
intersection function, 141
into in loop macro, 201
inventory function, 83
IP address, in socket address, 245
islands, preventing, 137–139
isomorphic item, 63
iterating
    across sequence, 167–170
    through lists, with format control
        sequences, 231–232
    through list values, 197

J

Java language, 10
Jones, Simon Peyton, 300
:junk-allowed parameter, 260
justified text, 228–231

K

key/value pair
    returning for alist, 112
    storage, 160
keyword parameter, 117–118, 122
    for find function, 81

known-city.dot-png file, 148
known-city-edges function, 146–147
known-city-nodes function, 146

L

labels, for graph nodes, 117–118
labels function, 29–30, 78
    for local function definition, 95
lambda calculus, 6, 105, 293
lambda function, 178, 179, 255, 314
    and closures, 326–327
    importance, 105
    purpose, 103–105
largest-cluster-size function, 424–425
launching website, 266–267
lazy-car command, 380
lazy-cdr command, 380
lazy command, 378–380
lazy-cons command, 380
lazy evaluation, 376–384, 423, 462
lazy-find-if function, 383
lazy game tree, 310
lazy lists
    adjusting AI functions to use,
        387–400
    converting between regular lists
        and, 381–382
    converting to regular lists, 382
    for Dice of Doom game tree, 384
    library for, 380
    mapping and searching, 383–384
lazy-mapcan function, 383, 385
lazy-mapcar function, 383
lazy-nil function, 381, 385
lazy-nth function, 383
lazy-null function, 381
legality of game move, 148
legal-tiles parameter, 407
length function, 166–167
less-than (<) function, with sort, 170
let* command, 140
let command, 28, 123, 140, 327, 340
    progn command and, 344
lexical variable, 123, 327–328
library, for lazy lists, 380
limit-tree-depth function, 388,
        395, 423
line breaks, 28

linking data pieces, cons function for,
        38–40
Lisp. *See also* Common Lisp (CL)
    basic etiquette, 24–25
    dialects, 15–18
        for scripting, 17
    features, 2–3
    Guess-My-Number game, 21–23
    origins, 4–9
    source of power, 10–11
    technologies supporting, comic
        book, 429–463
    up-and-coming dialects, 17
    valid expression example, 3
LispWorks, 18
list function, 41, 359
list-length function, 167
listp function, 170, 240
lists, 33, 37–42. *See also* association list
        (alist); lazy lists
    vs. arrays, 156–157
    association, 111–112
    benefits of using, 71
    calculating length, 51
    checking for membership, 60–61
    circular, 110–111
    control sequences for iterating
        through, 231–232
    dotted, 108–109
    empty, 39
        as false value, 50–51
        other expressions as disguises
            for, 51–52
    functions, 38–42
    iterating through with loop, 197
    joining multiple into one, 76
    macro for splitting, 346–347
    nested, 41–42
    of objects, 77–78
    pairs, 109–110
    sequence functions for, 166
    vs. structures, 165–166
    sum function for, 169
literal characters, 89
lit variable, and capitalization
        rules, 99
load command, 135
local functions, defining, 29–30

local variables
    defining, 28
    for value returned by read
        function, 88
log information, streams for, 249
long strings, 250
look function, 80, 93
lookup key, of hash table, 158
loop macro, 93, 136–137, 193,
        195–202
    breaking out, 198
    collect clause, 198
    counting from starting point to
        ending point, 197
    do token, 197
    iterating through list values, 197
    with multiple for clauses, 198–199
    nested, 199
    periodic table of, 200–201
    when token, 197
loops
    with dotimes function, 175
    for evolving environment,
        202–218
    and functional programming, 315
    getting out of infinite, 93
    preventing infinite, 111

M

machine language, 4
macroexpand command, 345, 348,
        349–350
macro expansion, 341–342
macros, 54, 82, 104–105, 339, 443. *See
        also* domain-specific
        language (DSL);
        programming language
    avoiding repeated execution,
        347–348
    avoiding variable capture,
        348–350
    dangers and alternatives, 352–353
    for defining new function, 370
    helper function, 358
    to implement lazy command, 379
    reader, 101
    recursive, 350–352
    simple example, 340–345

for splitting lists, 346–347
svg, 361–362
transformation, 342–344
main-loop function, 296, 298
make-array command, 154
make-city-edges function, 139, 140
make-city-nodes function, 143
make-edge-list function, 136, 140
make-hash-table command,
        157–158, 161
make-lazy function, 381
make-orc function, 181
make-person function, 164, 165
make-string-input-stream function,
        249, 263
make-string-output-stream
        command, 249
mapcan function, 146, 147, 314, 363
mapcar function, 74, 141, 359
mapc function, 118, 138, 162
map function, 169–170
maplist function, 126
map of city
    drawing, 145–149
    showing only visited nodes,
        146–148
mapping lazy lists, 383–384
mathematical functions,
        properties, 293
mathematical sets, hash tables for, 204
mathematical syntax, languages
        using, 6
max function, 212
maximize in loop macro, 201
McCarthy, John, 6–7
    "Recursive Functions of Symbolic
        Expressions and Their
        Computation by
        Machine," 7
member function, 60–61, 96
memoization, 328–331
memory, 5, 156
    software transactional, 461
Metaobject Protocol (MOP), 451
minimax algorithm code, game tree
        analysis with, 394
minimize in loop macro, 201
mod (remainder) function, 208

monetary floating-point value, 223
monster-attack function, 181
    for orcs, 182
    for slime mold, 185
monster-hit function, 176, 184
monsters. *See* Orc Battle game
monster-show function, for orcs, 182
MOP (Metaobject Protocol), 451
most-negative-fixnum, 397
most-positive-fixnum, 397
move function, 207–208
move in game, checking legality, 148
multiparadigm language, 18
multiple dispatch, 452
multiple-value-bind command, 159
mutations, 165, 210
    with reproduce function, 211
my-length function, 331–332
    custom, 345
    improving, 350–352

N

named in loop macro, 200
names of functions, available in
            defined functions, 29–30
namespaces, for variables and
            functions, 75
nconc in loop macro, 201
neato command (Graphviz), 115
negative infinity, 397
neighbors function, 142, 314–315,
            329–330
nested alists, 142
nested forms, 36
nested lists, 41–42
nested loop macro, 199
nested tags, in XML, 357
network computers, communication
            between, 245
never in loop macro, 201
new-game function, 144
    to draw known city, 147
#\newline, 89
new line
    control sequences for, 227–228
    in printed output, 226
    before printing, 87

nil, 38, 39, 52, 107
    lists not ending with, 109
    symmetry of () and, 49–52
nodes, 118
    for Congestion City, 142–144
    identifiers, converting, 116–117
nodes->dot function, 118, 119
nondeterministic programming, 454
nonvisible characters, literals for, 89
nth function, 156
nullary functions, 120
null function, 61–62
numberp function, 170
numbers, 34–35
    comparison, 65
    control sequences for formatting,
            225–226
num-players variable, 418

O

object-oriented programming (OOP)
            languages, 9, 163, 451
    vs. Lisp, 165
objects
    descriptions
        at specific location, 77–78
        visible, 78–79
    inventory check, 83–84
    picking up, 82–83
objects-at function, 78, 82, 83
on in loop macro, 201
OOP (object-oriented programming)
            languages, 9, 163, 451
    vs. Lisp, 165
optimizing functional code, 326
    closures, 326–328
    memoization, 328–331
    tail call optimization, 331–334
orc-battle function, 174, 187–188
Orc Battle game, 172–188
    global variables for player and
            monsters, 173–174
    helper functions for player
            attacks, 177–178
    main game functions, 174–175
    monster management functions,
            178–179

monsters, 179–186
    checking for dead, 179
    Cunning Brigand, 185–186
    functions for building, 174
    generic, 180–181
    hydra, 183–184
    Slimy Slime Mold, 184–185
    Wicked Orc, 181–182
    player management functions, 175–177
    starting game, 187–188
orc datatype, 181
or operator, 58
orthogonal issues, 387
output-stream-p function, 240
output streams, 238, 239–240
    with-open-file command for, 242

P

padded value, for format function, 223
padding parameter, for number width, 225
pairs, 109–110
pairs function, 351, 359
parallel games, web server for multiple, 410
parameters, quoting, 95
parametric polymorphism, 9
paranoid strategy, 418
parentheses ()
    for calling commands and functions, 22, 24
    empty lists, 25
        symmetry of nil and, 49–52
    for list of declared variables in let, 28
    for organizing code into lists, 33
parse-integer function, 260
parse-params function, 261
parse-url function, 261–262
path descriptions
    in game, 72–77
    multiple at once, 73–77
performance
    arrays vs. lists, 156–157
    cons cells and, 113
    for Dice of Doom game, 326–336
    functional programming and, 300

hash tables and, 160–161, 163
    tail calls and, 333
periodic table of loop macro, 200–201
permitted commands, adding to list, 368
person-age function, 164
pick-chance-branch function, 420–421
pick-monster function, 176
pickup function, 82
pi constant, 226
picture, from DOT file, 120–123
player-attack function, 176, 177
player function, 314
play-vs-computer function, 324–325, 389
play-vs-human function, 386
police roadblocks, 139
polygon function, 362–363
polygons, for die, 403
port
    number in socket address, 245
    taking control of, 246
port 80, 264
port 8080, 264
position function, 167, 261
positive infinity, 397
POST request, 258
power, 193
predicates, 78, 116
:pretty parameter, 117
prin1 function, 87
prin1-to-string function, 98, 116
princ function, 35, 90–91, 222, 223–224
print-circle variable, 111
printed representation, creating object from, 164
print function, 86–87
    priority use, 88
printing. *See also* format function
    creating stream for functions, 121
    multiple lines of output, 226–228
    to screen, 86–87
    text justification, 228–231
print-tag function, 358
problem solving, 20
progn command, 54
programming
    heuristic techniques, 389
    nondeterministic, 454

programming language. *See also* macros
  higher-order, 298–300
  learning, 2
properties in structures, 163
push function, 82–83, 112, 138, 240
  for hash table values, 162
pushnew command, 368, 370
Python, 9

Q

quasiquoting, 73
quit command, 19
quote command, 95
quoting, 37
quote-it function, 95

R

:radix parameter, 260
raise-price function, 445
RAM, 156
random edges
  generating, 135–136
  and island prevention, 137–139
random function, 177, 308, 363
random-monster function, 177
random-node function, 136
random numbers, generating, 177
random-plant function, 204
random walk, 363
randval function, 177, 180
range of function, 292
rate-position function, 323–324,
      330–331, 391
  new versions, 397
rational number, function
      returning, 34
RDF (Resource Description
      Framework), 3
read-char command, 241
reader, 33
reader macros, 101
read-eval-print loop (REPL), 19, 22
  loading game code from, 365–366
  setting up custom, 93–94
  testing, 99–100
read-from-string function, 95, 410

read function
  danger of, 101
  local variable for value
      returned by, 88
reading data, input streams for,
      240–241
read-line function, 91
recurse macro, 350–351
recursion, 30, 50, 332
  in macros, 350–352
reduced instruction set computer
      (RISC) hardware
      architecture, 8
reduce function, 167–169
  initial value for, 168
reference, generalized, 155
referential transparency, 293, 301
reinforcements, rules for choosing
      number in Dice of
      Doom, 425
remhash function, 209
remove-duplicates function, 141, 320
remove-if function, 320
remove-if-not function, 78, 138
repeat in loop macro, 200
REPL. *See* read-eval-print loop (REPL)
reproduce function, 210
  mutations with, 211
request body, 257
  parsing, 263
request handler, testing, 265–266
request-handler function, 264
request-handler parameter, 264
request header, 257
  parsing, 261–262
request parameters
  decoding lists of, 260–261
  decoding values for HTTP,
      259–260
  for web server, 258–261
Resource Description Framework
      (RDF), 3
resources, freeing up, 248–249
response body, 258
response header, 258
restarts, 444–445
return-from in loop macro, 200
return in loop macro, 200
return value, for command, 25

reverse function, 222
RISC (reduced instruction set computer) hardware architecture, 8
roll-dice function, 420
round function, 159
Ruby, 9
rule engine, 310
runtime, 342

S

say-hello function, 87–88
SBCL (Steel Bank Common Lisp), 18
scalable vector graphics (SVG). *See* SVG images
scenery description, association list for, 70–71
Scheme, 15
   namespace for, 76
   tail call optimization in, 333
score-board function, 390
screen, printing to, 86–87
Script-Fu Scheme, 17
scripting, Lisp dialects for, 17
searching
   lazy lists, 383–384
   sequence functions for, 167
security, eval function and, 92
self function, 351–352
self-referential data structures, 111
semantics, 31–32
Semantic Web, 3
sending message over socket, 246–248
sequence functions, 166
   for searching, 167
sequences, 166–170
   iterating across, 167–170
serve function, 263–265
server, for socket connection, 246
set-difference function, 139
setf function, 27, 83, 111, 329, 447
   for array, 154–155
   to change structure property, 164
shallow copy of structure, 211
Short Code, 5
shortcut Boolean evaluation, 59
show-monsters function, 179
shutting down CLISP, 19

side effects, 441
   of functional programming, 294, 300–301
signaling condition, for error handling, 254
sin function, 293
single quote ('), as data indicator, 37
slots, 163
smaller function, 27
socket, serve function creation of, 264
socket-accept command, 247
socket-connect command, 247
sockets, 244–249
   addresses, 245
   connections, 246
   sending message over, 246–248
socket-server-close command, 249
socket-server function, 246
socket streams, 238
software transactional memory, 461
some function, 167
sort function, 170
#\space, 89
special form
   if as, 53
   let command as, 340
special variable, 24
splash command, 371
split macro, 346–347
splitting lists, macro for, 346–347
#S prefix, for structures, 164
standard-output variable, 364
starting CLISP, 19
start-over function, 28
statistics, of dice rolls, 422
Steel Bank Common Lisp (SBCL), 18
Steele, Guy L., 16
streams, 121, 237–238
   bidirectional, 247
   closing on network computer, 248–249
   commands to interact with, 242
   for files, 242–243
   types, 238–241
string builders, 250
string datatype, 70
string-downcase function, 358
string-equal function, 65
stringp function, 170

strings, 35
  converting symbol list to, 98
  sequence functions for, 166
string streams, 238, 249–251
  debugging and, 250–251
  get-header function testing with, 262–263
Stroustrup, Bjarne, 10
structures, 163–166
  vs. lists in Lisp code, 165–166
  when to use, 165–166
subseq function, 170
substitute-if function, 116–117
substitute-if-not function, 117
sum function, for arrays and lists, 169
sum in loop macro, 196, 201
suspension, 120. *See also* thunks
Sussman, Gerald Jay, 16
SVG images
  attributes for, 361
  circles, 362
  Dice of Doom game board using, 402–408
  polygons, 362–363
  writing, 356–364
svg macro, 361–362
svg-style function, 362
SVG Web, 356
symbol-function command, 329
symbolp function, 170
symbols, 33–34
  benefits of using, 71
  comparing, 63
  converting list to string, 98
symmetry
  of () and nil, 49–52
  between code and data, 91–92
syntax
  building blocks for Lisp, 32–35
  and semantics, 31–32

T

#\tab, 89
tables
  output as, 228–229
  trick for creating pretty, 232–233
tab variable, 331

tag macro, 359–360
  to generate HTML, 360–361
tail call, 332
tail call optimization, 331–334
take-all function, 382
take function, 382
~t control sequence, 228–229
TCP/IP, 256
TCP packets, 245
technologies supporting Lisp, comic book, 429–463
terpri function, 226–227
test functions, 116
testing
  get-header function with string stream, 262–263
  user interface, 99–100
:test keyword parameter, 141
  to use equal, 204
text. *See also* strings
  breaking into equal length pieces, 232
  converting all caps to capitalized, 97
  justified, 228–231
  processing, 67
text game interface, 92–99
  testing, 99–100
the in loop macro, 200
then in loop macro, 201
thereis in loop macro, 201
threatened function, 391
threatened hex, in Dice of Doom, 390
three-way-if macro, 443
thunks, 120–121
  for creating graph picture, 123
tilde (~), for control sequences, 223
time command, 161
to in loop macro, 201
top-level definition of variable, 23
top-offset variable, 403
tree-like data, 113
true/false functions, 78
turn function, for animals, 208–209
tweak-text function, 98
type-checking, 166
  in generic functions, 167
type dispatching, 172

type-of function, 180–181
type predicates, for generic functions,
      170–172

U

uedges->dot function, 126
ugraph->dot function, 126
ugraph->png function, 126, 145
undirected graphs, 124–127
unless, 55
      in loop macro, 201
until in loop macro, 200
unwind-protect function, 256, 264
update-world function, 212
upfrom in loop macro, 201
upto in loop macro, 201
URLs for web pages, name/value
      pairs in, 260
user interface, 85
      command-line, 85
            printing to screen, 86–87
      for evolving environment game,
            213–214
      testing, 99–100
      for Wizard's Adventure Game,
            92–99
using in loop macro, 200
usocket, 245

V

vacuum-tube computer systems, 4
values function, 159
variable capture, 348–350
variables. *See also* global variables;
      local variables
      asterisks (*) in names, 23
      declaration in let command, 28
      defining, 140
      destruction, 327
      in functional programming,
            293, 301
      function to create unique
            name, 349
      lexical, 123, 328
      for location descriptions, 70
      modifying value, 447
      namespaces for, 75

variable shadowing, 333
versions of function, 172
vertical pipe (|), for case-sensitive
      symbols, 89
virtual memory paging, performance
      impact, 160
visible objects, describing, 78–79
visualizing graphs, 114
visual noise, 340

W

walk function, 81–82, 148
web-announce-winner function, 410
web forms, 258
web-handle-human function, 410–411
web-initialize function, 409, 410
web resources
      downloading CLISP installer, 18
      for Graphviz, 115
      Lisp projects, 3
web server, 256–265
      continuation-aware, 454
      how it works, 256–258
      interface for Dice of Doom,
            408–412
            for computer player, 412
            for human player, 410–411
            limitations, 409–410
      parsing request body, 263
      parsing request header, 261–262
      request parameters, 258–261
      serve function, 263–265
webserver.lisp file, 402
website
      dynamic, 265–267
      launching, 266–267
weld function, 367–368, 370–371
when in loop macro, 201
when token, 55, 197
while in loop macro, 200
winners function, 319–320
with in loop macro, 200
with-open-file command, 121, 122,
            123, 242–244
with-open-stream macro, 264
with-output-to-string macro, 250–251

Wizard's Adventure Game
basic requirements, 69–70
custom game commands, 365–373
dunk, 368–369
game-action macro, 369–371
welding, 366–368
custom interface, 92–99
DOT information for, 119–120
location descriptions, 71
look command, 79–80
map of house in alists, 114
object descriptions at specific
location, 77–79
object inventory check, 83–84
path descriptions, 72–77
picking up objects, 82–83
playing completed version,
371–373
scenery description with
association list, 70–71
walk function, 81–82
world for, 68–69
write-char command, 240

X

~x control sequence, 225
XML, 113
XML format
nested tags, 357
and SVG format, 357
xmlns attribute, 361

Z

zero, dividing by, 53

The Electronic Frontier Foundation (EFF) is the leading organization defending civil liberties in the digital world. We defend free speech on the Internet, fight illegal surveillance, promote the rights of innovators to develop new digital technologies, and work to ensure that the rights and freedoms we enjoy are enhanced — rather than eroded — as our use of technology grows.

PRIVACY EFF has sued telecom giant AT&T for giving the NSA unfettered access to the private communications of millions of their customers. eff.org/nsa

FREE SPEECH EFF's Coders' Rights Project is defending the rights of programmers and security researchers to publish their findings without fear of legal challenges. eff.org/freespeech

INNOVATION EFF's Patent Busting Project challenges overbroad patents that threaten technological innovation. eff.org/patent

FAIR USE EFF is fighting prohibitive standards that would take away your right to receive and use over-the-air television broadcasts any way you choose. eff.org/IP/fairuse

TRANSPARENCY EFF has developed the Switzerland Network Testing Tool to give individuals the tools to test for covert traffic filtering. eff.org/transparency

INTERNATIONAL EFF is working to ensure that international treaties do not restrict our free speech, privacy or digital consumer rights. eff.org/global

EFF is a member-supported organization. Join Now! www.eff.org/support

THE LINUX PROGRAMMING INTERFACE
A Linux and UNIX® System Programming Handbook

by MICHAEL KERRISK

The Linux Programming Interface is the definitive guide to the Linux and UNIX programming interface—the interface employed by nearly every application that runs on a Linux or UNIX system. In this authoritative work, Linux programming expert Michael Kerrisk provides detailed descriptions of the system calls and library functions that readers need to master the craft of system programming and accompanies his explanations with clear, complete example programs. Extensively indexed and heavily cross-referenced, *The Linux Programming Interface* is both an introductory guide for readers new to the topic of system programming and a comprehensive reference for experienced system programmers.

SEPTEMBER 2010, 1552 PP., $99.95, *hardcover*
ISBN 978-1-59327-220-3

AUTOTOOLS
A Practitioner's Guide to GNU Autoconf, Automake, and Libtool

by JOHN CALCOTE

The GNU Autotools is a group of utilities designed to make it easy for developers to create software that is portable across many Unix-like operating systems. In *Autotools*, author John Calcote begins with an overview of high-level concepts, then tackles more advanced topics, like using the M4 macro processor with Autoconf, extending the Automake framework, and building Java and C# sources. *Autotools* also includes a variety of complete projects that readers are encouraged to work through to gain a real-world sense of how to become an Autotools practitioner. For example, they'll turn the FLAIM and Jupiter projects' hand-coded, makefile-based build systems into powerful Autotools-based build systems.

JULY 2010, 360 PP., $44.95
ISBN 978-1-59327-206-7

THE ART OF ASSEMBLY LANGUAGE, 2ND EDITION

by RANDALL HYDE

Widely respected by hackers of all kinds, *The Art of Assembly Language* teaches programmers how to understand assembly language and how to use it to write powerful, efficient code. Using the proven High Level Assembler (HLA) as its primary teaching tool, *The Art of Assembly Language* leverages your knowledge of high-level programming languages to make it easier for you to quickly grasp basic assembly concepts. Among the most comprehensive references to assembly language ever published, *The Art of Assembly Language, 2nd Edition* has been thoroughly updated to reflect recent changes to the HLA language. All code from the book is portable to the Windows, Linux, Mac OS X, and FreeBSD operating systems.

MARCH 2010, 760 PP., $59.95
ISBN 978-1-59327-207-4

LEARN YOU A HASKELL FOR GREAT GOOD!

by MIRAN LIPOVAČA

Learn You a Haskell for Great Good! is a fun, illustrated guide to learning Haskell, a functional programming language that can confound even experienced coders. The book introduces programmers familiar with imperative languages (such as C++, Java, or Python) to the unique aspects of functional programming. Packed with jokes, pop culture references, and the author's own hilarious artwork, *Learn You a Haskell for Great Good!* eases the learning curve of this complex language and is the perfect starting point for any programmer looking to expand their horizons.

JANUARY 2011, 400 PP., $44.95
ISBN 978-1-59327-283-8

GRAY HAT PYTHON
Python Programming for Hackers and Reverse Engineers

by JUSTIN SEITZ

Gray Hat Python explains how to complete various hacking tasks with Python, which is fast becoming the programming language of choice for hackers, reverse engineers, and software testers. Author Justin Seitz explains the concepts behind hacking tools like debuggers, Trojans, fuzzers, and emulators. He then goes on to explain how to harness existing Python-based security tools and build new ones when the pre-built ones just won't cut it. The book teaches readers how to automate tedious reversing and security tasks; sniff secure traffic out of an encrypted web browser session; use PyDBG, Immunity Debugger, Sulley, IDAPython, and PyEMU; and more.

APRIL 2009, 216 PP., $39.95
ISBN 978-1-59327-192-3

PHONE:
800.420.7240 OR
415.863.9900
MONDAY THROUGH FRIDAY,
9 A.M. TO 5 P.M. (PST)

EMAIL:
SALES@NOSTARCH.COM

WEB:
WWW.NOSTARCH.COM

FAX:
415.863.9950
24 HOURS A DAY,
7 DAYS A WEEK

MAIL:
NO STARCH PRESS
38 RINGOLD STREET
SAN FRANCISCO, CA 94103
USA

ABOUT THE AUTHOR

Conrad Barski has an M.D. from the University of Miami and nearly 20 years of programming experience. This includes a stint developing an obscure Atari Jaguar game and working on many medical software projects. Barski is also an avid cartoonist, having created the popular alien Lisp mascot and many graphical tutorials. He currently develops cardiology software and lives in Washington, DC.

UPDATES

Visit *http://www.nostarch.com/lisp.htm* for updates, errata, and other information.

Land of Lisp is set in New Baskerville, TheSansMono Condensed, Futura, and Dogma.

This book was printed and bound by Transcontinental, Inc. at Transcontinental Gagné in Louiseville, Quebec, Canada. The paper is Domtar Husky 60# Smooth, which is certified by the Forest Stewardship Council (FSC). The book has an Otabind binding, which allows it to lay flat when open.